Booth and Schwarz: Residence, Domicile and UK Taxation

D1336363

Booth and Schwarz: Residence, Domicile and UK Taxation

Twentieth Edition

Jonathan Schwarz BA, LLB (Witwatersrand),
LLM (University of California, Berkeley), FTII
Barrister (Middle Temple)
Advocate of the High Court of South Africa
Barrister and Solicitor: Alberta, Canada

Bloomsbury Professional

LONDON · DUBLIN · EDINBURGH · NEW YORK · NEW DELHI · SYDNEY

BLOOMSBURY PROFESSIONAL
Bloomsbury Publishing Plc
41–43 Boltro Road, Haywards Heath, RH16 1BJ, UK

BLOOMSBURY and the Diana logo are trademarks of Bloomsbury Publishing Plc

First published in Great Britain 2018

British Library Cataloguing-in-Publication Data

A catalogue record for this book is available from the British Library.

ISBN:	PB:	978 1 52650 616 0
	ePDF:	978 1 52650 618 4
	ePub:	978 1 52650 617 7

Typeset by Compuscript Ltd, Shannon
Printed and bound by CPI Group (UK) Ltd, Croydon, CR0 4YY

To find out more about our authors and books visit www.bloomsburyprofessional.com. Here you will find extracts, author information, details of forthcoming events and the option to sign up for our newsletters

PREFACE

'you don't need a weatherman to know which way the wind blows'

Bob Dylan – Subterranean Homesick Blues, 1965

The United Kingdom, long an open economy and an open society, has thrived on rules built up over recent decades on the mobility of individuals, capital and business flowing from technological changes in transport and communication as well as a reduction in legal impediments to free movement. To the extent that tax rules influence or facilitate behaviours, recent trends suggest UK tax policy may be moving in a direction that inhibits such mobility. In 2008, a charge for access to the remittance basis on non-domiciled individuals who have been UK resident for more than seven years, puts the remittance basis beyond all but the wealthiest with significant foreign income or gains, for those who come to the UK for longer than that period. Key milestones that suggest such changes include:

- 29 March 2017, when the UK government gave notice of its intention to withdraw the United Kingdom from the European Union. The right of British citizens to reside in other Member States for work or retirement may be traded in order to make the tenure of other Europeans in the United Kingdom similarly insecure.
- 7 June 2017, when the United Kingdom signed the *Multilateral Convention to Implement Tax Treaty Related Measures to Prevent Base Erosion and Profit Shifting*. In exercising choices offered by the Convention, the United Kingdom signalled a change in resolving dual residence problems for companies and other legal persons from a rule-based system to an administrative discretion-based regime.
- 16 November 2017 saw royal assent to Finance (No 2) Act 2017 which put an absolute time bar on the ability of non-UK domiciled individuals to benefit from the remittance basis. The Act also makes it impossible for UK born individuals with a foreign domicile, but a UK domicile of origin, to ever benefit from the remittance basis if they return to the UK, even for short periods. These individuals will also be drawn into worldwide inheritance tax after short periods of UK residence. The deemed domicile rules, which look back to residence over 20 years, also serve to increase the need to understand the common law principles applicable before April 2013.

Ordinary residence continues to play a key role for National Insurance Contributions and tax credits. *Arthur v HMRC* and *Mackay v HMRC* both concern foreigners with varying degrees of residential connection with the UK. Both were found to be ordinarily resident in the UK. In *Arthur's* case, the result of this conclusion was that his wife, with whom he lived intermittently, was excluded from separately claiming tax credits.

Recent controversies on the residence of companies illustrate that no area of residence lies dormant. The First-tier Tribunal decision on corporate residence in *Development Securities (No 9) Ltd v HMRC* is framed by a tax avoidance plan that depended on non-residence of the participant for success.

The Court of Justice of the European Union has ruled in *P Panayi Accumulation & Maintenance Settlements v HMRC* that the UK exit charge on trusts migrating to another Member State infringes EU fundamental freedoms. Corporate migration, as well as migration of other taxpaying entities will be significantly impacted by BEPS actions as well as Brexit.

This 20th edition aims to provide a comprehensive treatment of the law of residence for tax of individuals companies, trusts and partnerships in light of the latest legislation, case law and HMRC practice. All forms of taxpayer are now subject to statutory residence rules in varying degrees. Both individuals and companies continue to be governed by common law principles. The statutory residence test as well as common law residence for individuals will continue to require examination for years because residence in the current year is significantly dependent on residence during the three preceding years.

My thanks go to Greg Kilminster, Dave Wright, Claire McDermott, Jane Bradford, Paul Crick and all the Bloomsbury Professional editorial and production team for all their hard work in bringing this edition to fruition, which is generally up to date to the beginning of February 2018.

Jonathan Schwarz
Middle Temple, London
February 2018

CONTENTS

TABLE OF STATUTES

[References are to paragraph number and appendices]

TABLE OF STATUTORY INSTRUMENTS

[References are to paragraph number]

TABLE OF HMRC MATERIAL

[References are to paragraph number and appendices]

TABLE OF EC MATERIALS AND INTERNATIONAL CONVENTIONS

[References are to paragraph number and appendices]

TABLE OF CASES

W

Y

Z

Decisions of the European Court of Justice are listed below numerically. These decisions are also included in the preceding alphabetical list.

ABBREVIATIONS

CPR	Civil Procedure Rules
CTA	Corporation Tax Act
DMPA 1973	Domicile and Matrimonial Proceedings Act 1973
FA	Finance Act
HMRC	Her Majesty's Revenue and Customs
ICTA 1970	Income and Corporation Taxes Act 1970
ICTA 1988	Income and Corporation Taxes Act 1988
IHTA 1984	Inheritance Tax Act 1984
IR	Inland Revenue
ITA 1918	Income Tax Act 1918
ITA 2007	Income Tax Act 2007
ITEPA 2003	Income Tax (Earnings and Pensions) Act 2003
ITTOIA 2005	Income Tax (Trading and Other Income) Act 2005
OECD	Organisation for Economic Co-operation and Development
PCTA 1968	Provisional Collection of Taxes Act 1968
TCEA 2007	Tribunals Courts and Enforcement Act 2007
TCGA 1992	Taxation and Chargeable Gains Act 1992
TIOPA 2010	Taxation (International and Other Provisions) Act 2010
TMA 1970	Taxes Management Act 1970

CHAPTER 1

United Kingdom taxation

I am a stranger and a sojourner with you

Genesis ch 23 v 4

1.01 State practice in exercising taxing jurisdiction

In the field of direct taxation, state practice in exercising taxing jurisdiction universally recognises that either the person subject to taxation, or the item of income (or gain), that is the object of taxation, must be within the territory of the taxing state. Taxation by the country of the source of the income is often described as 'limited taxation', in that the liability is limited to income (and gains) from sources within that state's territory. 'Unlimited liability', on the other hand, applies to persons whose personal connection, typically residence, is within the state's territory, because the liability is in respect of income (or gains) regardless of where they arise.[1]

Most states adopt a single factor connecting persons with their territory, namely residence. The UK has long adopted a more nuanced approach in relation to individuals, applying instead several connecting factors: residence, ordinary residence, domicile and nationality. In general, the more connected the person has been to the UK, the greater the exposure to UK taxation. This approach, has contributed to, and is a product of, an open economy, a diverse and tolerant society and a central position as a leading centre of international commerce, finance and creativity.

Recent reforms have eliminated ordinary residence as a factor,[2] narrowed the relevance of domicile[3] and introduced temporary non-residence[4] as well as residence with split-year treatment,[5] as new factors. These changes have increased complexity of the tax system exponentially. It is too soon to say what their effect will be on UK society and its economy.

---

1 For an examination of these issues worldwide, see 'Source and residence: new configuration of their principles' *Cahiers de droit international*, Vol 90a (International Fiscal Association, 2005).
2 See **2.1**, **4.01** and **4.12**.
3 See **1.8**.
4 See **2.42**.
5 See **2.30**.

Questions of sovereignty

1.02 The right to levy tax

It was 1199 when King John began to convert the elaborate and well-ordered fiscal system he had inherited from Henry I and Henry II into an instrument of arbitrary and merciless extortion, but it was not until 15 June 1215 that 'in a Thames-side meadow called Runnymede, ... the taxpayers ... combined to control the tax-imposer'[1] by forcing the monarch to set his seal to Magna Carta. Clause 12 of the charter provided that 'no scutage or aid shall be imposed in our Kingdom unless by the Common Council of our Realm' but, even then, the control was incomplete. In the fourteenth century, Edward III imposed massive taxation to finance his long war with France and the price of the people's consent to such taxation was that future taxation would be conditional on the 'common consent of prelates, earls, barons and other lords and commons of the realm'.[2]

Although this was 'a major step on the road to parliamentary control of taxation',[3] it was not until 1689 that the prerogative rights of the British monarchy were finally and completely abrogated in that regard. In 1681, Charles II had dissolved the Parliament and begun to rule absolutely. In 1685, he was succeeded by his brother James II and, in 1689, upon the accession to the throne of William and Mary, Parliament secured the passing of the Bill of Rights which vouchsafed for it ultimate supremacy. Ever since then, the British monarch has reigned but not ruled, so that today, just as in 1689, 'levying moneys for or to the use of the Crowne by pretence of prerogative without grant of Parlyament ... is illegal'.[4]

In recent years, as the sophistication, complexity and volume of tax legislation has grown, concerns have been expressed about the reality of Parliamentary control. A 2005 International Monetary Fund working paper found that the UK had some of the weakest powers in the world for budget scrutiny. The Tax Law Review Committee of the Institute for Fiscal Studies said in 2003, 'The truth of the matter is that the House of Commons has neither the time nor the expertise nor, apparently the inclination, to undertake any systematic or effective examination of whatever tax rules the government of the day places before it for approval.' A Confederation of British Industry task force report in 2008 concluded, 'it would not be unreasonable to say ... there is no genuine scrutiny of the finance bill under the present system.' To illustrate, Sch 7 to the Finance Act 2008 (the Remittance Basis) is some 50 pages in length and had 135 government amendments introduced at the committee stage but received the attention of the Public Bills Committee for less than a full day. In response to these criticisms, a Working Party chaired by Lord Howe of Aberavon published a report in July 2008 taking forward the Forsyth Tax Reform Commission's recommendations on the making of tax law.[5] A discussion document setting out the government's proposals shaping a new approach to tax policy-making was published as part of the 2011 Budget documents.[6] It proposed a more considered approach, including consultation on policy design and improved scrutiny of draft legislative proposals.

Schedule 45 to the Finance Act 2013, which introduced the Statutory Residence Test, is 67 pages in length. Together with Schedule 46 (abolition of ordinary residence), which is 20 pages, it commanded under 30 minutes of the Public Bills Committee's time. This legislation was however the subject of public consultation over a period of nearly two years.[7]

1 Arthur Bryant, *Set in a Silver Sea* (Collins) pp 130–132.
2 Bryant, p 226.
3 Bryant, p 226.
4 Bill of Rights 1688.
5 *Making Taxes Simpler. The final report of a Working Party chaired by Lord Howe of Aberavon* (July 2008).
6 HM Treasury and HM Revenue & Customs, *Tax policy making: a new approach* (June 2011).
7 See **1.28**.

1.03   Jurisdictional limitations

It is a matter of constitutional law that, because the sovereign power of Parliament is absolute, unless Parliament chooses voluntarily to abrogate its powers,[1] it may legislate contrary to the requirements of international law, for 'international law … yields to statute'[2] and, 'if the language of the statute is clear, it must be followed notwithstanding the conflict between municipal and international law which results'.[3]

The primary characteristic of law is that it is enforceable by sanction (ie fine, suspension of rights, imprisonment, etc). Before a court may order enforcement, however, it must be competent to hear and determine the alleged non-compliance, and, in the English courts, such competence rests solely on whether a claim has been served on the defendant in person. This – following from the fact that a writ is essentially an assertion of sovereignty and that sovereignty itself is territorial – gives rise to the

'… broad general universal proposition that English legislation … is applicable only to English subjects or to foreigners who by coming into this country, whether for a long or a short time, have made themselves during that time subject to English jurisdiction.'[4]

Personal taxing jurisdiction has developed by reference to these same common law principles in relation to the matters with which this book is concerned.

1 As, for example, when, on 1 January 1973, Britain acceded to the Treaty of Rome and became bound, as a European Community Member State, by certain Community legislation.
2 *Cheney v Conn* (1967) 44 TC 217 at 221, per Ungoed-Thomas J.
3 *Maxwell on the Interpretation of Statutes* (12th edn) p 183.
4 *Re Sawyers, ex p Blain* [1874–80] All ER Rep 708 at 710, per James LJ.

1.04   Enforcement overseas

Although the requirement of service of process on a defendant personally may prevent an action for the recovery of taxes from a person abroad being brought before an English court, what is to prevent such an action being brought before the court of the foreign state in which that person is present and being heard there in accordance with the principles of international law? The short answer is simply that 'it is the practice of nations not to enforce the fiscal legislation of other nations'.[1]

The principle on which this practice is based emerged over two centuries ago when, in upholding a French individual's claim for the purchase moneys due in respect of goods which were to be smuggled into England by their purchaser in violation of English revenue laws, Lord Mansfield enunciated the proposition that 'no country ever takes notice of the revenue laws of another'.[2] Stated thus, the proposition may be too wide – and may, indeed, no longer even be of application in the circumstances with which Lord Mansfield was concerned.[3] What may be said, however, is that:

'... a foreign government cannot come here – nor will the Courts of other countries allow our government to go there – and sue a person found in that jurisdiction for taxes levied and which he is declared to be liable to by the country to which he belongs.'[4]

The rationale behind the principle thus stated is that:

'... a claim for taxes is but an extension of the sovereign power which imposed the taxes, and ... an assertion of sovereign authority by one State within the territory of another ... is (treaty or convention apart) contrary to all concepts of independent sovereignties.'[5]

Were the payment of tax a contractual obligation, the situation would, of course, be different and the contract would be not only recognised but enforced if necessary by the courts of a foreign state in accordance with the principles of private international law. Tax collection is, however, 'not a matter of contract, but of authority and administration as between the State and those within its jurisdiction'.[6] Accordingly, foreign courts will not entertain a suit for the direct or indirect[7] enforcement of UK revenue laws and, this being so, the limitation implicitly imposed on the legislature's legislative power by the principle of action *in personam* cannot be circumvented (at least so far as revenue laws are concerned) by recourse to a foreign forum.

This principle is now increasingly limited by European Union law and international treaties. The EU Mutual Assistance in Recovery of Taxes Directive[8] requires Member States to collect unpaid taxes of all kinds on behalf of each other. Authority to extend this assistance beyond the European Union by treaty has existed since 2006.[9] In 2007 the UK signed the Multilateral OECD/Council of Europe Convention on Mutual Assistance in Tax Matters, which, likewise, facilitates collection of taxes by one signatory state for the others.[10] The UK has also started to include such provisions in its bilateral tax treaties.[11]

---

1 *Clark v Oceanic Contractors Inc* [1983] STC 35 at 41, per Lord Scarman.
2 *Holman v Johnson* (1775) 1 Cowp 341.
3 In *Regazzoni v K C Sethia (1944) Ltd* [1957] 3 All ER 286 at 292, Viscount Simonds said: 'It does not follow from the fact that today the court will not enforce a revenue law at the suit of a

foreign state that today it will enforce a contract which requires the doing of an act in a foreign country which violates the Revenue laws of that country.'

4 *King of the Hellenes v Brostrom* (1923) 16 Ll L Rep 167, per Rowlatt J.

5 *Government of India v Taylor* [1955] 1 All ER 292, per Lord Keith of Avonholm.

6 *Government of India v Taylor* [1955] 1 All ER 292, per Lord Somervell of Harrow.

7 In *Peter Buchanan Ltd and Macharg v McVey* [1954] IR 89, the director of a Scottish company made a deal with the Inland Revenue on which the Revenue authorities subsequently reneged. The director promptly stripped the company of its assets and removed them – along with his private assets and himself – to the Republic of Ireland where he proceeded to 'snap his hands in the face of the disgruntled Scottish Revenue'. The Inland Revenue, realising that a direct attempt to recover taxes through the courts of Eire would fail, attempted to do so indirectly by suing the director on the grounds that he had acted in breach of his duties as a director. The court looked beyond the action, however, and, seeing that it was no more than an indirect attempt to enforce UK revenue laws in the Republic of Ireland, dismissed it.

8 Current legislation is Council Directive 2010/24/EU on mutual assistance for the recovery of claims relating to certain levies, duties, taxes and other measures; implemented in the UK by FA 2006 s 173 and the MARD Regulations SI 2011/2931.

9 FA 2006 ss 173–176.

10 OECD/Council of Europe Convention on Mutual Assistance in Tax Matters signed by the UK on 24 May 2007.

11 See, for example, Protocol of 7 November 2007 to United Kingdom-New Zealand Double Taxation Convention of 4 August 1983 (SI 1984/365 as amended).

1.05 Territorial limits

In interpreting a Parliamentary enactment, however, the courts have been committed to carrying the principle of territorial sovereignty no further than they need. Almost a century ago, Lord Esher MR expressed his conviction that:

'Parliament ought not to deal in any way, either by regulation or otherwise, directly or indirectly, with any foreign matter or person which is outside the jurisdiction of our Parliament, and ... the Courts ought always to construe ... general words to apply only to the person or thing which will answer the description in them, but which person or thing is also within the jurisdiction of our Parliament.'[1]

Those same sentiments have been echoed by Lord Asquith, who was adamant that:

'... an Act of the Imperial Parliament today, unless it provides otherwise, applies ... to nothing outside the United Kingdom: not even to the Channel Islands or the Isle of Man, let alone a remote overseas colony or possession.'[2]

In the context of taxation, in *Clark v Oceanic Contractors Inc*[3], the House of Lords held that, because Oceanic, a non-resident company, had an address for service in the UK and carried out operations in the designated areas of the North Sea (the profits of which were to be treated under FA 1973 s 38(4) as profits from a trade carried on by it in the UK and, as such, to be liable to corporation tax, it had a trading presence in the UK and that such a trading presence was sufficient to impose an obligation on the company to operate a PAYE scheme for the collection of tax in respect of emoluments chargeable to tax under Schedule E.

Lord Scarman also noted in that case that 'the principle is a rule of construction only' and that 'British tax liability has never been exclusively limited to British subjects and foreigners resident within the jurisdiction'. Lord Wilberforce[4] referred to the 'territorial principle' as being 'really a rule of construction of statutes expressed in general terms'.

On the other hand in *Agassi v Robinson (HM Inspector of Taxes)*,[5] a non-resident company, set up by a famous tennis star, entered into endorsement contracts with two manufacturers of sports clothing and equipment, neither of which was resident or had a tax presence in the UK. The company received payments abroad from the manufacturers pursuant to the contracts. The House of Lords by a majority concluded that the foreign entertainers' tax applied to the payments as a matter of legislative intendment.

1 *Colquhoun v Heddon* (1890) 2 TC 621 at 626.
2 *A-G for the Province of Alberta v Huggard Assets Ltd* [1953] 2 All ER 951.
3 [1983] STC 35.
4 At p 427; 152.
5 [2006] UKHL 23.

Questions of territory

1.06 The territory of the UK

The UK has three constituent units, each subject to the ultimate sovereignty of the common Parliament at Westminster. The three units are England and Wales, Scotland, and Northern Ireland. Legislation has now been passed which establishes a Parliament for Scotland with powers of primary legislation in some areas, including a limited power to vary income tax; a National Assembly for Wales which has, jointly with Westminster, some powers of primary legislation; and an Assembly for Northern Ireland with powers of legislation in certain areas.[1] England, Wales and Scotland are described collectively as Great Britain,[2] and the UK consists of Great Britain and Northern Ireland.[3] Scotland is the only country within the UK that has an element of autonomy in relation to income tax. A 'Scottish taxpayer' may be liable to the Scottish rate of income tax under Part 4A, Chapter 2 of the Scotland Act 1998.[4] The Isle of Man and the islands of Jersey, Guernsey, Alderney, Sark, Herm and Jethou (ie the Channel Islands) are British Isles outside the UK[5] and have their own systems of private law and taxation.

1 Scotland Act 1998 and 2012, Government of Wales Acts 1998 and 2006, and Northern Ireland Act 1998.
2 Royal and Parliamentary Titles Act 1927.
3 Interpretation Act 1978 s 5 and Sch 1.
4 See **2.44** on the meaning of 'Scottish taxpayer'.
5 As to the Channel Islands not being part of the UK, see *Navigators and General Insurance Co Ltd v Ringrose* [1962] 1 All ER 97.

1.07   The territorial waters

In addition to the land mass described at **1.06** above, the UK includes territorial waters. These include internal waters such as rivers, lakes and the area of sea which lies upon the landward side of the low-water line along the coast (including the coast of all islands and low-tide elevations comprised in the territory) or, in the case of a bay, the area of sea which lies on the landward side of a straight line (not more than 24 miles in length) joining the low-water lines of the natural entrance points of the bay.[1] They include also the territorial sea which consists of those parts of the sea over which the UK's sovereignty is subject to the right of innocent passage by foreign ships[2] being any part of the open sea which lies within one marine league[3] on the seaward side of the base-line from which the areas of internal waters are determined.[4]

The relevance of territorial waters in the context of revenue law may not be immediately obvious. As we shall see, however, the precise place where a person is present or the time at which a person leaves the UK may be critical in the context of the establishment of non-resident tax status,[5] and that time is the time at which a person moves out of the UK's territorial waters (or out of the air space above them).

Another possible area of application is suggested by two cases brought by the Post Office under the Wireless Telegraphy Act 1949 s 14(7) against a so-called 'pirate' radio station in the Thames estuary. The defendants, who operated from Red Sands Tower, a structure which rests on the seabed more than three nautical miles from the nearest low-water lines of the Kent and Essex coasts, contended that their operations were performed on the high seas outside the UK's territorial waters and that they did not, therefore, come within the UK's jurisdiction. It was held, however, that the Red Sands Tower lies within the bay contained by a straight line drawn between the Naze and Foreness Point (the natural entrance points of that coastal indentation which forms part of the Thames estuary) and is accordingly within the internal waters of the UK.[6] Had Estuary Radio Ltd sought to escape UK taxation on the grounds advanced in its defence, it would, it seems, have been bound to fail for identical reasons.

It is worth noting that one of the questions raised in the cases described was whether or not the jurisdiction of a magistrates' court could extend over an area of territorial water. As the territorial waters in question adjoined the county of Kent, it was held that the Kent justices did indeed have jurisdiction. On the same premise, therefore, it seems clear that, where matters of revenue law are concerned in relation to persons or sources of income or gains within territorial waters, the General Commissioners (whose function is similar in connection with revenue law to that of the justices in connection with criminal law) appointed for the adjoining tax division will have jurisdiction to the same extent as they would have jurisdiction were the person or source located on the area of land contained within that division.

---

1 Territorial Waters Order in Council 1964, Arts 2–5.
2 Convention on the Territorial Sea and Contiguous Zone, Cmnd 2511, Art 11.
3 That is three nautical miles.
4 Territorial Waters Jurisdiction Act 1878 s 7.

5 See **2.01** in relation to the Statutory Residence Test and **5.08** for years to 5 April 2013 below. See also **9.16** below in relation to domicile.
6 *Post Office v Estuary Radio Ltd* [1967] 1 WLR 1396 and *R v Kent Justices, ex p Lye* [1967] 2 WLR 765.

1.08   Territorial extension

Although Parliament is not, for all the reasons stated thus far, presumed to generally legislate beyond the limits of the territory over which it has sovereignty, there is nothing to prevent it so doing if the inhibiting constraints of international law are removed by international treaty. This will, of course, happen only rarely, but one instance of its occurrence may be cited.

In 1958, the Geneva Convention on the Continental Shelf[1] secured agreement at international level concerning exploration or exploitation rights in relation to all resources in the seabed and subsoil of the North Sea continental shelf. Certain of that Convention's provisions were brought within the municipal law of the UK[2] by the Continental Shelf Act 1964 and that Act provided that areas of the continental shelf outside the UK's territorial waters might be designated by Order in Council[3] as areas within which the UK might exercise rights of exploration and exploitation.[4] The Act recognised that any areas so designated would not thereby become part of the UK[5] and, implicitly, that the sovereignty of Parliament would not extend to them.

Once the Order in Council had been made, however, Parliament decided to extend its revenue legislation so as to bring within the scope of the Taxes Acts any profits or gains from exploration or exploitation activities carried on in the designated areas. This territorial extension of the charge to tax was achieved by the Finance Act 1973.[6]

1 29 April 1958.
2 See **1.07** above.
3 Orders have been made in relation to the sea around the Orkneys and Shetlands, the sea west and north-west of the Shetlands, the sea off the west coast of Scotland, the Irish Sea, St George's Channel, the Bristol Channel, the sea south of Cornwall, the south-western approaches to the English Channel, the English Channel, the North Sea and the southern North Sea.
4 Continental Shelf Act 1964 s 1(7).
5 Continental Shelf Act 1964 s 1(1).
6 FA 1973 Sch 15.

1.09   The European Union

On 1 January 1973, the UK acceded to the Treaty of Rome which had come into effect on 1 January 1959 and had provided for the establishment of a European Economic Community. The Treaty on the Functioning of the European Union (TFEU) is now the foundation instrument for the European Union. While the European Union does not have a specific jurisdiction over direct taxation, EU law places limitations on the freedom of action of Member States in the field of direct taxation as a consequence of the duty of Member States to conform to the requirements of EU law.

There have been increasing numbers of cases going to the Court of Justice of the European Union over recent years, where taxpayers resident within a Member State have sought to challenge a Member State's residence-based rules on the ground that they are alleged to infringe the prohibitions in EU law against discrimination on grounds of nationality or the fundamental freedoms conferred by Union law. Chapter 11 below considers jurisprudence of the European Court in this regard in relation to residence.

In an advisory referendum on 23 June 2016, a narrow majority of voters expressed the view that the UK should leave the EU. The Government gave notice to this effect on 29 March 2017. The mechanism for withdrawal from the EU, which has not previously been invoked, is set out in Article 50 of the TFEU. Once notice of withdrawal is given to the EU Council under Article 50(1), withdrawal is automatic and, under Article 50(3), the EU treaties cease to apply two years after this notice is given. The implications of UK withdrawal from the EU are discussed in Chapter 10, at **10.05**.

Determinants of chargeability

1.10 Residence

Residence is the central pillar of personal taxing jurisdiction in the UK. It is the common thread found in relation to all taxes identified in this work. It is applied to natural persons (individuals), legal persons (companies) and notional persons (trusts or settlements). The task of giving meaning to the expression was largely left to the courts, with legislation addressing only limited issues for more than two centuries. Codification of the residence of trusts and estates was undertaken in 2006. These rules are analysed in Chapter 6. The residence of individuals was largely codified in 2013. The residence of individuals from 6 April 2013 is addressed in Chapter 2. The residence of individuals from that date is determined in part by their residential status for the three previous years. Accordingly, the residence of individuals up to that date is discussed in Chapter 3. The residence of companies remains a mixture of case law and statute and is examined in Chapter 7.

The overall effect of the regime introduced by Schedule 45 to the Finance Act 2013 is to establish the following categories of persons with residence related fiscal connections to the UK:

- UK residents: UK residents are liable to income tax and capital gains tax on income and capital gains wherever they arise, whether in or outside the UK. A subcategory of UK residents is those who are resident but not domiciled in the UK and whose foreign income and gains may be taxed on the remittance basis.
- Non-residents: non-residents are liable to income tax on income from sources within the UK and certain capital gains on the disposal of assets situated in the UK.
- UK residents with split-year treatment: this is a new legal category of status. Such individuals are not taxed as fully resident nor as fully non-resident individuals. Instead they are liable to income tax and capital gains tax in accordance with a lengthy list of amendments to the tax system where certain items qualify for special treatment.

- Temporary non-residents: these are individuals who are not resident in the UK but whose liability to tax on certain income and gains on a worldwide basis is suspended and conditional, pending their possible return to the UK within five years of having departed.

1.11   Ordinary residence

From 6 April 2013, ordinary residence is generally abolished as a connecting factor for taxation but continues to apply in relation to national insurance contributions and tax credits.[1] Ordinary residence has previously only applied to individuals for the purposes of income tax, capital gains tax and national insurance contributions. In some cases it may have served to extend taxing jurisdiction. Liability to capital gains tax was expressed to arise where the individual is either resident or ordinarily resident in the UK.[2] In other cases it limited taxing jurisdiction. The anti-avoidance provisions of ITA 2007 relating to transfers of assets only applied to individuals ordinarily resident in the UK.[3] It has an uneasy relationship with simple residence, requiring as it does a degree of settled purpose. Ordinary residence is considered in Chapter 4.

1   Finance Act 2013 Sch 46; Tax Credits (Residence) Regulations 2003, Reg 3(1).
2   TCGA 1992 s 2.
3   ITA 2007 Pt 13 Ch 2.

1.12   Domicile

Domicile is frequently used to identify the personal law applicable to an individual. It may be described as the country in which the person has his 'permanent home'. It is universally recognised that, though a person may change his shores, this personal law remains the same – except in certain extreme circumstances.

Questions of status and succession are determined according to the law of the domicile and it has been adopted as the criterion for determining the chargeability of a person to inheritance tax on a worldwide basis. The use of this ultimate, long-term connecting factor as a determinant of liability to income tax and capital gains tax has been a key factor in making the UK attractive to foreigners as a place to live and work. It has been widely regarded as an important contributor to the success of the UK, and London in particular, as the centre of international trade finance, investment, and of artistic and scientific creativity. The scope of domicile as a determining factor for tax purposes was dramatically narrowed by the Finance Act 2008, Sch 7. Only time will tell if the restriction of the remittance basis for longer-term non-domiciled residents wealthy enough to pay the £30,000 or £50,000 minimum tax on foreign income and related measures will result in the fairer tax system its advocates claim, or, be seen as a hubristic tax grab aimed at income and gains tenuously linked to the UK by the territoriality principle.

A comprehensive time limit for the non-domiciled individuals to be treated as such for tax purposes was announced in the Summer Budget of July 2015.[1] This was followed on 30 September 2015 by an HM Treasury consultation[2] on extending deemed UK domicile for income tax, capital gains tax and inheritance tax purposes to non-domiciled individuals who have been resident in the UK for 15 out of the preceding 20 years. In addition individuals who were born in the UK and who have a UK domicile of origin will be deemed UK domiciled for tax purposes while resident in the UK. Draft legislation was published in February 2016 for inclusion in the 2016 Finance Bill. In March the government announced that this is no longer to be addressed in the 2016 Finance Bill but in the 2017 bill instead. The changes are still intended to take effect from 6 April 2017. A further consultation was launched with revised draft legislation on 19 August 2016 but did not propose and change to these reforms or to the timetable.[3] The changes were finally enacted in F(No 2)A 2017 which received royal assent on 16 November 2017 but with effect from 6 April 2017.

The concept of domicile is examined in Chapter 9.

1 HMRC Technical Note, *Technical briefing on foreign domiciled persons changes announced at Summer Budget 2015* (8 July 2015).
2 HM Treasury Consultation document, *Reform of the taxation of non-domiciled persons* (30 September 2015).
3 HM Treasury Consultation Document, *Reforms to the taxation of non-domiciles: further consultation*, updated 19 August 2016.

1.13   Nationality

Nationality now has no impact on taxing jurisdiction of individuals. It is a factor in resolving dual residence of individuals for the purpose of the application of tax treaties.[1] This is considered at **2.45**. Citizenship of the EU is conferred on nationals of all Member States by Article 21 of the TFEU. The rights entailed by this additional citizenship are considered in Chapter 10.

1 See OECD Model Double Taxation Convention, Art 4(2)(c).

1.14   The remittance basis

Some individuals are charged to income tax and capital gains tax on certain kinds of income and gains on the remittance basis; tax liability is charged only on the income and gains which are remitted to the UK. Usually the remittance basis applies where the income or gains arise outside the UK and where the individuals are not domiciled and in some cases not ordinarily resident in the UK. The remittance basis dates from 1803 and remained largely unchanged over the last 90 years. The meaning of remittance is now the subject of detailed and lengthy statutory provisions introduced by Finance Act 2008, Sch 7.[1]

1 Contained in ITA 2007 Pt 14 Ch A1.

1.15   Attempts to narrow the remittance system

The remittance basis itself remained largely unchanged for over 80 years, although the scope of its application has become restricted over time.

By 1974, only non-domiciled individuals and trustees benefited from the remittance basis, and, for income other than employment income, non-ordinarily resident Commonwealth and Irish citizens. In 1974 a proposal to end the remittance basis completely for non-domiciled taxpayers who had been ordinarily resident for five out of the six previous years of assessment, by deeming such persons to be domiciled was abandoned.

1.16   Reform of residence rules

An attempt to reform the definition of residence itself in 1988 was made when the Inland Revenue published *Residence in the United Kingdom, The Scope of UK Taxation for Individuals, A Consultation Document*. In it a comprehensive reform was proposed under which residence would be determined only by physical presence in the UK.

Residence based on physical presence

The proposals were based on the US Federal Internal Revenue Code. An individual who was present in the UK for 183 days or more would, as now, be resident in that year for income tax and capital gains tax. An individual who was present for 30 days or less in a year would not be resident in that year. When an individual was present for between 30 and 183 days in a year, his residence would be determined by including not only the days spent in the UK during the year in question but also one-third and one-sixth of the days spent in the UK in the preceding year and the year before that respectively. Presence for any part of a day would count as presence for the whole day.[1]

Intermediate basis of taxation

Although the reform project was originally conceived only as a review of the residence tests, enthusiastic drafters of the document also proposed abolition of the remittance basis for non-domiciled residents. Residence would be the only affiliation test and an intermediate basis of taxation which would be applied to an individual's worldwide income depending on the length of an individual's residence in the UK. A graduated charge would apply to individuals who had been resident for 7 out of 14 years and only to those who had not previously been resident in this country for a continuous period of, say, 10 or 15 years.

The intermediate charge would apply to an individual's income and gains arising outside the UK. Liability would be based not on remittance but on a percentage of the total of worldwide income and gains, the percentage being determined by the number of years during which the individual had been resident in the UK in the previous, say, 14 years. The Inland Revenue suggested 15% in the case of one year's residence in the 14 years, increasing to 100% where the individual has resided for seven years out of the previous 14 years. The percentage would be applied to the individual's liability to tax on worldwide income and gains, taking account of any overseas tax paid. If the resultant figure were higher than the amount of tax payable on income and gains arising within the UK calculated in the normal way, then the individual's total tax charge for that year would be that higher figure. Otherwise total tax liability would be the amount of tax payable on the individual's income and gains arising within the UK.

Political unacceptability of the changes for non-domiciled residents effectively scuppered the project. No further changes in this area emerged during the period of Conservative government which ended in 1997.

---

1 *Residence in the United Kingdom, The Scope of UK Taxation for Individuals, a Consultation Document* (Inland Revenue, July 1988).

1.17   Criticisms of the system

In November 1994, the Rt Hon Gordon Brown MP, then the Shadow Chancellor of the Exchequer, issued a document entitled *Tackling Abuses – Tackling Unemployment.* It stated, *inter alia,* that:

> 'Taxation of non-residents, non-domiciles and those with off-shore accounts should be overhauled in line with the recommendations of the Inland Revenue. It is not fair that a wealthy few be allowed to work or live in the UK without making a fair contribution through taxation … In Britain it is easy for a few, even if they live or work here to avoid substantial amounts of tax through claiming to be non-resident or non-domiciled. The Tories have even widened the loopholes by scrapping the "available accommodation test" … Today it is possible for an individual to fly into Britain every day of the year and not be treated as resident as long as he is absent for a few hours of each day … People wishing to avoid substantial capital gains arrange to be non-resident for a year. Those who are non-domiciled are able to live in the UK free of tax … In 1988 the Inland Revenue recommended a radical new approach to residents and domiciles.'

Included in the materials of Chancellor Gordon Brown's 2003 Budget, was a document entitled *Reviewing the residence and domicile rules as they affect the taxation of individuals: a background paper* (published jointly by HM Treasury and Inland Revenue in April 2003). Through the use of a series of examples the paper identified a number of issues where there was unhappiness with the existing system. Most related to the benefits enjoyed by non-domiciled individuals and to somewhat anomalous results that can flow from various circumstances where residence is determined by counting days present in the UK.

The principles, it stated, which underpin the review are that the rules:

(a)   should be fair;
(b)   should support the competitiveness of the UK economy; and
(c)   should be clear, and easy to operate.

The questions that the government stated in the document that it was considering, and welcomed comments from others upon, were whether the current rules:

(a)   successfully identify those with a long-term connection to the UK who have an obligation to help support the UK exchequer on the basis of their worldwide income;

(b)   successfully identify those with a temporary connection to the UK, and ensure an appropriate contribution to the UK exchequer from those individuals;

(c)   provide objective criteria for determining when a long-term or temporary connection is severed, suspended or restored;

(d)   establish an appropriate divide between long-term and temporary connections to the UK;

(e)   play an appropriate role, alongside other policy instruments, in supporting the internationalisation of labour markets, and ensuring the competitiveness of UK firms in the international market for skills, entrepreneurship and expertise;

(f)   ensure that any difference in treatment between UK locals and visitors, and long- and short-term residents have a clear economic rationale;

(g)   take into account the equivalent arrangements in other countries;

(h)   are transparent, provide clear and unambiguous outcomes, and minimise the compliance burden on individuals and their employers; and

(i)   present minimal opportunities for exploitation or avoidance.

Again, these proposals seemed to be kicked into the political long grass, at least at the legislative level during the Brown Chancellorship. At an administrative level there were stirrings of action, tackling taxpayers regularly flying in and out of the UK, including airline pilots who claimed not to be resident, which produced decisions of the Special Commissioners and Tax Tribunal.[1] Similarly, seafarers have been in the sights of HMRC.[2]

---

1 Inland Revenue Tax Bulletin 52, April 2001, p 836, 'Mobile Workers'; *Shepherd v Revenue & Customs* [2005] UKSPC 484; *Gaines-Cooper v HMRC* [2006] UKSPC SPC568; *Barrett v Revenue & Customs* [2007] UKSPC SPC 639 and *Grace v Revenue & Customs* [2008] UKSPC SPC 663 and [2011] UKFTT 36 (TC); *Hankinson v HMRC* [2009] UKFTT 384 (TC); *Turberville v HMRC* [2010] UKFTT 69 (TC). See generally Chapters 2 and 4.

2 *Farquhar v Revenue & Customs* [2010] UKFTT 231 (TC); *Megwa v Revenue & Customs* [2010] UKFTT 543 (TC).

1.18   Remittance basis amendments

In his first Pre-Budget Report in November 2007, Chancellor Alistair Darling announced sweeping changes limiting the availability of the remittance basis, expanding the meaning of remittance and a change to the method of counting days in the UK for the purpose of determining residence. This was followed by a further consultation exercise launched by a document entitled *Paying a fairer share: a consultation on residence and domicile* on 6 December 2007 and ending on 28 February 2008. It sought views on whether the application of the remittance basis should be further limited. In the March 2008 Budget the Chancellor confirmed that there would be no more legislation in this area during the life of that Parliament.

Further changes to the remittance basis were proposed by Chancellor George Osborne in the 2011 Budget. In a document entitled *Reform of the taxation of non-domiciled individuals: a consultation* it proposed to increase the existing £30,000 annual charge to £50,000 for non-domiciled individuals who have been UK resident in 12 or more of the 14 years prior in which the remittance basis is claimed, permitting tax-free remittance overseas income and capital gains to the UK for the purpose of commercial investment in UK businesses and some technical simplifications. These proposals were made law in ITA 2007 s 809C by FA 2012 s 46 and Sch 12, para 2(3) for 2012–13 and subsequent years. The charge for those resident in the UK for at least 12 of the past 14 years was increased from £50,000 to £60,000 and a new charge of £90,000 for individuals who are resident in 17 or more years for 2015-16 and subsequent years by FA 2015 s 24(2)(e)(i).

1.19   Codification of the residence of individuals

A chain of events started in 2001 with the publication of a Tax Bulletin article on mobile workers, followed by a considerable amount of litigation on individual residence,[1] culminating in the hearing of the *Davies* and *Gaines-Cooper* judicial reviews of HMRC practice in the area.[2] The withdrawal of IR20 and two versions of HMRC6 in as many years gave rise to pressure to end the uncertainty in such an important area of tax law. The government announced that it proposed to enact a statutory residence test at Budget 2011 and a consultation document was issued on 17 June 2011 by HM Treasury and HM Revenue & Customs setting out their proposals to put the meaning of residence on a statutory basis. It was intended to supersede all existing legislation, case law and guidance for tax years following its introduction.[3] A further consultation document was issued on 21 June 2012 in response to the consultation including draft legislation.[4] A further draft of the legislation along with draft HMRC guidance was published in December 2012.[5] This was followed by the Finance Bill 2013 and amended draft HMRC guidance in May 2013.[6] The statutory residence test, enacted in FA 2013 Sch 45 is examined in detail in Chapter 2.

The government also announced at Budget 2012 its decision to abolish the concept of ordinary residence for tax purposes generally from 6 April 2013, which was accomplished by FA 2013 Sch 46 and discussed at **4.12**.

The stated aim of the statutory residence test was to provide a simple process and clear outcome for the vast majority of people whose circumstances are straightforward[7] and to provide a fair way of determining residence for those with more complicated affairs.[8] The first Consultative Document asserted that, in broad terms, the proposals reflect the HMRC interpretation of the case law with modifications. Thus it was proposed to take into account both the amount of time the individual spends in the UK and the other connections they have with the UK. However, to avoid the complexity of the case law examination of all facts and circumstances, the test was not proposed to take into account a wide range of connections in the belief that the relevant connections should be simply and clearly defined and the weight and relevance of each connection should be clear.[9] The first Consultative Document expressed the belief that individuals would be able to assess their residence status simply and without the need to resort to specialist advice. Sixty-seven pages of legislation and over one hundred pages of guidance may make this something of a challenge.

Schedule 45 to the Finance Act 2013 is unlikely to be the end of the history of the law of tax residence. HM Treasury Tax Information and Impact Notes for the SRT, published on 11 December 2012, included a commitment that 'this measure will be kept under review through communication with affected taxpayer groups'. On 3 December 2013 the Chartered Institute of Taxation wrote to HMRC recommending that the SRT be formally evaluated in April 2016 (ie three tax years after the SRT came into force), by an independent review, against its declared objectives, in order to assess whether those objectives are being achieved. No such review has been undertaken or announced.

1 See **3.18**.
2 See **3.27**.
3 HM Treasury and HM Revenue & Customs, *Statutory definition of tax residence: a consultation* (17 June 2011) (in this book the 'Consultative Document').
4 HM Treasury and HM Revenue & Customs, *Statutory definition of tax residence and reform of ordinary residence: a summary of responses* (21 June 2012) (in this book the 'Second Consultative Document').
5 HM Revenue & Customs, Guidance Note: Statutory Residence Test (SRT) (December discussion draft) (18 December 2012).
6 HM Revenue & Customs, Guidance Note: Statutory Residence Test (SRT) (May 2012).
7 Consultative Document para 3.2.
8 Consultative Document para 3.4.
9 Consultative Document para 3.4.

UK revenue law

1.20 Income tax

There are four UK direct taxes whose incidence is, to some extent, governed by the residence or domicile status of the person on whom the liability will fall: income tax, corporation tax, capital gains tax and inheritance tax. A detailed consideration of each of those taxes is beyond the scope of this work but, in this and the subsequent paragraphs, the relevance to each of territoriality and of a person's residence and domicile is noted. Income tax is the first to be considered.

Although income tax is 'one tax, not a collection of taxes essentially distinct',[1] it has, since 1803, been charged under one or other of a number of schedules each of which specifies a chargeable source of income. Income tax is now charged in accordance with the Income Tax Act 2007 (ITA), effective from 6 April 2007, the Income Tax (Earnings and Pensions) Act 2003 (ITEPA), effective from 6 April 2003, and the Income Tax (Trading and Other Income) Act 2005 (ITTOIA), effective from 6 April 2005. These Acts were passed by the UK Parliament as part of the Tax Law Rewrite Project, whose aim is to rewrite tax law in plain English and modern legislative drafting structure without changing the law. Some minor changes in the laws have been made but case law which used to appertain to the old schedular system may still be relevant in interpreting the new legislation.

Income tax is an annual tax, being reimposed for each new year of assessment[2] (ie a year which runs from 6 April in one calendar year to 5 April in the next following calendar year)[3] and thus, in principle, if income is to be charged to tax for say, 2014–15, income must arise in the year ended 5 April 2015.

The Income Tax (Earnings and Pensions) Act imposes a charge to income tax on employment income, being a charge which is described as a charge on general earnings and a charge on special employment income.[4] Chapter 4 of the Act sets out the rules applying to employees who are resident, ordinarily resident and domiciled in the UK, while Ch 5 of the Act sets out the rules applying to employees not resident, ordinarily resident and domiciled in the UK.

The Income Tax (Trading and Other Income) Act 2005 deals with sources of income other than employment and pensions: Pt 2 of ITTOIA 2005 deals with trading profits; Pt 3 with property income; Pt 4 with saving and investment income; Pt 5 miscellaneous income; and Pt 8 specifically with foreign income.

The penultimate income tax product of the Rewrite Project is the Income Tax Act 2007, which rewrites and in some cases repeals various provisions relating to income tax not dealt with by the two Acts mentioned above. The rules regarding residence are contained in Pt 14 of Ch 2. The Act came into force on 5 April 2007. Certain international provisions are also contained in the Taxation (International and Other Provisions) Act 2010 which has effect from 1 April 2010.

---

1 *A-G v LCC* (1900) 4 TC 265 at 293, per Lord Macnaghten.

2 The continuing structure is preserved by ICTA 1988 s 820, but the tax itself requires an annual parliamentary resolution (invested with statutory authority by PCTA 1968) to keep it alive pending the enactment of the annual Finance Act.

3 ITA 2007 s 4(3) and s 4(5).

4 Income Tax (Earnings and Pensions) Act 2003 ss 1(1), (8), 6, 7.

1.21 Corporation tax

The first product of the Rewrite Project for companies is the Corporation Tax Act 2009 (CTA 2009) which generally has effect for accounting periods ending on or after 1 April 2009.[1] Corporation tax is chargeable on the worldwide profits of any company resident in the UK. A non-resident company is, however, chargeable to corporation tax only if it carries on a trade in the UK through a permanent establishment in the UK, and, in that event, the profits brought into charge to corporation tax are those of, or attributable to, the permanent establishment.[2] The second corporate tax rewrite exercise is the Corporation Tax Act 2010 which includes the definition of permanent establishment.[3]

The profits chargeable to corporation tax are to be arrived at by aggregating with its chargeable gains its income computed on principles similar to income tax but now separately contained in the Corporation Tax Act.[4]

UK-resident companies are also liable to the controlled foreign companies' charge. This charge is analogous to corporation tax but is imposed by apportioning among UK-resident corporate shareholders with an interest in a non-resident company, the profits of the non-resident company (computed on the basis of it being a company resident in the UK) if that company is controlled by persons resident in the UK, but is resident in a country where its profits are subject to a level of taxation lower than that to which they would be subject in the UK.[5] Company residence is examined in Chapter 7.

---

1 CTA 2009 s 1329(1).
2 CTA 2009 s 5.
3 CTA 2010 Pt 24, Ch 2.
4 See generally CTA 2009 Pts 3 to 10.
5 TIOPA 2010 Pt 9A. See **7.22** below.

1.22   Capital gains tax

A charge to capital gains tax arises when a gain accrues to a person on the disposal or deemed disposal of a chargeable asset in a year of assessment during any part of which he is resident in the UK.[1] A chargeable gain accruing to a company is included in its profits for corporation tax purposes.[2]

A disposal occurs whenever the owner of the asset disposes (or is deemed to dispose) of his ownership, absolute and beneficial, of the whole or part of the asset; a chargeable asset is any asset (including incorporeal property) other than an individual's principal private residence,[3] gilt-edged securities and qualifying corporate bonds,[4] savings certificates and non-marketable securities,[5] life policies, and deferred annuities,[6] tangible moveable assets disposed of for £6,000 or less,[7] private motor vehicles,[8] certain interests under settlements,[9] decorations for valour etc,[10] debts other than debts on a security,[11] and foreign currency for personal expenditure.[12]

There is an annual exemption for individuals.[13] For the year 2014–15 it is £11,000.

Where a person has a foreign domicile, no capital gains tax is to be charged on a gain accruing to him from the disposal of an asset situated outside the UK except to the extent of any amounts received in the UK in respect of that gain.[14] Whether an asset is situated outside the UK or not is determined by the provisions of TCGA 1992 s 275.

Where a person is neither resident nor ordinarily resident in the UK but carries on a trade in the UK through a branch or agency, he is to be charged to tax on gains accruing to him from the disposal of assets situated in the UK and either held by the branch, or used in connection with the trade.[15]

---

1 TCGA 1992 ss 1 and 2(1).
2 See **1.21** above.
3 TCGA 1992 s 222.
4 TCGA 1992 s 115.
5 TCGA 1992 s 121.
6 TCGA 1992 s 210.
7 TCGA 1992 s 262.
8 TCGA 1992 s 263.
9 TCGA 1992 s 76.
10 TCGA 1992 s 268.
11 TCGA 1992 s 251.
12 TCGA 1992 s 269.
13 TCGA 1992 s 3.
14 TCGA 1992 s 12.
15 TCGA 1992 s 10.

1.23   Inheritance tax

Inheritance tax is a direct tax on transfers of value made on, or (at a tapered rate) during the seven years preceding, a person's death;[1] and on transfers by a close company or by an individual (during his life) into certain trusts.[2]

Transfers to a spouse are exempt from tax, provided that the spouse is domiciled in the UK,[3] as are gifts of £250 or less,[4] certain gifts in consideration of marriage,[5] and gifts to charities etc.[6] Where lifetime transfers by an individual are chargeable to tax, the amount brought into charge is to be reduced by an annual exemption.

Domicile is a key concept in relation to inheritance tax. If a person is domiciled in the UK, the transfer, during the last seven years of his life or upon his death, of any property to which he is beneficially entitled, wherever situated, is within the charge to tax. If, however, a person is domiciled outside the UK, only transfers of property situated in the UK will be within the charge.[7] Domicile has, however, an extended meaning for the purpose of inheritance tax as explained in Chapter 9 below.

1 IHTA 1984 Pt I as amended by FA 1986.
2 IHTA 1984 ss 3, 71 and 89; F(No 2)A 1987 s 96(2); FA 2006, Sch 20.
3 IHTA 1984 s 18.
4 IHTA 1984 s 20.
5 IHTA 1984 s 22.
6 IHTA 1984 ss 23–29.
7 IHTA 1984 s 6(1).

1.24   National Insurance Contributions

While not strictly a tax, National Insurance Contributions are often thought of by both those who pay and collect them in the same way as tax. In the international context, they share some of the same jurisdictional issues with income tax. Liability to pay Class 1, Class 1A, Class 1B or Class 2 contributions generally only falls on persons who fulfil prescribed conditions as to residence or presence in Great Britain.[1] The prescribed conditions refer to both residence and ordinary residence (but not domicile).[2] Unlike the income tax rules, mere presence by an employed earner at the time of employment may be sufficient to establish liability.[3] These expressions are undefined in the social security legislation and thus the case law on the meaning of those expressions is relevant to this area of law. HMRC do not apply their guidance set out in HMRC6 to the expressions for National Insurance Contributions purposes.[4]

1 Social Security Contributions And Benefits Act 1992 s 1(6).
2 Social Security (Contributions) Regulations 2001 (SI 2001/1004) reg 145.
3 Reg 145(1)(a).
4 HMRC6 (March 2009) side note to para 11 states: 'The terms "resident" and "ordinarily resident" do not have the same meaning for NICs as they do for tax and so the tax rules on residence and ordinarily residence set out in parts 2 and 3 of this guidance are not relevant to NICs. The replacement document RDR1 does not address the issue. Leaflet NI38 Social Security abroad gives guidance on the rules on residence and ordinarily residence which apply for National Insurance purposes.' For the HMRC view of ordinary residence as it relates to NICs, see **4.11** below. The leaflet offers no view on the meaning of the term 'resident'.

1.25 Value added tax (VAT)

Member States of the European Union are required to impose value added tax (VAT) under the VAT Directive.[1] Residential concepts are again relevant in determining taxing jurisdiction. While the place of supply of goods for VAT purposes is decided by reference to the goods supplied,[2] the place of supply of services is generally by reference to the location of the supplier or customer.[3] Thus, for example, the place of supply of services is the place where the supplier has established his business or has a fixed establishment from which the service is supplied, or, in the absence of such a place of business or fixed establishment, the place where he has his permanent address or usually resides.[4]

1 Council Directive 2006/112 on the common system of value added tax (the VAT Directive).
2 VAT Directive Title V, Chs 1, 2 and 4.
3 VAT Directive Title V, Ch 3.
4 VAT Directive, Art 43.

HMRC practices and concessions

1.26 Individual residence

The operation of the UK system of taxation has included concessions whereby the Revenue do not enforce the letter of the law and published practices as to how they apply the law. At first, it was thought that the authority for such concessions and practices lay in the Inland Revenue Regulations Act 1890 s 1(2) which provided that the Commissioners of Inland Revenue ('the Board') 'shall have all necessary powers for carrying into execution every Act of Parliament relating to inland revenue', but when, in 1947, three years after the first list of concessions had been published, Sir Stafford Cripps MP, the then Chancellor of the Exchequer, was asked to state their basis in law, he replied that they had been brought into existence 'without any particular legal authority under any Act of Parliament, but by the Inland Revenue under my authority'.[1]

From this clear admission of the fact that HMRC concessions and practices have no statutory foundation but represent merely the will of the Executive, it follows that – whether they work in favour of the Crown or the subject – they have no place in the law for 'the pretended power of suspending laws or the execution of laws by regall authoritie without consent of Parlyament is illegal'.[2]

In areas of law that are unclear or where its application can be uncertain, such as the subject of this work, the way in which the law is administered is of particular importance. There are few areas where Revenue practice has been more significant than in relation to the residence and ordinary residence of individuals. Revenue booklet IR20 was for decades the central statement of practice and concessions on individual residence, ordinary residence and domicile. The judicial attitude towards this code is plain. When, in

Reed v Clark,[3] Nicholls J was referred to IR20, he dismissed its authority in a single sentence: 'I do not see', he said, 'how this booklet affects any matter I have to decide.'[4]

Although IR20 was merely a statement of HMRC practice and, in certain respects, concessions, it had for some time been heavily relied on and widely regarded almost as a codification of the rules. There had been no cases before the Courts on residence for some 20 years after *Reed v Clark* in 1985. In 11 of the 15 decisions of the Special Commissioners and First-tier Tribunal since 2005 in this area, IR20 has received attention. In several, taxpayers had relied in varying degrees on IR20 in organising their living arrangements. The first case to disabuse taxpayers from the notion was *Shepherd v Revenue & Customs*.[5] In that case, Captain Shepherd, a British Airways pilot, knew that he would have to retire on 22 April 2000 when he attained the age of 55 years. He started to plan for his retirement in 1997 when he wrote to the Revenue and asked for guidance on retirement overseas; he did not mention any particular country. In reply he received a copy of the Revenue publication IR20 'Residents and non-residents'. On 17 September 1998 he wrote to the Revenue to say that, with one year and seven months to go before his retirement, he was considering moving abroad to minimise his tax liabilities. He understood that his time in the UK had to average less than 91 days over four years. He had applied for Cyprus residency and would move there when permission was granted. However, this would take a considerable time and so he might move to Switzerland or Eire in the meantime. The Revenue replied to say that he was responsible for determining his residency status but if he was in the UK for 183 days or more in a tax year then he would be regarded as resident here. He spent less than 91 days a year in the UK. When the question of his residence came before the Special Commissioners it was determined without reference to IR20. While the case was not about the application of IR20, it neatly illustrates the special credence given to it.

In the *Shepherd* case as well as in *Gaines-Cooper v HMRC*,[6] the taxpayers offered calculations of the number of days they had spent in the UK based on the practice in IR20 that the days of arrival and departure should be ignored. In *Gaines-Cooper* these calculations were not disputed for years from 1976 to 1979. They were disputed during the period 1992 to 2004. The Revenue calculations included the days of arrival and departure and recorded the number of visits and visits of more than one night. These gave a very different picture of the presence of Mr Gaines-Cooper. The Special Commissioner noted that on appeal the law rather than IR20 should apply.[7]

Following the decision in *Gaines-Cooper*, HMRC issued a statement aimed at clarifying the application of IR20.[8] It noted that some commentators had suggested that the decision in *Gaines-Cooper* means that HMRC has changed the basis on which it calculates the '91-day test' and declared this to be incorrect. It stated further that there has been no change to HMRC practice in relation to residence and the '91-day test', and that HMRC would continue to:

'• follow its published guidance on residence issues, and apply this guidance fairly and consistently;
• treat an individual who has not left the United Kingdom as remaining resident here;

- consider all the relevant evidence, including the pattern of presence in the United Kingdom and elsewhere, in deciding whether or not an individual has left the United Kingdom;
- apply the "91-day test" (where HMRC is satisfied that an individual has actually left the United Kingdom) as outlined in booklet IR20, normally disregarding days of arrival and departure in calculating days under this "test".'

It restated that:

'The guidance provided by booklet IR20 is general in nature. If, on the facts of the matter, a dispute arises over the application of this general guidance and the parties cannot resolve their dispute by agreement, the Commissioners will determine any appeals. The Commissioners are bound to decide the legal issues by reference to statute and case law principles rather than HMRC guidance. Where a dispute relates to particular facts the Commissioners will consider the evidence and make findings of fact to which they will apply the law.'

At the same time in January 2007 the long-standing Inspector's Manual, which contained further guidance on this area was withdrawn.

In *Genovese v HMRC*,[9] the taxpayer (who represented himself) based his case before the Special Commissioners that he was not ordinarily resident in the UK on the test in IR20 that relied on matters of intention and what an individual decides about living in the UK. In dismissing the appeal by reference to the legal tests, which were at variance, with the practice stated in IR20, the Special Commissioner expressed concern that all individuals in a similar position will have acted on the assumption that their position is governed by the practice set out in IR20, and in particular will have submitted returns on that basis. An individual who discovers that his tax position is not as it had been assumed to be is placed in a difficult position, as nothing can be done after the event to rearrange matters.[10]

In *Hankinson v HMRC*[11] the taxpayer contended that he had gone to live and work abroad full time and that he had met the criteria, including the number of return days, according to HMRC's practice at the time set out at para 2.2 of HMRC's booklet IR20.[12] His employment abroad was found not to have remotely been full time.[13] This contributed significantly to the Tribunal finding that he was negligent, thereby permitting a discovery assessment.[14] Mr Hankinson also launched judicial review proceedings on the application of IR20 which were adjourned until after the Tribunal decision.[15] Findings of fact in relation to IR20 as requested by the High Court that he did not work full time abroad within IR20 para 2.2 nor that he had 'a main employment abroad and some unconnected occupation in the UK at the same time' within para 2.5 effectively eliminated reliance on IR20. Two extra-statutory concessions address the treatment of individuals, coming to or leaving the UK part-way through a tax year as there is no legal rule splitting a tax year between periods of residence and non-residence. In the *Shepherd* case, at the hearing, Captain Shepherd had to accept that the Special Commissioners had no jurisdiction to consider the possible application of extra-statutory concession A11 (*Residence in the United Kingdom: year of commencement or cessation of residence*) which provided for the splitting of a tax year where an individual ceased to reside in the UK during a year of assessment.

Given the state of the law, taxpayers will often seek to rely on published practice or concession. Since, as the unfortunate Mr Genovese and others have found to their cost, such matters cannot form the basis of an appeal, the only remedy open to taxpayers where HMRC do not apply published practice or concessions is under administrative law principles on judicial review. Administrative law gives wide discretion to the Revenue in the application of concessions and administrative practice.

In *R v IRC, Ex Parte Fulford-Dobson*[16] the taxpayer sought application of the ESC D2 dealing with split tax years in relation to capital gains. Shortly before he left the UK mid-way through a tax year, his wife, who remained resident, gave capital assets to him which he sold after departing. The Court declined to interfere with a Revenue refusal to apply the concession on the basis that it was used for a tax avoidance purpose.

The broad effect illustrated by this case is that where taxpayers need to rely on concessions they are governed by administrative discretion rather than legal rights. This unsatisfactory approach has been criticised by the courts. In *Absolom v Talbot*,[17] Scott LJ observed: 'The fact that such extra-legal concessions have to be made to avoid unjust hardships is conclusive that there is something wrong with the legislation.' Perhaps the final death blow to extra-statutory concessions was the decision of the House of Lords in *R v Inland Revenue Commissioners, ex p Wilkinson*[18] where Lord Hoffmann said of the power to make such concessions:

'This discretion enables the Commissioners to formulate policy in the interstices of the tax legislation, dealing pragmatically with minor or transitory anomalies, cases of hardship at the margins or cases in which a statutory rule is difficult to formulate or its enactment would take up a disproportionate amount of Parliamentary time. The Commissioners publish extra-statutory concessions for the guidance of the public and Miss Rose drew attention to some which she said went beyond mere management of the efficient collection of the Revenue. I express no view on whether she is right about this, but if she is, it means that the Commissioners may have exceeded their powers under section 1 of TMA.'[19]

In light of the uncertainty now surrounding concessions, Finance Act 2008 s 160 now authorises HM Treasury by order to make provision for and in connection with giving effect to any existing HMRC concession.[20]

The procedural complexities where HMRC refused to apply IR20 are well illustrated in *Davies v HMRC*.[21] There HMRC asserted that the taxpayers were UK resident in 2001–02. The claimants challenged this both as a matter of law by appeal to the Special Commissioners and an application to the High Court for judicial review, arguing that they had a legitimate expectation to be treated in accordance with IR20. The judge stayed the application pending the appeal to the Special Commissioners. The Court of Appeal however restored the application for judicial review on the basis that, assuming it was well founded it might be pre-empted if the Special Commissioners' determination proceeded before it. It would also create a significant obstacle to the taxpayers in pursuing the judicial review claim as there was a real risk that a decision by the Special Commissioners might be seen as ruling out a claim on the basis of legitimate expectation.

When the substantive *Davies* judicial review was heard,[22] the taxpayers argued, on appeal, that HMRC failed correctly to interpret IR20, and had refused to apply IR20, properly construed, or, at the very least, attempted to apply a different and unannounced change to the interpretation and application which it had previously adopted. Moses LJ reiterated the well-established public law principle that a statement formally published by HMRC to the world might safely be regarded as binding, subject to its terms, or in any case falling clearly within them.[23] The real difficulty, he ruled, lay in the interpretation and their application of IR20 to the facts relating to these particular taxpayers, because the guidance may lead to a wide range of value judgments. For example, he asked:

> 'In 2.2, what is "full-time employment"? To what extent do remaining duties to be performed within the UK affect any conclusion that the work is full-time abroad? IR20 at 2.5 demonstrates that the issue may not be straightforward. Equally, 2.7–2.9 require judgements to be made as to whether a person has gone abroad "permanently" and whether the purpose for which a person has gone abroad is "settled".'[24]

Moses LJ found that these paragraphs in IR20 do not contain any bright-line test of certain application. They require consideration of particular facts and that a judgment be made on those facts. They underline the problem inherent in the guidance that a view will have to be taken on the facts, even though they are undisputed, and that there will be many cases in which opposite but equally reasonable views may be taken.[25]

The Supreme Court affirmed the Court of Appeal decision.[26] The court agreed that representations published by the Revenue are binding in relation only to cases falling clearly within them, the requirement that they should be 'clear, unambiguous and devoid of relevant qualification'. Furthermore, Lord Wilson said, for the majority of the Supreme Court, that:

> '[J]udgement about their clarity must be made in the light of an appraisal of all relevant statements in the booklet when they are read as a whole; and that, in that the clarity of a representation depends in part upon the identity of the person to whom it is made, the hypothetical representee is the "ordinarily sophisticated taxpayer" irrespective of whether he is in receipt of professional advice.'[27]

Reliance on IR20 was undermined by the health warning in the preface to the effect that the guidance was only general and set out only the 'main' factors to be taken into account, and a decision in relation to residence could be made only upon an evaluation of all the facts of the case.[28] He found that the relevant paragraphs were very poorly drafted and lacked the clarity required by the doctrine of legitimate expectation.[29]

In contrast, Lord Mance, in the minority, was of the view that IR20 was intended to obviate any need for a taxpayer to look further.[30] In his view, the natural meaning of the relevant parts of IR20 was that the appellants in this case could rely on the guidance to be treated as non-resident, even if this was not the case in strict law 'in the interests of good governance, clarity and transparency'.[31]

1 446 HC Official Report (5th Series) col 2266.
2 Bill of Rights 1688.
3 [1985] STC 323.
4 [1985] STC 323 at 347.
5 [2005] UKSPC 484.
6 [2006] UKSPC SPC568.
7 At para 99. In *Grace v HMRC* 92008 SpC 663 the taxpayer calculated days present in the UK, ignoring days of arrival and departure as well (at paras 18 and 19). See also *Karim v HMRC* [2009] UKFTT 368 (TC), at paras 21 and 22. In *Karim*, HMRC argued on the basis of the approach in IR20. In *Farquhar v HMRC* [2010] UKFTT 231, the taxpayer was a merchant seaman in full-time employment with a Norwegian company. The taxpayer and HMRC adopted different methods of counting days and in deciding when to start counting in the case of departure part-way through the year. In *Megwa v Revenue & Customs* [2010] UKFTT 543 (TC), another seafarer argued that the time when he became resident and ordinarily resident should be determined by reference to IR20 para 3.1. In *Ogden v HMRC* [2011] UKFTT 212 (TC) the taxpayer telephoned the Cambridge tax office and was told that if he did not exceed 90 working days whilst in Cambridge his other days would fall under a compassionate visit dispensation, but having spent more than 183 days in the year was resident as a matter of law.
8 HMRC Brief 01/07.
9 *Genovese v HMRC* [2009] UKSPC 741. Likewise, in *Tuczka v HMRC* [2010] UKFTT 53 (TC) the taxpayer, Dr Tuczka, had self-assessed himself as having become ordinarily resident from 6 April 2001 based purely on IR20 (at para 21).
10 At para 57.
11 *Hankinson v HMRC* [2009] UKFTT 384.
12 At para 11.
13 At para 107.
14 At para 109.
15 *R (on the application of Hankinson) v Revenue & Customs Commissioners* [2009] STC 2158.
16 [1987] STC 334.
17 (1944) 26 TC 166 at p 181.
18 [2005] UKHL 30.
19 At para [21].
20 At the time of publication, no such order has been made.
21 [2008] EWCA (Civ) 10 July 2008.
22 *Davies & Anor, R (on the application of) v HM Revenue & Customs* [2010] EWCA Civ 83.
23 At para 13.
24 At para 26.
25 At para 27.
26 *R (on the application of Davies & Anor) v Revenue & Customs Commissioners; R (on the application of Gaines-Cooper) v Revenue & Customs Commissioners* [2011] UKSC 47, [2011] STC 2249.
27 At para 29.
28 At paras 32 and 33.
29 At para 39.
30 At para 94.
31 At para 100.

1.27 Withdrawal of IR20

The withdrawal of IR20 announced on 2 April 2009 and the issue of the successor document, HMRC6, represented a departure more radical than any other in the 80 or so years since the practices it reflected were first developed.

The successor, HMRC6, which was made applicable from 6 April 2009 appeared to be at pains to avoid taxpayers placing any reliance on it. The point was made at great length in the introduction:

'1 Introduction and Glossary

This guidance outlines our (HMRC) view and interpretation of legislation and case law. The material is guidance only. It has no legal force, nor does it seek to set out regulation or practice. When it seeks to give practical examples of what the relevant law means, it contains HMRC interpretation of that law.

The guidance replaces IR20 Residents and non-residents: Liability to tax in the United Kingdom. Any practices associated with the IR20 – whether overtly expressed or not – will not apply from 6 April 2009, unless provided for outside the IR20 (in statute law, in case law, in published extra statutory concession, or in a guidance note).'

If there were any doubt about this intention it reiterated:

'The Purpose of this guidance

...

You are responsible for your own tax affairs in the UK but we might ask you about your tax affairs at some time. This guidance will tell you the main factors that we at HMRC take into account when deciding your residence, ordinary residence and domicile status for UK tax purposes. It is general guidance which is designed to help you reach a decision yourself. We accept that these are not straightforward subjects and our guidance might not cover all of the issues which affect you. You might find that your personal circumstances are more complex than the simple guidance we provide here and that you need to contact us to obtain further information or seek the services of a professional tax adviser.

The Self Assessment system also means that it is up to you to make a decision on whether or not you are resident in the UK for tax purposes. If you are resident, you will also have to decide whether you are not domiciled or not ordinarily resident in the UK as this may affect how any foreign income and/or gains that you have are taxed in the UK. If you decide that you are not resident, or not ordinarily resident, or not domiciled in the UK we would expect you to be able to support your conclusions with details on how you have reached them.'

No hint that this approach would be taken appeared from the invitation to comment on the rewrite of guidance. HMRC announced a rewrite of its guidance[1] indicating that 'we recognise that the time has come for a complete rewrite to reflect changing circumstances such as increased international mobility since the IR20 was first written'. The invitation to comment asked whether the scope of guidance in the current IR20 was about right, whether there were any areas or issues not covered which should be addressed, whether some of the content was unnecessary or irrelevant and, whether there were any particular issues where clearer guidance was required. The invitation concluded perplexingly: 'Please note that we are not inviting comments on the legislation, HMRC policy or practice on residence and domicile issues or on individual cases.'

The author's view is that HMRC6 offered little guidance on which individuals can rely. The content lacks the clarity of IR20 and is in some respects self-contradictory. HMRC6 appears to have been written principally to limit the scope for judicial supervision of the administration of this area of law. In addition to the general disclaimers, almost all the Revenue statements are qualified by the insertion of the word 'normally' or by the use of 'may' or 'might' rather than 'will.' As cases such as *Shepherd, Gaines-Cooper, Genovese* and *Davies* demonstrate, even in relation to IR20, relying on the guidance by a taxpayer is a risky proposition.[2]

HMRC6 was revised in December 2010 and the later edition is expressed to apply immediately from 31 December 2011, but with the proviso that the previous version may be used for tax liability before 6 April 2011. It will have no effect after 5 April 2013.

1 HMRC Consultative Document *Replacement Guidance for Residence and Domicile – an invitation to comment* 15 September 2008.
2 *Shepherd v Revenue & Customs* [2005] UKSPC 484; *Gaines-Cooper v HMRC* [2006] UKSPC SPC568; *Genovese v Revenue & Customs* [2009] UKSPC 741; and *Davies & Anor, R (on the application of) v HM Revenue & Customs* [2010] EWCA Civ 83.

1.28 Guidance and the statutory residence test

Although the Consultative Document expressed the belief that the statutory residence test will allow individuals to assess their residence status simply and without the need to resort to specialist advice, HMRC has issued a guidance note (RDR3)[1] setting out its views on the operation of the legislation. RDR3 is 105 pages long compared to the previous 86-page HMRC 6. It contains 73 examples to illustrate the application of the SRT and split-year treatment. The hoped-for simplicity has thus far evaded the legislative drafters. Express limitations on the extent to which the guidance may be relied on suggest that the issues that have dogged guidance on individual residence will not disappear. An HMRC online 'Tax Residence Indicator[2] also offers to check whether individuals are considered to be resident in the UK but not whether they meet the requirements for split-year treatment. It does not check the residence status of someone who died in the tax year. The indicator will helpfully perform calculations to deal with the many formulae and numerical thresholds contained in the statutory residence test. It is not authoritative and HMRC cautions that the results given rely on individuals inputting accurate information. In so doing explicit recognition is given of the need to interpret the concepts that constitute the test before any calculations can be made. Tax Residence Indicator invites users to use the RDR3 guidance in answering the questions posed by the online tool. HMRC recommends that taxpayers should keep the results for future reference in case of enquiry by them.

1 HMRC Guidance Note: Statutory Residence Test (SRT) ('RDR3') 22 August 2016. A draft version of RDR3 was published in May 2013 and the first version published on 28 August 2013 and amended several times since. HMRC guidance note RDR1: Residence, Domicile and the Remittance Basis (31 January 2018) also sets out HMRC guidance on the subject in less detail.
2 See http://tools.hmrc.gov.uk/rift/screen/SRT+-+Combined/en-GB/summary?user=guest.

CHAPTER 2

Residence of individuals: the Statutory Residence Test

'An Answer for you?' interrupted Deep Thought majestically. 'Yes, I have.'
'There really is one?' breathed Phouchg.
'To Everything? To the great Question of Life, the Universe and Everything?'
'Yes' said Deep Thought, 'Though I don't think that you're going to like it'
'Forty-two,' said Deep Thought, with infinite majesty and calm.

Douglas Adams, *The Hitchhiker's Guide to the Galaxy*

2.01 Introduction

The 'Statutory Residence Test'[1] (SRT) defines the tax residence of individuals from 6 April 2013.[2] The test is set out in Parts 1 and 2 of Schedule 45 to the Finance Act 2013. It determines the residence of individuals for the purposes of income tax, capital gains tax and, where relevant, corporation tax and inheritance tax.[3] The statutory residence test will determine whether an individual is resident or non-resident in the UK, including those cases where a tax liability of another actual or deemed person depends on the residence of another individual.[4] Thus, for example, the residence of a trust is determined by reference to the residence of the trustees.[5] In such a case the residence of a trust with individual trustees will be determined indirectly by the statutory residence test. It does not apply to National Insurance Contributions or for non-tax purposes.[6]

The UK, for this purpose, means the United Kingdom including the territorial sea of the United Kingdom.[7] 'Overseas' is defined to mean anywhere outside the UK.[8] The SRT only determines whether an individual is resident in the UK as a whole and not in one of the countries comprising the UK. For 'residence' in Scotland, see **2.44**. The SRT does not apply to individuals whose residential status is expressly dealt with differently in any other statute.[9] It replaces all other tests of residence so that the residential status of individuals is entirely governed by statute.[10]

The background to the adoption of the statutory residence test is considered in Chapter 1.

The overall effect of the statutory residence test and related rules contained in Schedule 45 to the Finance Act 2013 is to establish the following category of persons with residential fiscal connections to the UK:

- *UK residents*: UK residents are liable to income tax and capital gains tax on income and capital gains wherever they arise whether in or outside the UK.
- *Non-residents*: non-residents are liable to income tax on income from sources within the UK and certain capital gains on the disposal of assets situated in the UK.
- *UK residents with split-year treatment*: this is a new legal category of status, rather like the Flying Dutchman who was perpetually between ports. Such individuals are not taxed as fully resident nor as fully non-resident individuals. Instead they are liable to income tax and capital gains tax in accordance with a lengthy list of amendments to the tax system where certain items qualify for special treatment.
- *Temporary non-residents*: these are individuals who are not resident in the UK but whose liability to tax on a worldwide basis is suspended pending their possible return to the UK within five years of having departed. The list of items on which their liability to tax as a resident is suspended is likewise lengthy.

Drafting of the SRT

The drafting of the statutory residence test and related rules is less than satisfactory. It will be apparent to the reader from different drafting conventions adopted, that different parts of Schedule 45 have been drafted by different individuals and that little attempt has been made to harmonise or reconcile them. Secondly, the legislation has abandoned the clear language of the consultation documents which set out the government policy in favour of bland, uninformative, unmemorable phrases. Thus, for example, 'full-time work abroad' has given way to 'the third automatic overseas test'. 'International transportation workers' has given way to 'P' with a 'relevant job on board a vehicle, aircraft or ship'. The eight cases of split-year treatment are known by their case numbers. Some individual rules have lost conceptual coherence as the draft legislation developed. Whether this is a product of policy or drafting is far from clear. Words such as 'somewhere' in relation to a home or 'something' in relation to work, may leave the reader with the feeling that the drafters sought to evade rather than ensure the clarity and certainty that the statutory residence test was intended to produce. HMRC Guidance is contained in a new publication HMRC Guidance Note: Statutory Residence Test (SRT) ('RDR3'), which has been revised several times, most recently on 16 August 2016.

This chapter aims to explain and analyse the statutory test using ordinary language. Rather than speculating about the meaning of every ambiguous expression, a general caution about the precise meaning of the SRT is appropriate, until the tribunals and courts have had an opportunity to consider them in practice.

Consistent with the HMRC view of the case law, that residence should have an adhesive nature, the legislation aims to ensure that resident individuals cannot become and remain non-resident without significantly reducing the extent of their connection with the UK.[11] The legislative test has thus been designed to make it significantly harder to become non-resident when leaving the UK after a period of residence than it is to become resident when an individual comes to the UK. Once an individual has become resident and built up connections with the UK, they will be required to scale back their ties to the UK significantly or spend far less time here or a combination of the two before they can relinquish tax residence. On the other hand, individuals should not be resident if they have little connection with the UK.[12] In line with this approach, a distinction is made between:

- individuals who were not UK resident in all of the previous three tax years; and
- individuals who were resident in one or more of the previous three tax years.

1 Finance Act 2013 Sch 45, para 1(2). All statutory references in this chapter are to paragraphs of that Schedule unless stated otherwise.
2 See **2.41** for commencement and transitional rules.
3 Schedule 45 para 1(2) and (4), 2(1)–(3).
4 Schedule 45 para 2(2).
5 See generally, Chapter 6.
6 Schedule 45 para 1(4).
7 Schedule 45 para 145. See Chapter 1, paras **1.06** and **1.07** on the territorial extent of the United Kingdom.
8 Schedule 45 para 145.
9 Schedule 45 para 2(5). See **2.27** on the residence of members of Parliament and of the House of Lords and **2.28** on the residence of EU officials.
10 Schedule 45 para 2(1) and (2).
11 HM Treasury and HM Revenue & Customs, Statutory definition of tax residence: a consultation, 17 June 2011 (the 'Consultative Document') para 3.5.
12 Consultative Document para 3.6.

The statutory residence test

2.02 Basic rule

The basic rule of the statutory residence test is that an individual is resident in the UK for a tax year if, for that year, either (a) the automatic residence test, or (b) the sufficient ties test is met.[1] The basic rule is modified by the automatic residence test itself. The automatic UK test only applies if none of the automatic overseas tests is met. It is a requirement of the sufficient ties test that none of the automatic UK tests and none of the automatic overseas tests are met.[2]

The automatic residence test contains conclusive non-residence factors that would each be sufficient in themselves to make an individual resident. The sufficient ties test contains other connection factors and day counting rules which, taken together, may make an individual resident. If an individual satisfies neither test for a tax year, he will definitely be not resident in that tax year.

By this convoluted and circular route, a hierarchy for the application of the three parts of the statutory residence test is established. Firstly, if any of the automatic overseas tests are satisfied, that would be sufficient to make an individual not resident. Secondly, if an individual satisfies any of the automatic

UK (residence) tests, but none of the automatic overseas tests, that would itself be sufficient to make an individual resident. Thirdly, if none of the automatic UK tests and none of the automatic overseas tests are satisfied, then the sufficient ties test is engaged. The sufficient ties test contains other connecting factors and day counting rules which will need to be considered only by those whose residence status is not determined by the automatic tests.

The tests

There are four automatic UK tests, five automatic overseas tests and the sufficient ties test, summarised as follows:

Automatic UK tests:

- spending 183 days or more in a tax year in the UK (the 'first automatic UK test');[3] or
- having a home in the UK at which sufficient time is spent (and either having no home overseas or spending insufficient time at overseas homes) (the 'second automatic UK test');[4] or
- working full-time in the UK over a period of 365 days (the 'third automatic UK test');[5] or
- dying in a year after having been resident in the UK under the automatic residence test for each of the previous three tax years and having a home in the UK (the 'fourth automatic UK test').[6]

Automatic overseas tests:

- residence in the UK for one or more of the three tax years preceding the year, and spending less than 16 days in the year in the UK (the 'first automatic overseas test');[7] or
- residence in the UK for none of the three tax years preceding the year and spending less than 46 days in the year in the UK (the 'second automatic overseas test');[8] or
- working full-time overseas for the year, spending less than 91 days in the year in the UK and having no more than 31 days in the year on which the individual does more than three hours' work (the 'third automatic overseas test').[9]
- Dying in a year after having been UK resident for neither of the two preceding year tax years (or not UK resident in the previous year and the tax year before that was a split year in certain cases) and having spent less than 46 days in the UK in that year (the 'fourth automatic overseas test').[10]
- Dying in a year after having been UK resident for neither of the two preceding year tax years because of full-time work overseas in certain cases (the 'fifth automatic overseas test').[11]

Sufficient ties test

The sufficient ties test is met by spending the prescribed number of days in the UK in a tax year in conjunction with the following UK ties:

- a family tie;
- an accommodation tie;

- a work tie;
- a 90-day tie; and
- a country tie.[12]

The automatic tests turn on the application of four factors: physical presence in the UK; having and using a home in the UK; full-time work either in the UK or overseas; and death. In this chapter, each factor is discussed in turn as a determinant of residence rather than simply following the list of tests in the numerical order as set out in the legislation.

---

1 Schedule 45, para 3.
2 Schedule 45, para 5.
3 Schedule 45, para 7. See **2.06**.
4 Schedule 45, para 8. See **2.07**.
5 Schedule 45, para 9. See **2.12**.
6 Schedule 45, para 10. See **2.17**.
7 Schedule 45, para 12. See **2.05**.
8 Schedule 45, para 13. See **2.06**.
9 Schedule 45, para 14. See **2.13**.
10 Schedule 45, para 15. See **2.16**.
11 Schedule 45, para 16. See **2.16**.
12 Schedule 45, para 16. See **2.18** to **2.26**.

2.03 Physical presence: counting days

Physical presence in the UK is a central theme in the statutory test. A living individual who is not physically present in the UK at all in a tax year cannot satisfy any of the tests to qualify as a UK resident. All tests, other than the death-related automatic tests, expressly or by necessary implication require such presence. It is also a specific requirement throughout the split-year rules. A uniform manner of determining the number of days spent in the UK applies to all measures of physical presence in the UK for purposes of the SRT, but one.[1] Different rules, however, apply to determine time spent working,[2] at home or at any other place to live,[3] or seeing children.[4]

Unlike the previous HMRC practice, none of the time periods are averaged. The number of days present in, or absent from, the UK are measured strictly for each tax year concerned. This inflexibility is likely to produce harsh and arbitrary outcomes as few individuals live their lives by the UK tax calendar.

The number of days spent in the UK in a given period is determined by reference to the total number of days spent there, in the aggregate, in that period, whether continuously or intermittently.[5] A day counts as a day spent by an individual in the UK if he is present in the UK at the end of a day. Whether an individual is present in the UK, is a question of fact. The legislation makes explicit that a day does not count as a day spent in the UK if the individual is not present in the UK at the end of that day.[6] Two exceptions are made: in the case of transit passengers[7] and for circumstances beyond the individual's control.[8]

The first exception is where an individual arrives in the UK as a passenger on a particular day and leaves the UK the next day, and between arrival and departure, the individual does not engage in activities that are to a substantial

33

extent unrelated to his passage through the UK.[9] This is similar to the rule introduced by FA 2004 s 24. HMRC regard merely taking dinner or breakfast at an hotel, in the normal course of events, as related to passage. In contrast, enjoying a film at the local cinema or catching up with friends or a brief work-related meeting would be considered substantially unrelated to passage through the UK.[10] See the discussion and examples in RDR3, para 3.9. See also HMRC's previous practice in Chapter 5, at **5.09**.

Secondly, where an individual would not be present in the UK at the end of a day but for exceptional circumstances beyond his control that prevent him from leaving the UK, and the individual intends to leave the UK as soon as those circumstances permit, that day does not count as a day spent in the UK.[11] The relief is tightly drawn. The circumstances must both be exceptional and beyond the individual's control. In addition, the circumstances must be such that they prevent the individual from leaving. These expressions are undefined, but the legislation gives examples of circumstances that may be exceptional. They are national or local emergencies such as war, civil unrest or natural disasters, and a sudden or life-threatening illness or injury.[12] The relief does not appear apply to individuals who are compelled to come to the UK because of such circumstances. A British national who is evacuated to the UK from a foreign war zone is outside the exception. The same would be true for an individual evacuated to the UK for emergency medical treatment.

HMRC have devoted six pages of the Guidance in RDR3 to the subject of exceptional circumstaces[13] Whether circumstances can be regarded as exceptional for the purpose of the SRT will always depend on the particular facts, an individual's circumstances and the choices available to them.[14] Exceptional circumstances will normally apply where an individual has no choice concerning the time they spend in the UK or in coming back to the UK.[15] Thus where an individual with serious injury can be removed to hospital outside the UK, the failure to do so will not constitute exceptional circumstances.[16] Some concession appears to be made in very limited circumstances where an individual comes to the UK rather than merely remaining in the UK in circumstances beyond their control: where they are coming back to the UK to deal with a sudden life-threatening illness or injury to a partner or dependent child[17] a passenger (but not a crew member) on a commercial aircraft that is forced to make an emergency landing in the UK and there is no available onward flight to their original destination for two days afterwards[18] evacuation from a ship departing the UK for emergency medical treatment.[19] Where Foreign and Commonwealth Office advice is to avoid all travel to a region because of civil unrest or natural disaster, individuals who return to and stay in the UK while such advice remains at this warning level would 'normally' have days spent in the UK ignored during that period.[20]

HMRC do not consider travel problems, such as a delayed or missed flight due to traffic disruption, train delays or cancellations, or a car breakdown, as exceptional circumstances.[21]

In the view of HMRC, not only must the circumstances be beyond control, they must be beyond the individual's influence and unforeseeable.[22] The HMRC view plainly goes beyond the requirements of the statute. No more than 60 days in a year may be excluded from counting as presence in the UK on this ground.[23]

The fact that a day is spent in the UK, detained by exceptional circumstances, does not prevent the day counting as one spent working in the UK, at home or at any other place to live, or seeing children. Similarly, it does not impact on another day counting rules such as breaks between employments or in the availability of a home or a place to live.

---

1 Schedule 45, para 23(3). See **2.22**.
2 See **2.12** and **2.21**.
3 See **2.07** and **2.20**.
4 See **2.19**.
5 Schedule 45, para 24.
6 Schedule 45, paras 22(1) and 23(1).
7 Schedule 45, para 22(3).
8 Schedule 45, para 22(4).
9 Schedule 45, para 22(3).
10 RDR3 para 3.9.
11 Schedule 45, para 22(4).
12 Schedule 45, para 22(5).
13 See Appendix B.
14 RDR3, Annex B, para B3.
15 RDR3, Annex B, para B9.
16 RDR3, Annex B, Example B2 (a broken neck).
17 RDR3, Annex B, para B 12.
18 RDR3, Annex B, para B14.
19 RDR3, Annex B, ExampleB1.
20 RDR3, Annex B, paras B16 and 16.
21 RDR3, Annex B, para B20.
22 RDR3, Annex B para B13.
23 Schedule 45, para 6.

2.04   Day-count hyping

In certain circumstances an individual will be deemed to spend a day in the UK even if that individual is not actually present in the UK at midnight on the day concerned regardless of the exceptions for transit passengers and circumstances beyond the individual's control. This will be the case for individuals who: (a) have at least three UK ties for a tax year; (b) were resident in the UK for at least one of the three tax years preceding the tax year in question; and (c) are present in the UK at some point in the day but not at the end of the day ('qualifying days') for more than 30 days in a tax year. Such individuals must count any qualifying day in excess of 30 in the tax year as a day spent in the UK.[1]

Day-count hyping (given the anodyne 'deeming rule' label in RDR3) does not apply for the purposes of deciding whether an individual has a 90-day tie or in determining presence in the UK under the full-time work overseas test (the 'third automatic overseas test').[2]

The Second Consultative Document stated that a supplementary rule, which would apply only to those who are present in the UK on a large number of days without ever being in the UK at midnight on those days to minimise the potential for manipulation.[3] The stated policy was not to have such a rule affect those who legitimately commute to and from the UK frequently, especially if they do not have other significant ties to the UK. The day-count hyping deeming rule overshoots that objective and is not restricted to 'manipulators' of the normal day counting rule.

---

1 Schedule 45, para 23(2)–(4).
2 Schedule 45, para 23(5).
3 HM Treasury and HM Revenue & Customs, Statutory definition of tax residence and reform of ordinary residence: a summary of responses (June 2012) (the 'Second Consultative Document'), para 3.153.

2.05 Counting days: conclusive non-residence

The automatic overseas tests are designed to treat individuals as clearly not tax resident in the UK in certain circumstances without having to take account of the connections they have with the UK. This is the case when they are present in the UK for only a small number of days in a tax year. Two tests are almost entirely dependent on physical presence in the UK. An individual is conclusively not resident in the UK for a tax year if he:

- was resident in the UK in all of the previous three tax years and is present in the UK for fewer than 16 days in the current tax year but does not die in that year (the 'first automatic overseas test');[1] or
- was not resident in the UK in one or more of the previous three tax years and is present in the UK for fewer than 46 days in the current tax year (the 'second automatic overseas test').[2]

Different amounts of time that may be spent in the UK depending on previous residence, reflects the HMRC view of the case law, that residence should have an adhesive nature. As a result resident individuals cannot become and remain non-resident without significantly reducing the extent of their connection with the UK. The test has been designed to make it harder to become non-resident when leaving the UK after a period of residence than it is to become resident when an individual comes to the UK. Once individuals have become resident and built up connections with the UK, they will be required to scale back their ties to the UK significantly or spend far less time here or a combination of the two before they can relinquish residence. On the other hand, individuals should not be resident if they have little connection with the UK. The stated policy was that it is beneficial to encourage individuals to come to the UK and spend a limited amount of time here without necessarily becoming resident, such as investors assessing investment opportunities.[3] A holiday in the UK of little more than six weeks will take the occasional visitor out of automatic non-resident status.

---

1 Schedule 45, para 12.
2 Schedule 45, para 13.
3 Second Consultative Document para 3.154.

2.06 Counting days: conclusive residence

If none of the automatic overseas tests applies to treat an individual as conclusively non-resident, then the individual will be conclusively resident for a tax year if he is present in the UK for 183 days or more in a tax year (the 'first automatic UK test').[1] The application of the 183-day rule is neither new nor complex. Its operation is illustrated by the following example.

David and Edward visit the UK and both spend about six months here in one tax year. David comes to the UK for one continuous period and is treated as resident in the UK if he spends 183 days here. Edward visits for the same period but makes a few trips abroad from the UK during the year and is treated as not resident if days present are less than 183 in the tax year (subject to the second, third and fourth automatic UK tests and the sufficient ties test).[2] It will be apparent that this is the only simple test based on counting days present in the UK. Even the automatic overseas day counting tests described in **2.05** above require determination of residence in prior years under the whole of the SRT or the case law test for years prior to 6 April 2013 for their accurate application.

---

1 Schedule 45, paras 5(b) and 7.
2 Drawn from HM Treasury and HMRC, *Reviewing the residence and domicile rules as they affect the taxation of individuals: a background paper*, April 2003.

2.07   UK home: conclusive residence

The principle that an individual is resident where their home is, is enticingly simple. The most obvious cases cause no difficulty. It might be thought that in modern western society, most people have a home and that the vast majority have only one. This straightforward principle has been converted into a complex test that conflates the amount of time an individual needs to be at the home for it to qualify as such, and a mechanism to deal with those individuals who have a home in the UK and overseas.

An individual is automatically resident if: (a) he has a home in the UK during all or part of a year; (b) there is at least one period of 91 consecutive days, of which at least 30 days ('sufficient time') in the aggregate fall within the year in which he has no home overseas; and (c) he spends at least 30 days in the year at that UK home.[1] If the individual has one or more homes overseas during that 91-day period, and spends fewer than 30 days ('a permitted amount of time') in the aggregate, in the year at any of those overseas homes, but spends at least 30 days in the aggregate, in the year at the UK home, then the individual is likewise automatically UK resident.[2] The UK home test (the 'second automatic UK test') thus comprises two separate tests that treat an individual as conclusively resident if the automatic overseas tests do not apply.[3]

In each case an individual will spend a day at a home when he is present there for at least some of the time, no matter how short, on that day. Presence at a dwelling only counts when it is a home of the individual, so that presence there on any other occasion is disregarded. Looking round a property with a view to buying it, is given as an example of disregarded presence in the legislation.[4] Mere presence, rather than occupation is sufficient. Brief presence in this context may be contrasted with the accommodation tie which requires a night to be spent at the accommodation.

In the case of multiple overseas homes, presence at only one of them for less than 30 days may be sufficient to disapply the UK home test.[5] A generous rule applies to those who have more than one home in the UK. Each UK home must be looked at separately to see if the second automatic UK test is met, and the test is then met provided it is met in relation to at least one of those homes.

1 Schedule 45, paras 8(1), (2) and (4).
2 Schedule 45, paras 8(1), (3) and (5).
3 Schedule 45, para 5(b).
4 Schedule 45, para 8(6)(b).
5 Schedule 45, para 8(8).

2.08 What is a home?

However, even the most straightforward and common cases raise the question: 'What is a "home"?' Does a student who goes to study at an overseas university retain a home if their bedroom is kept available but they do not use it? What if the room is converted to a study by the student's parents? The ordinary meanings offered by the Oxford English Dictionary are:

'1.   The place where a person or animal dwells.
2. a.   A dwelling place; a person's house or abode; the fixed residence of a family or household; the seat of domestic life and interests. Also (chiefly in later use): a private house or residence considered merely as a building;'

Although this question gave rise to significant comment during the consultation process, Parliament declined to attempt a definition of the term. The HMRC response during the consultation was:

'The only home condition is not intended to set a low bar but is meant to be indicative of an individual who normally lives only in the UK. The vast majority of UK resident taxpayers will have only one place to live and this will be their home. It will typically be where they and their immediate family live for all, or the greater part, of their time.

The Government has carefully considered whether to further define in legislation what is meant by a home. It has concluded that it would be extremely difficult to provide a precise definition given the wide variety of living patterns adopted by individuals and their families. Any detailed definition would run the risk of inadvertently including or excluding certain individuals from the test because of the way in which they choose to live their lives. The Government is confident however, that the vast majority of people will know where their home is and whether that home is in the UK or overseas.'

Thus the question is ducked in the legislation. Instead, the following statutory explanation is provided:

'(1)   A person's home could be a building or part of a building or, for example, a vehicle, vessel or structure of any kind.
(2)   Whether, for a given building, vehicle, vessel, structure or the like, there is a sufficient degree of permanence or stability about [the person]'s arrangements

there for the place to count as [the person]'s home (or one of [the person]'s homes) will depend on all the circumstances of the case.

(3) But somewhere that [the person] uses periodically as nothing more than a holiday home or temporary retreat (or something similar) does not count as a home of [the person]'s.

(4) A place may count as a home of [the person]'s whether or not [the person] holds any estate or interest in it (and references to "having" a home are to be read accordingly).

(5) Somewhere that was [the person]'s home does not continue to count as such merely because [the person] continues to hold an estate or interest in it after [the person] has moved out (for example, if [the person] is in the process of selling it or has let or sub-let it, having set up home elsewhere).'[1]

Ownership or form of tenancy does not determine whether a place is a 'home'. It may be a home whether or not the individual holds any estate or interest in it. A home may be any place including a vehicle or vessel.[2] The legislation helpfully clarifies that a place that was a home does not continue as such merely because the individual continues to hold an estate or interest in it after having moved out. It also confirms that where an individual is in the process of selling a home, it will not continue to count as a home for the purpose of the test after they have moved out of the property.[3]

The requirement to be present for at least 30 days at a home will exclude some cases at the margins from the UK home test. However, very many individuals who either leave the UK or come to it, giving up their existing homes and acquiring a new home in the process will find themselves automatically resident under this test. Imperfect alignment of this test with the split-year treatment in Schedule 45, Part 3 will result in extended periods of taxation as a resident for them.[4]

Paragraph 25(2) suggests that 'a sufficient degree of permanence or stability about [the person]'s arrangements' are necessary to make a dwelling place count as a home. No indication of the degree is specified. It will depend on all the circumstances of the case. It is unclear how the requisite degree of permanence or stability will be interpreted in the context of the minimal 91-day period over which an individual having a home combined with will fall within this rule. If 91 days is sufficient, then paragraph 25(2) is otiose. On the other hand, if a broader examination of facts and circumstances is necessary and classification as a home during 30 days in a tax year is sufficient, then the 91-day period in paragraph 8(1)(c) is otiose. While residence is an annual attribute, the existence of a home in many cases take into account facts in more than one tax year.

The only qualitative indicator is that periodic use as nothing more than a holiday home or temporary retreat is not a home in this context. If the guideline is 30 days of presence in a tax year, will occupation for longer periods make a 'holiday home' a 'home'? Under the case law test of residence, occupation of a dwelling place for a portion of a year constitutes residence. In *Cooper v Cadwalader*[5] Mr Cadwalader was an American citizen who had a house in New York but spent two months of each year in occupation of, a furnished house in Scotland. Although the vocabulary is not identical, Mr Cadwalader undoubtedly had a home in Scotland, even if it was only used for holidays. Case law on the word 'temporary' indicated that it means casual as distinguished regular habits of life. Temporary purpose means the opposite of continuous purpose.[6] These cases suggest that periodic use as a regular matter will mean the accommodation is a home while casual use will not. In *Yates v Revenue & Customs*[7] Ms Yates rented a three-bedroom apartment in Estepona, on the southern coast of Spain, on an 11-month lease, which was renewed until November 2003, when she purchased another three-bedroom apartment in the same development. She stayed in them when living in Spain. HMRC accepted in the context of Art 4(2)(a) of the Spain-UK income tax treaty that these apartments were both permanent and available to her, but would not accept that they were 'homes' because they did not have the quality of being 'the seat of domestic life' inherent in the French word 'foyer', which is used to distinguish a house from a home. Tribunal Judge John Walters QC however found, on the facts, that it was clear that the Spanish apartments had the quality of being her 'homes'.[8] The application of the UK home test inevitably raises questions about the boundary between it and the 'place available to live' expression in the 'accommodation tie' test. The accommodation tie test must be applied in conjunction with physical presence as a 'sufficient ties' test. A detailed exposition of what will constitute 'place available to live', the purposes of the 'accommodation tie' as part of the sufficient UK ties test is provided[9] but no statutory explanation on what makes a place available to live a home. A home in the UK will always be a place to live in the UK, but a place to live may not always be a home. Uncertainty, in relation to the UK home test will mean that its reliability as an automatic test will be limited to individuals with no place to live overseas or those with no place to live in the UK in a tax year.

Although HMRC assiduously resist a definition of home for this purpose, their views on its application are set out in a ten-page appendix to their guidance on the SRT in RDR3 which is reproduced in full in Appendix 1. HMRC guidance on record keeping in connection with the question indicated a wide ranging enquiry into the full facts and circumstances of an individual's life going far beyond connection with a particular property.[10] This approach effectively revives the full enquiry into the pattern of living of individuals required by the previous case law and subverts the purpose of the SRT itself. Questions relating to whether an individual 'has a home' within the second automatic UK test in paragraph 8 are destined for early consideration by the tribunals and the courts.

Relevance of having a home

Whether an individual can be said to have a home is critical to the application of the SRT. It forms the basis of the second automatic UK test.[11] It is an element in the fourth automatic UK test (death after having been previously resident).[12] Having a home and when an individual starts or ceases to have one is relevant to split-year treatment under Case 2 (the partner of someone starting full-time work overseas),[13] Case 3 (ceasing to have a home in the UK),[14] Case 4 (starting to have a home in the UK only),[15] Case 7 (the partner of someone ceasing full-time work overseas)[16] and Case 8 (starting to have a home in the UK).[17]

---

1 Schedule 45, para 25.

2 Schedule 45, para 25(1).

3 Schedule 45, para 25(5).

4 See **2.30–2.40**.
5 *Cooper v Cadwalader* (1904) 5 TC 101.
6 See Chapter 5 at **5.05**.
7 *Lynette Dawn Yates v Revenue & Customs* [2012] UKFTT 568 (TC). HMRC are of the view that 'home' for SRT purposes is not the same as that term in treaty tie-breaker provisions. See RDR3, Annex A, para A5.
8 Schedule 45, para 116.
9 Schedule 45, para 34.
10 See Appendix 2.
11 See **2.07.**
12 See **2.19**.
13 See **2.34**.
14 See **2.35**.
15 See **2.36**.
16 See **2.39**.
17 See **2.40**.

Work

2.09 Introduction

Full-time work in the UK gives rise to automatic residence (the 'third automatic UK test'),[1] while full-time work overseas (the 'third automatic overseas test') means automatic non-residence.[2] The two tests are not symmetrical. The Second Consultation Document confirms that this asymmetry is intentional[3] and that the full-time work in the UK test will cause more employees to be resident in the UK in years of arrival and departure than under prior law.[4] Dying in a year after having been UK resident for neither of the two preceding year tax years because of full-time work overseas in certain cases (the 'fifth automatic overseas test')[5] further extends the relevance of full-time work. The legislation spells out in some detail what is meant by work, where it is done and the nature of working full time.

An individual who does not meet any of the conditions of the work-related automatic overseas test, nor the conditions of the work-related automatic UK test, would need to consider the application of the work-related significant UK ties test.[6]

Full-time work in or out of the UK also engages split-year treatment.[7]

1 See **2.12**.
2 See **2.11**.
3 Second Consultative Document, paras 3.97–3.105.
4 Second Consultative Document, para 3.99.
5 See **2.16**.
6 See **2.21**.
7 See **2.33, 2.34, 2.37, 2.38** and **2.39**.

2.10 What is work?

An individual is considered to be working (or doing work) at any time when he is 'doing something' in the performance of duties of his employment, or in the course of a trade carried on by the individual, alone or in partnership.[1] This rather amorphous expression, 'doing something', is not defined in the legislation but is elaborated in relation to both employment and trade.

'Employment' in this context has the meaning given in ITEPA 2003 s 4.[2] It therefore includes: (a) any employment under a contract of service; (b) any employment under a contract of apprenticeship; and (c) any employment in the service of the Crown. Employment further includes an office within the meaning of ITEPA 2003 s 5(3). It thus includes, in particular, any position which has an existence independent of the person who holds it and may be filled by successive holders. Nonetheless, a voluntary post for which the individual has no contract of service does not count as an employment for these purposes.[3]

'Trade' for this purpose,' also includes: (a) a profession or vocation; (b) anything that is treated as a trade for income tax purposes; and (c) the commercial occupation of woodlands (within the meaning of s 11(2) of ITTOIA 2005).'[4]

In each case, whether an individual is working (or 'doing something'), is essentially a question of fact to be determined by the terms of the employment relationship or the office and the scope and nature of the trade. This factual determination is supplemented by a hypothetical exercise required by sub-paragraphs 26(2), (3) and (8). In deciding whether 'something is being done' in the performance of duties of an employment, regard must be had to whether:

'if value were received by the individual for doing the thing, it would fall within the definition of employment income in section 7 of ITEPA 2003.'[5]

By contrast, in relation to doing something in the course of a trade, regard must be had to whether, if expenses were incurred by the individual in doing the thing, the expenses could be deducted in calculating the profits of the trade for income tax purposes.[6] In each case, for the purposes of sub-paragraphs 26(2) and (3) it must be assumed that the individual is chargeable to income tax under ITEPA 2003 or ITTOIA 2005. Thus, in assessing whether any activity undertaken by an individual is work, the individual must first be engaged in hypothetical employment or trade within the charge to tax. This hypothesis ensures that activities not giving rise to income not within the charge to tax (because, for example, they are performed outside the UK by a putative non-resident) are determined under the UK statutory rules. Secondly, the activity in question must be identified. Thirdly, in the case of employment, it must be decided whether the hypothetical employee would be rewarded for the activity. In the case of a trade, the test is not by reference to hypothetical income for the activity but rather by whether if hypothetical expenses were incurred, they would be deductible trading expenditure.

Time spent working may include being on call or standby, depending on the conditions of employment and the nature of duties. RDR3 Paragraph 3.18 and the examples therein indicate that HMRC does not accept that a self-employed individual is working when available for work in a similar way.

HMRC says that work includes 'where your employer instructs you to stay away from work, for example while serving a period of notice while you remain on the payroll.'[7] Some workers might be surprised to discover that their notice period spent enjoying the sights of London or the wilds of the Scottish highlands meant they were working in the UK!

The stated aim of this additional hypothetical approach is to depart from the traditional distinction between incidental duties which are largely ignored in determining the place of performance of duties of employment under ITEPA (ITEPA 2003 s 39) and other 'substantive' duties.[8] The Second Consultation Document acknowledges that this tightens the existing approach. Activities such as reporting, which have been regarded as incidental, will in future be something done in the performance of duties of employment. Activities that may be necessary such as attending a medical examination, for which, in isolation, an employee may not normally be rewarded, would be excluded. This suggests a very narrow class of activity. Whereas in the case of an employee the test is by reference to remuneration for the activity, in the case of a self-employed trader deductibility is the criterion. In neither case is it necessary for the employee to be actually rewarded for the activity or for the individual to actually be chargeable to income tax or entitled to a trade related deduction in respect of the activity. Training would normally be regarded as an incidental activity for employment. The legislation, however, deems time spent undertaking training as time spent working if the training is provided or paid for by the employer and is undertaken to help the individual in performing duties of the employment.[9] In the case of a trade, deductibility of the cost of the training in calculating the profits of the trade for income tax purposes is the criterion.[10]

Time spent travelling will also be time spent working according to rules similar to those applicable to training. Thus, if the cost of the journey could, if it were incurred by the individual, be deducted in calculating his earnings from that employment under ITEPA 2003, the journey will itself count as work. In the case of a trade, a journey is treated as work if the cost would be deductible in calculating the profits of the individual's trade under ITTOIA 2005.[11] Furthermore, if the individual does something else during the journey that would itself count as work, then the journey will also count as work. Modern working life is such that individuals who can keep a clear divide between work and non-work are becoming increasingly rare. 'Work' as defined, would include activities such as dealing with phone calls and emails, reading work-related documents, and even thinking about work. An individual catching up on a laptop or smartphone while en route for a holiday or weekend break would be working while on such a journey.

Economic activities that do not comprise employment or trade such as management of investments or property business[12] are not 'work' in this context.

---

1 Schedule 45, para 26.
2 Schedule 45, para 145.
3 Schedule 45, para 26(8).
4 Schedule 45, para 145.
5 Schedule 45, para 26(2).
6 Schedule 45, para 26(3).
7 RDR3 para 3.13.
8 Second Consultative Document, paras 3.22–3.32.
9 Schedule 45, para 26(5)(a).

10 Schedule 45, para 26(5)(b).
11 Schedule 45, para 26(4).
12 ITTOIA 2005, ss 264 and 265.

2.11 Location of work

Normally, identifying the place of performance of employment duties gives rise to little difficulty. The SRT specifies the location of work in detail. Work is deemed to be done where it is actually done, regardless of where the employment is held or the trade is carried on by the individual.[1] Thus, individuals with flexible working patterns or arrangements will find themselves working for these purposes when dealing with emails, engaged on the phone or reading work-related documents undertaken outside specific work-related visits. The stated policy is that using a specific number of hours to define a working day is the best approach to achieve a clear and objective definition for the purposes of the SRT.[2] Thus, the boundary in the work-related tests is drawn not by reference to the nature of the work but to the amount of time consumed by work-related activities.

The place of work by way of or in the course of travel, therefore, calls for particular consideration. An arbitrary line is drawn by reference to the point of embarkation. Work done by way of or in the course of travelling by air or sea or via a tunnel under the sea to or from the UK is treated as done overseas, including during the part of the journey in or over the UK.[3] Travelling to or from the UK begins when the individual boards the aircraft, ship or train that is bound for a destination in the UK or (as the case may be) overseas, and ends when the individual disembarks from that aircraft, ship or train.[4] These rules do not apply to international transportation workers who have specific provisions about the location of their work.[5]

1 Schedule 45, para 27(1).
2 Second Consultative Document, para 3.31.
3 Schedule 45, para 27(2).
4 Schedule 45, para 27(3).
5 Schedule 45, para 27(4). See **2.15**.

2.12 Full-time work

Full-time work is not used as an expression in the SRT legislation (although it does appear in the title of certain cases for split-year treatment and is used in HMRC guidance), but this status is described as whether an individual works sufficient hours in the UK or overseas as the case may be.[1] 'Sufficient hours', means work for 35 or more hours per week, on average, across a relevant reference period.[2] Where an individual holds more than one employment or carries on more than one trade during the reference period, the hours worked with respect to all of them are aggregated in determining whether he works sufficient hours there for the period.[3] Thus, any combinations of employments and self-employments have to be taken into account together for this purpose.

The period over which the 35 hours per week is to be measured may be reduced for several reasons.[4] First, a reduction in the length of the period may be made to take account of reasonable amounts of annual leave taken by the individual during the period.[5] Reasonable amounts of annual leave are to be assessed having regard to (among other things) the nature of the work, and the country or countries where the individual is working.[6] The reduction is by reference to leave taken and not leave entitlement. This will be relatively straightforward for employed individuals who take all their leave and have regular work patterns. It may give rise to difficulties in the case of less bureaucratic employment or self-employed traders who may not take leave in a formal sense or full entitlement, but, instead work fewer hours. While the country where work is performed may influence the reasonableness of the amount of leave, no reduction is made for weekends or public holidays or other non-working days. A non-working day for this purpose is any day of the week, month or year on which the individual is not normally expected to work according to his contract of employment or usual pattern of work, and does not in fact work.[7] The result is that an individual working in a country where there is a high statutory minimum holiday will be permitted a greater reduction in the length of the reference period compared to countries with no legal minimum and, for example, two weeks' holiday is the customary norm. On the other hand, an individual working in a country with many public holidays may need to work longer hours to catch up hours not worked on those days to meet the 35-hour average. Reasonable amounts of parenting leave may also be excluded. 'Parenting leave' is maternity leave, paternity leave, adoption leave or parental leave (whether statutory or otherwise).[8]

Absences from work during the period when the individual is on sick leave and cannot reasonably be expected to work as a result of the illness or injury also qualify to reduce the length of the period.[9] The rule requires not only that the person is on sick leave but also establishes an objective standard, that the illness or injury ought to prevent working. No other commonly recognised forms of leave, such as compassionate leave or study leave are referred to, although they may be embraced by annual leave.

An arbitrary formula applies to non-working days that are embedded within a period of leave to take into account leave being determined by reference to working days (and therefore in addition to other non-working days such as weekends and public holidays). Such non-working days only reduce the reference period if there are at least three consecutive days of leave taken before and after the non-working day or series of non-working days in question.[10]

If the individual changes employment during the period any gap of up to 15 days between the two employments may be deducted from the length of the period, but only if the individual does not work at all at any time between the two employments. If there is more than one change in employment during the reference period a maximum of 30 days may be deducted in determining the reference period. No equivalent rule is expressed in relation to individuals engaged in trade who cease to trade and start a new trade.[11]

The language used to describe the factors that permit a reduction in the reference period reflects an employment-focused perspective. It is less well adapted to trade carried on by an individual. In relation to an individual who carries on a trade annual leave or parenting leave means reasonable amounts of time off from work for the same purposes as the purposes for which annual leave or parenting leave is taken.[12]

---

1 Schedule 45, paras 9(1)(a) and 14(1)(a).
2 Schedule 45, paras 9(2) and 14(3). In each case this is only apparent by working through the steps set out in those paragraphs.
3 Schedule 45, paras 9(2) Step 2 and 14(3) Step 2.
4 Schedule 45, para 28. This is described as the 'Rules for calculating the reference period'.
5 Schedule 45, para 285(2)(a).
6 Schedule 45, para 128(4).
7 Schedule 45, para 28(6).
8 Schedule 45, para 28(2)(a).
9 Schedule 45, para 128(2)(b).
10 Schedule 45, para 28(2)(c) and 28(5).
11 Schedule 45, para 128(8) and (9).
12 Schedule 45, para 146.

2.13 Full-time work overseas: conclusive non-residence

The stated intention is that a UK-resident individual who leaves the UK to work abroad full-time should be non-resident for the duration of this work irrespective of the connections with the UK they leave behind, subject to certain conditions.[1]

An individual who works full-time overseas for a tax year is conclusively non-resident if the individual: (a) works sufficient hours overseas, as assessed, over the tax year; (b) has less than 31 days in the year on which he does more than three hours' work in the UK; (c) spends less than 91 days a year in the UK, excluding day-count hyped days; and (d) there are no significant breaks from overseas work during the year (the third automatic overseas test).[2]

No hours worked overseas count if worked on a day when the individual does more than three hours' work in the UK.[3] Thus an individual who works overseas all day for seven hours preparing for a meeting in the UK that day that lasts for over three hours, cannot count those hours worked towards the sufficient hours target.

There is a 'significant break from overseas work' if there are at least 31 consecutive days on which the individual does not do more than three hours' work overseas, or would have done more than three hours' work overseas but for being on annual leave, sick leave or parenting leave.[4] These limits are reduced pro rata for the overseas part of a year in which an individual qualifies for split-year treatment.[5] International transportation workers who have at least six cross-border work trips in a year are outside the scope of the third automatic overseas test.[6]

Assessment of whether sufficient hours have been worked overseas is by application of the following formula in para 14(3):

'(3) Take the following steps to work out whether P[the individual] works "sufficient hours overseas" as assessed over year X[the tax year in question]—

Step 1

Identify any days in year X on which P does more than 3 hours' work in the UK, including ones on which P also does work overseas on the same day.

The days so identified are referred to as "disregarded days".

Step 2

Add up (for all employments held and trades carried on by P) the total number of hours that P works overseas in year X, but ignoring any hours that P works overseas on disregarded days.

The result is referred to as P's "net overseas hours".

Step 3

Subtract from 365 (or 366 if year X includes 29 February)—

(a) the total number of disregarded days, and
(b) any days that are allowed to be subtracted, in accordance with the rules in paragraph 28 of this Schedule, to take account of periods of leave and gaps between employments.

The result is referred to as the "reference period".

Step 4

Divide the reference period by 7. If the answer is more than 1 and is not a whole number, round down to the nearest whole number. If the answer is less than 1, round up to 1.

Step 5

Divide P's net overseas hours by the number resulting from step 4.

If the answer is 35 or more, P is considered to work "sufficient hours overseas" as assessed over year X.'

Once days have been excluded because of UK work, permitted leave or gaps in employment, the resulting number of days is divided by seven to produce the number of weeks worked. A minimum average of 35 hours a week is required to work sufficient hours overseas. It should be possible to meet this test without the work starting or finishing in the tax year over which it is assessed, although the reference period will at least need to start and finish in that tax year. This feature (measurement over a tax year) distinguishes working overseas under the third automatic non-residence test from working in the UK under the second automatic UK test described in **2.14**.

---

1 Consultative Document, para 3.16.
2 Schedule 45, para 14.
3 Schedule 45, para 14(3) Step 1.
4 Schedule 45, para 29(2).
5 See **2.33**, **2.37** and **2.38**.
6 Schedule 45, para 14(4). See **2.15**.

2.14 Full-time work in the UK: conclusive residence

If one of the automatic overseas tests does not apply to treat an individual as conclusively non-resident, then the individual will be conclusively resident for a tax year if he works full-time in the UK. That is the case if the individual: (a) works sufficient hours in the UK, as assessed, over a period of 365 days, all or part of which falls within the tax year; (b) does more than three hours' work in the UK on more than 75% of the total number of days in that period on which the individual does more than three hours' work; (c) does more than three hours' work in the UK on at least one day which is both in that period and the tax year; and (d) during that period, there are no significant breaks from UK work (the third automatic UK test).[1]

No hours worked in the UK count if worked on a day when the individual does more than three hours' work overseas. A 'significant break from work' is a period of 31 days or more where there is no day in the period on which the individual does more than three hours' work in the UK which does not arise because he was on annual leave or on sick leave.[2]

The full-time work in the UK test does not apply to an individual who is an international transportation worker at any time in a year where he has at least six cross-border work trips in a year.[3]

This test equates work exclusively or predominantly in the UK with residence regardless of any other connecting factors. The meaning of full-time work in the UK is not symmetrical with the expression full-time work abroad for the purpose of the automatic overseas test, both in relation to the qualifying period, and the amount of working or other time spent in the UK. No justification for this is offered in either consultation document although the second accepted that this may cause more employees to be UK resident in the year of arrival or departure than under prior HMRC practice.[4]

Assessment of whether sufficient hours have been worked in the UK is similar to that for overseas work described in **2.13** and is by application of the following formula in para 9(3):

'(3) Take the following steps to work out, for any given period of 365 days, whether P[the individual] works "sufficient hours in the UK" as assessed over that period—

Step 1

Identify any days in the period on which P does more than 3 hours' work overseas, including ones on which P also does work in the UK on the same day.

The days so identified are referred to as "disregarded days".

Step 2

Add up (for all employments held and trades carried on by P) the total number of hours that P works in the UK during the period, but ignoring any hours that P works in the UK on disregarded days.

The result is referred to as P's "net UK hours".

Step 3

Subtract from 365—

(a)   the total number of disregarded days, and
(b)   any days that are allowed to be subtracted, in accordance with the rules in paragraph 28 of this Schedule, to take account of periods of leave and gaps between employments.

The result is referred to as the "reference period".

Step 4

Divide the reference period by 7. If the answer is more than 1 and is not a whole number, round down to the nearest whole number. If the answer is less than 1, round up to 1.

Step 5

Divide P's net UK hours by the number resulting from step 4.

If the answer is 35 or more, P is considered to work "sufficient hours in the UK" as assessed over the 365-day period in question.'

The stated purpose of the test is to provide a clear answer for individuals coming to the UK to work, including those who come to the UK partway through the tax year. The purpose of the rule is to provide certainty for this group, including the many expatriate employees who come from abroad to work on posts in the UK.[5] Unlike the prior HMRC practice, arrival in the UK for full-time work and split-year treatment are not fully aligned with each other and, while the tests for work-related residence and work-related split-year treatment will dovetail in many cases, there is no guarantee that they will.

Examples

The operation of this rule is illustrated by the following examples.[6]

Fergal

Fergal has his home in the Irish Republic and bases his life and family there. He is employed full-time as a scientist at a research establishment in Northern Ireland. Each morning he crosses the border to work and again in the evening when he returns home. He is conclusively resident in the UK.

Gail

Gail has her home in the United States and bases her life and family there. She works in the human resources department of a New York bank. She is seconded to the London branch to stand in for the head of human resources there during the London head's maternity leave from 1 December to 30 November. She works a 50-hour week in London for 34 weeks to enable her to go home to New York unofficially regularly for a week at a time. At home she does no more than an hour a day's work. Her four-week annual holidays are taken outside the UK. She is conclusively resident in the UK in both the year of her arrival and of departure.

Helene

Helene has her home in France and bases her life and family there. She works in the human resources department of a Paris bank and is required to cover for the head of human resources there during the London head's maternity leave from 1 December to 30 November while continuing her existing responsibilities and she regularly visits London during the week for this purpose so that she spends 75 days working there in the tax year she first visits, and 150 days in the second. On one third of the days that she works in the UK for at least three hours (including travelling time) she also works for three hours in Paris. She is not conclusively resident in the UK in either year.

---

1 Schedule 45, para 9(1).
2 Schedule 45, para 29(1).
3 Schedule 45, para 9(3).
4 Second Consultative Document, para 3.99.
5 Second Consultative Document, para 3.100.
6 These are adapted from HM Treasury and HMRC, *Reviewing the residence and domicile rules as they affect the taxation of individuals: a background paper*, April 2003.

2.15   International transportation workers

International transportation workers are singled out for special treatment. International transportation workers are those who have 'relevant jobs on board vehicles, aircraft or ships'.[1] In the case of employees, their duties are relevant if they are to be performed on board a vehicle, aircraft or ship while it is travelling.[2] In the case of self-employed individuals, the activities of their trade consist of work to be done or services to be provided on board a vehicle, aircraft or ship while it is travelling and which require them to be present (in person) on board the vehicle, aircraft or ship while it is travelling.[3] Substantially all of the trips made in performing those duties or carrying on those activities must involve crossing an international boundary at sea, in the air or on land.[4] Any duties or activities of a purely incidental nature are to be ignored in determining the character of the services.[5] A ship includes any kind of vessel (including a hovercraft) for this purpose.[6]

Neither the full-time work in the UK test (the 'third automatic UK test'), nor the full-time work overseas test (the 'third automatic overseas test') applies to an individual who is an international transportation worker at any time in a year in which he has at least six cross-border work trips in a year.[7] Their work in such cases is thus only relevant to the work tie for the sufficient ties test.[8] For that purpose, international transportation workers are assumed to do more than three hours' work in the UK on any day on which they start a cross-border trip that begins in the UK in their international transportation working capacity. They are also assumed to do fewer than three hours' work in the UK on any day on which such a cross-border trip ends in the UK. These assumptions apply whether or not the worker completes the journey on that day, regardless of how late in the day the journey begins, and whether or not the worker also starts other international journeys on the same day that begin overseas.[9]

Any day on which an international transportation worker has a trip that starts in the UK is deemed to be one on which the worker is assumed to do more than three hours' work in the UK and a trip that ends in the UK is assumed to be a day with less than three hours of work in the UK.[10]

A cross-border trip to or from the UK that is undertaken in stages is deemed to begin or end, as the case may be, on the day the UK border crossing begins or ends. Accordingly, any day on which a stage is undertaken solely within the

UK must be counted separately as a day on which the worker does more than three hours' work in the UK, if the trip lasts for more than three hours.[11]

---

1 Schedule 45, para 30.
2 Schedule 45, para 30(2)(a).
3 Schedule 45, para 30(2)(b) and (4).
4 Schedule 45, para 30(3).
5 Schedule 45, para 30(5). RDR3 give the example of a pilot whose job consists of making long-haul international flights and who also attends a training course. The duties spent undertaking training are incidental to the duties of flying the plane and so can be ignored (RDR3, para 3.27).
6 Schedule 45, para 145.
7 Schedule 45, paras 9(3) and 14(4)
8 See **2.21**.
9 Schedule 45, para 36.
10 Schedule 45, para 36(3).
11 Schedule 45, para 36(7).

2.16 Death: conclusive non-residence

The effect of death on residential status has neither been canvassed by the courts nor considered in previous HMRC published practice. Three automatic tests are included in the SRT. Two confer non-residence status and one confers UK residence. The first automatic overseas test, under which an individual is not resident if he has been resident in each of the three preceding years and spends less than 16 days in the UK, does not apply to a year in which the individual dies.[1] The other automatic tests, that do not concern the death of an individual, may be applicable in the year of death in appropriate circumstances. The work-related automatic tests are more likely to apply to individuals who die towards the end of a tax year, by which time the requirements of those tests may have been met.[2] The UK home test may be met at various times in the tax year.[3] If none of the automatic tests applies, then the sufficient ties test must be applied in the year of death. Mercifully, the legislature has not ventured a definition of death.

Where an individual dies in a tax year, and was not resident in the UK for either of the two tax years preceding the year, and spent less than 46 days in the UK in that year, then the individual is conclusively not resident in the year of death. If such an individual was not resident in the UK for the preceding tax year, and the tax year before that was a split year within Case 1 (starting full-time work overseas), Case 2 (the partner of an individual starting full-time work overseas) or Case 3 (ceasing to have a home in the UK), then the individual is similarly conclusively not resident in the year of death. These two tests together form the fourth automatic overseas test.[4] An individual who dies in a tax year, was not resident in the UK for either of the two preceding tax years under the third automatic overseas test (full-time work overseas) for each of those years and who would have met the third automatic overseas test (modified to take into account the death) for year of death is conclusively non-resident in the year of death. Similarly, if such an individual was not resident in the UK for the preceding tax year under the third automatic overseas test for that year, and the tax year before that was a split within Case 1 (starting full-time work overseas), the individual is conclusively non-resident in the year of death. The modifications of third automatic overseas test (full-time work overseas) for this purpose, limit the period over which days are disregarded because of work done in the UK and over which net overseas hours worked are calculated, as well as the reference period to start of the year up to the day before the date of death. These two tests together form the fourth automatic overseas test.[5]

---

1 Schedule 45, para 12(c).
2 See **2.13** and **2.14**.
3 See **2.07**.
4 Schedule 45, para 15.
5 Schedule 45, para 16. See **2.13** for the third automatic overseas test (full-time work overseas) and **2.33** for Case 1 (starting full-time work overseas) split-year treatment.

2.17   Death: conclusive residence

An individual who dies and is not conclusively non-resident under one of the automatic overseas tests will be UK resident in two circumstances: If an individual dies in a tax year, and was resident in the UK for each of the previous three tax years by meeting the automatic residence test, the previous year was not a split year or would not be a split year even on the assumption that the individual was not resident in the tax year of death, when the individual died, his only home was in the UK, then the individual is conclusively UK resident for that year. Secondly, if, at the time of death, such an individual had more than one home and at least one of them was in the UK, and he was not present at the overseas home on at least 30 days in the year, in the aggregate, for at least some of the time, no matter how short, or was similarly present there for at least some of the time each day of the year up to and including the date of death, then the individual is likewise conclusively UK resident for that year. If the individual had more than one home overseas at the time of death, sufficient presence at each overseas home must be tested separately. Unless the individual was sufficiently present at each of them, he will be UK resident. These tests together form the fourth automatic UK test.[1]

---

1 Schedule 45, para 10. See **2.07** and **2.08**.

2.18   The sufficient ties test: other connecting factors and day counting

The sufficient ties test applies only to those individuals whose residence is not determined by any automatic UK tests nor by any automatic overseas tests.[1] Under the sufficient ties test, an individual will be resident according to a scale of the number of days spent in the UK in a tax year in conjunction with five connecting factors. Separate scales apply to individuals who were UK resident in any of the three tax years preceding the year in question and to individuals who were not so resident in any of those three years. Individuals who were previously so resident will be UK resident when they spend fewer days in the UK with the same connecting factors as individuals who were not resident in any of the three preceding years. This reflects the principle that it is harder for anyone leaving to relinquish residence than it is for a newly arrived person to acquire it.

These connecting factors are:

- family – the individual's spouse or civil partner or common law equivalent or minor children are resident in the UK (a family tie);
- accommodation – the individual has a place to stay in the UK and makes use of it during the tax year (accommodation tie);
- work – the individual works in the UK for 40 days in the year (work tie);
- UK presence in previous year – the individual spent 90 days or more in the UK in either of the previous two tax years (90-day tie); and
- more time in the UK than in other countries – the individual spends more days in the UK in the tax year than in any other single country (country tie).

The chosen factors are mostly drawn from the case law indicators of residence: family – see **3.16**; accommodation – see **3.8** and **3.9**; work – see **3.17**; presence in previous year – see **3.11** and **3.14**. More time spent in the UK than any other country as a connecting factor is not an established principle. In *Grace v Revenue & Customs*[2] a comparison was made by the First-tier Tribunal between time spent in the UK and South Africa which led to a conclusion of dual residence. In *Gaines-Cooper v Revenue & Customs*[3] an examination of the total travel pattern of Mr Gaines-Cooper was explained by reference to his 'unusual background'.[4] The Special Commissioners did not include the comparison as a factor in coming to their conclusion and none of the cases cited by them was in support of such a proposition. Certainty is increased by limiting the factors only to those specified. The country tie is only a connecting factor for individuals who were UK resident in one or more of the three years preceding the year of arrival.

---

1 See **2.02**.
2 [2011] UKFTT 36 (TC).
3 [2006] UKSPC SPC 568.
4 [2006] UKSPC SPC 568. at para 92.

2.19 Family tie

An individual has a family tie for a year if, in that year, the individual has a 'relevant relationship' with another person who is resident in the UK for that year.[1] Regardless of the number of relevant relationships an individual has, he will only have one family tie. The legislation specifically prohibits the residence of the family member from being tested by reference to the individual whose residence is tested.[2] Thus, the family member with whom the individual has a relevant relationship must be resident in the UK for other reasons. This prevents circularity that might arise if the status of both individuals was mutually dependent on the status of each other.

A 'relevant relationship' is one between a husband or wife or between civil partners if they are not separated at the time, as well as between persons living together as husband and wife or, if they are of the same sex, as civil partners.[3]

For this purpose, 'separated' means separated under an order of a court of competent jurisdiction, by deed of separation, or in circumstances where the separation is likely to be permanent.[4]

Whether individuals are legally married or are civil partners is a legal question. Similarly, whether individuals are legally separated by order of a court or by deed of separation is a largely legal and relatively easily evidenced by the relevant legal documents.

On the other hand, whether individuals are living together as husband and wife or as civil partners, not only requires interpretation of that expression but also a detailed examination into intimate elements of the lives of the individuals concerned. The right to equal treatment means that both kinds of relationships are likely to be tested in the same way.[5] A thorough examination of the legally relevant characteristics of cohabitation was undertaken by the Court of Appeal in *Amicus Horizon Ltd v Mabbot & Anor*[6] where Lord Justice Ward said:

> 'One does not have to spend too much time in the Family Division to realise that husbands and wives live their married lives in many and various ways, yet always at its heart marriage is a serious but public commitment to have and to hold the other as one's husband or one's wife and in whatever religious or civil form the promises are made, in essence always to love and to cherish until death us do part. A married couple share their lives and make their home together. They bear equal responsibilities for bringing up their children. They offer each other love, commitment and support. Lord Nicholls of Birkenhead spoke of the "intimate mutual love and affection and long term commitment that typically characterise the relationship of husband and wife" *Fitzpatrick v Sterling Housing Association* Ltd [2001] 1 AC 27 at page 24, and Lord Slynn of Hadley said at page 38: "The hall marks of the relationship were essentially that there should be a degree of mutual inter-dependence, of the sharing of lives, of caring and love, of commitment and support."'[7]

Lord Justice Ward adopted comments in the speech of Baroness Hale in the House of Lords in *Ghaidan v Godin-Mendoza* where she said:

> 'Some people, whether heterosexual or homosexual, may be satisfied with casual or transient relationships. But most human beings eventually want more than that. They want love. And with love they often want not only the warmth but also the sense of belonging to one another which is the essence of being a couple. And many couples also come to want the stability and permanence which go with sharing a home and a life together, with or without the children who for many people go to make a family.'[8]

In *Nutting v Southern Housing Group*,[9] the relationships were described thus:

> 'In my judgment the relationship, to come within this subsection, cannot have a single (or even a simple) definition. Human relationships are too complex and varied for that to be the case. There are, however, indicia. I have chosen to put them by questions, which must be asked in the affirmative as follows:
>
> (a)   Have the parties openly set up home together?
> (b)   Is the relationship an emotional one of mutual lifetime commitment rather than simply one of convenience, friendship, companionship or the living together of lovers?

(c)   Is the relationship one which has been presented to the outside world openly and unequivocally so that society considers it to be of permanent intent—the words 'till death us do part' being apposite?

(d)   Do the parties have a common life together, both domestically (in relation to the household) and externally (in relation to family and friends)?

The above indicia (which may overlap) must principally be objectively assessed by reference to what the outside world can see (albeit that the domestic aspect may not be viewable without visitors) and the indicia at (b) must also be assessed by reference to the viewpoint of the parties themselves, so far as that can be ascertained on evidence. In that regard the relationship of the spouse does have some subjective element to it, but accompanying its subjectivity there must be express or implied communication of one party to the other by way of a demonstration of a lifetime emotional commitment. Whist the length of time which the relationship has been in existence is irrelevant to the above indicia, it may sometimes corroborate them or even, in appropriate cases, be of sufficient length to satisfy a court that they are satisfied that the relationship of spouse exists.'

HMRC practice may be indicated by their approach in relation to similar expressions in relation to tax credits:

'These "signposts" are the only indicators to help form a sustainable view of whether two people are living together as husband and wife or as civil partners for the purposes of a tax credits claim. The weight and worth of each indicator will vary from relationship to relationship and an officer of HMRC should conclude their decision on the balance of evidence, based on all the facts.

The signposts include:

- living in the same household
- stability of the relationship
- financial support
- sexual relationship
- dependent children
- public acknowledgement.'[10]

A parent of a child under the age of 18 also has a 'relevant relationship' with that child.[11] There are three exceptions to this rule, one relating to seeing the child and two dealing with children in full-time education. Firstly, there will be no family tie for the parent for a year in which the parent sees the child in the UK on fewer than 61 days in total in the year. If the child turns 18 during the year, then there will be no family tie for the parent for a year in which the parent sees the child in the UK on fewer than 61 days in total during the part of the year before the day on which the child turns 18.[12] A day on which the parent sees the child counts as a day if the parent sees the child in person for all or part of the day.[13]

Secondly, a child in full-time education in the UK may be ignored for this purpose in certain circumstances. That will be the case if he is resident in the UK for the year, but would not be resident if the time spent in full-time education in the UK in that year were disregarded. Time spent in full-time education is the time spent there during term-time. Furthermore, half-term breaks and other breaks when teaching is not provided during a term are treated as part of term time for this purpose.[14] The whole of the SRT must be applied to the child but in doing so, time spent in full-time education is excluded in determining days present in the UK. The child may well still be UK resident in his own right, but will not be a family tie for a parent.

Thirdly, if the child spends less than 21 days in the UK outside term-time, he is treated as not resident in the UK for the year for this purpose. Full-time education in the UK, for the purpose of the family tie test, must be at a university, college, school or other educational establishment in the UK.[15] In *Barry v Hughes*,[16] a hospital unit for training mentally challenged individuals was not an educational establishment. It was not within the expression 'university, college, school or other educational establishment', because of the word 'educational'. In that context, education was considered to be devoted exclusively to training of the mind and not manual skills.

1 Schedule 45, para 32(1).
2 Schedule 45, para 33(2).
3 Schedule 45, para 32(2)(a) and (b).
4 Schedule 45, para 32(5).
5 *Ghaidan v Godin-Mendoza* [2004] UKHL 30, [2004] 3 WLR 113, [2004] 2 AC 557.
6 *Amicus Horizon Ltd v Mabbot & Anor* [2012] EWCA Civ 895.
7 Schedule 45, para 16.
8 Schedule 45, para 142.
9 *Nutting v Southern Housing Group* [2004] EWHC 2982, [2005] HLR 25.
10 HMRC Tax Credits Manual TCTM09341, last updated 06.09.2011.
11 Schedule 45, para 32(2)(c).
12 Schedule 45, para 32(3).
13 Schedule 45, para 32(4).
14 Schedule 45, para 33(4), (5)(b) and (6).
15 Schedule 45, para 33(3).
16 *Barry v Hughes* 48 TC 586; [1973] STC 103, Ch D.

2.20 Accommodation tie

Accommodation is referred to for the purposes of this tie as a 'place to live' in the UK.[1] An individual is considered to have a 'place to live' in the UK if his home or at least one of those homes, if there are more than one, is in the UK.[2] Home in this context must have the same meaning as in the 'second automatic UK test' (the 'UK home' test).[3] In addition an individual is considered to have a 'place to live' in the UK if he has a holiday home or temporary retreat (or something similar) in the UK, or if accommodation is otherwise available to the individual where he can live when in the UK.[4] While the expression is undoubtedly widely drawn, it is not without limits. The individual must be able to live at the place. This would exclude, for example, a sleeping pod at an employer's premises designed only for exceptional overnight stays. A 'place to live' connotes a minimum level of facility to enable human habitation is required.

An individual has an accommodation tie for a year if he has a place to live in the UK that is available to him during the year for a continuous period of at least 91 days.[5] This connotes a degree of entitlement. Accommodation may be available even if the individual holds no estate or interest in it and has no legal right to occupy it.[6] The place must be at the disposal of the individual. Thus an hotel room is not available unless it is booked, or a friend's or family member's home is not normally available without an invitation. Despite this, if there is a gap of fewer than 16 days between periods in the year when a particular place is available to an individual, then that place is to be treated as continuing to be available during that gap.[7] This has a surprising effect for intermittent users of certain kinds of accommodation. An individual who stays at the same hotel or company flat one night every two weeks, will have it available throughout that period. Eight such stays will make it available for 91 days.

The individual must spend at least one night at that place in that year to have an accommodation tie.[8] If the accommodation belongs to a close relative of the individual, then he must spend at least 16 nights at that place in that year.[9] For this purpose, a close relative is a parent or grandparent, a brother or sister, a child aged 18 or over, or a grandchild aged 18 or over, in each case whether by blood or half-blood or by marriage or civil partnership.[10]

While the legislation goes into great detail in prescribing when a day is spent in the UK, at a home or working, it is silent on when a night is spent at a place to live. The ordinary meaning of the expression implies both physical presence there for a significant time from evening to morning as well as its use as a dwelling during that time such as for sleeping. Visiting a grandparent or adult child for dinner would not, for example, qualify as spending a night there.[11] In *R v National Insurance Commissioner, ex parte Secretary of State for Social Services*,[12] Lord Widgery CJ observed that 'night' is one of the commonest English words in its ordinary usage, it does have different shades of meaning and the decision of the correct shade of meaning to give to the word in a particular context requires consideration of the context and thus becomes a matter of construction and therefore a matter of law.' He held that the word 'night' does not mean the period between sunrise and sunset but refers to that period of inactivity beginning with the time when, in accordance with its domestic routine, the household in which the disabled person lives closes down for the night in the context of s 4(2)a of the National Insurance (Old Persons' and Widows' Pensions and Attendance Allowance) Act 1970, which entitles a disabled person to an attendance allowance if he requires, *inter alia*, prolonged or repeated attention during the night.

---

1 Schedule 45, para 34(1)(a).
2 Schedule 45, para 34(3)(a).
3 See **2.08**.
4 Schedule 45, para 34(3)(b) and (c).
5 Schedule 45, para 34(1).
6 Schedule 45, para 34(4).
7 Schedule 45, para 34(2).
8 Schedule 45, para 34(1)(c).
9 Schedule 45, para 34(5).
10 Schedule 45, para 34(6).
11 See *Amicus Horizon Ltd v Mabbot & Anor* [2012] EWCA Civ 895, at para 4 for an example of the ordinary use of the expression.
12 *R v National Insurance Commissioner, ex parte Secretary of State for Social Services* [1974] 3 All ER 522, at 526.

2.21 Work tie

An individual has a work tie for a year if he works in the UK for at least 40 days (whether continuously or intermittently) in the year. Working in the UK for a day, means doing more than three hours' work in the UK on that day.[1] For the meaning of work, see **2.10** and for the place where work is undertaken, see **2.11**. The special rules that apply to the work of international transportation workers are discussed at **2.15** above.

Eight five-day weeks of working under half a day in the UK may result in a work tie. The effect of this rule may also be illustrated by the following example:

Ian and Isobel, who live and work in the Netherlands, are sent to work on a project in the UK. They both work in the UK for 130 hours on the project in a year. Ian works for three-and-a-quarter hours on each of 40 days in the UK. He has a work tie. Isobel works six and a half hours on each of 20 days in the UK and has no work tie.

---

1 Schedule 45, para 35.

2.22 90-day tie

An individual has a 90-day tie for a year if he has spent more than 90 days in the UK in the tax year preceding the year in question, the tax year before that tax preceding year, or in each of those tax years.[1] Thus, while there is no mechanism for averaging presence in the UK over a period of time, an individual who has spent 91 days or more will find themselves put into a category where they will either need to spend much less time in the UK or eliminate other factors. For example, an individual who was not resident in the previous two years, spent 91 days in the UK in a year and who otherwise has two connecting factors could only spend 45 or fewer days in the UK for three years thereafter without becoming UK resident. The 90-day tie is applied in mechanical fashion. Thus an individual who is resident in the UK in the two previous years on a basis that is not by reference to time spent, such as having a UK home will still need to count days spent in the UK for this purpose. The day-count hyping rule described in **2.04** does not apply to determine whether an individual has a 90-day tie.

---

1 Schedule 45, para 37.

2.23 Country tie

An individual has a country tie for a year if the country in which he spends the greatest number of days in the year is the UK. If the individual spends the same number of days in two or more countries in a year, and that number is the greatest number of days spent by him in any country in the year, the individual has a country tie for the year if one of those countries is the UK.[1]

Presence in a country at the end of a day means that a day is spent in that country.[2]

A 'country' as defined for this purpose 'includes a state or territory'.[3] This raises the question of the operation of this tie in relation to federal systems. In relation to the United States of America, for example, is each state in the Union a 'country' for the purpose of this tie? The answer may have a significant impact on the existence of a country tie. An individual who spends a quarter of the year in each of say New York, Florida and the UK with the balance in a variety of places around the world, would have a country tie if New York state and Florida are each counted as separate countries but would not, if the United States of America as a whole is the relevant country. Would the question be answered differently if the three jurisdictions were the Netherlands, the UK and Spain? No official guidance is given on this important question. Any answer is likely to produce anomalous results with individuals in similar circumstances being treated differently as a result of widely differing constitutional systems. The UK is treated as one country for the purpose of this rule, but the legal ties that bind its constituent countries of England and Wales, Scotland and Northern Ireland together provide no clear test for comparing other jurisdictions.

---

1 Schedule 45, para 38.
2 Schedule 45, para 38(3). For some inexplicable reason, the drafter of this part of the Schedule has chosen to call this the 'midnight test'. This is defined to mean the end of the day!
3 Schedule 45, para 145.

2.24 The sufficient ties test: day counting for former non-residents

The residence status of individuals who were not resident in any of the previous three tax years[1] is judged by reference to combinations of four ties, namely, a family tie, a work tie, an accommodation tie and a 90-day tie.

Connecting factors combine with days spent in the UK to determine residence as follows:

Fewer than 46 days	Always non-resident
46–90 days	4 ties – resident
91–120 days	3 or more ties – resident
121–182 days	2 or more ties – resident
183 days or more	Always resident

---

1 Schedule 45, para 19.

2.25 The sufficient ties test: day counting for former residents

The residence status of individuals who were resident in one or more of the previous three tax years[1] is judged by reference to combinations of five ties, namely, a family tie, a work tie, an accommodation tie, a 90-day tie and a country tie. Connecting factors combine with days spent in the UK to determine residence as follows:

Fewer than 16 days	Always non-resident
16–45 days	4 or more ties – resident
46–90 days	3 or more ties – resident
91–120 days	2 or more ties – resident
121–182 days	1 or more ties – resident
183 days or more	Always resident

1 Schedule 45, para 18.

2.26 The sufficient ties test: day counting in the year of death

If residence is not determined by any of the automatic tests, the sufficient ties test will apply in the year of death. Death in a year changes the number of days of UK presence that make the individual resident. The ties will be determined in the normal way in the year of death, although the death may affect the existence of a tie. There is no reduction in the number of days in any of the ties by reason of death. Any individual spending less than 46 days in the UK will require four factors to be resident.[1]

In addition, if the death occurs before 1 March the number of days presence required is reduced by multiplying the number of days, in each case, by the number of whole months in the year after the month in which the individual died, divided by 12. If, the result is not a whole number, it is rounded up if the result is 0.5 or more, and, otherwise, down.[2]

HMRC have produced the following tables to show the application of the tests by reference to the date of death of the individual.[3] In each case, the number of days shown will result in UK residence:

Individuals who were not resident in any of the previous three tax years before the year of death

No of ties	Date of death											
	6 Apr to 30 Apr	1 May to 31 May	1 Jun to 30 Jun	1 Jul to 31 Jul	1 Aug to 31 Aug	1 Sep to 30 Sep	1 Oct to 31 Oct	1 Nov to 30 Nov	1 Dec to 31 Dec	1 Jan to 31 Jan	1 Feb to 29 Feb	1 Mar to 5 Apr
	Days spent in UK in year of death											
All 4 ties	4–7	8–15	11–22	15–30	19–37	23–45	27–52	31–60	34–67	38–75	42–82	46–90
At least 3 ties	8–10	16–20	23–30	31–40	38–50	46–60	53–70	61–80	68–90	76–100	83–110	91–120
At least 2 ties	Over 10	Over 20	Over 30	Over 40	Over 50	Over 60	Over 70	Over 80	Over 90	Over 100	Over 110	Over 120

Individuals who were resident in one or more of the previous three tax years before the year of death

No of ties	Date of death											
	6 Apr to 30 Apr	1 May to 31 May	1 Jun to 30 Jun	1 Jul to 31 Jul	1 Aug to 31 Aug	1 Sep to 30 Sep	1 Oct to 31 Oct	1 Nov to 30 Nov	1 Dec to 31 Dec	1 Jan to 31 Jan	1 Feb to 29 Feb	1 Mar to 5 Apr
	Days spent in UK in year of death											
At least 4 ties	0–4	0–7	0–11	0–15	0–19	0–22	0–26	0–30	0–34	0–37	0–41	0–45
At least 3 ties	5–7	8–15	12–22	16–30	20–37	23–45	27–52	31–60	35–67	38–75	42–82	46–90
At least 2 ties	8–10	16–20	23–30	31–40	38–50	46–60	53–70	61–80	68–90	76–100	83–110	91–120
At least 1 tie	Over 10	Over 20	Over 30	Over 40	Over 50	Over 60	Over 70	Over 80	Over 90	Over 100	Over 110	Over 120

1   Schedule 45, para 20.
2   Schedule 45, para 20(4).
3   RDR3 para 4.11. Tables C and D.

2.27   Residence of MPs and members of the House of Lords

The residential status of members of Parliament and the House of Lords is not governed by the SRT. Individuals who, for any part of a tax year are members of the House of Commons and of the House of Lords are treated as resident in the UK for the whole of that tax year. This treatment applies for the purposes of income tax, capital gains tax, and inheritance tax.[1]

For this purpose, an individual becomes a member of the House of Commons when (having been elected to that House) he makes and subscribes the oath required by the Parliamentary Oaths Act 1866 (or the corresponding affirmation), and ceases to be a member of that House when the Parliament to which he was elected is dissolved, or the individual's seat is otherwise vacated.[2] An individual is a member of the House of Lords if the individual is entitled to receive writs of summons to attend that House except in the case of an archbishop or bishop.[3]

1   Constitutional Reform and Governance Act 2010, s 41.
2   Section 41(4).
3   Section 41(5) and (6).

2.28   EU officials

Employees of European Union institutions are subject to deemed residence rules for tax purposes under Art 13 of the 7th Protocol on the Privileges and Immunities of the European Union annexed to the Treaty on European Union. Officials and servants of the EU who establish their residence in the territory of a Member State other than their country of residence for tax purposes at the time of entering the service of the Union, solely by reason of the performance of their duties in the service of the Union, are deemed to be tax resident in their home Member State. This deemed residence applies both in the country of their actual residence and in their home Member State, spouses have the same deemed tax residence, to the extent that they are not separately engaged in a gainful occupation, as do dependent children.

2.29   An annual attribute

The rule that residence in the UK means residence for the whole tax year is codified in the statutory residence test. Thus an individual who, in accordance with the statutory residence test, is resident (or not resident) in the UK for a tax year is taken for the purposes of any enactment relating to a relevant tax to be resident (or not resident) there at all times in that tax year.[1]

1   Schedule 45, para 2(3).

Split-year treatment

2.30 Introduction

Under the SRT an individual is either resident or not resident in the UK for the whole of a tax year. However, in reality, individuals become and cease to reside in the UK at different times during the year. In principle this leads to a situation where an individual is liable to UK tax on worldwide income and gains as well as the other tax consequences of UK residence for the whole tax year even though in ordinary terms they are not resident or living in the UK. Statutory split-year treatment is set out in Part 3 of Schedule 44 to the Finance Act 2013.

Meaning of split year

A tax year is a 'split year' for an individual who is resident in the UK for that year, and falls within one of the prescribed cases involving either their actual or deemed departure from the UK or their actual or deemed arrival in the UK.[1]

The first three cases apply to departures from the UK and the last five apply to arrivals in the UK. The cases are:

Case 1 (starting full-time work overseas);[2]
Case 2 (the partner of someone starting full-time work overseas);[3]
Case 3 (ceasing to have a home in the UK);[4]
Case 4 (starting to have a home in the UK only);[5]
Case 5 (starting full-time work in the UK);[6]
Case 6 (ceasing full-time work overseas);[7]
Case 7 (the partner of someone ceasing full-time work overseas);[8]
Case 8 (starting to have a home in the UK).[9]

The cases are closely connected with certain of the automatic tests both for UK and overseas residence. Thus split-year treatment is available for individuals who start or cease full-time work overseas and their accompanying spouses and civil partners. These relate to the 'third automatic overseas test'.[10] Individuals who start full-time work in the UK and their accompanying spouses and civil partners may likewise qualify. These relate to the 'third automatic UK test'.[11] There are no automatic tests of residence for accompanying spouses and civil partners whose status must be determined by other tests. As a result, the split-year cases for such individuals are more complex.

Individuals who move to or from the UK in non-work related circumstances may also qualify for split-year treatment if they start or cease to have a home in the UK or if they start or cease to have their only home in the UK. These cases are all closely connected with the 'second automatic UK test'.[12]

No split-year treatment is available in respect of the automatic tests that operate by reference to physical presence only,[13] nor where the sufficient ties test determines residence.[14] In addition, individuals who meet the related automatic tests will still need to meet the detailed particular conditions of the case in question.

1 Schedule 45, para 43(1).
2 Schedule 45, para 44. See **2.33**.
3 Schedule 45, para 45. See **2.34**.
4 Schedule 45, para 46. See **2.35**.
5 Schedule 45, para 47. See **2.36**.
6 Schedule 45, para 48. See **2.37**.
7 Schedule 45, para 49. See **2.38**.
8 Schedule 45, para 50. See **2.39**.
9 Schedule 45, para 51. See **2.40**.
10 See **2.13**.
11 See **2.14**.
12 See **2.07**.
13 See **2.05** and **2.06**.
14 See **2.18**.

2.31   The effect of a split year

A split year is divided into a UK part and an overseas part. Intuition might lead one to regard the individual as UK resident for the UK part and not-resident for the overseas part. This is not, however, the case. The effect of a tax year being a split year is to 'relax' the effect of treating individuals who are UK resident 'for' a tax year as being UK resident at all times in that year.[1] This is achieved by the special charging rules introduced by the amendments made to TCGA 1992, ITEPA 2003 and ITTOIA 2005 by paragraphs 57–101 of Schedule 45 so as to alter the incidence of taxation of certain sources of income and gains. There is no comprehensive split-year treatment for all sources other than as specifically introduced by these amendments. In all other respects, individuals with split-year treatment remain to be taxed as residents.[2] Somewhat obscurely, this status is reinforced by para 42 which states that 'The existence of special charging rules for cases involving split years is not intended to affect any question as to whether an individual would fall to be regarded under double taxation arrangements as a resident of the UK.'

Although the statutory residence test determines whether an individual is resident or non-resident in the UK, including where a tax liability of another actual or deemed person depends on the residence of another individual, this rule is disapplied in the case of split years. Thus split-year treatment does not apply in determining the residence status of personal representatives.[3] Split-year treatment applies in determining the residence status of the trustees of a settlement only to the extent section 475 of ITA 2007 and section 69 of TCGA 1992, are amended by paragraphs 102 and 103 of Schedule 43.[4]

'The UK part' of a split year is the part of a year that is not 'the overseas part'.[5] Because the special charging rules do not simply exclude foreign income and gains during the overseas part of the year, an elaborate and convoluted definition of the overseas part by reference to the period before arriving in the UK or after leaving as the case may be linked to each of the cases.[6] Identification of the overseas part follows analysis of the cases which give rise to split years. These are each discussed below.

1 Schedule 45, para 40(1).
2 Schedule 45, para 40(3).

3 Schedule 45, para 41(a).
4 Schedule 45, para 41(b). See Chapter 6, para **6.06**.
5 Schedule 45, para 56.
6 Schedule 45, para 53.

2.32 Which split-year case applies?

Individuals who move to or from the UK may well qualify for split-year treatment under more than one case. Since the division of the year into UK and overseas parts is by reference to different criteria, a hierarchy is established for the application of the cases. For individuals leaving the UK, Case 1 (starting full-time work overseas) takes priority followed by Case 2 (the partner of someone starting full-time work overseas) and then Case 3 (ceasing to have a home in the UK).[1]

A complex hierarchy applies to individuals moving to the UK. Firstly, where an individual works overseas and moves to work in the UK, then if Case 6 (ceasing full-time work overseas) and Case 5 (starting full-time work in the UK) both apply and the split-year date in relation to Case 5 is earlier than the split-year date in relation to Case 6, Case 5 has priority. Otherwise, Case 6 has priority.[2]

Secondly, where a non-working spouse overseas starts to work full time in the UK, then if Case 7 (the partner of someone ceasing full-time work overseas) (but not Case 6 (ceasing full-time work overseas)) applies and if Case 5(starting full-time work in the UK) also applies and the split-year date in relation to Case 5 is earlier than the split-year date in relation to Case 7, Case 5 has priority. Otherwise, Case 7 has priority.[3]

Thirdly, if two or all of Cases 4 (starting to have a home in the UK only), 5 (starting full-time work in the UK) and 8 (starting to have a home in the UK) apply but neither Case 6 (ceasing full-time work overseas) nor Case 7 (the partner of someone ceasing full-time work overseas), the Case which has priority is the one with the earliest split-year date.[4] But if, in these circumstances, two or all of the cases which apply share the same split-year date and that date is the only, or earlier, split-year date of the cases which apply, the cases with that split-year date are to be treated as having priority.[5]

1 Schedule 45, para 54.
2 Schedule 45, para 55(1).
3 Schedule 45, para 55(3).
4 Schedule 45, para 55(4) and (5).
5 Schedule 45, para 55(6).

2.33 Case 1: Starting full-time work overseas

Split-year treatment is available in the year in which an individual starts working full time overseas. In order to qualify for split-year treatment in a year when the individual starts full-time work overseas, he must, firstly, have been resident in the UK for the previous tax year for any reason (whether or not it was a split year),[1] and, secondly, also not be resident in the UK for the next tax year by reason of the full-time work abroad (third automatic overseas) test.[2] The second requirement, although inherent in the case raises practical difficulties for taxpayers in filing returns by the deadline of 31 January in the year after the tax year ends. Taxpayers will only know that they have met this requirement by the following 6 April and amended returns may be required.

The third requirement is that there is a period in the year which starts on the day the individual does more than three hours' work overseas and ends on the last day of the tax year during which the individual meet the requirements for full-time work overseas.[3] This means working sufficient hours overseas assessed over that period without any significant breaks from overseas work and not exceeding the permitted limit for days on which more than three hours' work is done in the UK.[4] Whether sufficient hours are worked overseas is determined in the same way as for the third automatic overseas test by reference to the number of days from the date on which overseas work starts to the end of the tax year. The normal permitted limit for work in the UK of 30 days a year under the third automatic overseas test is reduced by the proportion of the year before starting full-time work overseas. Similarly, the permitted limit for days spent in the UK (90 days a year under the third automatic overseas test) is reduced by the same proportion.[5] This proportion is determined by reference to the number of whole months in the year before the day full-time work overseas starts.[6]

HMRC have produced the following table[7] to show the permitted limits for Case 1:

Overseas part of year starts on

	6 Apr to 30 Apr	1 May to 31 May	1 Jun to 30 Jun	1 Jul to 31 Jul	1 Aug to 31 Aug	1 Sep to 30 Sep	1 Oct to 31 Oct	1 Nov to 30 Nov	1 Dec to 31 Dec	1 Jan to 31 Jan	1 Feb to 29 Feb	1 Mar to 31 Mar	1 Apr to 5 Apr
Permitted limit on days where you can work more than three hours and maximum number of days that can be subtracted for gaps between employments	30	27	25	22	20	17	15	12	10	7	5	2	0
Permitted limit on days spent in the UK	90	82	75	67	60	52	45	37	30	22	15	7	0

The overseas part of a split year for Case 1 is the period from when full-time work overseas starts to the end of the year. If there is more than one period of full-time work overseas (without significant breaks), the overseas part starts at the part beginning of the longest of those periods.[8]

1 Schedule 45, para 44(2).
2 Schedule 45, para 44(4).
3 Schedule 45, para 44(3).
4 Schedule 45, para 44(5).
5 Schedule 45, para 44(5).
6 Schedule 45, para 44(8) and (9).
7 RDR3, para 5.13, Table E.
8 Schedule 45, para 53(2).

2.34 Case 2: Spouse or partner of someone starting full-time work overseas

A spouse or civil partner of an individual who qualifies for split-year treatment under Case 1 (starting full-time work overseas) by accompanying the working spouse or civil partner overseas may also qualify for split-year treatment.[1] An individual qualifies for split-year treatment in this case firstly, if he or she was resident in the UK for the previous tax year (whether or not it was a split year) for any reason and, secondly, is not resident in the following year under any part of the SRT. Thirdly, the individual must have a partner who qualifies for split-year treatment under Case 1 for either the relevant year or the previous tax year.[2]

Fourthly, the individual must move overseas on a particular day in the year so he or she can continue to live together while his or her spouse or civil partner is working overseas.[3] When an individual 'moves' overseas it may give rise to difficulties of interpretation and application in practice. In *R (on the application of Davies & Anor) v Revenue & Customs Commissioners; R (on the application of Gaines-Cooper) v Revenue & Customs Commissioners*,[4] the Supreme Court spent some time considering whether a taxpayer 'left' the UK within the meaning of Booklet IR20. Lord Wilson, speaking for the majority of the court, concluded that the individual 'was required to "leave" the UK in a more profound sense than that of travel, namely permanently or indefinitely or for full-time employment.'[5] and Lord Hope agreed that a distinct break with the UK was required.[6] Even if a mere departure meets the statutory requirement, in many cases further evidence of the context of a particular departure may be required to show which of several departures constituted the 'move'. Fifthly, the individual must either have no home in the UK at any time, or spend the greater part of the time living in the overseas home where the individual has homes in both the UK and overseas during the period from the 'deemed departure day' to the end of the year.[7] Identification of the date of the move may cause difficulties given modern travel patterns as illustrated by *Kimber v HMRC*[8] where the taxpayer arrived and departed physically several times for different purposes in the course of moving from one country to another.

Sixthly, the individual may spend no more days in the UK than the permitted limit during the period from the deemed departure date to the end of the year.

The permitted limit for days spent in the UK is 90 days a year reduced by the proportion of the year before the deemed departure day. This proportion is determined by reference to the number of whole months in the year before the deemed departure day.[9]

The 'deemed departure day' depends on whether the working spouse or civil partner qualifies for split-year treatment under Case 1 for the year of departure, or the previous tax year of the accompanying spouse or civil partner. If it is in the year of departure, the 'deemed departure day' is the later of the day the individual moves overseas and the first day of the overseas part of the relevant year for the working spouse or civil partner under Case 1. If it is in the previous tax year, the 'deemed departure day' is the day the individual moves overseas.[10]

The overseas part of the split year is the part beginning with the deemed departure day.[11]

---

1 Schedule 45, para 45.
2 Schedule 45, para 45(3).
3 Schedule 45, para 45(4).
4 *R (on the application of Davies & Anor) v Revenue & Customs Commissioners; R (on the application of Gaines-Cooper) v Revenue & Customs Commissioners* [2011] UKSC 47.
5 Schedule 45, para 45.
6 Schedule 45, para 63.
7 Schedule 45, para 45(5).
8 [2012] UKFTT 107 (TC). See **5.02**.
9 Schedule 45, para 45(5)(c) and (9).
10 Schedule 45, para 45(7) and (8).
11 Schedule 45, para 53(3).

2.35 Case 3: Ceasing to have a home in the UK

Although Case 3 is headed 'ceasing to have a home in the UK', it may be more accurately described as leaving the UK to live overseas, given the requirements of the Case.[1] In order to qualify for split-year treatment in a year under Case 3, an individual must, firstly, have been resident in the UK for the previous tax year for any reason (whether or not it was a split year), and, secondly, also not resident in the UK for the next tax year for any reason.[2] Thirdly, at the start of the relevant year, the individual must have had one or more homes in the UK but ceased to have any home in the UK on a day in the relevant year and thereafter have no home in the UK for the rest of that year.[3] A day must be found when the individual no longer has a home in the UK. In straightforward cases this may entail a sale, lease, removal of furniture and belongings or simply leaving. The scheme of the SRT clearly contemplates that a UK home may be downgraded to a place to stay. This break will demand a detailed examination of all facts and circumstances of an individual's habitation as suggested in HMRC guidance on record keeping found in Appendix 2.[4]

Thirdly, the individual must spend fewer than 16 days in the UK from the day on which he ceases to have a home in the UK.[5]

Fourthly, within six months from the day on which he ceases to have a home in the UK, the individual must have a 'sufficient link' with a country overseas.[6] A 'sufficient link' exists with a country overseas if he is a resident for tax purposes in accordance with the domestic laws of that country, has been present in that country at the end of each day of the six-month period or the individual's only home is in that country or, if he has more than one home, they are all in that country.[7]

The overseas part of the split year is the part from the deemed departure day to the end of the tax year.

---

1 Schedule 45, para 46.
2 Schedule 45, para 46(2) and (5).
3 Schedule 45, para 46(3).
4 RDR 3, para 7. See Appendix 2.
5 Schedule 45, para 46(4).
6 Schedule 45, para 46(6) and (7).
7 Schedule 45, para 53(4).

2.36   Case 4: Starting to have a home in the UK only

Two cases permit split-year treatment in the year when an individual starts to have a home in the UK. Case 4 deals with individuals starting to have a home in the UK only, while Case 8 deals with individuals starting to have a home in the UK.

An individual may qualify for split-year treatment under Case 4 if he, firstly, was not resident in the UK for the previous tax year for any reason, and, secondly, did not have his only home in the UK (or if the individual had more than one home, one of them is outside the UK) at the start of the relevant year but on a day in that year the individual's only home is in the UK (or if the individual had more than one home, all of them are in the UK) (the 'only home test') and that remains the case for the rest of that year.[1]

Thirdly, for the part of the year before the day the only home test is met, the individual must not have sufficient UK ties under the sufficient ties test, modified to take into account that the period will be less than a full year. The permitted limit for days spent in the UK during that period is reduced by the proportion of the year from the day the only home test is met to the end of the year. This proportion is determined by reference to the number of whole months in the year from the day the only home test is met. The existence of a family tie must, however, be determined by reference to the whole year.[2]

The overseas part of the split year is the part before the day the only home test is met.[3]

---

1 Schedule 45, para 47(2)–(5).
2 Schedule 45, para 47(6) and (7).
3 Schedule 45, para 53(5).

2.37   Case 5: Starting full-time work in the UK

Split-year treatment is available in the year in which an individual starts working full time in the UK.[1] In order to qualify for split-year treatment in a year when the individual starts full-time work overseas, he must, firstly, have been non-resident for the previous tax year for any reason.[2]

The second requirement is that there is at least one period of 365 days which starts on the day in the year the individual does more than three hours' work in the UK and during which at least 75% of the total number of days in the period on which the individual works for more than three hours are days on which the individual works in the UK for more than three hours. Thirdly, the individual must meet the requirements for full-time work in the UK. This means working sufficient hours in the UK assessed over that period. Fourthly, there must be no significant breaks from UK work.[3]

Fifthly, for the part of the year before the day full-time work in the UK starts, the individual must not have sufficient UK ties under the sufficient ties test, modified to take into account that the period will be less than a full year.[4] The permitted limit for days spent in the UK during that period is reduced by the proportion of the year from the day full-time work in the UK starts. This proportion is determined by reference to the number of whole months in the year from the day full-time work in the UK starts. The existence of a family tie must, however, be determined by reference to the whole year.[5]

HMRC have produced the following table[6] to show the permitted limits for Case 4:

	Day before satisfying only home or having a UK home tests is											
	6 Apr to 30 Apr	1 May to 31 May	1 Jun to 30 Jun	1 Jul to 31 Jul	1 Aug to 31 Aug	1 Sep to 30 Sep	1 Oct to 31 Oct	1 Nov to 30 Nov	1 Dec to 31 Dec	1 Jan to 31 Jan	1 Feb to 29 Feb	1 Mar to 5 Apr
For 15 substitute	1	2	4	5	6	7	9	10	11	12	13	14
For 45 substitute	4	7	11	15	19	22	26	30	34	37	41	45
For 90 substitute	7	15	22	30	37	45	52	60	67	75	82	90
For 120 substitute	10	20	30	40	50	60	70	80	90	100	110	120

The overseas part of a split year is the period before full-time work in the UK starts. If there is more than one period of full-time work in the UK (without significant breaks), the overseas part starts at the beginning of the first of those periods.[7]

---

1 Schedule 45, para 48.
2 Schedule 45, para 48(2).
3 Schedule 45, para 48(3).
4 Schedule 45, para 48(3)(c) and (5).
5 Schedule 45, para 48(7).
6 RDR3 para 5.26, Table F.
7 Schedule 45, para 53(6).

2.38   Case 6: Ceasing full-time work overseas

Split-year treatment may be available in the year in which an individual ceases working full time overseas.[1] In order to qualify the individual must firstly have been non-resident for the previous tax year by reason of working full time overseas (the third automatic overseas test). Secondly, the individual had been resident for one or more of the four tax years immediately preceding that year. Thirdly, the individual is resident in the UK for the next tax year (whether or not it is a split year).[2]

The third requirement is that there is at least one period in the year which starts on the first day of the year and ends on another day in the tax year when the individual does more than three hours' work overseas, during which the individual meets the requirements for full-time work overseas. This means working sufficient hours overseas assessed over that period without any significant breaks from overseas work and not exceeding the permitted limit for days on which more than three hours' work is done in the UK. In addition, the individual must also not work in the UK more than three hours per day or spend more time in the UK in that year beyond the permitted limit from the time he starts to work full-time overseas.[3]

Whether sufficient hours are worked overseas is determined in the same way as for the third automatic overseas test by reference to the number of days from the beginning of the year to the date on which overseas work ends.[4] The normal permitted limit for work in the UK (30 days a year under the third automatic overseas test) reduced by the proportion of the year before starting full-time work overseas. Similarly, the permitted limit for days spent in the UK is 90 days a year under the third automatic overseas test is reduced by the same proportion. This proportion is determined by reference to the number of whole months in the year before the day full-time work overseas starts.[5]

HMRC have produced the following table[6] to show the permitted limits for Case 6:

	6 Apr to 30 Apr	1 May to 31 May	1 Jun to 30 Jun	1 Jul to 31 Jul	1 Aug to 31 Aug	1 Sep to 30 Sep	1 Oct to 31 Oct	1 Nov to 30 Nov	1 Dec to 31 Dec	1 Jan to 31 Jan	1 Feb to 29 Feb	1 Mar to 5 Apr
							UK part of year starts on					
Permitted limit on days where you can work more than three hours in overseas part of the year or maximum number of days which may be subtracted from the reference period on account of gaps between employment	2	5	7	10	12	15	17	20	22	25	27	30
Permitted limit on days spent in the UK in overseas part of year	7	15	22	30	37	45	52	60	67	75	82	90

The overseas part of a split year for Case 6 is the period from the start of the year to the day when full-time work overseas ends. If there is more than one period of full-time work overseas (without significant breaks), the overseas part ends on the last day of the longest of those periods.[7]

---

1 Schedule 45, para 49.
2 Schedule 45, para 49(2) and (4).
3 Schedule 45, para 49(3).
4 Schedule 45, para 49(5) and (7).
5 Schedule 45, para 49(8) and (9).
6 RDR3 para RDR3, para 5.37, Table G.
7 Schedule 45, para 53(7).

2.39   Case 7: The partner of someone ceasing full-time work overseas

A spouse or civil partner of an individual who qualifies for split-year treatment under Case 6 (ceasing full-time work overseas) by accompanying the working spouse or civil partner overseas may also qualify for split-year treatment.[1]

The requirements to qualify are that the individual, firstly, was not UK resident for the previous tax year for any reason, secondly, is UK resident for the next tax year (whether or not it is a split year) and thirdly, has a spouse or civil partner who qualifies for split-year treatment for the relevant year or the previous year. Fourthly, the individual must move to the UK to continue to live together with his spouse or civil partner on their return or relocation to the UK.[2]

Fifthly, the individual must either have no home in the UK at any time, or spend the greater part of the time living in the overseas home where the individual has homes in both the UK and overseas during the period from the beginning of the relevant year to the 'deemed arrival day'.[3] Sixthly, the individual may spend no more days in the UK than the permitted limit during the period from the beginning of the relevant year to the 'deemed arrival day'.[4] The permitted limit for days spent in the UK is 90 days a year reduced by the proportion of the year after the deemed arrival day. This proportion is determined by reference to the number of whole months in the year after the deemed arrival day.[5]

The 'deemed arrival day' depends on whether the working spouse or civil partner qualifies for split-year treatment under Case 6 for the year of arrival, or the previous tax year of the accompanying spouse or civil partner. If it is in the year of arrival, the 'deemed arrival day' is the later of the day the individual moves to the UK and the first day of the UK part of the relevant year for the working spouse or civil partner under Case 6. If it is the previous tax year, the 'deemed arrival day' is the day the individual moves to the UK.[6]

The overseas part of the split year is the part before the deemed arrival day.[7]

---

1 Schedule 45, para 50.
2 Schedule 45, para 50(2)–(4) and (6).
3 Schedule 45, para 50(5)(a).
4 Schedule 45, para 50(5)(b).
5 Schedule 45, para 50(9) and (10).

6 Schedule 45, para 50(7).
7 Schedule 45, para 53(8).

2.40   Case 8: Starting to have a home in the UK

An individual will qualify for split-year treatment if he was, firstly, not resident in the UK for the previous tax year and secondly, is resident in the UK for the tax year after the relevant year and that is not a split year.[1] Thirdly, the individual had no home in the UK at the start of the relevant year but he starts to have a home in the UK for the first time in that year, and continues to have a home in the UK for the rest of that year and for the whole of the next tax year.[2] Fourthly, the individual must not have sufficient UK ties for the part of the relevant year before the day starts to have a home in the UK for the first time.[3] The sufficient ties test is modified to take into account that the period will be less than a full year.[4] The permitted limit for days spent in the UK during that period is reduced by the proportion of the year from the day the only home test is met to the end of the year. This proportion is determined by reference to the number of whole months in the year from the day the only home test is met.[5] The existence of a family tie must, however, be determined by reference to the whole year.[6]

The overseas part of the split year is the part before the day the individual starts to have a home in the UK.[7]

1 Schedule 45, para 51(2) and (5).
2 Schedule 45, para 51(3).
3 Schedule 45, para 51(4).
4 Schedule 45, para 51(6).
5 Schedule 45, para 51(6) and (7).
6 Schedule 45, para 51(8).
7 Schedule 45, para 53(9).

2.41   Dual residence

The concept of dual residence has disappeared as a matter of domestic law under the statutory residence test. The legislation only determines whether an individual is resident in the UK and provides no basis for determining whether an individual is also resident elsewhere. Dual residence will therefore only arise and be relevant where an individual is resident in another country for the purposes of that country's tax system. Where the other country is a party to a tax treaty with the UK, then dual residence may be resolved for the purposes of the application of that treaty, at least in treaties patterned on the OECD model.

A glaring omission from the legislation is treating individuals who are resident in another contracting state under a tiebreaker as non-UK resident for all purposes in the same way that companies are so treated under CTA 2009 s 18. The application of this principle to individuals would bring coherence and consistency to the UK tax system. It would also help to reduce some of the harsh and surprising results of the current legislative proposals.

2.42   Temporary non-residence

Parliament has extended the jurisdiction to tax on a worldwide basis over individuals who succeed in breaking the residential ties but who become UK resident again within five years of ceasing to be so. Temporary non-residents – that is individuals who have been tax resident in the UK and become not resident for a period of less than five tax years – will be liable to tax in respect to several items of income and capital gains tax on certain gains realised after departure from the UK in the year they resume UK residence.[1] Remittance basis taxpayers who are temporary non-residents are similarly liable to tax in the year of return on remittances made in the intervening years.[2] The tax regime for temporary non-residents is set out in Part 4 of Schedule 43 to the Finance Act 2013.

Part 4 of Schedule 43 is headed 'anti-avoidance'. The consultative document asserts that the statutory residence test:

'... will therefore need to counteract the risk of individuals creating artificial short periods of non-residence, during which they receive a large amount of income (which accrued during periods of UK residence) free of UK tax and then bring the income back into the UK tax free.'[3]

The notion of 'artificial non-residence' is surprising given the entirely factual nature of residence both under existing law and the statutory test. The statutory residence test in many respects specifies a particular period or set of conditions quite precisely. HMRC guidance on the General Anti-Abuse Rule in FA 2013, Part 5, says that in such cases, 'taxpayers are entitled to assume that they are on the right side of the line if they have satisfied the statutory condition and there is no contrivance about what they have done.'[4] The provisions existing prior to FA 2013 relating to temporary non-residents demonstrate the fallacy of a link between more certain rules introduced in the SRT and the behaviour the regime for temporary non-residents is aimed at. The temporary non-residents rules apply in any event equally to tax sinners and saints alike. No distinction is made between a short period of non-residence that is motivated by tax considerations, a spell of overseas employment, or a gap year.

The temporary non-residence rules depart from other aspects of the statutory residence regime in that, an individual, who is resident in the UK under domestic law, is only resident for the purpose of these rules, if he is also not resident in another country for the purposes of a tax treaty at any time in the tax year. This status is labelled 'sole UK residence'. The same principle applies to split years. The UK part of a split year is only a period of residence for these rules if the individual is also not resident in another country for the purposes of a tax treaty at any time in the UK part of the tax year.[5] Thus, in applying these rules, a period of UK residence requires both residence in the UK as a matter of domestic law and, where relevant, under any applicable tax treaty. The corollary is that an individual may be UK resident as a matter of domestic law but have a period of temporary non-residence under these rules if they are treaty resident in another country at any time in the tax year or UK part of a split year.

Individuals who cease to be resident may be treated as temporarily non-resident. This will potentially be applicable to an individual who has been a sole UK resident for four out of the seven years immediately preceding the year of departure.[6] Any year in which the individual has split-year treatment is included as a year of residence for this purpose. An individual departs either by ceasing to be resident or becomes treaty non-resident.[7] An individual returns when he is resident and not a treaty non-resident.[8]

An individual is 'temporarily non-resident' if his temporary period of non-residence is five years or less.[9] The temporary residence period is measured from the end of a period of sole UK residence to the start of the next period of sole UK residence (called the 'period of return'). For this purpose, a 'residence period' is either a full tax year, or in the case of an individual with a split year, the overseas part or the UK part of that split year. The five-year period is therefore by reference to time elapsed and not to tax years, as was the case previously.

---

1 These items are identified in Schedule 45 paras 116–144 by amendments throughout the tax legislation and in the Temporary Non-Residence (Miscellaneous Amendments) Regulations 2013 (SI 2013/1810) in force from 12 August 2013.
2 Schedule 45, para 118.
3 Consultative Document, para 3.50.
4 This principle is articulated in HMRC'S GAAR GUIDANCE (Approved by the Advisory Panel with effect from 15 April 2013) PART D – Examples D2.4.1.
5 Schedule 45, para 112.
6 Schedule 45, para 110(1)(c).
7 Schedule 45, paras 110(1)(d).
8 Schedule 45, para 114 and 115.
9 Schedule 45, para 110(1)(d).

2.43   Commencement and transitional rules

The statutory residence test and the statutory split-year treatment generally have effect for determining whether individuals are resident or not and in calculating an individual's liability to income tax or capital gains tax for the tax year 2013–14 or any subsequent tax year. The split-year treatment and the temporary non-residence rules have effect if the year of departure is the tax year 2013–14 or a subsequent tax year.[1]

Transitional rules apply for a limited period. If it is necessary to determine whether an individual was resident or not resident in the UK for a tax year before the tax year 2013–14 (a pre-commencement tax year) for the purpose of determining residence in 2013–14, 2014–15 or 2015–16 then the existing case law and statutory rules described in Chapters 3 and 5 apply. However, an individual may elect, in respect to one or more pre-commencement tax years, for the question to be determined instead in accordance with the statutory residence test by notice in writing to HMRC. Such a notice must be given no later than the first anniversary of the end of year for which the question is relevant and is irrevocable.[2]

Where such an election is made, the SRT rules are modified in their application to years before 2013–14. In applying the fourth automatic UK test to an individual, residence on any basis, and not only automatic residence will govern. In applying the fifth automatic overseas test, the deceased individual must have been non-resident in those previous tax years (the earlier year will meet this condition if ESC A11 applied to a departure from the UK that year).[3] Split-year treatment in the earlier years under the relevant Extra-Statutory Concessions is given statutory effect by reference to the actual or deemed departure.[4] The existing temporary non-resident provisions, as in force immediately before the day on which the Finance Act enacting the statutory residence test is passed, continue to have effect on and after that day in any case where an individual's year of departure is a tax year before the tax year 2013–14.[5] The existing temporary non-resident provisions are:

- s 10A of TCGA 1992 (chargeable gains);
- s 576A of ITEPA 2003 (income withdrawals under certain foreign pensions);
- s 579CA of ITEPA 2003 (income withdrawals under registered pension schemes); and
- s 832A of ITTOIA (relevant foreign income charged on remittance basis).[6]

Where those provisions continue to have effect, the question of whether a person is or is not resident in the UK for the tax year 2013–14 or a subsequent tax year is to be determined in accordance with the statutory residence test, but the effect of the new statutory split-year treatment is to be ignored. Whether an individual met the requirements for UK residence four out of the seven years preceding departure is determined for earlier years under the prior law.[7]

---

1 Schedule 45, para 153.
2 Schedule 45, para 154.
3 Schedule 45, para 154(5).
4 Schedule 45, paras 155 and 156. See **5.02**.
5 Schedule 45, para 158.
6 Schedule 45, para 157.
7 See Chapters 3 and 5.

2.44   Scottish taxpayers

Scotland is the only country within the UK that has an element of autonomy in relation to income tax. A 'Scottish taxpayer' may be liable to the Scottish rate of income tax under Part 4A, Chapter 2 of the Scotland Act 1998. The expression 'Scottish taxpayer' is used rather than 'Scottish resident' although the definition bears the hallmarks of residence.

A Scottish taxpayer is an individual who is resident in the UK for income tax purposes and meets any one of three conditions.[1]

The first condition applies to an individual who has a closer connection with Scotland than with any other part of the UK for any year. This will be the case if in that year he has only one place of residence in the UK and that place is Scotland provided he lives at that place for at least part of the year.[2] An individual who has two or more places of residence in the UK, is a Scottish taxpayer if his main place of residence in the UK is in Scotland for at least part of the year and he lives at a place of residence in Scotland for at least part of the year. In addition, the times in the year when his main place of residence is in Scotland must comprise (in aggregate) at least as much of the year as the times when his main place of residence is in any one other part of the UK.[3] A 'place' includes a place on board a vessel or other means of transport.[4]

HMRC guidance[5] on the application of these tests is hardly unequivocal. HMRC consider that an individual's 'place of residence' is 'a place that a reasonable onlooker, with knowledge of the material facts, would regard as the dwelling in which that person habitually lives: in other words his or her home.'[6] Where, in a tax year, an individual has two or more 'places of residence' in the UK, HMRC say that:

'A "main place of residence" is not necessarily the residence where the individual spends the majority of their time, although it commonly may be. A "main place of residence" is the "place of residence" with which the individual can be said to have the greatest degree of connection.'

This is a matter of fact and all of the facts and circumstances of the particular case must be considered.[7] An individual's election of 'main residence' for CGT purposes will not determine 'main place of residence' for Scottish taxpayer purposes.[8] The factors that HMRC regard as indicative are similar to their approach to the meaning of 'home' for purposes of the Statutory Residence Test.[9]

Scottish taxpayer status will be dependent on whether a 'close connection' with Scotland or another part of the UK exists. Central to that test is establishing an individual's 'main place of residence'.

The second condition is that the individual spends more days of a year in Scotland than in any other part of the UK. A day spent in Scotland or elsewhere in the UK is spent there only if the individual is there at the end of the day. An individual is not treated as being in the UK at the end of a day if on that day he arrives in the UK as a passenger and departs from the UK on the next day, and during the time between arrival and departure does not engage in activities which are to a substantial extent unrelated to his passage through the UK.[10]

Thirdly, members of Parliament for constituencies in Scotland, members of the European Parliament for Scotland, and members of the Scottish Parliament are all Scottish taxpayers.[11]

---

1 Scotland Act 1998, s 80D.
2 Section 80E(2).
3 Section 80E(3).
4 Section 80E(4).
5 HMRC, Scottish Taxpayer Technical Guidance Manual (3 November 2015).
6 HMRC, Scottish Taxpayer Technical Guidance Manual STTG3400.
7 HMRC, Scottish Taxpayer Technical Guidance Manual STTG3700.
8 HMRC, Scottish Taxpayer Technical Guidance Manual STTG3100.
9 See **2.08** and STTG3700 and STTG5000.
10 Section 80F.
11 Section 80D(4).

2.45 Residence for tax treaty purposes

It will be apparent that an individual may be resident in the UK for tax purposes although also living elsewhere. In most, but not all cases, residence in another country will entail a liability to tax in that country as well. The UK has entered into over 120 treaties with the objective of the prevention of, or relief from, double taxation (ie the taxation of the same income or gains by both the UK and the foreign state concerned).[1] A double tax treaty generally protects a person against double taxation by allocating taxing jurisdiction between the contacting states and providing that income arising in one state is not to be charged to tax in the hands of a resident of the other state, or affords him relief by providing that, where he is charged to tax on income accruing to him in the source state, he is to be given exemption or a credit for that tax in the state of which he is resident.

Included in the mechanisms for allocating taxing jurisdiction are rules for determining which residence status of the two is to prevail for the purposes of the treaty where both states claim taxing rights on the basis that the taxpayer is resident in each state.

Most modern treaties to which the UK is a party follow the Model Double Taxation Convention on Income and Capital published by the Organisation for Economic Co-operation and Development, Paris. Although the model has been amended several times, the provisions dealing with residence have in essence remained constant since the 1963 OECD Draft Double Taxation Convention. The current form, as it applies to individuals reads as follows:

'**Article 4:** Residence
(1)   For the purposes of this Convention, the term "resident of a Contracting State" means any person who, under the laws of that State, is liable to tax therein by reason of his domicile, residence, ... or any other criterion of a similar nature; the term does not include any person who is liable to tax in that Contracting State only if he derives income or capital gains from sources therein.
(2)   Where by reason of the provisions of paragraph (1) of this Article an individual is a resident of both Contracting States, then his status shall be determined in accordance with the following rules:
(a)   he shall be deemed to be a resident of the Contracting State in which he has a permanent home available to him; if he has a permanent home available to him in both Contracting States, he shall be deemed to be a resident of the Contracting State with which his personal and economic relations are closer (centre of vital interests);
(b)   if the Contracting State in which he has his centre of vital interests cannot be determined, or if he has not a permanent home available to him in either Contracting State, he shall be deemed to be a resident of the Contracting State in which he has an habitual abode;
(c)   if he has an habitual abode in both Contracting States or in neither of them, he shall be deemed to be a resident of the Contracting State of which he is a national;
(d)   if he is a national of both Contracting States or of neither of them, the competent authorities of the Contracting States shall settle the question by mutual agreement.'

In *Hankinson v HMRC*[2] the First-tier Tribunal found the taxpayer was resident and ordinarily resident in the UK during 1998–99. Mr Hankinson had entered into a service agreement with a Dutch subsidiary of a company that he was indirectly interested in, to work in the Netherlands from 23 February 1998 for a period of a minimum of 15 months, while remaining as non-executive chairman of the parent company. On 2 January 1999 he became ill on a flight to Barbados where he had booked a holiday from 2 to 30 January 1999. He returned to the UK on 30 April 1999 but did not return to work in the Netherlands again, and retired from the service of the Dutch company on about 15 August 1999 and from his non-executive chairmanship of the parent company on 31 August 1999. He contended, somewhat optimistically, that he was nonetheless resident in the Netherlands for the purposes of the UK-Netherlands tax treaty. The case concerned a capital gain made in March 1999 which falls within the UK tax year 1998–99 and the Dutch tax year 1999. The overlap of tax years was from 1 January to 5 April 1999.

The only evidence before the tribunal on residence in the Netherlands was advice from Mr Hankinson's Dutch accountants that residence in principle is a question of facts and circumstances and that in view of Mr Hankinson's wife not living in the Netherlands while he was working full-time (as they were instructed) in the Netherlands, 'it is not very likely that Dutch tax authorities will regard you as a resident of the Netherlands'. During 1999 he spent only five days in the Netherlands to collect his belongings from the apartment after the employment contract had apparently been terminated. The tribunal had no hesitation in deciding as a fact, even in the absence of any expert evidence on Dutch law, that the Dutch authorities would not regard him as a resident of the Netherlands. Accordingly Mr Hankinson was held to be a resident of the UK and not of the Netherlands for the purpose of Art 4(1) of the treaty.[3]

Consequently, it was unnecessary to determine his status under the tie-breaker in Art 4(2) of the treaty. Nonetheless, the tribunal examined the tie-breaker as if Mr Hankinson were also a resident of the Netherlands. Each of the rules listed in Art 4(2) is to be applied sequentially.[4]

The first of these is that he is deemed to be a resident of the state in which he has a permanent home available to him. According to the OECD Commentary to the Model Convention 'any form of home may be taken into account (house or apartment belonging to or rented by the individual, rented furnished room).[5] If that is to be so, 'home', in the context of Art 4(2)(a), may be taken to be similar to 'place of abode' as described at **2.08** to **2.09** above.[6] Permanence is however essential. According to the commentary, this means that 'the individual must have arranged to have the dwelling available to him at all times, continuously, and not occasionally and retained [the home] for his permanent use as opposed to staying at a particular place under such conditions that it is evident that the stay is intended to be of short duration'. This rules out the possibility that a house, etc which is let between visits might be a 'permanent home' for tie-breaker purposes.

If a person has a permanent home in both states (but not if he has a permanent home in neither), then he shall be deemed to be a resident of the state with which his personal and economic relations are closer (centre of vital interests).

The meaning of the words in parentheses is by no means clear, but the OECD Commentary provides some guidance by stating that:

> '… regard will be had to his family and social relations, his occupations, his political, cultural or other activities, his place of business, the place from which he administers his property etc … but … considerations based on the personal acts of the individual must receive special attention'.[7]

If a person's centre of vital interests are divided equally between the two states concerned, or if the person concerned has no permanent home, then the person is to be regarded as resident in the state 'in which he has an habitual abode'. The OECD Commentary suggests that the place where he spends more time tips the balance in favour of that state.[8] Furthermore, the French version of the text is '*où elle séjourne de façon habituelle*', which indicates that what is being referred to is the state in which a person habitually *stays*.

Where, even after the application of these tests, the question of a person's residence remains unresolved, nationality becomes the deciding factor. If the person is a national of both states or of neither of them, then the competent authorities of the contracting states are required to settle the question by mutual agreement.

A more extensive application of the tie-breaker was necessary in *Yates v Revenue & Customs*.[9] Ms Yates was found to be resident in both the UK and Spain under their respective domestic tax laws in each of 2003–04, 2004–05 and 2006–07 when certain capital gains were realised. Prior to moving to Spain, she lived together with her husband in a jointly purchased residential property, near Nottingham ('Kingston Hall'). In March 2000, Ms Yates rented a three-bedroom apartment, on the southern coast of Spain on an 11-month lease which was renewed until November 2003. She then purchased another three-bedroom apartment in the same development. In applying the tie-breaker in Art 4(2)(a) of the Spain-UK Income tax treaty, the tribunal found that she had permanent homes in both states. Therefore, it was necessary to examine whether in the relevant years Ms Yates's personal and economic relations (centre of vital interests) were closer to Spain or to the UK.

The tribunal concluded that her centre of vital interests was retained in the UK. Her husband, who remained UK resident throughout, was the centre of her vital interests. He was unable to join her in Spain while she was there (except for occasional but regular visits) because of his business commitments in the UK. Other significant relationships were with her parents, who lived in the UK, and her siblings, who lived in the UK, except for a sister in Italy. They far outweighed in significance and importance any social ties she may have formed in Spain. The main factor connecting Ms Yates to Spain was the desirability of residence there for health reasons. This, the tribunal ruled, was not a factor of importance to consider in locating Ms Yates's centre of vital interests. Her economic relations were also with the UK as she was financially dependent on her husband. As a result, she was a resident of the UK and not Spain for treaty purposes. The tribunal observed, *obiter*, that, had it been necessary to apply the habitual abode test in Art 4(2)(b) of the treaty, she would probably have had an habitual abode in Spain, and not the UK, having regard to the day-count. Both the *Hankinson* and *Yates* decisions emphasise that the tie-breaker is a series of successive tests. If one is satisfied then, the later tests do not apply.

---

1 Such treaties are given effect in domestic law by Order in Council made under the authority of TIOPA 2010 s 2.

2 *Hankinson v HMRC* [2009] UKFTT 384 (TC).

3 At para 63.

4 Although unnecessary for the decision, the judge in *Hankinson* set out his views *obiter* on the operation of the tie-breaker in Art 4(2). Another case in the UK where the residence

tie-breaker provisions of Art 4(2) were invoked is *Squirrell v Revenue & Customs* [2005] UKSPC SPC 00493 (23 June 2005). The taxpayer left the UK on October 2000, moving to the US where he was treated as resident for the whole of 2000. He was resident in the UK in the tax year 1999–2000 when he received a termination payment from his UK employer. Although Art 4(2) of the US-UK treaty was referred to, no claim had been made in either country to determine his residence status for the purposes of the treaty by going through the tie-breaker provisions in turn. In any event the Special Commissioner concluded that the taxpayer's UK tax treatment was the same regardless of where he was resident for purposes of the treaty. See generally Jonathan Schwarz, *Schwarz on Tax Treaties* (5th Edition, Croner-i, 2018), Ch 6 on treaty residence.

5 Commentary to Art 4, para 13.
6 It is interesting to note that, in *R v Hammond* (1852) 17 QB 772, Lord Campbell CJ said (at 780 and 781) that 'a man's residence, where he lives with his family and sleeps at night, is always his place of abode in the full sense of that expression'.
7 Commentary to Art 4 para 15.
8 Commentary to Art 4 para 17.
9 *Lynette Dawn Yates v Revenue & Customs* [2012] UKFTT 568 (TC).

CHAPTER 3

Residence of individuals: case law test

Come, give us a taste of your quality.

Shakespeare Hamlet Act 2 Sc 2

3.01 Introduction

The Income Tax Act 1806 (which is the foundation on which the present system of direct taxation rests) accorded clear recognition to this limitation by making 'residence' in Great Britain (now the UK) the chief determinant of chargeability where there would not otherwise be a sufficient connection between the sovereign territory and the source of the profits or gains which Parliament had resolved to tax. Residence, as interpreted by the courts is, as we shall see, a concept rooted in, but of greater durability and more nuanced than, the concept of presence[1] and, as a determinant of chargeability to tax, survived for over 200 years. Finance Act 2013 Sch 45 abolished the case law interpretation with effect from 6 April 2013.[2] Nonetheless, because the statutory residence test[3] determines residence, in part, by reference to residence in the three years preceding the year in question, the case law test remains relevant. In this context, the meaning of residence as described in this chapter will be an ingredient in deciding the residence of individuals until 5 April 2018. The knock-on effect of residence in previous years will mean its relevance remains for a further three years thereafter.

Individuals may need to consider the law in this chapter (and in Chapter 5) in deciding whether to make the election provided in FA 2013 Sch 45, para 153 in order to compare their status in the years 2010–11, 2011–12 and 2012–13 for the purpose of applying the statutory residence test.[4]

The case law on residence discussed in this chapter remains applicable to National Insurance Contributions.

---

1 As to whether it follows from this that a person cannot be regarded as resident in the UK for a tax year during which he has at no time been physically present within the territorial bounds of the UK, see **5.14** below.
2 FA 2013 Sch 45, paras 1, 2 and 153.
3 See Chapter 2.
4 See **2.43**.

The nature of residence

3.02 A qualitative attribute

It has often been observed that, in legislating for the imposition of taxation on the basis of 'residence', Parliament omitted, or declined, to give the term 'residence' any statutory definition. That omission created an immediate difficulty which very soon required judicial resolution for, in the absence of a statutory definition, the word 'residence' has 'no technical or special meaning'[1] and must, therefore, according to accepted principles of construction, be given the meaning it would bear 'in the speech of plain men'.[2] To put it another way: if Parliament uses a word without explaining what it means by that word, it must be assumed to be using that word 'in its common sense'.[3] But what *is* the common sense of 'residence' or any of its variants? As Rowlatt J has said:

> 'When you speak of a person residing, do you mean that he has attributed to himself a quality which makes him describable in that way with reference to a place, or do you mean that he is really there?'[4]

If 'residing' means no more than 'is really there', 'residence' becomes a mere synonym for 'physical presence' and that, as we saw in Chapter 1, is what Parliament sought to avoid. Presence is an attribute which is far too easily acquired or shed for it to serve as an adequate determinant of chargeability to tax, and residence instead of presence was chosen to fill that role because of its ability to provide a more enduring territorial link. Residence can play the part assigned to it, however, only if it carries the *first* of the two senses which Rowlatt J has indicated it may bear and, accordingly, the judiciary has consistently held that, in the context of fiscal legislation, 'residence' is to be regarded only 'as signifying an attribute of the person'.[5] Therefore, one must never, in the context of a fiscal statute, 'think of "residence" in the sense of a house or place of residence',[6] and the same is true of all the variants – 'resident', 'reside', 'resides', 'residing', etc. 'Resident', for example, 'indicates a quality of the person and is not descriptive of ... property, real or personal'.[7]

Attributes or qualities of the person defy encompassment in a form of words. They have no concrete reality. Their existence may only be inferred or deduced from a person's particular pattern of behaviour in particular circumstances, and rarely, if ever, will the pattern or the circumstances in any two cases be quite the same. 'Residence', taken as a term expressing a quality of the person,

> '... is not a term of invariable elements, all of which must be satisfied in each instance. It is quite impossible to give it a precise and inclusive definition. It is highly flexible, and its many shades of meaning vary not only in the contexts of different matters, but also in different aspects of the same matter. In one case it is satisfied by certain elements, in another by others, some common, some new.'[8]

To bring a person within, or to exclude a person from, the charging sections of a taxing statute solely by reference to a determinant of such inexactitude is, clearly, far from satisfactory and, indeed, brings the Taxes Acts close to defeating the maxim that a taxing statute must impose a charge in clear terms or fail. As Viscount Sumner has pointed out, however, 'the words are plain and it is only their application that is haphazard and beyond all forecast'.[9]

The Royal Commission on the Taxation of Profits and Income[10] believed that a precise definition would benefit the Inland Revenue. The Commission's report concluded by recommending further statutory provisions in this area but, apart from legislation introduced in 1956 in relation to persons working abroad,[11] that recommendation was never implemented.

Instead, the Inland Revenue further developed its own code of practice[12] which, though of no legal standing,[13] has been generally applied with a degree of inflexibility normally accorded only to statutory instruments. This placed the taxpayer in the worst of all possible positions for, though the code is far from being comprehensive or the balanced summary of case law principles which the Inland Revenue held it out to be, the taxpayer will frequently find that he has no option but to employ the appeal machinery, applying the law, if he wishes to challenge the code on any point.

---

1 *Lysaght v IRC* (1928) 13 TC 511 at 536, per Lord Warrington of Clyffe.
2 *Lysaght v IRC* (1928) 13 TC 511 at 529, per Viscount Sumner.
3 *Lysaght v IRC* (1928) 13 TC 511 at 534, per Lord Buckmaster.
4 *Levene v IRC* (1928) 13 TC 486 at 492.
5 *Pickles v Foulsham* (1923) 9 TC 261 at 274, per Rowlatt J.
6 *Pickles v Foulsham* (1923) 9 TC 261 at 274, per Rowlatt J.
7 *Lysaght v IRC* (1928) 13 TC 511 at 528, per Viscount Sumner.
8 *Thompson v Minister of National Revenue* [1946] SCR 209 at 224, per Rand J, quoted with approval by Wynn-Perry J in *Miesegaes v IRC* (1957) 37 TC 493 at 497.
9 *Levene v IRC* (1928) 13 TC 486 at 502.
10 Final Report, 1955, Cmd 9474, para 292.
11 See **5.16** to **5.20** below.
12 Previously contained in Booklet IR20, the last version of which was published in July 2008, *Residents and non-residents: liability to tax in the UK*. The subsequent HMRC view is contained in HMRC6. The last edition was issued on 31 December 2011 and applicable from 6 April 2011 to 5 April 2013.
13 See **1.26** above.

3.03 A question of fact and degree

The absence of a statutory definition of the term 'residence' is yet more far-reaching in its consequences than even the foregoing paragraphs might suggest. If the Taxes Acts contained such a definition, then it would be open to the courts[1] to decide whether or not a person had come within that definition, for 'a proper construction of … statutory language is a matter of law'.[2]

As we have seen, however, the Taxes Acts give no definition of the word 'residence' and the judiciary has inclined to the view that 'it is not possible to frame one'.[3] Accordingly, whether a person is resident or not is, within the present state of affairs, a question not of law but of fact.

Because of the way in which the appeal procedure operates, however, it falls not to the courts but to the Commissioners to consider what Rowlatt J called the 'bundle of actual facts'[4] and to form from those facts the 'impression or opinion' in accordance with which a finding of 'resident' or 'non-resident' will be made. As Nicholls J put it in *Reed v Clark*:[5]

> 'The key word "residing" is not defined by statute ... Thus the task of the fact-finding tribunal in the present case was to consider and weigh all the evidence and then, giving the word "residing" its natural and ordinary meaning, reach a conclusion on the factual question of whether or not the taxpayer was residing in the UK in the year of assessment.'[6]

Once such a conclusion has been reached, the appellate court's powers of intervention become very limited. Its role is restricted by statute[7] to the hearing and determination only of questions of law arising on the case stated by the General Commissioners for its opinion or on appeal from the Special Commissioners which means that:

> '... when commissioners have made findings of fact, their decision is not open to review provided (a) they had before them evidence from which such findings could properly be made and (b) they did not misdirect themselves in law.'[8]

Thus, a finding by the Commissioners that a person is resident in the UK in a year of assessment 'only raises a question of law if it can be contended that it is impossible to draw that conclusion of fact as to residence in the United Kingdom from the facts set out in the case'.[9] By reason of the very inexactitude of the term 'resident', such a contention will rarely be upheld, and this places the taxpayer in an unenviable position.

The facts on which the Commissioners make their findings as to residence or non-residence differ from case to case, but have tended to be facts concerning a person's physical presence in the UK or absence from it, facts concerning his history of residence or non-residence, facts concerning his present habits and manner of life, facts as to his nationality, facts as to the purpose, frequency, regularity and duration of his visits to the UK or to places overseas, facts as to ties of family and ties of business in the UK, and facts as to the maintenance or availability of a place of abode in the UK.

Such facts do not all carry equal weight and, indeed, facts which in one case carry no weight at all may, in another case, be so significant as to completely tip the scales. This is what is meant when residence is referred to (as, from time to time, it has been) as a 'question of degree'. A visit to the UK this year may signify little, a visit next year may signify not much more, but visits year after year may, in the context of the particular circumstances of a case, push the needle to that point on the Commissioners' scale which reads 'resident'. It is then that the questions of degree resolve themselves into a finding of fact and it is that finding of fact which the courts are powerless to disturb unless 'no person acting judicially and properly instructed as to the relevant law could have come to the determination under appeal'[10] or 'no reasonable person could have arrived at the same conclusion as the Commissioners'.[11]

---

1 Ie, on an appeal from a decision of the Commissioners.
2 *IRC v Fraser* (1942) 24 TC 498 at 501, per Lord Normand LP.
3 *Levene v IRC* (1928) 13 TC 486 at 497, per Lord Hanworth MR.
4 *Lowenstein v De Salis* (1926) 10 TC 424 at 437.

5 [1985] STC 323.
6 [1985] STC 323 at 338.
7 TMA 1970 ss 56(6), 56A.
8 *Reed v Clark* [1985] STC 323 at 336–337, per Nicholls J.
9 *Bayard Brown v Burt* (1911) 5 TC 667 at 670, per Hamilton J.
10 *Edwards v Bairstow and Harrison* (1955) 36 TC 207 at 229, per Lord Radcliffe.
11 *Pilkington v Randall* (1966) 42 TC 662 at 674, per Salmon LJ.

3.04 A personal attribute

Because residence is a 'quality of the person'[1] and, therefore, a 'question …
of degree',[2] it follows that a spouse's residence status is not governed by her
co-spouse's status but is determined by her own circumstances.

Recognition as a person as a matter of law carries with it the implication that
residential status is capable of being conferred. Because corporate bodies such
as limited companies are legal persons independent of their members under
English law, they too will either possess or lack UK residence status. 'Resident'
is, however, 'a term exceedingly unsuited to describe a legal "person"'[3] and,
accordingly, a corporation's residence status can be determined only 'by
analogy from natural persons'.[4] So it has been with partnerships during the
years in which they were given quasi personality for income and corporation
tax purposes.[5] A partnership is not a legal entity under English law and its
residence status, too, was arrived at by analogy. Trusts and settlements present
even greater conceptual difficulties, for a trust or a settlement is a proprietary
relationship.[6] It does become necessary in some circumstances to determine its
residence status. All these matters are discussed in depth in Chapters 6 and 7.

1 *IRC v Lysaght* (1928) 13 TC 511 at 528, per Viscount Sumner.
2 *IRC v Lysaght* (1928) 13 TC 511 at 536, per Lord Warrington of Clyffe.
3 *Todd v Egyptian Delta Land and Investment Co Ltd* (1928) 14 TC 119 at 140, per Viscount
Sumner.
4 *Todd v Egyptian Delta Land and Investment Co Ltd* (1928) 14 TC 119 at 140, per Viscount
Sumner.
5 Repealed by FA 1995 s 117; see now ITTOIA 2005 Pt 9.
6 See for example *Green v Russell* [1959] 2 QB 226 (CA) per Romer LJ, at 241.

3.05 An annual attribute

In *Levene v IRC*,[1] Viscount Sumner said that 'the taxpayer's chargeability
in each year of charge constitutes a separate issue',[2] and, in so saying, gave
recognition to the fact that income tax is an annual tax. It is an annual tax
in that the charge must be reimposed by Parliament in the Finance Act each
year and it is an annual tax in that the charge is made upon the annual income
(ie, the income of the year of charge). As was noted in Chapter 1, however,
residence is a principal determinant of chargeability and it will come as no
surprise, therefore, to learn that residence is an annual attribute (ie an attribute
which endures for a year).

This was brought out very clearly in the case of *Thomson v Bensted*[3] where
it was held that, although during the tax year 1911–12 Mr Thomson had

actually spent only four or so months at his home in Scotland and had spent the remainder of the year in West Africa, he was resident in the UK 'during the whole year, in the sense of the ... Acts'.[4]

It is quite possible to argue that what was being recognised in the *Thomson* case was not so much that residence is an annual attribute but simply that Mr Thomson had a quality of residence which, because it had been acquired at some time in the past and because it extended into the foreseeable future, was not disturbed or impaired by the periods of time he spent abroad. That argument did not hold good, however, in the case of *Back v Whitlock*.[5] There, Rowlatt J said that if a person were to become a new permanent resident in the UK only two days before the end of a year of assessment he would be just as chargeable to tax as would someone who had resided here throughout the year. It could surely not be contended that such a person, *de facto*, had the quality of residence prior to the date on which his period of actual residence began and, indeed, Rowlatt J did not base his statement on that ground. It was rather that:

> '... there is no question under the Income Tax Acts of any apportionment or adjustment for Income Tax in time, with regard to the date when a person became resident and so became taxable.'[6]

This same principle emerged more clearly, but in relation to a person who had permanently left the UK, in *Neubergh v IRC*[7] when Brightman J had to decide whether a Mr Felix Neubergh, who had lived in the UK since 1919 but had permanently departed on 26 January 1968, was nevertheless liable to the special charge on investment income imposed by the Finance Act 1968 on persons domiciled in the UK in the tax year 1967–68 or resident in the UK in that fiscal year and throughout the nine preceding years. Having first asked the question: 'Was the taxpayer resident in the UK in the tax year 1967–68 and throughout the nine preceding years?',[8] he declared that 'the answer to that question can only be Yes'.[9] His grounds for such a conclusion were that, in accordance with the reasoning in *Mitchell v IRC*[10] 'residence during a part of the year is clearly sufficient'.[11]

It was in the case of *Gubay v Kington*,[12] that the point was finally made clear but in obscure circumstances. The case concerned the chargeability or otherwise of Mr Gubay to capital gains tax on the disposal of shares to his non-resident wife in a tax year during only part of which he was *de facto* resident in the UK. The question arose in the context of whether Mrs Gubay was 'living with her husband' for the then regime of joint taxation of spouses. Where one of the spouses is, and the other one is not, resident in the United Kingdom 'for a year of assessment', was the woman deemed not to be 'living with her husband' throughout that year of assessment? The argument with which Mr Gubay succeeded before the House of Lords was not the argument on which he had gone to the High Court and then to the Court of Appeal. In the lower courts, he had argued that, as he was actually resident in the UK for only six and a half months in the tax year 1972–73 he could not be said to be resident 'for the year of assessment' 1972–73 for income tax and could not, therefore, be charged with capital gains tax on the notional gain accruing to him on the disposal of shares made to his non-resident wife during that year. This argument was dismissed in both courts. In the High Court, Vinelott J said:

'The words "resident in the UK for a year of assessment" are frequently used by judges and textbook writers to describe the situation of a taxpayer who, because he was resident in the UK for part of a year of assessment, is assessable to tax from all sources of income arising during that year of assessment. In effect, the words "resident in the UK for a year of assessment" are used to predicate of the taxpayer that he had the status or quality of being a resident in the UK for tax purposes during the year of assessment.'[13]

In the Court of Appeal, Sir John Donaldson MR, said:

'Being resident in the UK may be a status or a fact. Where it is a status, it is something which is either enjoyed (if that be the right word) or not enjoyed for a whole tax year.'[14]

It has thus been placed beyond doubt that any person who possesses or acquires the attribute of residence for part of a tax year will, unless a statute or an extra-statutory concession or a rule of practice dictates otherwise,[15] be regarded as being resident for the whole of that year; and both residence and its related concept of ordinary residence[16] may, therefore, in general terms, be said to be annual attributes, enduring for the whole of any fiscal year in which they are enjoyed, however briefly.

---

1 *Levene v IRC* (1928) 13 TC 486.
2 *Levene v IRC* (1928) 13 TC 486 at 501.
3 (1918) 7 TC 137.
4 (1918) 7 TC 137 at 145, per the Lord President.
5 (1932) 16 TC 723.
6 (1932) 16 TC 723 at 726.
7 [1978] STC 181.
8 [1978] STC 181 at 184.
9 [1978] STC 181 at 185.
10 (1951) 33 TC 53.
11 *Neubergh v IRC* [1978] STC 181 at 185.
12 [1983] STC 443.
13 *Gubay v Kington* [1981] STC 721 at 735.
14 *Gubay v Kington* [1983] STC 443 at 451.
15 No statute other than TCGA 1992 s 2(1) presently so provides, but extra-statutory concessions and HMRC practice did. See **5.21** below.
16 See Chapter 4.

3.06   The judicial principles

Although, as has been explained, the question of whether or not a person possesses the quality of residence is a question of fact, and although the task of the judiciary is limited to that of examining the facts on which the Commissioners reach their decisions and seeing whether anyone acting judicially and properly instructed as to the relevant law could have arrived at the decisions at which the Commissioners have arrived,[1] judges have, in the course of carrying out their examinations, tended to underline significant facts, formulate principles and outline approaches which would lead them to one conclusion or another – even if, at the end of the day, they are obliged, in the absence of any obvious error of law on the part of the Commissioners, to uphold a decision which they themselves might not have reached. It is these general principles which will now be considered.

---

1 See **3.03** above.

3.07 The Shepherd/Grace syntheses

As the size of this work indicates, explaining the undefined statutory expression and distilling the cases is no easy or brief task. From a practical perspective, a brief statement of principles is most desirable. In *Shepherd v HMRC*,[1] the first published decision of the Special Commissioners dealing with residence, an attempt was made to synthesise the principles relating to residence and ordinary residence thus:

1   that the concepts of residence and ordinary residence are not defined in the legislation; the words therefore should be given their natural and ordinary meanings (*Levene*);
2   that the words 'residence' and 'to reside' mean 'to dwell permanently or for a considerable time, to have one's settled or usual abode, to live in or at a particular place' (*Levene*);
3   that the concept of 'ordinary residence' requires more than mere residence; it connotes residence in a place with some degree of continuity (*Levene*); 'ordinary' means normal and part of everyday life (*Lysaght*) or a regular, habitual mode of life in a particular place which has persisted despite temporary absences and which is voluntary and has a degree of settled purpose (*Shah*);
4   that the question whether a person is or is not resident in the UK is a question of fact for the Special Commissioners (*Zorab*);
5   that no duration is prescribed by statute and it is necessary to take into account all the facts of the case; the duration of an individual's presence in the UK and the regularity and frequency of visits are facts to be taken into account; also, birth, family and business ties, the nature of visits and the connections with this country, may all be relevant (*Zorab*; *Brown*);
6   that a reduced presence in the UK of a person whose absences are caused by his employment and so are temporary absences does not necessarily mean that the person is not residing in the UK (*Young*);
7   that the availability of living accommodation in the UK is a factor to be borne in mind in deciding if a person is resident here (*Cooper*) (although that is subject to ICTA 1988 s 336 (now ITA 2007 s 831);
8   that the fact that an individual has a home elsewhere is of no consequence; a person may reside in two places but if one of those places is the UK he is chargeable to tax here (*Cooper* and *Levene*);
9   that there is a difference between the case where a British subject has established a residence in the UK and then has absences from it (*Levene*) and the case where a person has never had a residence in the UK at all (*Zorab*; *Brown*);
10   that if there is evidence that a move abroad is a distinct break that could be a relevant factor in treating an individual as non-resident (*Combe*); and

11   that a person could become non-resident even if his intention was to mitigate tax (*Reed v Clark*).[2]

On appeal to the High Court,[3] only the statutory provisions of ICTA 1988 ss 334 and 336 (now ITA 2007 ss 829 and 831) were addressed. However, Lewison J 'detected no error of law' in the Special Commissioner's conclusion.[4] The same synthesis was restated in *Gaines-Cooper*.[5] A similar but not identical summary was adopted by Lewison J in *Grace v Revenue & Customs Commissioners*[6] on appeal from the same Special Commissioner who decided *Shepherd* and in which the same Counsel appeared for HMRC. Lewison J's summary there is as follows:

'1   The word "reside" is a familiar English word which means "to dwell permanently or for a considerable time, to have one's settled or usual abode, to live in or at a particular place": *Levene v Commissioners of Inland Revenue* (1928) 13 TC 486, 505. This is the definition taken from the Oxford English Dictionary in 1928, and is still the definition in the current online edition;

2   Physical presence in a particular place does not necessarily amount to residence in that place where, for example, a person's physical presence there is no more than a stop gap measure: *Goodwin v Curtis* (1998) 70 TC 478, 510;

3   In considering whether a person's presence in a particular place amounts to residence there, one must consider the amount of time that he spends in that place, the nature of his presence there and his connection with that place: *Commissioners of Inland Revenue v Zorab* (1926) 11 TC 289, 291;

4   Residence in a place connotes some degree of permanence, some degree of continuity or some expectation of continuity: *Fox v Stirk* [1970] 2 QB 463, 477; *Goodwin v Curtis* (1998) 70 TC 478, 510;

5   However, short but regular periods of physical presence may amount to residence, especially if they stem from performance of a continuous obligation (such as business obligations) and the sequence of visits excludes the elements of chance and of occasion: *Lysaght v Commissioners of Inland Revenue* (1928) 13 TC 511, 529;

6   Although a person can have only one domicile at a time, he may simultaneously reside in more than one place, or in more than one country: *Levene v Commissioners of Inland Revenue* (1928) 13 TC 486, 505;

7   "Ordinarily resident" refers to a person's abode in a particular place or country which he has adopted voluntarily and for settled purposes as part of the regular order of his life, whether of short or long duration: *R v Barnet LBC, ex p Shah* [1983] 2 AC 309, 343;

8   Just as a person may be resident in two countries at the same time, he may be ordinarily resident in two countries at the same time: *Re Norris* (1888) 4 TLR 452; *R v Barnet LBC, ex p Shah* [1983] 2 AC 309, 342;

9   It is wrong to conduct a search for the place where a person has his permanent base or centre adopted for general purposes; or, in other words to look for his "real home": *R v Barnet LBC, ex p Shah* [1983] 2 AC 309, 345 and 348;

10   There are only two respects in which a person's state of mind is relevant in determining ordinary residence. First, the residence must be voluntarily adopted; and second, there must be a degree of settled purpose: *R v Barnet LBC, ex p Shah* [1983] 2 AC 309, 344;

11   Although residence must be voluntarily adopted, a residence dictated by the exigencies of business will count as voluntary residence: *Lysaght v Commissioners of Inland Revenue* (1928) 13 TC 511, 535;

12 The purpose, while settled, may be for a limited period; and the relevant purposes may include education, business or profession as well as a love of a place: *R v Barnet, LBC ex p Shah* [1983] 2 AC 309, 344;

13 Where a person has had his sole residence in the United Kingdom he is unlikely to have ceased to reside in the United Kingdom (or to have "left" the United Kingdom) unless there has been a definite break in his pattern of life: *Re Combe* (1932) 17 TC 405, 411.'

On appeal,[7] Lord Justice Lloyd noted that the Special Commissioner's list in *Shepherd* summarised the relevant factors in much the same way and, ignoring, as being less relevant, points which relate to ordinary residence, he added the following three items in her list, despite the overlap between the two lists:

'• no duration is prescribed by statute and it is necessary to take into account all the facts of the case; the duration of an individual's presence in the United Kingdom and the regularity and frequency of visits are facts to be taken into account; also, birth, family and business ties, the nature of visits and the connections with this country, may all be relevant (*Zorab*; *Brown*);

• the availability of living accommodation in the United Kingdom is a factor to be borne in mind in deciding if a person is resident here (*Cooper*) (although that is subject to s 336);

• the fact that an individual has a home elsewhere is of no consequence; a person may reside in two places but if one of those places is the United Kingdom he is chargeable to tax here (*Cooper* and *Levene*).'[8]

While undoubtedly a handy list, caution must be exercised in treating these lists as comprehensive statements of the law. Indeed, it may be questioned the extent to which some cases establish principles of law at all, or whether they are merely illustrations of a very broad test based on facts and circumstances. This need for caution is underlined by the fact that while referring to these summaries, the Court of Appeal fell short of endorsing them as all-embracing. Lloyd LJ observed that they set out a number of relevant factors and noted, 'the incidental advantage of identifying almost all the decided cases to which I need to refer.'[9] In the High Court, Lewison J noted that there was considerable agreement about the law between the parties. The decision, however, relies on older tax cases and does not cite the more recent line of non-tax cases in the High Court that deal with residence in the context of the jurisdiction of the English courts for the purposes of the Civil Jurisdiction and Judgments Act 1982.[10] In *OJSC Oil Company Yugraneft (In Liquidation) v Roman Abramovich and others,* Christopher Clarke J, a judge with considerable experience in private client matters, underlined that 'resident for jurisdiction purposes but not resident for tax purposes is a distinction to be avoided if possible.'[11] In *Hankinson v HMRC*, the First-tier Tribunal, while accepting that changing communications and social conditions have to be dealt with in the context of reviewing residence, distinguished the non-tax decision in *Deripaska* as having a different emphasis in that it was not considering the shedding of a previously existing status, but the acquisition of residence with a degree of permanence or continuity.[12]

When *Grace* was reheard before the First-tier Tribunal,[13] the confusion between residence and ordinary residence in the recitation of the governing principles by the Court of Appeal was identified. The First-tier Tribunal was required only to decide whether Mr Grace was UK resident. Accordingly,

Judge Mosedale omitted the seventh, eighth, tenth and twelfth principles set out by the Court of Appeal on the basis that they addressed ordinary residence exclusively.[14] The distinction between residence and ordinary residence is considered more fully in Chapter 4.

---

1 *Shepherd v Revenue & Customs* [2005] UKSPC 484.
2 *Shepherd* para 58.
3 [2006] EWHC 1512 (CH); STC 1821.
4 At para [23].
5 *Gaines-Cooper v Revenue & Customs Comrs* [2007] UKSPC 568 at para 165.
6 *Grace v Revenue & Customs Commissioners* [2008] EWHC 2708 (Ch) at para 3.
7 *Grace v Revenue & Customs Commissioners* [2009] EWCA Civ 1082.
8 At paras 5 and 7.
9 At paras 3, 5 and 6.
10 *Dubai Bank Ltd v Abbas* [1997] ILPr 308, *High Tech International v Deripaska* [2006] EWHC 3276 (QB) and *OJSC Oil Company Yugraneft (In Liquidation) v Roman Abramovich and others* [2008] EWHC 2613 (Comm).
11 At para 461 where Christopher Clarke J noted that Mr Abramovich 'is not treated as resident in the UK for tax purposes. His non-resident status has never been challenged by the Inland Revenue. It is submitted on his behalf that this must be an important factor, not least because the courts have sought to give the word the same "*ordinary*" meaning in both tax cases (such as *Levene*) and jurisdiction cases (such as *Abbas*). It makes sense to do so.'
12 *Hankinson v HMRC* [2009] UKFTT 384 (TC) at para 29.
13 *Grace v Revenue & Customs* [2011] UKFTT 36 (TC).
14 At paras 18–24.

A place of abode

3.08 Occupation of a dwelling house

In *Levene v IRC*,[1] Lord Cave said:

> 'The word "reside" is a familiar English word and is defined in the Oxford English Dictionary as meaning "to dwell permanently or for a considerable time, to have one's settled or usual abode, to live in or at a particular place". No doubt this definition must for present purposes be taken subject to any modification which may result from the terms of the Income Tax Act and Schedules; but subject to that observation, it may be accepted as an accurate indication of the meaning of the word "reside".'[2]

Those words are a useful reminder that, although, as has been pointed out,[3] we must not think of residence in terms of bricks and mortar, we must not overlook the fact that the primary meaning of residence is to do with a person's inhabitation of bricks and mortar – or their equivalent.[4] Thus, in *Lloyd v Sulley*,[5] the President of the Court of the Exchequer said of Mr Lloyd's castle in Scotland and his town house and country villa in Italy:

> 'They are places to which it is quite easy for [him] to resort as his dwelling place whenever he thinks fit, and to set himself down there with his family and establishment. That is a place of residence, and if he occupies that place of residence for a portion of a year he is then within the meaning of the Clause as I read it, residing there in the course of that year.'[6]

The same was true of Sir C H Coote. He had a house in Ireland which he occupied for the greater part of each year and a house in Connaught Place, London, in which he stayed from time to time for a few weeks. The Court of the Exchequer held that he was resident in Great Britain and 'clearly within the Act'.[7]

Both these judgments were followed in the case of *Cooper v Cadwalader*.[8] Mr Cadwalader was an American citizen who had a house in New York but spent two months of each year in occupation of Millden Lodge, a furnished house in Forfar in Scotland, which he leased and kept available for his use throughout each year. Was Mr Cadwalader resident in the UK? Lord Adam was in no doubt as to the answer:

> 'Can it be said that during ... these two months in which he is residing continuously in Millden Lodge that he is not residing there? Where is he residing? He is residing ... in Millden Lodge, and therefore residing in the UK; and if that be so, then it humbly appears to me that he is a person in the sense of the Act residing in the UK, and assessable under the Act.'[9]

In *High Tech International v Deripaska*,[10] Mr Deripaska, a Russian billionaire, owned two valuable homes in England, one in Weybridge and the other in Belgrave Square, together worth approximately £40 million. It was submitted that the Belgrave Square property was his home when he was in England. However, Edy J observed that Mr Deripaska had either completed or had under construction, a total of over 20 houses in various parts of the world and concluded that the requirement for a degree of permanence or continuity applied even in the context of a second or third home. He considered the evidence as to Mr Deripaska's movements, which showed that he spent 'up to 90 days' a year in England. In finding that there was no good arguable case that Mr Deripaska was resident in England he said:

> '[Mr Hunter] accepted that the matter of residence is not to be judged according to "a numbers game", and that it is appropriate to address the quality and nature of the visits in question. Mr Deripaska is, if I may say so, very much a modern phenomenon. It makes it very difficult to draw useful comparisons with precedents from a different era. He is truly an international businessman and jets about the world for frequent and brief business meetings. Miss Page may have hit the nail on the head when she considered the ordinary meaning of "residence". While it may make sense to speak of Mr Cadwallader being resident in Scotland for the months of August and September, or of Mr Theron being resident during his monthly visits, it hardly rings true to say of Mr Deripaska that he was resident for (say) last Tuesday afternoon or next Thursday morning. It would be a misuse of language.'

In the *Abramovich* case several residential properties in England had been transferred to his former wife in a divorce settlement and his use of a single, albeit very expensive property in London in the context of other properties abroad and in particular in Russia which he regarded as home did not indicate that it was his usual or settled place of abode.[11]

---

1 (1929) 13 TC 486.
2 (1929) 13 TC 486 at 505.

3 At **3.02** above.

4 In *Bayard Brown v Burt* (1911) 5 TC 667, it was accepted that an ocean-going yacht anchored in territorial waters was Mr Bayard Brown's place of abode, and in *Hipperson v Electoral Registration Officer for the District of Newbury* [1985] 2 All ER 456, Sir John Donaldson MR (at 462) rejected the submission that women living in tents, vehicles and benders (a form of tent) on Greenham Common in furtherance of their protest concerning cruise missiles could not be said to have a home in the camp: 'It may be unusual to make one's home in a tent, bender or vehicle, but we can see no reason in law why it should be impossible.' In *Makins v Elson* [1977] STC 46, it was further held that a wheeled caravan, jacked up and resting on bricks, with water, electricity and telephone services installed, was a dwelling house, while in *R v Bundy* [1977] 2 All ER 382, even a motor car in which a certain Mr Bundy had been living rough was held to be his place of abode when sited – though not while in transit.

5 (1884) 2 TC 37.

6 (1884) 2 TC 37 at 41.

7 *A-G v Coote* (1817) 2 TC 385.

8 (1904) 5 TC 101.

9 (1904) 5 TC 101 at 107.

10 *High Tech International v Deripaska* [2006] EWHC 3276 (QB) at para 24. See also *Cherney v Deripaska* [2007] EWHC 965 (Comm) per Langley J, at para 45.

11 *OJSC Oil Company Yugraneft (In Liquidation) v Roman Arkadievich Abramovich and others* [2008] EWHC 2613 (Comm), at para 487.

3.09 Ownership irrelevant

The general principle which has been discussed in the foregoing paragraphs is that a person cannot possess a dwelling place in the UK and occupy it, however briefly, during a tax year without becoming resident in the UK for that tax year. But is 'possess' the correct word? Sir C H Coote owned his house in London,[1] Thomas Lloyd owned his castle in Minard,[2] Robert Thomson owned his house in Hawick,[3] and John Cadwalader leased Millden Lodge from the Earl of Dalhousie.[4] Captain Loewenstein did not possess his accommodation.[5] He was a Belgian subject with a home in Brussels, who visited 'Pinfold', a furnished hunting box at Melton Mowbray in Leicestershire, each year for the purpose of fox hunting. The property was owned by the Belgian Breeding Stock Farm Company Ltd, a company in which he had a controlling interest and of which he was a director. In no year did he spend as many as six months in the UK and he claimed, therefore, that, on the basis of ITA 1918 Sch 1, Rule 2 of the Miscellaneous Rules of Schedule D (now ITA 2007 s 831),[6] he was exempt from tax under Schedule D. That exemption is discussed in Chapter 5 and does not concern us here, but Rowlatt J's view of Captain Loewenstein's central argument is of present concern. On the question of the necessity of a 'proprietorial interest', Rowlatt J said:

'I cannot see what difference that makes … this man had this house at his disposal, with everything in it or for his convenience, kept going all the year round, although he only wanted it for a short time. Luckily, he was in relation with a Company who were the owners of it, and he could do that without owning it. It is an accident. It might well have been that he could do that with a relation, or a friend, or a philanthropist, or anybody; but in fact there was this house for him … He has got this house to come to when he likes; he does not own it; he has got no proprietary interest in it, but it is just as good as if he had for the purpose of having it for a residence, and there it is.'

In the light of this pronouncement, a general principle has been asserted that an individual may be held to be resident here notwithstanding that he does not possess the accommodation, provided that the accommodation is available for the individual throughout the tax year even though he occupies it only briefly during that year. This thinking plainly influenced the High Court in *Grace* where the availability of the accommodation was regarded as decisive.[7] By comparison, in *Cherney v Deripaska*, Langley J reached the conclusion that Mr Deripaska was not resident in England. He said:

'The "quality" of the use of the house is, I think, equally important. In many ways its use by Mr Deripaska resembles that of a private hotel. It is infrequent, intermittent, and generally fleeting. The house has the character of continuity and permanence; its use does not.'[8]

It should be noted that the precise form which the accommodation takes is irrelevant. An ocean-going yacht permanently moored in the UK's territorial waters has been held to be a dwelling-house for these purposes[9] and so, too, in other circumstances, has a wheeled but immobilised caravan to which electricity, water and telephone services had been supplied.[10]

The entry of a person's name on an electoral roll may be evidence of the availability of accommodation.[11]

The effect of ITA 2007 ss 831 and 832,[12] which provides that the existence or otherwise of available accommodation must be disregarded in determining whether, for the purpose of those provisions, an individual is in the UK for some temporary purpose and not with a view to or intent of establishing his residence here will be considered at **5.06** below.[13] The presence or otherwise of available accommodation has been treated as relevant to assist in determining whether an individual is generally resident in the UK or not.[14]

---

1 *A-G v Coote* (1817) 2 TC 385. See **3.08** above.

2 *Lloyd v Sulley* (1884) 2 TC 37. See **3.08** above.

3 *Thomson v Bensted* (1918) 7 TC 137.

4 *Cooper v Cadwalader* (1904) 5 TC 101. See **3.08** above.

5 *Loewenstein v De Salis* (1926) 10 TC 424 at 438.

6 See **5.02** below.

7 *Grace v Revenue & Customs Commissioners* [2008] EWHC 2708 (Ch) at para 40 and [2009] EWCA Civ 1082 at para 24. This appears to confuse the discussion in *Levene* that living in a hotel or a series of hotels can amount to residence with the impermanence normally associated with staying in an hotel. The same confusion is apparent in the HMRC submissions at the rehearing of *Grace* [2011] UKFTT 36 (TC) at para 130.

8 *Cherney v Deripaska* [2007] EWHC 965 (Comm) at para 45.

9 *Bayard Brown v Burt* (1911) 5 TC 667.

10 *Makins v Elson* [1977] STC 46.

11 See paras 6 and 5 respectively of the cases stated by the Commissioners in *Lloyd v Sulley* (1884) 2 TC 37 at 38 and *Cooper v Cadwalader* (1904) 5 TC 101 at 103.

12 Originally enacted as FA 1993 s 208.

13 ITA 2007 ss 831 and 832.

14 See *Grace v Revenue & Customs Commissioners* [2009] EWCA Civ 1082 at para 7, approving Special Commissioner Dr Brice in *Shepherd v HMRC* [2005] UKSPC 404, at paras 49 and 58 relying on *Cooper v Cadwalader* in this respect.

Physical presence

3.10 Duration of presence

There are many situations in which the principle of occupation of available accommodation is of no application. If residence is not synonymous with mere physical presence, then the mere fact of presence in the UK ought not to constitute residence there. However, a person may be in the UK without ever acquiring a 'settled or usual abode'[1] but that will not necessarily prevent him from being attributed with the status of UK residence. As Viscount Sumner has said:

> 'Although setting up an establishment in this country, available for residence at any time throughout the year of charge, even though used but little, may be good ground for finding its master to be "resident" here, it does not follow that keeping up an establishment abroad and none here is incompatible with being "resident here" if there is other sufficient evidence of it.'[2]

The point is graphically made in *Reid v IRC*[3] by Lord Clyde, the Lord President of the Court of Session:

> '... take the case of a homeless tramp, who shelters to-night under a bridge, to-morrow in the greenwood and as the unwelcome occupant of a farm outhouse the night after. He wanders in this way all over the United Kingdom. But will anyone say he does not *live* in the United Kingdom? – and will anyone regard it as a misuse of language to say he *resides* in the United Kingdom. In his case there may be no relations with family or friends, no business ties, and none of the ordinary circumstances which create a link between the life of a British subject and the United Kingdom; but, even so, I do not think it could be disputed that he *resides* in the United Kingdom. There are other and very different kinds of tramps, who – being possessed of ample means, and having the ordinary ties of birth, family, and affairs with the United Kingdom or some part of it – yet prefer to enjoy those means without undertaking the domestic responsibility of a home, and who move about from one house of public entertainment to another – in London today, in the provinces to-morrow, and in the Highlands the day after. They too are homeless wanderers in the United Kingdom. But surely it is true to say they *live* in the United Kingdom, and *reside* there? The Section of the Act of Parliament with which we are dealing speaks of persons "residing", not at a particular locality, but in a region so extensive as the United Kingdom.'[4]

Although the person at the centre of the *Reid* case was a woman who possessed many links with the UK other than mere presence, the principal point which the Lord President was making was that the duration of a person's presence may alone in exceptional cases be sufficient to transform mere presence into residence. Nothing but presence attaches the homeless tramp to the UK, yet if that presence endures for a significant length of time, the whole of his time in the example given by Lord Clyde, it alone will be sufficient to imbue the tramp with UK residence status.[5] Lord Blackburn, in a concurring judgment, referred to a person spending 365 days a year, each in a different hotel,[6] and while accepting the Special Commissioners' decision on the facts, regarded residing outwith the UK for the greater part of the year as inconsistent with residence.[7]

Presence in the UK for 183 days within a tax year is one of the criteria to engage the application of ITA 2007 s 831[8] and, as such, will be a significant length of time, but if the case does not fall within that section the question what is a significant length of time will be one for the Tax Tribunal to decide.

In the reported cases, the physical presence which has resulted in the attribution of residence has always been for periods amounting to less than 183 days, but in each case there have been connecting factors other than time to which weight has also had to be given. Apart from the 183-day test for statutory purposes, there is no fixed amount of presence that gives rise to or negates residence.

On re-hearing *Grace*,[9] the First-tier Tribunal was invited to compare the number of days spent in the UK by Mr Grace with the number of days spent in the UK by taxpayers in the early cases.[10] By taking those cases in which the individual was found to be not resident, it was argued that Mr Grace ought not to be found UK resident. Judge Mosedale, in rejecting the contention, observed that trying to make such comparisons shows how difficult they can be.[11] She concluded that lower day counts do not preclude a finding of residence.[12] Apart from confirming that physical presence alone is not determinative, no guidance is given, nor any rational explanation for the significance of varying amounts of time spent in the UK.

---

1 See **3.08** above for the Oxford English Dictionary definition of residence quoted by Lord Cave in *Levene v IRC* (1928) 13 TC 486.
2 *Lysaght v IRC* (1928) 13 TC 511 at 528.
3 (1926) 10 TC 673.
4 (1926) 10 TC 673 at 679.
5 As to whether a person can be attributed with residence status without ever setting foot in the UK during a tax year, see **5.14** below.
6 At p 681.
7 At p 682.
8 See **5.03** and **5.09** to **5.10** below.
9 *Grace v Revenue & Customs* [2011] UKFTT 36 (TC).
10 At para 150.
11 At para 159.
12 At para 162.

3.11 Regularity and frequency of visits

Closely linked to the element of time or duration is the element of regularity and frequency. The duration of a person's physical presence in the UK during any one tax year may not be sufficiently significant for it to transform the presence into residence, but presence of insignificant duration in a succession of tax years may be sufficient to effect the transformation. This principle is well illustrated by the case of *Kinloch v IRC*.[1] Although Mrs Kinloch spent the greater part of her time abroad, she visited the UK each year, sometimes for only a few days, other times for weeks or even months. The pattern of her visits from 1921–22 to 1927–28 was as follows: 66 days in 1921–22, 40 days over three visits in 1922–23, 177 days over five visits in 1923–24, five months, 12 days over three visits in 1924–25, 145 days over four visits in 1925–26, 141 days over five visits in 1926–27, and 156 days over four visits in 1927–28. In 1924–25, the Inland Revenue challenged Mrs Kinloch's assertion that she was not resident in the UK and the question was taken before the Special Commissioners. They decided that Mrs Kinloch was correct: she was not resident in the UK; and, accordingly, for the following two years the Inland Revenue followed the Commissioners' ruling. In 1927–28, however, the Inland Revenue again challenged Mrs Kinloch's non-resident status, and this time the Inland Revenue's contention was upheld: the Commissioners found that:

'... having regard to the continuance through the series of years of the regular and lengthy visits to the United Kingdom the circumstances were different from those under consideration when the appeal for the earlier year was heard,'[2]

and that Mrs Kinloch was resident in the UK. In 1927–28, she 'crossed the line, and ... now she is resident here'.[3] But what was the line Mrs Kinloch had crossed? Rowlatt J seems to have thought it was the line of duration of presence. He said that in 1927–28 Mrs Kinloch had stayed in the UK rather longer than previously; but that was not so: her visits in 1927–28 were of shorter duration than her visits in either 1923–24 or 1924–25. The line can only have been the line of frequency and regularity. Although a pattern had begun to emerge by the third year of Mrs Kinloch's visits, that pattern was neither sufficiently clear nor sufficiently well established for it to have transformed her presence into residence; but, by the fifth year, her continued visits had remedied those defects. In the case of *Levene v IRC*[4] a similar pattern had emerged. Mr Levene, whose circumstances are fully described at **5.15** below, had

'... elected in each [of the four years from 1920–21 to 1924–25] to adopt a regular system of life in accordance with which he and his wife made their abode and lived in this country for a period of between four and five months in each year, and ... they were therefore resident in the United Kingdom not merely in the sense of being present here but in the fuller sense of making their home here.'[5]

Two recent decisions involving airline pilots flying in and out of the UK illustrate how similar patterns of presence may produce differing outcomes. In *Shepherd*[6] the Special Commissioner, Dr Brice, found that in 1998–99 the taxpayer was in the UK (not including the days of arrival and departure) for 92 days and in 1999–2000 for 80 days. By comparison, in *Grace*[7] it was found that he was present in 1997–98 for 41 days, in 1998–99 for 71 days and in 1999–2000 for 70 days (not including the days of arrival and departure). This translated into 86, 146 and 136 days including the days of arrival and departure in each of those years. Shepherd was found to be resident while Special Commissioner, Dr Brice, found Grace was not.[8]

These findings of Dr Brice were revisited when *Grace* was re-heard by the First-tier Tribunal who found that he was UK resident.[9] The taxpayer and HMRC adopted differing approaches to the counting of days. Excluding days of arrival and departure markedly reduced presence (unsurprising in the case of aircrew on international flights). HMRC included fractions of days which the judge accepted. The judge noted that evidence of overnight flights was not presented (somewhat surprising again in the case of a long-haul pilot flying west to east) and did not deal with the obvious issue that most long-haul travel from east to west involves departure in one country (eg Japan) and arrival in another (eg the UK) on the same day under each local time but on different days viewed from one time zone only. Much turned on a comparison of the time spent in the UK with that spent in South Africa. Somewhat more time was spent in the UK. Except when working, Mr Grace never spent less than seven days consecutively in South Africa. He spent more than seven consecutive days in the UK on only three occasions over six years but only if days of sickness and grounding and days of departure and arrival were excluded. Only the fact of presence in the UK and not the reason was relevant in counting days present. This point was harshly brought home in *Ogden v HMRC*[10] where the taxpayer was present in the UK for more than 183 days in the tax year principally due to his son in the UK becoming seriously ill and requiring a heart and lung transplant as the only option for his survival. HMRC were sympathetic to the appellant's circumstances but the law had to be applied.[11]

In *Abramovich*, evidence of presence was categorised as either full or part days in the UK of which Mr Abramovich spent between 153 and 189 in the UK but of these, whole days present in the UK ranged from 25 to 110 and was found not to be resident.[12]

---

1 (1929) 14 TC 736.
2 (1929) 14 TC 736 at 738.
3 (1929) 14 TC 736 at 738, per Rowlatt J.
4 (1928) 13 TC 486.
5 (1928) 13 TC 486 at 499.
6 *Shepherd v Revenue & Customs* [2005] UKSPC 484.
7 *Grace v Revenue & Customs* [2008] UKSPC SPC 663.
8 The High Court appeared to decide the question on other grounds including that there was no distinct break with the UK: *Grace v Revenue & Customs Commissioners* [2008] EWHC 2708 (Ch) at para 43. See para **5.14** below.
9 *Grace v Revenue & Customs* [2011] UKFTT 36 (TC) at paras 74–103.
10 *Ogden v Revenue & Customs* [2011] UKFTT 212 (TC).
11 At para 15.
12 *OJSC Oil Company Yugraneft (In Liquidation) v Roman Arkadievich Abramovich and others* [2008] EWHC 2613 (Comm) at para 467.

3.12 Revenue practice

Perhaps the most extreme case bearing on the principle of regular visits is that of *Lysaght v IRC*.[1] Since 1920, Mr Lysaght had lived in Ireland with his wife and family and had had no definite place of abode in the UK. Each month, however, he visited England to attend a meeting of the directors of John Lysaght Ltd and remained here on company business for about a week on each occasion. During his visits to the UK he stayed either at the home of his brother or in hotels. The total number of days spent in the UK for the three years 1922–23, 1923–24 and 1924–25 were 101, 94 and 84 respectively. The Special Commissioners held that Mr Lysaght was resident in the UK for each of those years and the House of Lords felt itself bound to uphold their decision on the grounds that the question of residence is a question of degree and fact and not a question of law.[2] Their Lordships' support for the Commissioners was by no means unqualified, however, and Viscount Cave LC went so far as to say:

'There appears to me to be no reason whatever for holding that [Mr Lysaght] is resident ... in this country. It is true that he comes here at regular intervals and for recurrent business purposes; but these facts, while they explain the frequency of his visits, do not make them more than temporary visits or give them the character of residence in this country.'[3]

For reasons such as these, Viscount Cave thought the Crown's appeal should have been dismissed; Lord Warrington of Clyffe doubted that he would have come to the Commissioners' conclusion; Viscount Sumner could see several points in Mr Lysaght's favour but could find no error of law which would enable him to interfere with the Commissioners' decision; and only Lord Atkinson and Lord Buckmaster clearly felt that the Commissioners' decision was the correct one. For all this, however, it is the *Lysaght* case, tainted with uncertainty and stretching the concept of residence almost to its breaking point, on which the Revenue built its former rule concerning the frequency and regularity of visits to the UK.[4]

As explained at **5.12** below, until 6 April 2009, HMRC regarded three months as equivalent to 91 days, and it may easily be calculated that Mr Lysaght's annual average was that less only one day! Although, as we shall see later,[5] it was Mr Lysaght's strong business link with the UK which, clearly, combined with the frequency and regularity of his visits so as to give his presence here the quality which transformed it into residence, the Revenue rule betrayed no recognition that any such link is a necessary ingredient in the transformational process. Notwithstanding this, the practice functioned as an important guide to the conduct of individuals and as a safe harbour for those able to fall within its terms.

Following the decision in *Gaines-Cooper*, HMRC issued a statement aimed at clarifying the application of IR20 on the question as to when it regards the counting of days present to be relevant as follows:[6]

'In considering the issues of residence, ordinary residence and domicile in the Gaines-Cooper case, the Commissioners needed to build up a full picture of Mr Gaines-Cooper's life. A very important element of the picture was the pattern of his presence in the UK compared to the pattern of his presence overseas. The Commissioners decided that, in looking at these patterns, it would be misleading to wholly disregard days of arrival and departure. They used Mr Gaines-Cooper's patterns of presence in the UK as part of the evidence of his lifestyle and habits during the years in question. Based on this, and a wide range of other evidence, the Commissioners found that he had been continuously resident in the UK. From HMRC's perspective, therefore, the "91-day test" was not relevant to the Gaines-Cooper case since Mr Gaines-Cooper did not leave the UK.'

The practice of determining residence simply by reference days present was finally abandoned by the adoption of HMRC6. In its introduction to residency, HMRC6 states:

'The terms "residence" and "ordinary residence", are not defined in the Taxes Acts. The guidance we give on these terms throughout this guidance is largely based on rulings of the Courts and how we interpret them and put them into practice on a day to day basis. This guidance tells you the main factors we take into account when deciding your residence and ordinary residence status. Your status is determined by the facts of your particular case. It is not simply a question of the number of days you spend in the country.'[7]

Explanations of residence and non-residence are offered in the HMRC6 glossary which read:

'Resident

The number of days you are present in the country is only one of the factors to take into account when deciding your residence position.

If you are in the UK for 183 days or more in the tax year, you will always be resident here. There are no exceptions to this. You count the total number of days you spend in the UK – it does not matter if you come and go several times during the year or if you are here for one stay of 183 days or more. If you are here for less than 183 days, you might still be resident for the year.

You should always look at the pattern of your lifestyle when deciding whether you are resident in the UK. Things you should consider would include what connections you have to the UK such as family, property, business and social connections. Just because you leave the UK to live or work abroad does not necessarily prove that you are no longer resident here if, for example, you keep connections in the UK such as property, economic interests, available accommodation, and social activities or if you have children in education here.

For example, if you are someone who comes to the UK on a regular basis and have a settled lifestyle pattern connecting you to this country, you are likely to be resident here.'[8]

'Non-resident

If you do not meet the requirements to be resident in the UK for income and capital gains tax purposes, you will be "non-resident". If you are not resident in the UK you might not have to pay UK tax on some of your income and gains.

If your normal home is outside the UK and you are in the UK for fewer than 183 days in the tax year you may be non-resident. But you might still be resident even if you spend fewer than 183 days in a tax year in the UK (see 1.5.23). Being resident in the UK is not simply a question of the number of days you spend in the country.'[9]

Despite these statements, HMRC6 continues to refer to day counting tests in the context of individuals becoming or ceasing to be UK resident.[10] Their application of these tests is far from clear but it would seem that to the extent in the past the practices in IR20 functioned as safe harbours in practice, they do not under HMRC6.

---

1 (1928) 13 TC 511.
2 See **3.03** above.
3 *Lysaght v IRC* (1928) 13 TC 511 at 532.
4 IR20 (July 2008), para 3.3.
5 At **3.17** below.
6 HMRC Brief 01/07.
7 HMRC6, para 1.2.
8 HMRC6, para 1.5.22. The same points are restated at para 2.2 'UK Residence'.

3.13 Future conduct

Before leaving this discussion of the acquisition of residence status through regular and frequent visits, something must be said about the fact that a determination of residence status on those grounds in many cases involves the simultaneous consideration of a number of tax years. In the *Levene* case, it was objected that such a global consideration was wrong in law since it involved the taking into account in earlier years of conduct which only occurred subsequently. Viscount Sumner did not accept that this was at all erroneous:

'I agree that the taxpayer's chargeability in each year of charge constitutes a separate issue, even though several years are included in one appeal, but I do not think any error of law is committed if the facts applicable to the whole of the time are found in one continuous story. Light may be thrown on the purpose with which the first departure from the United Kingdom took place, by looking at his proceedings in a series of subsequent years. They go to show method and system and so remove doubt which might be entertained if the years were examined in isolation from one another.'[1]

1 *Levene v IRC* (1928) 13 TC 486 at 501.

3.14 Previous history

If it is permissible to look at a person's conduct in years subsequent to the year for which a determination of residence status is being sought,[1] it is certainly permissible to look at a person's conduct in previous years, and this was Viscount Sumner's initial approach in the *Levene* case.[2] Having decided that for the first year in question, 1920–21, Mr Levene was resident in the UK, Viscount Sumner took Mr Levene's conduct in that year as a reference against which to examine each of the subsequent years in question and concluded that 'no material change occurred in his way of living'.[3] It followed, therefore, that Mr Levene was resident in each of the subsequent years also.

This same approach was adopted by the Special Commissioners in the case of *Miesegaes v IRC*.[4] Stanley Miesegaes was a Dutch national who was at boarding school in Harrow from 1939 until July 1951. The years for which his residence status was in question were 1947–48 to 1951–52. Having found that Mr Miesegaes was resident for the years 1947–48 to 1950–51, the Special Commissioners had still to decide his residence status for the year 1951–52. At the start of that tax year, Mr Miesegaes was in Holland but he was in the UK from 15 April to 17 August. On 17 August he left the UK to continue his education in Switzerland. The Commissioners decided the question for 1951–52 by looking back to the previous years. The four months' presence in 1951–52 was, they said, 'in continuation of what we found to be his residence here for the previous four years and we found that he was resident in the UK for 1951–52 also'.[5] The Commissioners' decision was upheld by both the High Court and the Court of Appeal, and it is clear, therefore, that the principle applied by the Commissioners will stand: UK residence status, once acquired, will endure in succeeding years unless there is some change in a person's manner of life of such significance as to throw the question of his residence status into doubt.

---

1 See **3.13** above.
2 *Levene v IRC* (1928) 13 TC 486.
3 *Levene v IRC* (1928) 13 TC 486 at 501.
4 (1957) 37 TC 493.
5 (1957) 37 TC 493 at 495.

Connecting factors

3.15   The ties of birth

Clearly, the less conclusive the elements of duration, frequency and regularity of presence where a person's residence status has been called into question are, the more important will be the other elements that may, in any particular case, be indicative of that status. One element which obviously carried some weight with the Lord President in the case of *Reid v IRC*[1] was the tie of nationality. Miss Reid, he said 'is a British subject',[2] and the suggestion would seem to be that the link thus subsisting between Miss Reid and the UK must necessarily have tinged her periods of presence here with the hue of residence – though the tie of nationality can never alone do more than that. Prior to the enactment of ITA 2007 ss 831 and 832, a British subject whose ordinary residence had been in the UK found it more difficult than a foreign national to divest himself of UK residence status[3] and, the possible rationale behind that section – that a British subject may be supposed to wish to cultivate and preserve, rather than sever, his links with the UK – has had a place in the approach to questions of residence even where the statutory provisions were of no direct application. Viscount Cave recognised this in the *Levene* case when he said:

> 'The most difficult case is that of a wanderer who, having no home in any country, spends a part only of his time in hotels in the United Kingdom and the remaining and greater part of his time in hotels abroad ... If ... such a man is a foreigner who has never resided in this country, there may be great difficulty in holding that he is resident here. But if he is a British subject the Commissioners are entitled to take into account all the facts of the case.'[4]

The link of nationality is, then, of greater importance than it is often acknowledged to be for, if a person is found to be joined to the UK by that link, the Commissioners have not only the right but also the duty to look much more closely at the circumstances surrounding that person's presence here than would otherwise be the case. A practical example of the difference in approach is given by the *Zorab* case which is described at **5.05** below. Mr Zorab had been born in India and had spent all his life there until his retirement from the Indian Civil Service. Upon his retirement, however, he began to spend almost half of each year in the UK, yet, despite the duration and regularity of his visits, the Commissioners found that he was not resident here. His nationality was a decisive factor. 'This gentleman,' said Rowlatt J, 'is a native of India'.[5]

---

1 (1926) 10 TC 673.
2 (1926) 10 TC 673 at 679.
3 See **5.14**ff below.
4 *Levene v IRC* (1928) 13 TC 486 at 506.
5 *IRC v Zorab* (1926) 11 TC 289 at 292. See also Christopher Clarke J at para 460 on the Russian origin and citizenship of Mr Abramovich in *OJSC Oil Company Yugraneft (In Liquidation) v Roman Arkadievich Abramovich and others* [2008] EWHC 2613 (Comm).

3.16 The ties of family

As well as being a British subject, Miss Reid[1] had a sister who lived in London. Viewed in isolation, that fact may not seem of particular significance but it was one of the elements listed by Lord Clyde as contributing to the finding that she was resident in the UK. 'Her family ties', he said, 'are with this country'.[2]

So it was, too, with Mr Levene and his wife:

'They ... came to visit their relatives in England, and (on one occasion) to make arrangements for the care of a brother of [Mr Levene] who is mentally afflicted [and] to visit the graves of his parents.[3]

His family ties are in this country, his wife having five sisters and he himself six brothers and sisters residing here.'[4]

In the *Levene* case, Lord Hanworth MR had said in the Court of Appeal that an important characteristic factor to look for in determining whether or not a man possesses the quality of residence is 'if he returns to and seeks his own fatherland in order to enjoy a sojourn in proximity to his relations and friends',[5] and this characteristic was very much in evidence in the *Kinloch* case referred to at **3.11** above. Mrs Kinloch was a British subject and a widow who had lived in India from 1909 to 1919. From 1919 onwards she made frequent and regular visits to the UK in each tax year but her presence here throughout was coloured by the fact that her son was attending boarding schools in England and that:

'... her various objects in coming to the United Kingdom were to take her son to and from school, to attend to his outfitting, to consult with his doctor, dentist and oculist, to interview those having charge of him, to be with him during illness and to attend his confirmation.'[6]

Although, as has been noted,[7] the decisive factor in the Commissioners' decision that Mrs Kinloch was resident in the UK was the frequency and regularity of Mrs Kinloch's visits here, her family ties with this country were undoubtedly of weight and had a bearing on their determination for here was a lady:

> '... who spends a good deal of her time in this country but without any settled home, living in hotels here and abroad, but having a reason for coming here, because she has a son who is being educated here and who is sometimes ill, and so on.'[8]

Family ties have featured in virtually all the recent decisions. In some it showed ties in the UK: Captain Shepherd stayed with his wife from whom he was separated but remained good friends;[9] Mr Gaines-Cooper came to be with his wife and child;[10] Mr Barrett stayed with his partner and children when in the UK.[11] In others they have not shown such ties: Mr Abramovich came, prior to his divorce, to see his children who were being educated in England and thereafter mostly saw them outside the country;[12] Mr Grace had no contact with his estranged wife and children when living in the UK which continued after he departed to live in South Africa where his extended family lived;[13] Mr Deripaska's wife and children only used their Belgravia house when they briefly visited London.[14]

---

1 *Reid v IRC* (1926) 10 TC 673.
2 *Reid v IRC* (1926) 10 TC 673 at 679.
3 *Levene v IRC* (1928) 13 TC 486 at 504, per Viscount Cave LC.
4 *Levene v IRC* (1928) 13 TC 486 at 508, per Lord Warrington of Clyffe.
5 *Levene v IRC* (1928) 13 TC 486 at 497.
6 *Kinloch v IRC* (1929) 14 TC 736 at 738.
7 At **3.11** above.
8 *Kinloch v IRC* (1929) 14 TC 736 at 739, per Rowlatt J.
9 *Shepherd v Revenue & Customs* [2005] UKSPC 484 at para 45.
10 *Gaines-Cooper v HMRC* [2006] UKSPC SPC568 at para 166.
11 *Barrett v Revenue & Customs* [2007] UKSPC SPC 639 at para 36.
12 *OJSC Oil Company Yugraneft (In Liquidation) v Roman Arkadievich Abramovich and others* [2008] EWHC 2613 (Comm) at para 486.
13 *Grace v Revenue & Customs* [2008] UKSPC SPC 663 at paras 13 and 16. He did have two girlfriends in the UK over the period, one of which also spent time with him in South Africa, while his relationship with the other broke up as she did not want to go there: [2011] UKFTT 36 (TC) at paras 115–119.
14 *Cherney v Deripaska* [2007] EWHC 965 (Comm) at para 45.

3.17 The ties of business

Another factor which, in the *Reid* case,[1] Lord Clyde singled out as being relevant to the finding that the taxpayer possessed UK residence status was that 'her business matters (including her banking) are conducted here'.[2] That tie was of particular importance in the case of Mr Lysaght. It has already been explained[3] that the element of frequency and regularity in Mr Lysaght's visits to the UK was thought by the House of Lords to be barely sufficient to justify the finding of residence returned by the Commissioners. This feeling was present in each of the lower courts, too, and it seems clear that it was only the strong business link between Mr Lysaght and the UK which, in the view of Lawrence LJ, added a support which would enable the Commissioners' decision to stand:

'The case is near the line but in my opinion the determining factor is that the post which [Mr Lysaght] holds in John Lysaght Ltd causes him to come regularly to England and to stay in the UK for a substantial period in each year. The fact that [Mr Lysaght] stays regularly in England for about three months of the year for the discharge of his duties as the servant of an English company in my opinion constitutes him a person who is ... resident ... in the UK.'[4]

Mr Levene, too, had ties of business which contributed to the finding that he was resident in the UK:

'He had gone out of business in England and had broken up his establishment, but he still had in England business interests connected with his Income Tax assessments.'[5]

Included in ties of business may be ties of communication. People wishing to get in touch with Miss Reid did so 'c/o Commercial Bank, Glasgow', thus 'the address by which she can be found at any time is in this country'[6] and this factor too was added to the list of those which weighed in favour of Miss Reid's residence in the UK.

The insertion of a UK address for Captain Loewenstein[7] in the annual return of the Belgian Breeding Stock Farm Company Ltd weighed against his assertion that he was not resident in the UK:

'At any rate this gentleman's return to the Registrar of Joint Stock Companies shows him as a Director and having his usual residence at "Pinfold". Now it is said that this was only done for convenience ... The Commissioners say they do not accept that view, and they certainly are entitled to say that, and I am bound by it.'[8]

In *Gaines-Cooper* the taxpayer was involved in several foreign-based businesses that operated around the world including operations in the UK where he regularly visited for business purposes.[9] In contrast, Langley J, in *Cherney v Deripaska* [2007] EWHC 965 (Comm), accepted that Mr Deripaska who had substantial interests in a number of businesses, most particularly in Russia, had '*significant business interests in England*' which appear to have included an English-based service company and several English business advisers, but were a minimal part of his interests and notwithstanding that, Mr Deripaska was not resident in England.[10] In *Abramovich* the court found that the defendant's interest in buying Chelsea Football Club was only as a hobby in which the £500 million invested was more than he could ever see returned from it. He had no executive role and had no other business interests in the UK. He similarly had no role in a service company established in England to provide services to his properties and investments outside Russia.[11] In *Grace*, the taxpayer, a pilot, only came to the UK in the course of his employment duties flying in and out of the UK. Such ties of employment seem to have supported the conclusion of Lewison J that Mr Grace was UK resident.[12] However, the Court of Appeal distinguished the presence of Mr Grace in the UK for the purpose of applying the ordinary meaning of residence and the application of the statutory test in what is now ITA 2007 s 831. It was fair to say that employment was the only purpose in Mr Grace being in the UK. That did not make him resident on the ordinary meaning but was relevant to the question.[13] On re-hearing, the First-tier Tribunal applied the ruling of the Court of Appeal that employment in the UK is not determinative.[14] It was noted that most of Mr Grace's work was performed outside the UK; he would fly planes out of the UK on long-haul flights and only bring them back again a couple of days later. The judge preferred to decide on the basis of what he was doing when he was in the UK but not working.

1 *Reid v IRC* (1926) 10 TC 673.
2 *Reid v IRC* (1926) 10 TC 673 at 679.
3 At **3.11** above.
4 *Lysaght v IRC* (1928) 13 TC 511 at 525.
5 *Levene v IRC* (1928) 13 TC 486 at 500, per Viscount Sumner.
6 *Reid v IRC* (1926) 10 TC 673 at 679, per the Lord President.
7 *Loewenstein v De Salis* (1926) 10 TC 424. See **3.09** above.
8 *Loewenstein v De Salis* (1926) 10 TC 424 at 436, per Rowlatt J.
9 *Gaines-Cooper v HMRC* [2006] UKSPC SPC568 at paras 91 and 166.
10 *Cherney v Deripaska* [2007] EWHC 965 (Comm) at para 39.
11 *OJSC Oil Company Yugraneft (In Liquidation) v Roman Arkadievich Abramovich and others* [2008] EWHC 2613 (Comm) at paras 487–484.
12 *Grace v Revenue & Customs Commissioners* [2008] EWHC 2708 (Ch) at para 41.
13 *Grace v Revenue & Customs Commissioners* [2009] EWCA Civ 1082 at para 40.
14 *Grace v Revenue & Customs* [2011] UKFTT 36 (TC) at paras 144–147.

3.18 Other ties

In the *Reid* case,[1] the Commissioners noted that, when the house in Glasgow in which Miss Reid had once lived was given up, Miss Reid 'sent three trunks with clothes, jewellery, and a few other personal effects to a store in London and has since, on one or two occasions, been to the store to fetch or put back various articles',[2] and this fact, that 'her personal belongings not required when she is travelling are kept in store in London',[3] duly weighed against her when the question of her residence status was decided.

The ties of religious observance also may weigh against a person's claim to be non-resident. Mr Levene, on occasions, visited the UK 'to take part in certain Jewish religious observances'.[4] This, accordingly, became a factor in the determination of his residence status.

Membership of clubs and societies in the UK will also be a factor of importance.[5] Continued membership will indicate an intention to return and will weigh against any claim that ties with the UK have been broken.

The list of possible links with the UK which may so colour a person's presence here as to transform it into residence is inexhaustible. All such links will be of importance, however, should it ever become necessary for the question of a person's residence status to be determined.

1 *Reid v IRC* (1926) 10 TC 673.
2 *Reid v IRC* (1926) 10 TC 673 at 676.
3 *Reid v IRC* (1926) 10 TC 673 at 679, per the Lord President.

4 *Levene v IRC* (1928) 13 TC 486 at 509, per Lord Warrington of Clyffe.
5 See paras 2(6) and 2(m) respectively of the cases stated by the Commissioners in *Lysaght v IRC* (1928) 13 TC 511 at 514 and *Withers v Wynyard* (1938) 21 TC 724 at 727.

Intent and legality

3.19 Involuntary or unintentional presence

While positive intentions may contribute to the transformation of presence into residence, negative intentions will not prevent such a transformation taking place if other indicia would lead to the conclusion that a person is resident in the UK.

In *Bayard Brown v Burt*,[1] Mr Brown, who had lived on an ocean-going yacht in UK territorial waters for the last 20 years, contended that 'it was the intention to go to sea at any moment, and the ship could be steamed out of port at an hour's notice',[2] but he was nonetheless held to be resident in the UK.

In *Lysaght v IRC*[3] it was shown that Mr Lysaght visited the UK only in fulfilment of his business obligations and not from personal choice. Lord Buckmaster held, however, that this was no bar to residence:

'A man might well be compelled to reside here completely against his will; the exigencies of business often forbid the choice of residence and though a man may make his home elsewhere and stay in this country only because business compels him, yet none the less, if the periods for which and the conditions under which he stays are such that they may be regarded as constituting residence, it is open to the Commissioners to find that in fact he does so reside.'[4]

During the years for which his residence status was in question, Stanley Miesegaes was a schoolboy boarding at Harrow. His counsel argued that a stay at a boarding school could not constitute residence because 'it is not voluntary residence; and it is institutional. If one asked a schoolboy ... where he lived, he would never say that he lived at his public school'.[5] Pearce LJ could not accept that argument, however:

'Lord Buckmaster's remarks [in the *Lysaght* case] as to the exigencies of business seem equally applicable to the exigencies of education. Education is a large, necessary and normal ingredient in the lives of adolescent members of the community, just as work or business is in the lives of its adult members ... In this case the school terms at Harrow dictated the main residential pattern of the boy's life ... It would be erroneous to endow educational residence with some esoteric quality that must as a matter of law, remove it from the category of residence.'[6]

It was neither business nor education that constrained Lord Inchiquin to stay in the UK for most of 1940–41 and 1941–42: 'The only reason he was there was because his military duties kept him there.'[7] He had, furthermore, before the outbreak of the Second World War, formed the intention of returning to Dromoland Castle, his ancestral home in Ireland, and had carried out that intention as soon as he managed to obtain indefinite release from active service. None of this was, however, of the least effect:

> 'I am quite unable to say that where you find a man has at all times before the war been resident in this country and you find him continuing to serve in this country in His Majesty's Forces during the war, the mere fact that he had, before the outbreak of war, formed the intention of going to live elsewhere makes it impossible to say, as the Commissioners have found, that he was resident in this country during the period of his military service.'[8]

In *Re Mackenzie*[9] it was held that an Australian lady who, four months after arriving in England in 1885, was certified to be insane and detained in an asylum for the 54 years ending with her death in 1939, was resident in the UK for each of those years:

> 'Her residence in England became permanent, no doubt, by reason of her mental condition and the fact that she required care and attention, but I think it may fairly be said that, in the ordinary course of her life as events happened, she resided in England.'[10]

The same would, it seems, be true of a person imprisoned in the UK. In *Todd v Egyptian Delta Land and Investment Co Ltd*,[11] Viscount Sumner said:

> 'A man may change his residence at will, except that a certain duration of time or fixity of decision is requisite, and, but for the peculiar cases of a convict in gaol or a lunatic lawfully detained in a madhouse, I do not think that residence is ever determined for a natural person simply by law.'[12]

The rationale behind all the decisions referred to above is very simply put. Residence depends upon the fact of residing not (except in the context of ITA 2007 ss 831 and 832)[13] upon the intent or wish to reside. Just as a person is none the less present for not wanting to be where he is, so they cannot be the less resident for not wishing to be where they reside. It must be noted, however, that this does not hold true in questions of ordinary residence. There, as explained in Chapter 4, the voluntary adoption of an abode in a particular place or country is essential.

In *Kimber v HMRC*,[14] the intention to stay in the UK, albeit on a settled basis only at a future date, was decisive in converting presence in the UK on an annual holiday into residence during the holiday stay (see **5.02** below for details of the case). By contrast, in *Broome v HMRC*,[15] there was significant evidence to show that Dr Broome intended to leave the UK indefinitely. However, he developed no real and closer connection to his new country of residence – there was no evidence that he did, or ever intended to declare to the French authorities that he had become resident in France. He gave a UK postal address in post-2000 tax returns, in his French property tax declaration, for his French bank account and for other purposes. Despite presence in the UK of between three and seven weeks in each tax year, he was found to have remained UK tax resident. While there is a danger of reading too much into cases of taxpayers representing themselves in the Tribunal, these First-tier

Tribunal decisions do illustrate the influence of the individual's intention when making inferences by reference to more objective facts.

---

1 (1911) 5 TC 667.
2 (1911) 5 TC 667 at 672.
3 (1928) 13 TC 511.
4 (1928) 13 TC 511 at 534.
5 *Miesegaes v IRC* (1957) 37 TC 493 at 500, per Pearce LJ.
6 *Miesegaes v IRC* (1957) 37 TC 493 at 501.
7 *Inchiquin v IRC* (1948) 31 TC 125 at 130, per Singleton J.
8 *Inchiquin v IRC* (1948) 31 TC 125 at 134 and 135.
9 (1940) 19 ATC 399.
10 (1940) 19 ATC 399 at 404, per Morton J.
11 (1928) 14 TC 119.
12 (1928) 14 TC 119 at 140.
13 See **5.05** below.
14 [2012] UKFTT 107 TC.
15 [2001] UKFTT 760 TC.

3.20 Unlawful presence

If, as has been demonstrated at **3.19** above, residence is not necessarily a matter of volition, neither is it necessarily a matter of lawful presence. Mr Bayard Brown[1] had no right to anchor his yacht in the tidal waters off Brightlingsea but that did not alter the fact that he was residing there:

> 'Residence is something which depends upon the fact of residing and not upon the legal right to reside.'[2]

The question of the effect of unlawful or illegal presence on residence status was fully explored by Sir John Donaldson MR in the case of *Hipperson v Electoral Registration Officer for the District of Newbury*.[3] The case concerned the right of women living in tents and vehicles on Greenham Common, in the furtherance of their protest against the presence of cruise missiles, to be placed on the electoral register of the District of Newbury. Under the Representation of the People Act 1983 s 1(1), such a right rests on a person being 'resident' in the relevant district on a specified date, and it was contended that the Greenham women could not be resident in the District of Newbury as they were present there in breach of the bylaws and of the Highways Act 1980 s 137. In rejecting this submission, Sir John Donaldson MR pointed out that:

> '... the consequences of holding that ... residence must not involve the commission of a criminal offence and, a fortiori, that the residence must be lawful in the sense of not involving a breach of the civil rights of others are startling in the extreme. A whole range of citizens would be disqualified. The county court judge gave, as an example, the occupation as a living room or workroom of a room which is immediately over a cesspool, midden or ashpit contrary to s 49 of the Public Health Act 1936. He could also have referred to breach of conditions relating to the use of caravans under s 269 of the same Act, to the continued occupation of premises to which a closing order has been applied under the Housing Acts, to the use of

premises for residential purposes in breach of an enforcement notice under the Town and Country Planning Acts and to adverse possession of residential premises contrary to s 7 of the Criminal Law Act 1977. If the scope of the disqualification is to be extended from the illegal to the unlawful, all those who remain in occupation of residential premises when a possession order has been made would be disqualified.'[4]

The Master of the Rolls concluded his rejection of the submission by declaring that 'residence ... does not depend on law for its existence'.[5]

---

1 See **5.08** below.
2 *Bayard Brown v Burt* (1911) 5 TC 667 at 672, per Kennedy LJ.
3 [1985] 2 All ER 456.
4 [1985] 2 All ER 456 at 463.
5 [1985] 2 All ER 456 at 463.

3.21 Dual and multiple residence

In *A-G v Coote*,[1] for instance, one of the questions was whether Sir C H Coote could possess the quality of UK residence for a year of assessment during which he undoubtedly possessed the quality of Irish residence. The court found his Irish residence to be no barrier at all. Baron Wood said:

> 'It is no uncommon thing for a gentleman to have two permanent residences at the same time, in either of which he may establish his abode at any period, and for any length of time. This is just such a case.'[2]

The same question arose in *Cooper v Cadwalader*.[3] The fact that Mr Cadwalader was clearly resident in New York did not prevent him being found to be resident in the UK also.

It must be understood that these cases did not establish that a person may be resident *consecutively* in two or more places during a year, but that a person may *simultaneously* be resident (ie possess the quality of residence) in two or more places for the same year. This both follows from and supports the proposition that residence is an annual quality which endures for the whole of any tax year in which it is enjoyed, however briefly.

This proposition was implicitly confirmed by Viscount Cave LC when, in *Levene v IRC*,[4] he said:

> 'A man may reside in more than one place ... he may have a home abroad and a home in the UK, and in that case he is held to reside in both places and to be chargeable with tax in this country.'[5]

In *Lysaght v IRC*,[6] Viscount Sumner admitted that it runs counter to our normal mode of thought to think of such people as Mr Cadwalader[7] as being resident in the UK:

> 'Who in New York would have said of Mr Cadwalader: "His home's in the Highlands; his home is not here?" ... One thinks of a man's settled and usual place of abode as his residence, but the truth is that in many cases in ordinary speech one residence at a time is the underlying assumption and though a man may be the occupier of two

houses, he is thought of as only resident in the one he lives in at the time in question. For Income Tax purposes such meanings are misleading. Residence here may be multiple and manifold.'[8]

It is now an established principle, therefore, that the possession of residence status in relation to some foreign place or country is not on its own sufficient to prevent a person becoming attributed with UK residence status.[9]

---

1 (1817) 2 TC 385.
2 (1817) 2 TC 385 at 386.
3 (1904) 5 TC 101.
4 (1928) 13 TC 486.
5 (1928) 13 TC 486 at 505.
6 (1928) 13 TC 511.
7 *Cooper v Cadwalader* (1904) 5 TC 101. See **3.08** above.
8 *Lysaght v IRC* (1928) 13 TC 511 at 528 and 529.
9 *Grace v Revenue & Customs Commissioners* [2008] EWCA Civ 1082 at paras 8 and 20.

CHAPTER 4

Ordinary residence

'Sark.'
'Yes, sir,' said the man in the little quayside hut. 'A return fare. Six shillings.'
'A single, my friend,' said Mr Harold Pye.

Mervyn Peake *Mr Pye* Ch 1

4.01 Introduction

The concept of ordinary residence was almost entirely eliminated for tax purposes from 6 April 2013[1] as a major simplification of the tax system. Transitional rules are discussed in **4.12** below. Certain specific statutory regimes replace ordinary residence with tests for eligibility by reference to years of residence. Transitional rules permit individuals who were ordinarily resident at the end of the 2012–13 year to remain within those regimes for a limited period.

Ordinary residence will remain relevant for:

- eligibility for blind person's allowance which is linked to ordinary residence in Scotland or Northern Ireland rather than in the UK under ITA 2007 s 38;
- exemption condition under ITTOIA 2005 s 693 for income from Ulster Savings Certificates which is linked to ordinary residence in Northern Ireland.

Ordinary residence remains a connecting factor for National Insurance Contributions.

It has been noted at **1.10** above that residence *simpliciter* as interpreted by the courts as a determinant of chargeability may be seen as that same principle carried one stage further. However, ordinary residence is 'a more elusive concept than simple residence. On one Revenue view, it can also be more adhesive, in that a person can remain ordinarily resident even though physically absent from the country throughout the year (and, accordingly, not resident)'.[2] Ordinary residence is, in fact,

> '... a point on a scale which ranges from mere presence in this country through "resident" ... to "domicile" which is widely used to specify the nature and quality of the association between person and place which brings the person within the scope of that particular enactment.'[3]

In the context of the Taxes Acts, the term 'ordinarily resident', like the term 'resident', had 'no ... technical or special meaning'[4] and was, therefore, given its natural and ordinary meaning.[5] The courts, however, found some difficulty in deciding not only what that natural meaning might be but also how ordinary residence differs from residence *simpliciter* – though the fact that there is a difference between the two terms was evident from the legislation itself.

While residence is the central determinant of liability, ordinary residence was a determinant of liability only in certain special cases. In some circumstances it limited liability to UK taxation for those whose connection with the UK is more tenuous. Thus, Pt 8 of ITTOIA 2005 charged the 'relevant foreign income' of individuals who were resident but not ordinarily resident. Employment earnings of such individuals from duties performed outside the UK were likewise chargeable on the remittance basis.[6] A further graduation was found in the case of employees who are both resident and ordinarily resident but not domiciled in the UK. The 'overseas earnings' of such individuals were taxable on the remittance basis.[7] The parallel limited application of ITEPA 2003 Pt 7 (Employment Related Securities) to such individuals was modified by Finance Act 2008.[8]

On the other hand, the higher degree of connection with the UK was required before certain anti-avoidance legislation is applicable. ITA 2007 Pt 13 (Tax Avoidance), Ch 2 (Transfer of Assets Abroad) was only applicable to individuals ordinarily resident in the UK at the material time.

Ordinary residence was also perhaps used in an attempt to extend taxing jurisdiction. It is apparent that ordinary residence is a more enduring personal attribute than residence *simpliciter*, and TCGA 1992 s 2(1) prior to 6 April 2013 may suggest that Parliament had sought to rely on it to impose a charge on a wider range of person:

> 'Subject to any exceptions provided by this Act, a person shall be chargeable to capital gains tax in respect of chargeable gains accruing to him in a year of assessment during any part of which he is resident in the United Kingdom, or during which he is ordinarily resident in the United Kingdom.'

In other words, on this approach a person who succeeds in divesting himself of the quality of residence *simpliciter* (by, perhaps, absence from the UK for an entire tax year) would, if he remains ordinarily resident here, remain within the charge to capital gains tax on any disposals made during that year.[9]

'Ordinary residence' is a term which is undefined by statute, the question whether or not a person possesses the attributes which that term signify is a question not of law but of fact. The discussion at **3.03** above concerning the determination of questions of fact is, therefore, of equal relevance whether residence *simpliciter* or ordinary residence is the attribute in question.

---

1 FA 2013 Sch 46.

2 Inland Revenue explanatory note relating to a proposed amendment to Finance Bill 1974, cl 18. HM Treasury and HM Revenue & Customs *Statutory definition of tax residence: a consultation* (June 2011), para 6.6.

3 *R v Barnet London Borough, ex p Shah* [1980] 3 All ER 679 at 681, per Ormrod J.

4 *Levene v IRC* (1928) 13 TC 486 at 507, per Lord Warrington of Clyffe.

5 See **3.02** above.

6 ITEPA s 26 (before 6 April 2013).
7 ITEPA ss 21–24 (before 6 April 2013).
8 Schedule 7 para 22.
9 But see further **4.03** below.

Concept and application

4.02   The meaning of ordinary residence

Although the question of whether a person is 'ordinarily residing in the UK' is a question of fact, the meaning of those words is a matter of statutory interpretation and thus a matter of law. As such, the words were given careful consideration by the Court of Session in 1926 and by the House of Lords in two leading tax cases decided in 1928. In each case the court made it clear that it was construing the words as bearing their natural and ordinary meaning.

In the case of *Reid v IRC*[1] Lord Clyde LP firmly rejected Miss Reid's argument that, even if she was resident in the UK by reason of her visits and the various ties which bound her to this country, she could not be ordinarily resident since she had always spent the greater part of each year abroad:

'The argument was that the meaning of the word "ordinarily" is governed – wholly or mainly – by the test of time or duration. I think it is a test, and an important one; but I think it is only one among many. From the point of view of time, "ordinarily" would stand in contrast to "casually". But [Miss Reid] is not a "casual" visitor to her home country; on the contrary she regularly returns to it, and "resides" in it for a part – albeit the smaller part – of every year. I hesitate to give the word "ordinarily" any more precise interpretation than "in the customary course of events", and anyhow I cannot think that the element of time so predominates in its meaning that, unless [Miss Reid] "resided" in the United Kingdom for at least six months and a day, she could not be said "ordinarily" to reside there in the year in question.'[2]

This point was taken up in the case of *Levene v IRC*[3] by Rowlatt J who said:

'"Ordinarily" may mean either preponderatingly in point of time or time plus importance, or it may mean habitually as a matter of course, as one might say: in the ordinary course of a man's life, although in time it might be insignificant … I think that "ordinary" does not mean preponderatingly, I think it means ordinary in the sense that it is habitual in the ordinary course of a man's life, and I think a man is ordinarily resident in the United Kingdom when the ordinary course of his life is such that it discloses a residence in the United Kingdom …'[4]

In the House of Lords, Lord Warrington of Clyffe affirmed this view, saying of ordinary residence that it is:

'… impossible to restrict its connotation to its duration. A member of this House may well be said to be ordinarily resident in London during the Parliamentary session and in the country during the recess. If it has any definite meaning I should say it means according to the way in which a man's life is usually ordered.'[5]

119

In that same case, the Lord Chancellor, Viscount Cave, said:

> 'The expression "ordinary residence" ... is contrasted with ... occasional or temporary residence; and I think it connotes residence in a place with some degree of continuity and apart from accidental or temporary absences. So understood, the expression differs little in meaning from the word "residence" ...'[6]

In *Lysaght v IRC*[7] Viscount Sumner said:

> 'I think the converse to "ordinarily" is "extraordinarily", and that part of the regular order of a man's life, adopted voluntarily and for settled purposes, is not "extraordinary".'[8]

In 1981, the words 'ordinarily resident' again fell to be construed by the courts and, in *R v Barnet London Borough, ex p Shah*,[9] Lord Denning MR said:

> 'The words "ordinarily resident" mean that the person must be habitually and normally resident here, apart from temporary or occasional absences of long or short duration.'[10]

The conclusions of the House of Lords in *Shah* were summarised by Special Commissioner Clark in *Genovese v Revenue & Customs*[11] as follows:

> 'In *Shah*, the House of Lords considered the natural and ordinary meaning of the words "ordinarily resident". Lord Scarman, with whose speech the other Lords all concurred, expressed the following conclusions:
>
> (1) Following *Levene* and *Lysaght*, the words are to be construed in their natural and ordinary meaning as words of common usage in the English language (341H);
> (2) The words are not to be interpreted as comparable with domicile (343C);
> (3) They do not imply an intention to live in a place permanently or indefinitely (343E–F);
> (4) Unless the statutory framework or legal context requires a different meaning, the words refer to a person's abode in a particular country which he or she has adopted voluntarily as part of the regular order of his or her life for the time being, whether of short or long duration (343G);
> (5) The mind of the individual is relevant in two (and only two) particular respects. The residence must be voluntarily adopted, and there must be a degree of settled purpose, having sufficient continuity to be described as settled (344B–C);
> (6) The purpose, while settled, may be for a limited period, and common reasons for a choice of regular abode include education, business or profession, employment, health, family, or merely love of the place (344C);
> (7) The "real home" test is wholly inconsistent with the natural and ordinary meaning of the words as construed in *Levene* and *Lysaght* (345D);
> (8) The test requires objective examination of immediately past events, and not intention or expectation for the future (345F–H).'[12]

---

1 (1926) 10 TC 673.
2 (1926) 10 TC 673 at 680.

3 (1928) 13 TC 486.
4 (1928) 13 TC 486 at 493.
5 (1928) 13 TC 486 at 509.
6 (1928) 13 TC 486 at 507.
7 (1928) 13 TC 511.
8 (1928) 13 TC 511 at 528.
9 [1982] 1 All ER 698.
10 [1982] 1 All ER 698 at 704.
11 *Genovese v Revenue & Customs* [2009] UKSPC 741.
12 *Genovese v Revenue & Customs* [2009] UKSPC 741 at para 35. The case must be approached with some caution since the appellant was unrepresented. See also the summary in *Grace v Revenue & Customs Commissioners* [2008] EWHC 2708 (Ch) at para 39(vii) to (x).

4.03   The relation of residence to ordinary residence

Lord Denning's interpretation of the words 'ordinarily resident'[1] expands Viscount Cave's phrase 'with some degree of continuity' into 'habitually and normally' and takes ordinary residence to be residence *simpliciter* which is customary, usual and confirmed by habit. Thus, Miss Reid was ordinarily resident because the residence status she attracted to herself by reason of the regularity of her visits to the UK[2] and her various links with this country[3] was confirmed by habit as being residence of a customary and usual kind rather than residence which was exceptional, unusual or accidental.

Although Miss Reid undoubtedly had engaged in a great deal of wandering – one month in France, next month in Spain, the month after in Austria, the month after that in Portugal – the Commissioners decided no: Miss Reid every year, without fail (though only for some three and a half months) returned to the UK and it was this factor which added the quality of ordinariness to her residence *simpliciter*.

It should be noted, however, that had the regularity of Miss Reid's visits to the UK and her links with this country not, in the opinion of the Commissioners, been sufficient to imbue her with the quality of UK residence *simpliciter*, she could not, within either Viscount Sumner's, Viscount Cave's or Lord Denning's understanding of the term, have been attributed with the quality of being ordinarily resident during the years in question. In law, ordinary residence springs from residence *simpliciter*, and if residence *simpliciter* is never acquired then ordinary residence cannot be acquired either. Viscount Cave said:

'I find it difficult to imagine a case in which a man while not resident here is yet ordinarily resident here.'[4]

The link between ordinary residence and residence *simpliciter* in the manner described is again highlighted in the *Miesegaes* case,[5] where the Special Commissioners considered that they had:

'... first [to] decide whether [Mr Miesegaes] was resident in the United Kingdom in each of the years in question, and, second, if he was so resident, whether his residence had the quality of ordinary residence,'[6] and Morris LJ commented:

'It seems to me that the Special Commissioners were correct in their approach when they decided that first they should consider whether [Mr Miesegaes] was resident in the United Kingdom in each of the years in question and, in the second place, whether his residence had the quality of ordinary residence.'[7]

TCGA 1992 s 2(1) is drafted on the assumption that a person may be ordinarily resident in the UK without being resident *simpliciter* here, which provides that, subject to certain exceptions:

'… a person shall be chargeable to capital gains tax in respect of chargeable gains accruing to him in a year of assessment during any part of which he is resident in the UK, or during which he is ordinarily resident in the UK.'

The contrary is the basis for the income tax legislation discussed in **4.01** above. In *Gaines-Cooper*, it was the appellant's case that it was not possible to be ordinarily resident in the UK for any year in which one was not resident and that as the appellant was not resident in the UK for the years in question he was not ordinarily resident in those years either. The conclusions of Special Commissioners Brice and Hellier were:

'[T]hat the Appellant was resident in the United Kingdom in the years of assessment under appeal and that his residence here was continuous in the sense that it continued from year to year. It was ordinary and part of his everyday life bearing in mind that his everyday life was far from ordinary. We are also of the view that the Appellant would still be ordinarily resident in the United Kingdom even if there were an occasional year when he was not resident here.'[8]

Little reasoning is provided in support of this proposition other than that the concept of 'ordinary residence' requires more than mere residence but connotes residence in a place with some degree of continuity and 'ordinary' means normal and part of everyday life. In *Grace*, Special Commissioner Brice decided that:

'[If] an individual is not resident in the United Kingdom, then it is difficult to find that he is ordinarily resident here. I have concluded that the Appellant was not resident in the United Kingdom and also conclude that he was not ordinarily resident here.'[9]

On appeal, the parties agreed that the questions of residence and ordinary residence stand or fall together.[10] In *Genovese*, an unrepresented taxpayer, who was apparently resident throughout the period in question, tried unsuccessfully to argue that he was not ordinarily resident. In concluding that Mr Genovese was ordinarily resident, Special Commissioner Clark found that:

'[T]he taxpayer's primary reason for his presence in the UK was employment. Mr Genovese had chosen to come to work in London, and the consequence was that he had to remain here while working for UBS until he or UBS decided that he should take up duties elsewhere. His presence in the UK for this purpose, coupled with the presence of his family and the taking up of accommodation in the London flat, did amount to voluntarily adopting an abode in the UK.'[11]

In *Tuczka v HMRC*[12] the Upper Tribunal rejected a submission that for a person to be ordinarily resident in the UK, he must have the intention of staying here permanently or at least for an indefinite period. It was argued that, if an individual intends to remain only for a limited period, his stay would be temporary which precluded a finding of ordinary residence.[13] The Upper Tribunal likewise rejected an alternative submission, that an intention to reside here for only two and a half years, or 33 months, was too short to constitute a 'settled purpose'.[14] The distinction between residence *simpliciter* and ordinary residence is not as wide or as basic as was suggested on behalf of Dr Tuczka. 'That,' said Mr Justice Roth, 'may explain why the researches of counsel found no reported tax case where residence was not in issue and the only question was whether the taxpayer was also ordinarily resident.'[15]

While these cases illustrate that as a matter of fact, residence *simpliciter* and ordinary residence will normally coincide, in the author's view they must coincide as a matter of statutory construction. The addition of the word 'ordinary' merely qualifies an existing residence *simpliciter* by the addition of certain elements. It is not a separate legal notion of residence. The First-tier Tribunal in *Carey v HMRC*[16] came to the opposite conclusion where both parties agreed that the taxpayer had ceased to be resident and only ordinary residence was in issue. The Tribunal accepted that such cases were rare but relied on the fact that TCGA 1992 ss 2 and 16 are expressed to apply to a person who is either resident or ordinarily resident. The issue arose in relation to a claim for a capital loss of £145,827 on the disposal of shares acquired by the exercise of an option over shares in his employer, to be set off against the corresponding employment income of £145,827 arising in that year from the exercise of the option. Such relief was only available under ITA 2007 s 131 if he was ordinarily resident. On 4 January 2011 Mr Carey informally left his UK employment to embark on what he described as sabbatical leave without pay and then left the UK on 15 January 2011 to take up a post in Rwanda to work in impoverished areas of the developing world. He did so until 10 April 2012 after which he set up his own business in East Africa. He did not return to the UK at all in the 2011–12 tax year but said that he intended to do so for social reasons. Formal employment with his UK employer terminated on 11 December 2011. There was no evidence that he ever returned to the UK. The decision is wrong both in principle and on the facts. The assumption on which TCGA 1992 s 2(1) is drafted is erroneous. Although a person cannot be ordinarily resident in the UK unless he is also resident *simpliciter* here, a person may, in certain circumstances be resident *simpliciter* in the UK, year after year, without being ordinarily resident here. Those circumstances will subsist where a person's residence *simpliciter* lacks one or more of the elements emphasised by Lord Scarman when he said:

'I unhesitatingly subscribe to the view that 'ordinarily resident' refers to a man's abode in a particular place or country which he has adopted voluntarily and for settled purposes as part of the regular order of his life for the time being, whether of short or long duration.'[17]

It is to these three key features of voluntary adoption, settled purpose and the regular order of life – none of which is essential to the acquisition of residence *simpliciter* status but all of which are essential to the acquisition of ordinary residence status – that we must now turn our attention.

1 See **4.02** above.
2 See **4.02** above.
3 See **3.15–3.18** above.
4 *Levene v IRC* (1928) 13 TC 486 at 507.
5 *Miesegaes v IRC* (1957) 37 TC 493.
6 *Miesegaes v IRC* (1957) 37 TC 493 at 495.
7 *Miesegaes v IRC* (1957) 37 TC 493 at 502.
8 *Gaines-Cooper v HMRC* [2006] UKSPC SPC568 at para 190.
9 *Grace v Revenue & Customs* [2008] UKSPC SPC 663 at para 49.
10 *Grace v Revenue & Customs Commissioners* [2008] EWHC 2708 (Ch) at para 1.
11 *Genovese v Revenue & Customs* [2009] UKSPC 741 at para 42.
12 *Tuczka v Revenue & Customs* [2011] UKUT 113 (TCC). The converse may be true however. In *Megwa v Revenue & Customs* [2010] UKFTT 543 (TC), the taxpayer intended to make the UK his home and became ordinarily resident (and resident) on the day he moved there with his family.
13 At para 16.
14 At para 17.
15 At para 18.
16 *Carey v HMRC* [2015] UKFTT 0466 (TC).
17 *Shah v Barnet London Borough Council* [1983] 1 All ER 226 at 235.

Essential elements

4.04   A voluntarily adopted place of abode

It is clear from the facts of the case in which Viscount Sumner gave his interpretation of the words 'ordinarily residing' that he cannot have used the words 'adopted voluntarily' in the sense of 'free of any kind of external constraint' for Mr Lysaght was in Great Britain only because his business commitments compelled him to be here. He would, no doubt, have preferred to be at home in Ireland rather than in the Spa Hotel in Bath, but in choosing to be a director of John Lysaght Ltd he had accepted that he would have to spend one week or so of each month in the UK. The phrase 'adopted voluntarily' must, therefore, have been understood by Viscount Sumner as being not inconsistent with submission to such constraints as a person's chosen order of life imposed upon him.

On the face of it, however, the first case which came before the courts following the *Lysaght* case and which centred on the phrase 'adopted voluntarily' took the meaning of those words some way beyond that. It concerned Miss Mackenzie, an Australian, who, at the age of 28, came on a visit to England with her mother. There was no evidence as to how long the visit was intended to last but, in the event, Miss Mackenzie, having stayed here four months, remained here until her death at the age of 82 because, after spending those four months here, she was, in 1885, certified as insane and detained, first in Holloway Mental Hospital until 1893, then in the Coppice Lunatic Hospital at Nottingham until her death. The case was an estate duty case which arose because of a disagreement over the meaning of the words 'ordinarily resident' in F(No 2)A 1915 s 47(1), and counsel for the administrator of Miss Mackenzie's estate submitted that:

'Miss Mackenzie could not be said to be ordinarily resident in September, 1885, when she was certified as of unsound mind, and that during the whole of the rest of her life she was under constraint and unable to exercise any will of her own, and that that period, the last 54 years of her life, cannot be taken into account at all as making her ordinarily resident in this country ... [T]he words of Viscount Sumner "adopted voluntarily" indicate that no residence can be treated as ordinary residence unless it is the result of a voluntary act on the part of the person residing there.'[1]

Morton J could not agree:

'The matter does not wholly depend on choice ... I do not understand Viscount Sumner ... as saying that a period of residence in this country which is involuntary must be wholly disregarded for the purpose of ascertaining whether or not a person is ordinarily resident, and it must not be left out of account that Miss Mackenzie came to this country, one presumes, voluntarily at the age of 28, and, as a result of the circumstances ... described, never left it.'[2]

Morton J then went on to comment on some hypothetical case submitted by counsel for the administrator of Miss Mackenzie's estate:

'They put the case of a prisoner of war who has come to this country and been detained here, it might be, for a year. They say that he would not be ordinarily resident, because the element of constraint is present. They take again the case of a foreigner with a home abroad, who comes to this country on a visit and commits some crime or offence against the laws of this country, and is imprisoned for a considerable time, and ultimately dies in this country. There, they say, he would not be held to be ordinarily resident ... [S]uch cases must be dealt with on their particular facts, if and when they arise, but I can well imagine, in the case of a prisoner of war, that, if a man had a permanent residence in Germany and came over here in an aeroplane to attack this country, and was captured and kept here for a considerable period, it might well be held that his ordinary residence was his home in Germany.'[3]

Comparing Morton J's judgment as regards Miss Mackenzie and his views on the hypothetical case of the German prisoner of war, it is clear that it was in Miss Mackenzie's initial voluntary entry to the UK for an indefinite period that he found a justification for holding her to have been ordinarily resident here throughout all the years which followed. What he seems to have been saying is that the words are 'voluntarily adopted' not 'voluntarily continued and pursued'. If the beginning is a voluntary matter it is of no consequence that the continuance is enforced. Thus, the hypothetical German could not be ordinarily resident in the UK since his initial entry to this country would not be a matter of free will but of military orders emanating from those in command over him. Indeed, during the 1939–45 war, members of the allied forces who became resident in the UK were generally treated by the Inland Revenue as not ordinarily resident and so, too, were refugees and displaced persons.

This understanding of Viscount Sumner's words seems perfectly reasonable and the implicit rephrasing of 'adopted voluntarily' as 'adopted (but not necessarily continued) voluntarily' does them no violence.

It has been suggested, however, that in *Shah v Barnet London Borough Council*[4] Lord Scarman rejected this approach and, despite his explicit acceptance of the authority of Viscount Sumner's dictum,[5] so qualified Viscount Sumner's words as to rob them of any meaning. What Lord Scarman said was this:

> 'The residence must be voluntarily adopted. Enforced presence by reason of kidnapping or imprisonment, or a Robinson Crusoe existence on a desert island with no opportunity of escape, may be so overwhelming a factor as to negative the will to be where one is.'[6]

The relation of the second sentence to the first in this quotation is by no means clear, but if, as one writer has suggested,[7] it is to be taken as meaning that:

> '... to be ordinarily resident an individual must have adopted his residence voluntarily, except for extreme cases such as imprisonment or a desert island existence with no opportunity to escape where the imposed circumstances will override the individual's intention,'

then 'adopted (but not necessarily continued) voluntarily' has become 'adopted voluntarily or involuntarily', which is a quite different matter. It is suggested that the correct approach to Lord Scarman's second sentence must be to take it as a list of circumstances in which a place of abode will be involuntarily adopted and in which, accordingly, the attribution of ordinary residence will *not* ensue. This alternative way of reading Lord Scarman's remarks implies the insertion of a perfectly logical additional sentence between the two quoted so that the passage reads as follows:

> 'The residence must be voluntarily adopted. [Only if a person is where he is because at some point he has chosen to be there can the kind of residence known as ordinary residence ensue; but being where one is is not always a matter of choice.] Enforced presence by reason of kidnapping or imprisonment, or a Robinson Crusoe existence on a desert island with no opportunity of escape, may be so overwhelming a factor as to negative the will to be where one is.'

The *Mackenzie* case discussed above is not the only case where, on the face of it, the court appeared to set aside Viscount Sumner's requirement that residence must be voluntarily adopted before it can become ordinary residence. *Miesegaes v IRC*[8] concerned the residence status of Stanley Miesegaes who, during the years 1947–48 to 1951–52, had been a schoolboy boarding at Harrow. Counsel for Mr Miesegaes argued that even if Mr Miesegaes had been resident *simpliciter* in the UK during those years, such residence could not have constituted ordinary residence because it had not been voluntary residence; it had been institutional. Pearce LJ could not accept that argument. Referring to Viscount Sumner's interpretation of the words 'ordinarily resident' which he later quoted, he said:

'Education is too extensive and universal a phase to justify such descriptions as "unusual" and "extraordinary" ... The argument based on the institutional or compulsory nature of a boy's life at school is misleading. The compulsion is merely the will of his parents who voluntarily send him to that school. It would be hazardous, and in my opinion irrelevant, to investigate whether adolescents are residing voluntarily where their lot is cast and how far they approve of their parents' choice of a home or school.'[9]

Far from constituting a rejection of Viscount Sumner's test, however, those words are a strong affirmation of it. Pearce LJ is saying not that one can set aside Viscount Sumner's words but that, in order to give them due weight in circumstances where the person concerned is not a person of full capacity, one must have regard to the will of the person's parents, trustees or guardians in determining whether or not his place of abode has been adopted voluntarily. That is because, in law, an *incapax* has no will but the will of those who are legally responsible for him.[10] Accordingly, during the years 1947–48 to 1951–52, Stanley Miesegaes was ordinarily resident in Harrow because he was resident *simpliciter* in Harrow for each of those years for the settled purpose of being educated and cared for there and Harrow had been voluntarily adopted *by his father* (who, until his death on 10 July 1948, had custody and control of Stanley at all material times) as Stanley's place of abode.

These two principles concerning the ordinary residence status of a person who, in law, has no will of his own were brought together in the case of *R v Waltham Forest London Borough Council, ex p Vale*.[11] Judith Vale, a severely mentally handicapped child born in London in 1956, was, in 1961, moved by her parents to Dublin where, because of her handicap, she was, until May 1984, boarded at various rural community homes. The last of these was Camp Hill at Wexford. In 1978, her parents returned to England and took up residence in the London Borough of Waltham Forest, visiting Judith two or three times a year. In 1984, Judith became so severely disturbed that, on 6 May, her parents brought her from Ireland to live with them until such time as she could be accommodated at Stoke Place, a residential home in Buckinghamshire. In the event, Judith was placed there just one month later on 6 June 1984. Judith's parents sought the funding of this placement from the London borough in which they lived but this was refused on the ground that Judith was not ordinarily resident within the borough at the time of her placement in the home in Buckinghamshire and that, under the National Assistance Act 1948 s 24(1), this relieved the borough of responsibility. Judith's parents sought a judicial review of that decision and Taylor J held that:

'Where the propositus ... is so mentally handicapped as to be totally dependent upon a parent or guardian, the concept of her having an independent ordinary residence of her own which she has adopted voluntarily and for which she has a settled purpose does not arise. She is in the same position as a small child. Her ordinary residence is that of her parents because that is her "base" ... It may well be that if the parents delegate their guardianship of her to a school or home for greater or shorter periods she will acquire a second ordinary residence at that establishment ... It may well be therefore that in the present case Judith, although ordinarily resident with her parents throughout, had a second ordinary residence at Camp Hill for the duration of her stay there, and again acquired a second ordinary residence when she went to

Stoke Place. For the period May to June 1984, however, she had only one ordinary residence: at home.'[12]

It would seem to be established, therefore, that an infant or incapacitated person will be ordinarily resident wherever his parents, trustees or guardians are ordinarily resident and, if the person resides elsewhere in accordance with the will of those having legal responsibility for him and as part of the settled order of his life, in that other place also. In cases where there is no incapacity, however, a person's residence must be voluntarily adopted by the person himself before it can acquire the character of ordinary residence.

1 *Re Mackenzie* (1940) 19 ATC 399 at 402 and 403.
2 *Re Mackenzie* (1940) 19 ATC 399 at 403 and 404.
3 *Re Mackenzie* (1940) 19 ATC 399 at 403 and 404.
4 [1983] 1 All ER 226.
5 See **4.03** above.
6 *Shah v Barnet London Borough Council* [1983] 1 All ER 226 at 235.
7 J L Wosner, 'Ordinary Residence, the Law and Practice' [1983] *British Tax Review* 347 at 348.
8 (1957) 37 TC 493.
9 (1957) 37 TC 493 at 501.
10 Had this principle been invoked in the *Mackenzie* case, Miss Mackenzie's ordinary residence status could have been established on grounds far more convincing than those on which it was established.
11 11 February 1985, QB. Unreported except in (1985) *The Times,* 25 February.
12 (1985) *The Times,* 25 February, QB.

4.05   Settled purposes

In *Shah v Barnet London Borough Council,*[1] Lord Scarman said that ordinary residence was dependent not only on a person's voluntary adoption of an abode in some place or country, but also on:

'... a degree of settled purpose. The purpose may be one or there may be several. It may be specific or general. All the law requires is that there is a settled purpose. This is not to say that the propositus intends to stay where he is indefinitely; indeed his purpose, while settled, may be for a limited period. Education, business or profession, employment, health, family or mere love of the place spring to mind as common reasons for a choice of regular abode. And there may well be many others. All that is necessary is that the purpose of living where one does has a sufficient degree of continuity to be properly described as settled.[2]

In *Reid v IRC,*[3] the settled purpose of Miss Reid in spending some three and a half months in the UK each year was chiefly, it seems, to visit her homeland and her sister.

In *Lysaght v IRC,*[4] the settled purpose of Mr Lysaght's three months' residence in the UK each year was business. He came here to attend directors' meetings of John Lysaght Ltd and to deal with business matters arising in connection with that company.

In *Levene v IRC,*[5] the settled purposes of Mr Levene's regular periods of residence in the UK were to obtain medical advice, to visit relatives, to take part in Jewish religious observances, to visit the graves of his parents and to deal with his tax affairs.

In *Reed v Clark*,[6] the settled purpose of Dave Clark in going to Los Angeles and staying there throughout the tax year 1978–79 was to work there and to avoid a UK tax liability on income of $450,000. In his judgment of the case, Nicholls J said:

'Artificial tax avoidance schemes do not find much favour with the courts today. In this case the position, as I see it, is that when deciding issues of residence, ordinary residence and occasional residence all the reasons (including any desire to avoid a liability to UK income tax) underlying a person's being in a particular place are part of the overall picture. They are part of the material to be looked at and considered when deciding those issues. The presence of a tax avoidance intention may help to show, for instance, why a person went abroad at all, or at the particular time he did, how long he intended to remain away, or where his home in fact was in the year of assessment. But residence abroad for a carefully chosen limited period of work there … is no less residence abroad for that period just because the major reason for it was the avoidance of tax. Likewise with ordinary residence.'[7]

Although the cases cited above provide examples of settled purposes, they provide no detailed explanation of the term itself. Thus, the question what is meant by 'settled purpose' remained unanswered until it came to the fore in the case of *Shah v Barnet London Borough Council*.[8] That case concerned the eligibility of students for local authority grants in connection with their education. Such eligibility depends on whether or not a student is 'ordinarily resident' in the UK; but, in the Education Act 1962, as in the Taxes Acts, the term 'ordinarily resident' is undefined. Several of the education authorities involved tried to suggest that education could not be a settled purpose for the purposes of establishing ordinary residence and that, to establish a settled purpose:

'… there must be shown an intention to live here on a permanent basis as part of the general community; if a person's presence here was for a 'specific or limited purpose only', eg to pursue a course of study, he would not be ordinarily resident.'[9]

Lord Scarman, however, firmly rebutted that suggestion:

'A man's settled purpose will be different at different ages. Education in adolescence or early adulthood can be as settled a purpose as a profession or business in later years … study can be as settled a purpose as business or pleasure. And the notion of permanent or indefinitely enduring purpose as an element in ordinary residence derives not from the natural and ordinary meaning of the words "ordinarily resident" but from a confusion of it with domicile.'[10]

Earlier,[11] Lord Scarman had said, 'all that is necessary is that the purpose of living where one does has a sufficient degree of continuity to be properly described as settled'. A settled purpose is, therefore, a purpose which, though it need not provide a person with a motivation for becoming permanently or indefinitely present in a particular place, will provide him with the motivation to be more than transitorily or fleetingly present there. The purpose must, in other words, have a certain intrinsic durability. The difference between the two kinds of purpose may be illustrated by contrasting the motivation of the man who takes a holiday in the Cotswolds with that of the man who makes being in the Cotswolds part of his life; or the motivation of the woman who pays a visit to her invalid mother with that of the woman who makes caring for her invalid mother part of her life. In the first of both cases, the purpose is essentially transitory and results in a deviation from the person's normal mode of life; but in the second of both cases the purpose has an inbuilt element of continuity which results in the normal mode of life itself being modified so as to accommodate the presence of the person in the place in question. In either case the purpose which possesses an intrinsic element of continuity may, of course, be terminated very shortly after the mode of life has been altered to accommodate that purpose: the man may discover a preferred alternative to the Cotswolds and may further modify his mode of life so as to exclude presence in the Cotswolds and allow for presence in Tenerife; and the woman's mother may die. But in neither case can the early termination of the purpose change the settled nature it once possessed or retrospectively divest the person of the ordinary residence status to which it will have given rise.

How small a degree of continuity of purpose is needed for a purpose to be settled is well illustrated in *University College London v Newman*.[12] Edward Newman was a New Zealand citizen who, in 1977, left New Zealand and, after travelling extensively, arrived in the European Community in August 1978 whereupon, using France as his base, he became,

> '... a rather aimless drifter who has spent his time in what is inelegantly but descriptively called colloquially "bumming" around Europe.'[13]

In October 1983, however, he embarked upon a degree course at University College London and claimed to be eligible for lower rate fees on the grounds of having been ordinarily resident within the European Community during the course of the three years ended 1 September 1983 within the terms of the Education (Fees and Awards) Regulations 1983 Sch 2(2). In the Westminster County Court, McDonnell J held that he had not been ordinarily resident as claimed, but, in the Court of Appeal, his judgment was reversed. Croom-Johnson LJ said that Mr Newman,

> '... had been living in the EC for the necessary three years. But was he "ordinarily resident"? He has put down roots nowhere. He used France "as my base for travelling". He went from country to country, in short spells, returning again and again. His work record is spasmodic, and was described by the judge as "the token effort required to ensure that he receives social security payments".'[14]

Nevertheless, Croom-Johnson LJ concluded that if McDonnell J had asked himself 'Has Mr Newman been shown to have been ordinarily resident in the EEC for the three qualifying years'? and had he applied Lord Scarman's test (ie had Mr Newman's purpose of living where he did a sufficient degree of continuity to be properly described as settled?), the answer would have to be 'yes ... Mr Newman was ordinarily resident, after his casual fashion, somewhere in the EC for the whole of the qualifying three years'.[15]

It was accepted in the Court of Appeal that Mr Newman had not been ordinarily resident in any particular European Community Member State during the three-year period, but that is not relevant to the point being made. On the basis of the court's judgment, Mr Newman would have been ordinarily resident in the UK had he confined himself to merely 'bumming around' England, Scotland, Wales and Northern Ireland. 'Bumming around' may be a settled purpose.

In *Turberville v HMRC*[16] the appellant, born in Aberdeen, was a successful senior executive in the oil industry whose career had taken him from New Zealand in 1979 through Saudi Arabia, Malaysia, Nigeria, the US and the UK among others. He was sent to the UK by Shell in February 1997 and worked for them there until October 1998. He left them for a Dallas-based group but after a short break he was based in the UK for them until the beginning of July 2001 when he went to Dallas. He lost his job in Dallas at the end of October 2002 that would contractually have continued until June 2004. A consulting agreement required him to help in the UK until 31 January 2003, which in practice ended in November 2002. He had rented an apartment in Monaco from 1 December 2002, acquiring a *carte de sejour* there. He travelled between the UK and Monaco on five occasions between 27 November 2002 and 4 January 2003, finally driving to Monaco on 9 January 2003. Although he was ordinarily resident in the UK by July 2001, he was found to have lost that status when he left on 1 July 2001 (although this was only effective for the tax year 2002–03 since the 2001–02 year could not be split). The time he spent in the UK after October 2002 cannot be treated as part of a pattern starting from his residence in the UK before going to Dallas. It was held to be physical presence that was no more than a stop-gap measure.

Voluntarily adopted residence in the UK is itself insufficient to constitute ordinary residence. The individual must also have a settled purpose. In *Ward v HMRC*,[17] the taxpayer was an Australian citizen, seconded to London to work for a UK company within an Australian banking group until March 2009. For personal reasons, he asked to extend his secondment to June 2009. His employer agreed, but he was required to vacate his company-provided accommodation. His work permit was extended for six months. Then his intention was to move back to Australia at the end of the extended secondment and his furniture and other personal effects, including his car, were sent to Australia in anticipation of his return. Due to illness in his girlfriend's family, and his girlfriend becoming pregnant, he requested and was granted a further extension to April 2010 on the basis that he would both revert to working for an Australian group company and transfer back to the Australian payroll, from July 2009. He applied for an extension of his work permit to October 2010. He married in September 2010, and returned to Australia in January 2011. The First-tier Tribunal ruled that although he remained voluntarily in the UK during the tax years 2009–10 and 2010–11, he did not have a sufficient settled purpose to be part of the ordinary pattern of his life. Thus Mr Ward was resident but not ordinarily resident for those years.

In contrast, another peripatetic Australian who came to work in the UK, where he lived with his family during the three years in which his status was disputed, was found to be ordinarily resident. In *Mackay v HMRC*,[18]

Mr Mackay had voluntarily, but reluctantly, come to the UK to work. His work required a substantial amount of travel. His engagement involved a series of short-term projects, could be summarily terminated and two prospective sales of the business made his work precarious. He also decided, before coming to the UK, that he would, in any event, leave the UK within three years, even if this meant resigning. The First-tier Tribunal found that the UK was his base both for work and domestically.[19] He had a settled purpose of fulfilling the duties of his employment which was sufficient to make him ordinarily resident. The Tribunal accepted that the purpose for which an individual is in the UK can change and that different purposes should not necessarily be looked at together over a period.[20] Employment here was a single purpose. A temporary purpose in the context of employment was described as 'something intended, planned or expected to be much shorter than 18 months, not something which merely might be shorter.'[21] After reviewing various time periods in several decisions, Judge Hellier held that the period for which Mr Mackay intended or expected to be in the UK from the beginning of 2005 was sufficient to be settled, with the result that he was ordinarily resident in all three years.[22]

---

1 [1983] 1 All ER 226.
2 [1983] 1 All ER 226 at 235.
3 (1926) 10 TC 673.
4 (1928) 13 TC 511.
5 (1928) 13 TC 486.
6 [1985] STC 323.
7 [1985] STC 323 at 346.
8 [1983] 1 All ER 226.
9 [1983] 1 All ER 226 at 237.
10 [1983] 1 All ER 226 at 236, 238 and 239.
11 [1983] 1 All ER 226 at 235.
12 CA, 19 December 1985. Unreported except in (1986) *The Times*, 8 January.
13 (1986) *The Times*, 8 January, CA.
14 (1986) *The Times*, 8 January, CA.
15 (1986) *The Times*, 8 January, CA.
16 *Turberville v HMRC* [2010] UKFTT 69 (TC).
17 *Ward v HMRC* [2016] UKFTT 0114 (TC).
18 *Mackay v HMRC* [2017] UKFTT 0441 (TC).
19 *Mackay v HMRC* [2017] UKFTT 0441 (TC), at para 126.
20 *Mackay v HMRC* [2017] UKFTT 0441 (TC), at para 116.
21 *Mackay v HMRC* [2017] UKFTT 0441 (TC), at para 134.
22 *Mackay v HMRC* [2017] UKFTT 0441 (TC), at paras 137 and 138.

4.06 Regular order of life

Given that a person voluntarily adopts the UK as a place of abode and comes here in pursuit of one or more settled purposes, over what period must he be present here in pursuit of those purposes before his presence becomes part of the 'regular order' of his life and before he can thus be attributed with ordinary residence status? The body of case law preceding the *Shah* case[1] had suggested that the answer is three or more years – not because any of the judges hearing the cases concerned had declared that that was the required period but because, in every instance, the appellants had, in fact, visited the UK in three or more consecutive years before the Revenue chose to assert that the status of ordinary residence had been acquired and before the Commissioners (subsequently supported by the courts) upheld its assertion that that was so. The point was crisply made by First-tier Tribunal Judge Clark in *Tuczka v HMRC*[2] that:

'[T]he suggestion … that a longer period of time would be necessary to establish that a pattern of residence had become "habitual" is not consistent with the authorities. … We feel that the examination of the "three-year practice" in paragraph 3.9 of HMRC's booklet IR20 and the search for some form of linkage between that and the background law led to an over-emphasis on the question of the length of … stay in the UK. It is clear that Lord Scarman's reference in *Shah* (at 342) to Lord Denning's use of the expression "habitually and normally resident here" was intended to emphasise two features mentioned by Viscount Sumner in *Lysaght*, namely residence adopted voluntarily and for settled purposes; the word "habitually" did not imply a period of time, but related to the quality of the manner of residence in the UK.'

Where the settled purpose involves not merely visits to the UK but continuous presence here, a person's presence in the UK will necessarily have become part of the regular order of his life after only a few days have elapsed, and – just as early termination or fulfilment of the purpose will not retrospectively rob that purpose of any settled nature it possessed[3] – early termination or fulfilment of the purpose will not prevent the person's presence here from being presence as part of the regular order of his life. In the *Shah* case, Lord Scarman had said:

'If there be proved a regular, habitual mode of life in a particular place, the continuity of which has persisted despite temporary absences, ordinary residence is established provided only it is adopted voluntarily and for a settled purpose.'[4]

Likewise, in *Reed v Clark*,[5] Nicholls J was satisfied that a period of just over a year abroad was not too short a period for a person to have established an ordinary residence overseas.

The test which Nicholls J would (following Lord Scarman) seem to have been applying, however, was: did the period of residence in question, however long or short, represent an intrusion into or a deviation from the person's regular and habitual mode of life, or was it, in fact, a component part of the person's regular and habitual mode of life for the time being? If it was intrusive or deviatory it could not be ordinary residence, but if it was a component part of the normal pattern it could not be other than ordinary residence.

This would seem to bring the matter round full circle. In the *Levene* case, Lord Hanworth had said:

'I find it difficult to attach any distinction of meaning to the word "ordinarily" as affecting the term "resident", unless it be to prevent facts which would amount to residence being so estimated on the ground that they arose from some fortuitous cause, such as illness of the so-called resident or of some other person, which demanded his continuance at a place for a special purpose otherwise than in accordance with his own usual arrangements and shaping of his movements …'[6]

In other words, residence always will be ordinary residence unless it either lacks settled purpose or is enforced. That was the stance of the courts in 1928 and that, despite Revenue insistence (not always to the taxpayer's detriment) during the intervening years that ordinary residence necessitates the establishment of an annually recurrent pattern of residence *simpliciter*, has now been affirmed by the courts as being their stance today.

One further point must be made. Viscount Cave,[7] Lord Denning[8] and Lord Scarman[9] all made reference to the irrelevance of temporary absences in the context of the 'regular order of life' which is under discussion here. What each was saying is that once a person has, by reason of his voluntary presence in the UK in pursuit of one or more settled purposes, made his presence here part of the regular order of his life for the time being and thus attracted to himself the status of ordinary residence, his absence from the UK will not affect that status provided that the absences are temporary, occasional or accidental. It is worth observing that this principle of disregarding temporary absences provides additional support for the proposition that a person who makes voluntary regular visits to the UK in pursuit of settled purposes is ordinarily resident here. If the periods between visits are treated as temporary absences from the UK and are disregarded, the visitor's periodic presence in the UK is, effectively, transformed into a continuous presence. In *Karim v HMRC*[10] the taxpayer, who had moved to Portugal, could not substantiate first, that she was in the UK because of her mother's illness or, secondly, that she was here to wind up her affairs and thus her visits were not transient or to supply passing needs.

Ordinary residence is not in contrast to 'occasional' residence. It is enough that the residence 'is not casual and uncertain but that the person held to reside does so in the ordinary course of his life'. In *Arthur v Revenue And Customs*,[11] Mr and Mrs Arthur married in Ghana in 2008. At the time, Mrs Arthur was living in the UK and her husband in Ghana. He visited his UK resident wife and children intermittently and worked for a period and claimed the Jobseekers Allowance while living with his wife in the UK. He had obtained indefinite leave to remain in the UK and was registered to vote. This was sufficient to conclude that Mr Arthur was 'ordinarily resident' at the relevant time since a 'settled purpose' can be 'a specific limited purpose', for 'a limited period' and adopted 'for the time being, whether of short or long duration.' This was the case even if visits to the UK were for special occasions (the birth of his daughter, helping his wife to move house, the birth of his son), and to help take care of their children.[12]

---

1 *Shah v Barnet London Borough Council* [1983] 1 All ER 226 at 236.
2 *Tuczka v HMRC* [2010] UKFTT 53 (TC) at para 55. Upheld by the Upper Tribunal [2011] UKUT 113 (TCC) at para 14.
3 See **4.05** above.
4 *Shah v Barnet London Borough Council* [1983] 1 All ER 226 at 236.
5 [1985] STC 323.
6 *Levene v IRC* (1928) 13 TC 486 at 496.
7 *Levene v IRC* (1928) 13 TC 486 at 507.
8 *R v Barnet London Borough, ex p Shah* [1982] 1 All ER 698 at 704.
9 *Shah v Barnet London Borough Council* [1983] 1 All ER 226 at 236.
10 *Karim v HMRC* [2009] UKFTT 368 (TC) at para 40.
11 *Arthur v Revenue & Customs* [2017] EWCA Civ 1756.
12 *Arthur v Revenue & Customs* [2017] EWCA Civ 1756 at paras 31 and 32.

4.07 Unlawful residence

It has already been explained that residence is a question of fact not of law[1] so that, unless an Act contains specific provision to the contrary, residence does not need to be lawful for it to be residence which is voluntarily adopted and for a settled purpose as part of the regular order of a person's life. Thus although a deserting seaman who is living in the UK in breach of the immigration laws cannot be ordinarily resident here for the purposes of the Commonwealth Immigration Acts since those Acts make specific provision to that effect,[2] he may be ordinarily resident here for tax purposes since the Taxes Acts contain no such prohibiting provision. The principle underlying these rules is that a person who would appear to be ordinarily resident to anyone observing the way in which he is living but who is not entitled lawfully so to live cannot be allowed to benefit from his apparent status but 'for the purposes of taxation he will not be allowed to deny his apparent status'.[3] This, according to Oliver LJ in *R v Secretary of State for Home Department, ex p Margueritte*[4] made 'good common sense'.

1 See **3.22** above.
2 *Re Abdul Manan* [1971] 2 All ER 1016.
3 *R v Barnet London Borough Council, ex p Shah* [1982] 1 All ER 698 at 706, per Eveleigh LJ.
4 [1982] 3 All ER 909.

4.08 Dual or no ordinary residence

An individual may be ordinarily resident in two places at one and the same time was established in bankruptcy law in *Re Norris, ex p Reynolds*[1] and has been admitted in tax law also:

> 'I am not sure there is anything impossible in a person "ordinarily residing" in two places.'[2]

> 'I think … that a man can have two ordinary residences not because he commonly is to be found at those places, but because the ordinary course of his life is such that he acquires the attribute of residence at those two places.'[3]

That a person may be ordinarily resident in two countries at the same time was confirmed by the House of Lords in *Shah*.[4]

That a person may be ordinarily resident nowhere was affirmed in *University College London v Newman*.[5] Croom-Johnston LJ said:

> 'I agree that it is possible for someone to be ordinarily resident nowhere. People who spend their lives sailing about the world are such. So are the well-known class of tax-evaders who move on from country to country, always one move ahead of the tax man.'[6]

1 *Re Norris, ex p Reynolds* (1888) 4 TLR 452.
2 *Reid v IRC* (1926) 10 TC 673 at 680, per Lord Clyde LP.

3 *Levene v IRC* (1928) 13 TC 486 at 494, per Rowlatt J.
4 *R v Barnet LBC, ex parte Shah* [1983] 2 AC 309 at p 342.
5 CA, 19 December 1985. Unreported except in (1986) *The Times*, 8 January.
6 (1986) *The Times*, 8 January, CA. See also *Turberville v HMRC* [2010] UKFTT 69 (TC) at para 9, which involved a peripatetic executive rather than a tax-evader.

Revenue practice

4.09   IR20

HMRC practice in relation to ordinary residence as set out in IR20[1]departed significantly from the common law meaning of the expression. *Genovese v Revenue & Customs*[2] is a stark reminder. He arrived in London on 1 July 1998 to work for UBS, and initially lived in employer-provided accommodation. In September 1998, he entered into a tenancy agreement for a flat whereupon his wife and son joined him. Their furniture was shipped to London, but was placed in storage as the flat was furnished. He continued to work for UBS. In 1999 the terms of his employment contract were changed from expatriate to local. As each one-year term of the tenancy agreement for the flat expired, he renewed it for a further one-year term, until September 2001 when the new agreement was negotiated to provide a term of a further year. This contained a right to renew for a further year subject to a three-month early termination provision. (Strictly, all the terms of these agreements were for just under one year.) By March 2002, he had obtained approval for a property loan and on 28 March 2002 was able to make an offer, subject to survey and to contract, to purchase the property.

Mr Genovese had relied on published HMRC guidance to self-assess himself as resident but not ordinarily resident for 2001–02. Paragraph 3.9 of booklet IR20 sets out the following practice for longer term visitors:

> 'You will be treated as ordinarily resident from the beginning of the tax year after the third anniversary of your arrival if you come to, and remain in, the UK, but you
>
> • do not originally intend to stay for at least three years, and
> • do not buy accommodation or acquire it on a lease of three years or more.'

In supporting his position, Mr Genovese emphasised the unstructured nature of employment plans in the world of merchant banking; there was no certainty that an employee would remain in the UK, even if there was any form of annual plan relating to the particular employee. The conversion of his terms of employment from an expatriate contract to a 'local hire' contract was more likely to have been a decision based on cost grounds than one as to any kind of guarantee of continuing employment in the UK. He argued that the presence of a foreign national's family was not an indication of habitual residence. Putting down children's names for school places was not an indication of an intention to remain in the UK until the children reached a certain level in their education, but simply a prudent step in ensuring that places would be available if ultimately required. Mr Genovese had been far from settled in his employment in 2002; employment prospects were precarious. He had needed to house the family in the short term, and it made economic sense to buy rather than pay rent, but he had not purchased a house in 2001–02.

In applying the 'common law test' to find Mr Genovese ordinarily resident, Special Commissioner Clark observed that this conclusion was at variance with IR20. He noted that:

'Comparison of the various factors comprising the common law test with the factors considered relevant under HMRC's practice shows in particular that IR20 is concerned with matters of "intention" and what the individual "decides". The difference appears to stem from a fundamental difference of approach. The common law test is applied retrospectively to determine whether the individual coming to the UK has or has not become ordinarily resident. Booklet IR20 is concerned with a provisional decision whether or not, on the basis of information available at a much earlier stage, the individual appears to have become ordinarily resident. For this purpose, the individual's intentions and decisions need to be taken into account in order to arrive at an appropriate taxation treatment for the initial stages of his period in the UK.'[3]

The Special Commissioner did not consider that an offer would amount to a purchase within the terms of para 3 of Statement of Practice 17/91 but declined to decide whether this would have affected the outcome. In light of the withdrawal of IR20 from 6 April 2009,[4] readers are directed to the previous edition of this work for more detailed analysis of IR20 in light of the law on ordinary residence.

---

1 See IR20 (July 2008).
2 *Genovese v Revenue & Customs* [2009] UKSPC 741.
3 *Genovese v Revenue & Customs* [2009] UKSPC 741 at para 56.
4 *Genovese v Revenue & Customs* [2009] UKSPC 741 at para 55.

4.10   HMRC6

The subsequent HMRC interpretation of ordinary residence in HMRC6 is fundamentally different from its predecessor. As with residence *simpliciter*, the subject is explained in part in the Glossary which reads:

'Ordinarily Resident/Ordinary Residence

"Ordinary residence" is different from "residence". It is not defined in tax law and our guidance is based on cases heard by the Courts. For example, if you are resident in the UK year after year, this would indicate that you "normally" live here and you are therefore "ordinarily resident" here.

If you are resident here your ordinary residence position in the UK generally matters only if you have income from outside the UK. Income from outside the UK can include earnings for duties performed outside the UK.

Resident but not Ordinarily Resident

You can be resident in the UK but not ordinarily resident here. When we talk about someone being "not ordinarily resident in the UK" we mean that although they are resident in the UK for a particular tax year, they normally live somewhere else. For example, if you are resident in a tax year because you have been in the country for more than 183 days but you normally live outside the UK, it is likely that you are not ordinarily resident.'[1]

As is the case with the glossary explanation in respect of residence, it is difficult to extract a precise meaning from this description. The meaning of the expression is left to part 3 of the document. The discussion in part 3 now reflects, in part, the legal position, interspersed with elements that reflect the practice previously found in IR20. The subject is introduced as follows:

'**What does Ordinary Residence mean?**

Ordinary residence is different from "residence". The word "ordinary" indicates that your residence in the UK is typical for you and not casual. It is important not to confuse ordinary residence with domicile (see part 4).

If you have always lived in the UK then you are ordinarily resident here.

When you come to the UK you do not have to intend to remain in the UK permanently or indefinitely in order to be ordinarily resident here. It is enough that your residence has all the following attributes.

- Your presence here has a settled purpose. This might be for only a limited period, but has enough continuity to be properly described as settled. Business, employment and family all provide a settled purpose, but this list is not exhaustive.
- Your presence in the UK forms part of the regular and habitual mode of your life for the time being. This pattern can include temporary absences from the UK. If you come to live and work in the UK for three years or more then you will have established a regular and habitual mode of life here from the start.
- You have come to the UK voluntarily. The fact that you chose to come to the UK at the request of your employer rather than seek another job does not make your presence here involuntary.'[2]

These comments loosely follow the exposition of Lord Scarman in *Shah*.[3] Paragraph 3.2 continues:

'The pattern of your presence, both here in the UK and overseas, is an important factor when you are deciding if you are ordinarily resident in the UK. You will also need to take into account your reasons for being in, coming to, or leaving the UK and your lifestyle and habits. Parts 7 and 8 will help you with this, as they explain the considerations for those coming to and departing from the UK.

You can be ordinarily resident in the UK and, at the same time, be ordinarily resident in another country.

It is possible to be resident in the UK and be not ordinarily resident here. This means that although you are resident in the UK during a tax year, your residence does not have one or more of the factors that would make you ordinarily resident.

It is also possible (but unusual) to be not resident in the UK but remain ordinarily resident here. If you normally live in the UK you might become not resident solely for one tax year. As you would usually be resident in the UK and this is where you have your normal home, family ties and other social connections, you might still be ordinarily resident here.'[4]

Although the assertion that an individual may be ordinarily resident in the UK but not resident was dropped in the glossary contained in the 2011 version of HMRC6, this is still claimed in Part 3 in relation to capital gains.[5] This places HMRC in the camp of those who view it tentatively as possible (but rare) to be not resident but ordinarily resident in the UK. HMRC now suggest (rather than mandate) the counting of days to determine ordinary residence. How this helps an individual who is resident to decide whether that status also has the attributes to confer ordinary residential status is far from clear. The same day counting is used as benchmark of residence *simpliciter*[6] and just as the number of years alone are insufficient to convert residence to ordinary residence, so too, the number of days spent visiting are insufficient. An important departure from IR20 in this part of HMRC6 is the removal of references to matters of 'intention' and what the individual 'decides' that Special Commissioner Clark found inconsistent with the common law position in *Genovese*.[7] They are however repeated in HMRC6, Part 7. The three-year test to determine if residence is regular and habitual which is unsupported by law and owes its origin to IR20 para 3.8 has likewise disappeared from the definition in Part 3 but is retained in Part 7 which reads:

'**7.7.4 Ordinary Residence – the years after you arrive**

You will become ordinarily resident in a tax year after the year of your arrival if:

- you have been here for three years from the date of your arrival, even though you did not originally intend to stay and have not bought or acquired accommodation on a lease of three years or more – you will become ordinarily resident in the UK from the beginning of the tax year in which the third anniversary of your arrival falls – see example 1 at 7.8, or
- you decide, after you arrive, to stay in the UK for three years or more from the date of your arrival – you will become ordinarily resident in the UK from the beginning of the tax year in which you make that decision. If you make that decision after you arrived but still in the year of arrival, you will be ordinarily resident from the day you arrived in the UK – see example 2 at 7.8, or
- you buy or acquire accommodation on a lease of three years or more – You will become ordinarily resident from 6 April in the tax year in which you bought or leased the accommodation. If the only reason for you becoming ordinarily resident is because you have accommodation here, then as long as you dispose of the accommodation and leave the UK within three years of your arrival, you will be not ordinarily resident – see example 3 at 7.8.'

Secondly, the statement in HMRC6 para 7 appears to alter the former practice relating to residence of only short duration, which could work in the taxpayer's favour by resulting in the non-attribution of ordinary residence status in certain instances where such attribution is due in law. Residence *simpliciter* in only a single tax year will also, in law, take on the character of ordinary residence if the three judicially prescribed conditions are met.[8] Paragraph 7.7.4 appears to retain the earlier view.

The effect of the existence or otherwise of available accommodation in determining whether an individual is in the UK for some temporary purpose and not with a view to or intent of establishing his residence here will be considered at **5.06** below. While ITA 2007 ss 831 and 832 altered the law in respect of residence *simpliciter* for those purposes, the presence or otherwise of available accommodation can still be relevant in assisting in determining whether an individual is generally ordinarily resident in the UK or not. In cases where the individual is in the UK for a purpose that is more than temporary, this may be a somewhat academic exercise. If it is possible for an individual to be not resident but nonetheless ordinarily resident in the UK, then the question will not be theoretical.

The description includes a reiteration of the HMRC view on dual ordinary residence:

> 'You can be ordinarily resident in the UK and, at the same time, be ordinarily resident in another country. Your ordinary residence in another country does not prevent you being ordinarily resident in the UK.'

---

1 HMRC6 para 12.15.
2 HMRC6 para 3.2.
3 *R v Barnett LBC, ex parte Shah* [1983] 2 AC 309 at p 236.
4 HMRC6 para 3.1. See also HM Treasury and HM Revenue & Customs, *Statutory definition of tax residence: a consultation* (17 June 2011), para 6.6.
5 See **4.05** above.
6 See **5.12** below and the examples in HMRC6.
7 See **4.09** above.
8 See IR20 (December 2010) paras 3.4, 3.5 and 3.7.

4.11   National Insurance Contributions

HMRC take the view that ordinary residence does not have the same meaning for National Insurance Contributions as it does for income tax and capital gains tax.[1] Their position on the meaning of the expression for National Insurance purposes is as follows:

'Ordinarily residence

You are ordinarily resident in a particular country if you:

- normally live there, apart from temporary or occasional absences, and
- have a settled and regular mode of life there.

You may be ordinarily resident in:

- a place from which you are temporarily absent, or
- two places at once, in some circumstances.'[2]

While in HMRC6 the focus is on individuals coming to or visiting the UK, the focus in NI38 is on individuals leaving the UK. Their position is:

'When you go abroad, there are a number of factors which are considered in deciding whether or not you are ordinarily resident in the UK. For example:

Factor	Indication that you are
You return to the UK from time to time during the period of employment abroad.	Continued ordinarily resident. The more frequent or the longer the returns, the stronger the indication that you are.
Visits to your family who have remained at your home in the UK, or holidays spent at your home in the UK.	Ordinarily resident.
Visits in connection with the overseas work, eg for briefing or training or to make a report.	Not such a strong indication that you are ordinarily resident.
Partner and/or children are with you during your overseas employment.	Not ordinarily resident, especially, if you do not retain a home in the UK or only make occasional visits to the UK.
You maintain a home in the UK during your absence.	Ordinarily resident.
You have lived in the UK for a substantial period.	The longer the period, the stronger the indication that you are despite the period of employment abroad.
You will return to the UK at the end of your employment abroad.	The earlier the return, the stronger the indication that you are.'[3]

1 HMRC6 (March 2009) side note to IR20 (July 2008) para 11 states: 'The terms "resident" and "ordinarily resident" do not have the same meaning for NICs as they do for tax and so the tax rules on residence and ordinarily residence set out in parts 2 and 3 of this guidance are not relevant to NICs. Leaflet NI38 Social Security abroad gives guidance on the rules on residence and ordinarily residence which apply for National Insurance purposes.'
2 Leaflet NI38, p 11.
3 HMRC Booklet NI 38 March 2008, p 12.

4.12 Abolition of ordinary residence for income tax and capital gains tax: transitional measures

The government announced at Budget 2012 its decision to abolish the concept of ordinary residence for tax purposes generally from 6 April 2013[1] as a major simplification of the tax system. Specific statutory regimes will be enacted to replace the existing overseas work-day relief for employees who are not UK domiciled and resident but not ordinarily resident under ITEPA 2003 ss 22–24 and for the Seafarers Earnings Deduction under ITEPA 2003 Pt 5, Ch 6.

In addition, the government does not wish to change the law and the existing reference to ordinary residence will remain in place for:

- eligibility for blind person's allowance which is linked to ordinary residence in Scotland or Northern Ireland rather than in the UK under ITA 2007 s 38;
- exemption condition under ITTOIA 2005 s 693 for income from Ulster Savings Certificates which is linked to ordinary residence in Northern Ireland; and
- certification of diplomatic exemption which is linked to ordinary residence outside the UK under ITA 2007 s 841.[2]

Transitional provisions will allow individuals who are not ordinarily resident at the end of the 2012–13 tax year to continue to benefit for a maximum of two tax years thereafter as long as they would have continued to qualify for the tax treatment in question under the existing rules. These apply to the remittance basis,[3] overseas workday relief, transfer of assets abroad, Seafarers Earnings Deduction and foreign service relief.[4]

The government does not think transitional provisions are needed for any other tax provisions linked to ordinary residence, but has invited comments on whether any of the consequential changes have a disproportionate impact on particular individuals, allowing for the fact that there will be transitional grandfathering provisions, and whether transitional provisions are needed for any other places where ordinary residence influences tax liability.[5]

---

1 Schedule 46, paras 24, 70 and 111.
2 HM Treasury and HM Revenue & Customs, *Statutory definition of tax residence and reform of ordinary residence: a summary of responses* (June 2012) (the 'Second Consultative Document'), para 4.9.
3 Schedule 46, para 25.
4 Schedule 46, para 71.
5 Second Consultative Document, para 4.12.

CHAPTER 5

Individuals coming to and departing from the UK

They sailed away for a year and a day,
To the land where the Bong-tree grows.

Edward Lear *The Owl and the Pussy-Cat*

5.01 Introduction

The introduction of the statutory residence test and the statutory regime for split-year treatment from 6 April 2013 by FA 2013 Sch 45, makes this chapter, in conjunction with Chapter 3, relevant from that date in deciding whether individuals are resident in a particular year by reference to their residential status in the preceding three years. It describes the law and HMRC practice prior to that date. It is therefore necessary to consider this chapter along with Chapter 3 in deciding whether to make the election provided in FA 2013 Sch 45, para 153, in order to compare their status in the years 2010–11, 2011–12 and 2012–13 for the purpose of applying the statutory residence test. See **2.01**.

The discussion in Chapter 3 of the meaning given by the courts to the jurisdictional connection of residence status as it applies to individuals was modified by limited, but important, statutory provisions which imposed certain overriding tests and rules. The statutory provisions were themselves a patchwork and developed over time. Furthermore, HMRC had adopted certain extra-statutory concessions in areas where there were obvious shortcomings in the legal position and whose impact was significant on mobile individuals. While it is a self-evident proposition that an individual who never leaves the UK is always resident and ordinarily resident and that an individual who never comes to the UK is never resident or ordinarily resident, it is the degree and nature of movement between those extremes that may give rise to a change in status that form the subject matter of these chapters.

5.02   Split tax years

As has been repeatedly noted, the Taxes Acts did not recognise that a person may be resident in the UK for part of a tax year and non-resident for the balance. The consequence of this extraordinarily blinkered view was that, for example, a person leaving the UK on 7 April and returning on the following 4 April was nonetheless resident for the whole of the tax year running from 6 April to the following 5 April.[1]

There had been no inclination to allow taxpayers moving to or from the UK to divide a tax year between periods of non-residence by statute. Instead, the Revenue allowed this split by concession in the case of individuals. This concessionary treatment was unique among concessions in that provision is made for claiming this treatment appears on the individual's self-assessment form.[2] Separate concessions applied for income tax[3] and capital gains tax[4] and the conditions for their application were not identical. Neither treated the individual as non-resident for all purposes during the relevant part of the tax year. Furthermore, the concessionary treatment described in the two ESCs was not addressed in HMRC6.

One of the challenges in this area is to decide when exactly an individual becomes resident. The ease of modern travel and communication mean that individuals may arrive and depart physically several times in the course of moving from one country to another. In *Kimber v HMRC*,[5] the taxpayer who had previously lived in Japan disposed of shares on 12 August 2005. Was he UK resident on that date? It was agreed that he was non-UK resident between the years 1989 and 1994 and also from 17 September 1997 until at least 17 July 2005. He was in the UK between 17 and 30 July 2005, for the regular holiday he and family had taken during all the years when he had been non-resident. During that period the family stayed in Kent with his mother. On 30 July, he and his family then flew to Italy for a four-week holiday booked months before, when he had been living in Japan. On 28 August, he and his family returned to the UK from Italy, and it was accepted that from that date onwards he was UK-resident.

When Mr Kimber arrived in the UK, it remained a distinct possibility, or indeed even the greater likelihood, that he would sign up to work in Hong Kong. While on holiday he met with another prospective employer and before leaving the UK on 30 July, signed an agreement to work for them in the UK from September. While on holiday he found a property available to rent on a furnished basis in Norfolk near to where his children were to start school as arranged while he was living in Japan. The lease was to commence on 1 September 2005. Although it was unclear when he had signed it, a printed date at the bottom of the first page of the lease which contained the names and address in Kent of the appellant and wife, was 27 July 2005.

The First-tier Tribunal decided that at some time before 30 July, even if not on 17 July, Mr Kimber formed the intention to stay in the UK permanently and then became resident.[6]

Alternatively, when he and his family arrived in the UK on 17 July, he was not coming to the UK for a temporary purpose, but knew that, with the interval of a pre-booked holiday in Italy apart, he and his family were returning to the UK, and very specifically to Norfolk.[7]

---

1 See a more extreme illustration in *Reviewing the residence and domicile rules as they affect the taxation of individuals: a background paper* (published jointly by HM Treasury and Inland Revenue in April 2003), Example 4.
2 See Non-resident etc pages box 9.3.
3 Extra-statutory Concession A11.
4 Extra-statutory Concession D2.
5 [2012] UKFTT 107 (TC).
6 At para 23.
7 At para 23.

5.03 Income Tax Act 2007

The Income Tax Act 2007 (ITA) became law from 5 April 2007. It is a product of the Tax Law Rewrite Project.[1] ITA 2007 rewrites, and in some cases repeals, various provisions covering most of the rules relating to income tax which were not dealt with by the project's two previous Acts: the Income Tax (Earnings and Pensions) Act 2003 (ITEPA) and the Income Tax (Trading and Other Income) Act 2005 (ITTOIA). The rules regarding residence are contained in ITA 2007 Pt 14 Ch 2.[2] The rewritten legislation continues to adopt separate rules for employment and other income.

Although the project is intended to produce a restatement of existing law, acknowledged changes have been made. Thus, the reference in ICTA 1988 s 336 (Persons arriving in the UK) and to 'six months' in s 336 is replaced by a reference to '183 days' in the successor provisions (ITA 2007 ss 831 and 832).[3] ICTA 1988 s 334 (Persons leaving the UK) is replaced by ITA 2007 s 829. This new section expands the scope of the rule beyond Commonwealth and Irish citizens who were the only subjects of the predecessor rules in ICTA 1988 s 334.[4] Additionally, the rewrite project did not succeed in producing provisions entirely consistent with each other in the language used. This was tidied up by Finance Act 2008 s 24 but differences remain. Despite the changes, much of the case law pertaining to the previous, now repealed legislation is still likely to be relevant in the construction and application of the new sections, although, as will be apparent from the following discussion, the analysis is not always clear or convincing. They do not form a complete code and the relationship between them is opaque.

---

1 See **1.20** above.
2 Section 829 – Residence of individuals temporarily abroad; s 830 – Residence of individuals working abroad; s 831 – Foreign income of individuals in the UK for temporary purpose; s 832 – Employment income of individuals in the UK for temporary purpose; s 832 – Employment income of individuals in the UK for temporary purpose and s 833 – Visiting forces and staff of designated allied headquarters.
3 Rewrite: Explanatory Notes, Annex 1, Change 124.
4 Rewrite: Explanatory Notes, Annex 1, Change 123.

Individuals coming to the UK

5.04 Deemed residence or non-residence

In 1889, Sir E Clarke who was at that time the Solicitor General had the task of replying to a clearly astonished and disbelieving Lord Chancellor (Halsbury, no less) who had asked him:

> 'Do you contend that a subject of a foreign state residing here, carrying on a business abroad from which profits are derived, but not one farthing of which is earned in this country or ever comes here, is liable to pay Income Tax thereon in consequence of simply residing here?'

His answer was:

> 'Yes, subject to this limitation: he must be residing here; he must not be here merely for a temporary purpose. If he is residing here there is no hardship. Persons residing here and enjoying the protection of the laws of this country ought to bear its burdens.'[1]

It was perhaps just such sentiment that guided Parliament when it included in the taxing statutes the predecessors of ITA 2007 ss 831 and 832. The provisions date back at least to the Income Tax Act 1842. The function of this rule is to keep out of the income tax net the foreign income of any genuine short-term visitor who might otherwise find himself attributed with the quality of residence in the UK by reason of his visits here or other factors. TCGA 1992 s 9(3) which, on the face of it, has, in part, similar objectives with regards to capital gains tax presents special difficulties and is discussed at **5.11** and **5.12** below.

Separate provisions apply to employment income[2] and other income from other sources[3] but are now identical (except for the wording in italics). ITA 2007 s 831(1)[4] reads:

> 'Subsection (2) applies in relation to an individual if–
>
> (a) the individual is in the United Kingdom for some temporary purpose only and with no *view to* establishing the individual's residence in the United Kingdom, and
> (b) during the tax year in question the individual spends (in total) less than 183 days in the United Kingdom.
>
> In determining whether an individual is within paragraph (a) ignore any living accommodation available in the United Kingdom for the individual's use.'

If both (a) and (b) are satisfied, the individual's liability to income tax is determined according to ITA 2007 s 831(2) by treating the individual generally as non-UK resident. If (a) is satisfied but (b) is not, then the individual is treated as resident for s 831 purposes.

In relation to employment income section 832(1) reads:

'Subsection (2) applies in relation to an individual if–

(a)   the individual is in the United Kingdom for some temporary purpose only and with no *intention of* establishing the individual's residence in the United Kingdom, and

(b)   during the tax year in question the individual spends (in total) less than 183 days in the United Kingdom.

In determining whether an individual is within paragraph (a) ignore any living accommodation available in the UK for the individual's use.'

Similarly, if both (a) and (b) are satisfied, the individual's liability to income tax is determined according to ITA 2007 s 832(2) by treating the individual as non-UK resident. If (a) is satisfied but (b) is not, then the individual is treated as resident for s 832 purposes.

The benefit of s 832 is extended by concession to determine the status of an individual accompanying or later joining a spouse who goes abroad for full-time employment.[5] Special rules contained in TCGA 1992 s 11 and ITA 2007 s 833 for visiting forces and civilians employed by them as well as NATO and other allied headquarters personnel allow such individuals to retain their non-resident status.

Individuals who spend 183 days or more in the UK are dealt with in the legislation as follows:

'831(4) Subsection (5) applies in relation to an individual if subsection (2) would have applied in relation to the individual but for subsection (1)(b).

(5) Apply the rules set out in subsection (2) in determining the individual's liability for income tax.

But–

(a)   instead of treating the individual as non-UK resident in relation to the income and for the purposes mentioned in those rules, treat the individual as UK resident ...'[6]

By this obscure language, an individual who has no view or intent to establish their residence in the UK, but who spends 183 days or more in the UK during a tax year, is deemed to be resident in the UK. Since an individual in the UK for that period who does intend to establish residence will probably have met the case law criteria discussed in Chapter 3, most cases of presence for that period will result in UK residence in any event. The inflexibility of the rule and its potentially harsh effect is demonstrated by *Ogden v Revenue & Customs,*[7] where the taxpayer had been a Jersey resident since 1988. In early 2002 his son, who was seriously ill, was admitted to Papworth Hospital in Cambridge for a heart and lung transplant which was the only option for his survival. In August 2002, when his son's health became of great concern, Mr Ogden took leave from his employer to be with his son at the hospital. His son died on 13 October 2002 and when he returned to work he was fired from his job for no apparent reason. As a result Mr Ogden spent more than 183 days in the UK in 2002–03. The duties in the UK for which he was remunerated fell far short of what his normal duties would have been had his son not been so seriously ill. The First-tier Tribunal found he was deemed resident in the UK. The application of these provisions where individuals spend less than 183 days has not been uncontentious either. The precise relationship between these provisions and the case law criteria in Chapter 3 remains unresolved. At the re-hearing of *Grace* before the First-tier Tribunal, the parties were agreed that the effect of the statute was to override the common law in certain cases and allow a resident person to be subject to tax as if he was non-resident.[8]

---

1 *Colquhoun v Brooks* (1889) 2 TC 490 at 492.
2 Section 831(1).
3 Section 831(1).
4 See **5.03** above.
5 Extra-statutory Concession A 78.
6 ITA 2007 s 831(4) and (5). Section 832(3) and (4) are to the same effect in relation to employment income.
7 *Ogden v Revenue & Customs* [2011] UKFTT 212 (TC).
8 *Grace v Revenue & Customs* [2011] UKFTT 36 (TC) at para 8.

5.05 Temporary purpose

The expression 'temporary purpose' in ITA 2007 s 831(1)(a) and its predecessors is not without difficulty as is illustrated by the case of Mr Cadwalader, an American citizen, who was ordinarily resident in New York but who rented a house and shooting rights in Scotland and there spent some two months of each year. Was visiting Scotland each year for the shooting season a temporary purpose? The Commissioners seem to have been of the opinion that it was for they found against the Crown. The Court of Exchequer, however, reversed their decision. Lord McLaren said:

> 'I don't think that Mr Cadwalader is in a position to affirm, when he comes year after year during the currency of his lease to spend the shooting season in Scotland, that he is here for a temporary purpose only. I don't mean that you might not frame a definition which would bring this within the scope of temporary purposes, but taking the ordinary meaning of the word, I should say that temporary purposes means casual purposes as distinguished from the case of a person who is here in the pursuance of his regular habits of life … [The word] "temporary" … means that it is casual or transitory residence, as distinguished from a residence, of which there may be more than one, but which may be habitual or permanent.'[1]

In the previous chapter, we saw that a purpose which results in a person becoming present in the UK as part of the regular order of his life is properly describable as a 'settled purpose'.[2] What Lord McLaren is saying, therefore (in the current vocabulary of the law of residence), is that the terms 'settled purpose' and 'temporary purpose' are mutually exclusive and that for a purpose to be a temporary purpose it must be a non-settled purpose (ie a purpose which, if it brings a person to the UK, does so only in deviation from the regular order of his life).

The Inland Revenue was quick to take up Lord McLaren's definition and, over the years following the *Cadwalader* case, the Crown's rejection of many an individual's claim to exemption was based on a contention that the person 'was in this country in pursuance of his regular habits of life and therefore not "for some temporary purpose only"'. Thus it was in the case of Mr Zorab.[3]

Mr Zorab was a native of India who had lived there all his life and held office in the Indian Civil Service. In May 1920, however, he left India on two years' furlough at the end of which he intended to (and did) retire from the Indian Civil Service. In 1920–21 he spent a little over five months in the UK, just short of six months in 1921–22, 1922–23 and 1923–24, and a little short of five months in 1924–25. The remainder of each year he spent in Paris or Belgium. He had no business interests in the UK and his visits here were made solely with the object of seeing his friends. The Crown contended that Mr Zorab's visits were not 'for some temporary purpose only' within the meaning of rule 2 of the Miscellaneous Rules of Schedule D but that he was 'in this country in pursuance of his regular habits of life'. The Commissioners found against the Crown, however, and Rowlatt J upheld their decision. Contrasting the case of Mr Zorab with that of someone who, when absent from the UK, has links here which perpetuate and particularise his attachment to the UK (a house, a bank account, stored furniture and the like),[4] he said of Mr Zorab:

'This gentleman seems to be a mere traveller .... He is a native of India, he has retired from his work there and he really travels in Europe. All that can be said about it is that in the course of his habitual travels he spends a considerable period every year in England.'[5]

This judgment reinforces what has been said earlier,[6] namely, that mere recurrence of visits is by no means conclusive proof of the existence of a settled purpose. A person may visit the UK in each of a succession of years and yet each visit may (to use Lord McLaren's words in the *Cadwalader* case) be only 'casual or transitory' and possess a temporary character. Indeed, Viscount Cave LC argued in his dissenting speech in *Lysaght v IRC*[7] that although Mr Lysaght made monthly visits from Ireland to England for the purpose of attending directors' meetings and stayed for about one week on each occasion, that did not make his visits 'more than temporary visits or give them the character of residence in this country'.[8] In this respect he endorsed Sargant LJ who, in the Court of Appeal below, said the purpose of the taxpayer in the UK (as an advisory director of an English company) 'could fairly be described as "temporary" notwithstanding that it was of a regularly recurrent character'.[9]

In *Gaines-Cooper v Revenue & Customs Comrs*[10] the Special Commissioners held that what is now s 831 did not apply because a decision to visit the UK on a large number of days each year to be with one's wife and child was not a 'temporary purpose'. The Special Commissioner expressed the rule as follows:

'We conclude that a temporary purpose is a purpose lasting for a limited time; a purpose existing or valid for a time; a purpose which is not permanent but transient; a purpose which is to supply a passing need. "Temporary purpose" means a casual purpose as distinguished from the case of a person who is here in pursuance of his regular habits of life. Temporary purpose means the opposite of continuous purpose. A decision to visit the United Kingdom for a few months each year to shoot (ignoring the availability of living accommodation) is not a temporary purpose (*Cadwalader*).'[11]

The Special Commissioner also rejected the general proposition that because a visit is short it must necessarily be for a temporary purpose, dismissing the views of Viscount Cave described above without analysis as a dissenting opinion that did not establish any binding principle. In the author's view, neither of these statements meet the exposition of Lord McLaren in *Cadwalader* cited above.

In *Grace v Revenue & Customs*[12] Special Commissioner Dr Brice said that Mr Grace 'only visited the United Kingdom because his long-haul flights started and ended there',[13] that his residence in Cape Town was punctuated 'only by the need to visit the United Kingdom for the purposes of his work'[14] and consequently his presence was 'for temporary and occasional purposes only'.[15] On appeal to the High Court[16] in overturning the ruling of the Special Commissioner, Lewison J held that

'[W]hat is important is that the adjective "temporary" in section [831] is not descriptive of the taxpayer's presence. That is dealt with by the deeming provision which requires the aggregation of the time spent in the UK during the year of assessment. Rather, the adjective "temporary" is descriptive of the taxpayer's purpose: that is to say the reason why he is in the United Kingdom.'[17]

Mr Grace, he said, would continue to be present in the UK to fulfil those duties in subsequent years, unless and until he changed jobs or retired. On this basis, Lewison J ruled that presence in the UK in order to fulfil duties under a permanent (or at least indefinite) contract of employment cannot be described as casual or transitory.[18]

For the purposes of whether a person is in the UK for a temporary purpose and not with any view or intent of establishing residence here, the question whether the person has available accommodation here must be disregarded.[19]

The Court of Appeal agreed that the section did not relieve Mr Grace from UK residence. The statutory rule was only in issue before the Court of Appeal, however, in the sense that the Special Commissioner was said to have misdirected herself in applying the non-statutory tests of residence by the way in which she had applied what is now s 831.[20]

The long-standing practice of HMRC is to disregard days spent in the UK because of exceptional circumstances beyond the individual's control as long as days spent in the UK are less than 183 days.[21] Specific foreign political emergencies have been recognised. Recent examples include unrest in the Middle East and North Africa where individuals were evacuated to the UK in 2010. Similarly, additional days spent in the UK purely because of the closing of the skies caused by volcanic ash from Iceland in 2010 may be disregarded. Although no legal basis for the practice is specified, it would appear to be recognition of the application of the temporary purpose principle in ITA 2007 s 831 to each individual period of presence separately.

1 *Cooper v Cadwalader* (1904) 5 TC 101 at 109.
2 See **4.05** and **4.06** above.
3 *IRC v Zorab* (1926) 11 TC 289.
4 See Ch 2 above.
5 *IRC v Zorab* (1926) 11 TC 289 at 292.
6 See **4.05** above.
7 *Lysaght v IRC* (1928) 13 TC 511. Viscount Sumner, on the other hand, saw Mr Lysaght's commitment to monthly attendance at directors' meetings in the UK as a settled purpose (a term which Viscount Sumner coined in the *Lysaght* case) and, accordingly, he held that Mr Lysaght's visits to the UK were precluded from possessing the temporary character which might have brought them within the scope of what is now ITA 2007 s 831(1).
8 *Lysaght v IRC* (1928) 13 TC 511 at 532.
9 *Lysaght v IRC* (1928) 13 TC 511 at 521.
10 *Gaines-Cooper v Revenue & Customs Comrs* [2007] UKSPC 568.
11 At para 178.
12 *Grace v Revenue & Customs* [2008] UKSPC SPC 663.
13 *Grace v Revenue & Customs* [2008] UKSPC SPC 663 at para 37.
14 *Grace v Revenue & Customs* [2008] UKSPC SPC 663 at para 54.
15 *Grace v Revenue & Customs* [2008] UKSPC SPC 663 at para 58.
16 *Grace v Revenue & Customs Commissioners* [2008] EWHC 2708 (Ch).
17 *Grace v Revenue & Customs Commissioners* [2008] EWHC 2708 (Ch) at para 16.
18 *Grace v Revenue & Customs Commissioners* [2008] EWHC 2708 (Ch) at para 16.
19 ITA 2007 s 831(1); **5.07** below.
20 *Grace v Revenue & Customs Commissioners* [2009] EWCA Civ 1082.
21 See, eg IR20 (2008) paras 2.2 and 2.8, HMRC 6 (2010) para 2.2.

5.06   View or intent of establishing residence

If the expression 'temporary' discussed in **5.05** encompasses only the most casual of purposes, then it is modified by the additional requirement that the individual has no view or intention (depending on whether s 831 or s 832 is in issue) of establishing their residence in the UK. This was viewed by Lord McLaren in *Cadwalader* as giving rise to two separate elements which he explained thus:

> 'Now, the exemption is one that walks upon two legs. It is, first, that the party is not here for a temporary purpose only; and secondly, that he is here not with a view or intent of establishing a residence. If the argument is lame on one of the legs, then the party does not get the benefit of the exemption, because he must be able to affirm both members of the double proposition.'[1]

However Lord McLaren himself observed the conceptual link later on in his judgment when he said: 'Temporary purpose means the opposite of continuous and permanent residence.'[2]

This bifurcated approach is not without its difficulties and while breaking a provision down into its constituent elements is often an aid to comprehension, the conceptual link between the purpose of the presence and the view or intent to establish residence is inescapable. Some of the difficulty in separating the two is apparent from the judgment of Lord McLaren himself in construing the second limb independently, when said of the phrase:

> 'There might, I think, be a possible room for difference of opinion as to the meaning of the words "view or intent of establishing a residence". The words are somewhat

vague, but they seem to me to recognise what may be called a constructive residence as distinguished from actual residence.'[3]

In the case of Mr Cadwalader, this meant leasing a furnished house which, though he actually occupied it for only two months in each year, was maintained for him and placed at his disposal so that he was able to occupy it whenever he chose. In Lord McLaren's view, the essence of constructive residence was held to be that a person 'has a residence always ready for him if he should choose to come to it',[4] not that when in the UK he necessarily ever does set foot there. As Lord McLaren has said:

'If you are looking forward to it … that makes you liable to taxation, because in order to get the benefit of the exemption you must say that you have no view and no intention of acquiring a residence there.'[5]

Lord McLaren was there using the term 'looking forward' not in its modern sense of 'anticipating with pleasure' but in its plain sense of seeing oneself in occupation of the dwelling place in question at some future time. In ITA 2007 s 831 and its predecessors, the 'view or intent of establishing … residence' is not necessarily a view or intent in relation to the particular visit in question. The Lord President expressed the point thus:

'I do not think that the Appellant can reasonably maintain that he is in the United Kingdom "for some temporary purpose only, and not with any view or intent of establishing his residence therein," in the sense of the section, as he took Millden with the view of establishing his residence there during a material part of each year and maintaining his connection with it as tenant during the rest of the years, and he has a residence always ready for him if he should choose to come to it.'[6]

Likewise, a century before *Cadwalader*, in *A-G v Coote*[7] the court had to decide whether Sir C H Coote, who was domiciled in Ireland and spent most of his time there but visited a furnished house which he owned in Connaught Place, London, for a few weeks each year, fell within the excepting provisions of ITA 1806 s 51. It was held that:

'The fact of the defendant's domicile has nothing to do with the question, nor has the time of his residence any effect on the construction of the words of the Act; for if the defendant came here for the purpose of establishing a residence it were enough, although he should reside here only two weeks.'[8]

As Baron Graham made clear, the availability of the accommodation was the all-important fact, not the actual duration of Sir C H Coote's stay in it:

'At any period of the year he might have come to Connaught Place, where he would have found his house ready for him,'[9]

These early cases focus on the particular premises that the individuals acquired and the proprietary dimension of residence. However, residence in this sense is a reference to the personal attributes discussed in Chapter 3 rather than the physical place of abode. Even if the approach was correct at the time, it is no longer the case from 1993–94 in light of the exclusion of the availability of accommodation for the purposes of ITA 2007 ss 831(1) and 832(1).[10] This second meaning of residence as a personal attribute has been applied by the Special Commissioners in recent decisions without analysis.[11]

A more difficult question arises as to when the provisions may be invoked. In *Shepherd v Revenue & Customs Commissioners,*[12] Lewison J said that:

'It is true that the phrase "Not with the intention of establishing his residence" seems to presuppose that the taxpayer has no residence in the United Kingdom, since if a taxpayer already has a residence in the United Kingdom, he can hardly be said to be here with the intention of establishing one. Whatever the difficulties of construction may be about that particular limb, they do not, in my view, arise in the present case.'[13]

However, he later acknowledged that it is not correct to simply say that the provisions apply when a person who is not resident makes occasional visits to the UK,[14] but nonetheless upheld the conclusion of the Special Commissioner that:

'[L]eaving aside the availability of living accommodation, all the relevant factors mentioned above point to the conclusion that after October 1998 the appellant was not in the United Kingdom for temporary purposes only. He was here in order to continue to carry out the duties of his permanent employment; to visit the Boat Show and to celebrate the Millennium; to enjoy other periods here, and to stay with his family and no doubt visit his friends. He had already established his residence here. Thus, in my view, s [831] does not apply to the appellant.'[15]

In *Grace v Revenue & Customs Commissioners,*[16] the same learned judge acknowledged that[17] '[S]ection [831] provides an exemption for a taxpayer if he would otherwise be held to be resident in the United Kingdom.' This time, there was no discussion about any view or intent to establish residence. He continued:

'Thus even if (contrary to the Special Commissioner's decision) Mr Grace cannot take advantage of section [831], HMRC would still have to establish that he was resident in the United Kingdom on common law grounds (or by virtue of section [829]) …. If a person is in the United Kingdom for a temporary purpose, then section [831] operates as a deeming provision. If he has not spent six months in aggregate in the United Kingdom he must be treated as non-resident. Conversely if he has spent six months here then he must be treated as resident. Accordingly if Mr Grace was not here for some temporary purpose, then the deeming provision would not come into play and section [831] would not apply to him at all.'[18]

The question of intent was considered by the Special Commissioners in *Gaines-Cooper v HMRC*[19] but again without a real attempt to delve into its meaning. Special Commissioners Brice and Hellier ruled that:

'The second cumulative requirement in section [831(1)(a)] is the absence of an intention on the part of the taxpayer to establish his residence in the United Kingdom …. We are … of the view that the Appellant had no subjective intention of establishing his residence here for the purposes of the Taxes Acts and would have done quite a lot to ensure that residence with that meaning was not established but that does not mean that objectively he was not resident here.

Because the requirements of a temporary purpose and no intention to establish residence are cumulative and not alternative, and as we have found that the Appellant was not here for a temporary purpose, we conclude that the exemption in section [831(2)] does not apply to the Appellant.'[20]

In, most cases, as with *Grace*, attention has been given to temporary purpose only. In the author's view, the preferable construction is that a single composite test is intended whereby temporary purpose is qualified by the absence of a view or intent to establish residence. The class of visitor who qualifies for the exemption is made so narrow by the contrary view, that it is doubtful whether it really qualifies the ordinary meaning of the word resident. In *Gaines-Cooper*, the Special Commissioners rejected the general proposition that because a visit is short it must necessarily be for a temporary purpose.[21] Taken to its logical conclusion, an individual who comes to the UK every year for a few days, say to attend Glynbourne, would not benefit from these provisions but would be compelled to rely instead on the case law meaning examined in Chapter 3. On such an analysis, these provisions, despite the elaborate language, would merely restrict the case law meaning to individuals present for less than 183 days in a tax year. On the contrary, in the author's view, a short visit is, by its nature, evidence of a temporary purpose. It is only where short visits are so frequent, proximate to each other and extend over long time periods that a purpose beyond this may be indicated.

---

1 *Cooper v Cadwalader* (1904) 5 TC 101 at 108.
2 *Cooper v Cadwalader* (1904) 5 TC 101 at 109.
3 *Cooper v Cadwalader* (1904) 5 TC 101 at 109.
4 *Cooper v Cadwalader* (1904) 5 TC 101 at 106, per the Lord President.
5 *Cooper v Cadwalader* (1904) 5 TC 101 at 109, per Lord McLaren.
6 *Cooper v Cadwalader* (1904) 5 TC 101 at 106.
7 *A-G v Coote* (1817) 2 TC 385.
8 *A-G v Coote* (1817) 2 TC 385 at 385, per Richards CB.
9 *A-G v Coote* (1817) 2 TC 385.
10 See para **5.07** below.
11 See *Shepherd v Revenue & Customs* [2005] UKSPC 484 at para 70; *Gaines-Cooper v HMRC* [2006] UKSPC SPC568 at paras 182 and 183; *Grace v Revenue & Customs* [2008] UKSPC SPC663 at para 59.
12 *Shepherd v Revenue & Customs Commissioners* [2006] EWHC 1512 (Ch).
13 *Shepherd v Revenue & Customs Commissioners* [2006] EWHC 1512 (Ch) at para 15.
14 *Shepherd v Revenue & Customs Commissioners* [2006] EWHC 1512 (Ch) at para 18.
15 *Shepherd v Revenue & Customs Commissioners* [2006] EWHC 1512 (Ch) at para 19.
16 *Grace v Revenue & Customs Commissioners* [2008] EWHC 2708 (Ch).
17 *Grace v Revenue & Customs Commissioners* [2008] EWHC 2708 (Ch) at para 8.
18 *Grace v Revenue & Customs Commissioners* [2008] EWHC 2708 (Ch) at para 8.
19 *Gaines-Cooper v HMRC* [2006] UKSPC SPC568.
20 *Gaines-Cooper v HMRC* [2006] UKSPC SPC568 at paras 182 and 183.
21 *Gaines-Cooper v HMRC* [2006] UKSPC SPC568 at para 181.

5.07 Available accommodation

In determining whether an individual is in the UK for some temporary purpose only and with no *view to* establishing the individual's residence, any living accommodation available in the UK for the individual's use is to be ignored.

Prior to the introduction of the rule, the principle appeared to be that no one who has a place of residence in the UK, maintained and available for his use, can be free of a view or intent of establishing his residence in the UK. In 1926, Captain Loewenstein[1] noted that in both the *Coote* case and the *Cadwalader* case the persons attributed with a view or intent of establishing residence had proprietary interests in the dwelling houses concerned and he contended that unless there was such a proprietary interest the principle was of no application.

As has been noted at **3.09** above, Captain Loewenstein was a Belgian subject, resident in Brussels, who visited a property at Melton Mowbray in Leicestershire each year for the purpose of fox hunting. The property was a furnished hunting box called 'Pinfold' which was owned by The Belgian Breeding Stock Farm Company Ltd, a company in which Captain Loewenstein had a controlling interest and of which he was a director. In no year did he spend as many as six months in the UK and he claimed, therefore, that, on the basis of ITA 1918 Sch 1, rule 2 of the Miscellaneous Rules of Schedule D (now ITA 2007 s 831(1)), he was exempt from tax under Schedule D. Rowlatt J did not agree. Taking up the question of the application of rule 2, he said:

> 'It really comes to this, – whether it is of the essence of the case that a man should be treated under the Rule ... as coming here with a view to establishing his residence, and not for a temporary purpose only, that he should have at any rate a proprietary interest, such as a lease or something of that sort, in the house. I cannot see what difference that makes ... this man had this house at his disposal, with everything in it or for his convenience, kept going all the year round, although he only wanted it for a short time. Luckily, he was in relation with a Company who were the owners of it, and he could do that without owning it. It is an accident. It might well have been that he could do that with a relation, or a friend, or a philanthropist, or anybody; but in fact there was this house for him ... He has got this house to come to when he likes; he does not own it; he has got no proprietary interest in it, but it is just as good as if he had for the purpose of having it for a residence, and there it is.'[2]

The *Loewenstein* case therefore established that to have a place of abode in the UK at one's disposal *de facto* was sufficient, if a person set foot in the UK, to attribute that person with a view or intent of establishing residence here, whether the place of abode was *actually* occupied or not. The 'place of abode' test was pressed to its fullest extent by the Inland Revenue until the law was changed by FA 1993 s 208(1)(4), since when *Loewenstein* ceased to be applicable law. Depending upon the view taken of the precise function of ITA 2007 ss 831 and 832, it may more generally abolish the availability of living accommodation as an element in determining residence.

---

1 *Loewenstein v De Salis* (1926) 10 TC 424.
2 *Loewenstein v De Salis* (1926) 10 TC 424 at 437 and 438.

5.08 Actual presence

It may be noted that the 'physical presence' of 183 days' duration which will result in a visitor to the UK becoming attributed with residence status for the purposes of ITA 2007 ss 831 and 832 need not be on-shore physical presence. The UK consists of territorial land and territorial waters, and the territorial waters include both inland waters and the territorial sea. It was this fact which Mr Bayard Brown, an American citizen living on a yacht anchored in the tidal waters off Brightlingsea within the Port of Colchester, appears to have overlooked when he sought to avoid UK taxation. The yacht had, under the harbour-master's sufferance, been anchored off the Essex coast for some 20 years and though it had no lawful right to be there, the Court of Appeal recognised that, in point of fact, it *was* there and that Mr Bayard Brown was upon it 'for more than six months' in the year 1908–09. Accordingly, as the yacht was within the UK's territorial waters, 'in the body of the County of Essex', Mr Bayard was chargeable to income tax 'as a person residing in the UK'.[1]

---

1 *Bayard Brown v Burt* (1911) 5 TC 667.

5.09   Determining presence

The amount of time 'spent' in the UK determines the application of the statutory residence rules. As stated at **5.03** above, until 2007 the 'six-month test' as provided in ICTA 1988 s 336, applied continuously until it was replaced by ITA 2007 ss 831 and 832 as well as TCGA 1992 s 9(3) by the '183-day test'.

Donovan J, in the case of *Wilkie v IRC*[1] gave a judicial answer to the question of what was meant by 'six months'. Mr Wilkie had spent his working life in India but visited the UK when on leave every few years. At 2pm on 2 June 1947, he and his wife arrived in England by air for one such visit, intending to return to India not later than the end of November, but, unfortunately, Mr Wilkie had to undergo a medical operation in October and was not discharged from hospital until 10 November. Thereupon he booked a flight from Poole for 30 November – the earliest date on which a flight to India was available – but, on 14 November, those flight arrangements were cancelled by the airline and, in consequence, he was unable to actually leave the UK until 10am on 2 December 1947.

The Crown contended: (a) that a fraction of a day falls to be treated as a full day; and (b) that 'six months' means six lunar months of 28 days each. By Inland Revenue reckoning, therefore, Mr Wilkie had actually resided in the UK for 184 days and had fallen to be treated as resident (by reason of his actual residence for a period equal in the whole to six months in 1947–48) after 168 days.

Mr Wilkie, on the other hand, contended: (a) that fractions of a day fall to be taken account of as fractions; and (b) that 'six months' means six calendar months. By his reckoning, therefore, he had actually resided in the UK for 182 days and 20 hours and would not have fallen to be treated as resident (on the grounds of actual residence equal in the whole to six months in 1947–48) unless he had stayed in the UK for 183 days, ie until 2pm on 2 December, four hours after his actual time of departure.

Donovan J allowed Mr Wilkie's appeal, holding that, because under the Interpretation Act 1889 s 3, 'month' in all Acts passed since 1850 means calendar month unless a contrary intention appears, '"six months" … means six calendar months'[2] and that when computing the length of a person's stay in the UK,

'… there is nothing in the language of the Rule to prevent hours being taken into the computation; but that, on the other hand, since what has to be determined is the period of actual residence it is legitimate to do so.'[3]

Accordingly, in order to determine whether or not a person falls to be treated as resident under the six-month rule, one has simply to:

'… look at complete days of actual residence … and at the hours in the case of days when the Appellant was here for a part of the day and elsewhere for the rest; and then see whether or not it all adds up to the amount of time that there is in six months.'[4]

In a letter to the Consultative Committee of Accountancy Bodies dated 4 March 1983, the Inland Revenue commented that:

'The treatment for residence purposes, as outlined in paragraph 8 of Booklet IR20,[5] was adopted in 1972 following a review of our practice in the light of the decision in *Wilkie v IRC* (1952) 32 TC 495. That case established the principle that, in deciding whether a temporary visitor had actually resided in the UK for a period equal to six months, periods of time in terms of hours were relevant for days of less than total residence. In view of the difficulties which would arise in following the strict rule it was decided to regard 183 days as equal to six months and to disregard days of arrival and departure in making the count.'[6]

The boundary has been shifted to limit the time that an individual might spend in the UK without becoming resident by the Finance Act 2008. Measurement of days spent in the UK from 6 April 2008 is determined by detailed statutory rules added by FA 2008 s 24 amending ITA 2007 ss 831 and 832 as well as TCGA 1992 s 9 by the addition of the following:

'(1A) In determining whether an individual is within subsection (1)(b) treat a day as a day spent by the individual in the United Kingdom if (and only if) the individual is present in the United Kingdom at the end of the day.
(1B) But in determining that issue do not treat as a day spent by the individual in the United Kingdom any day on which the individual arrives in the United Kingdom as a passenger if—
(a) the individual departs from the United Kingdom on the next day, and
(b) during the time between arrival and departure the individual does not engage in activities that are to a substantial extent unrelated to the individual's passage through the United Kingdom.'

The changes to the legislation introduced in the clause are in respect of the 183-day test only. However, HMRC have stated that where their practice requires the use of day counting to determine residence for tax purposes, that practice will also be changed in line with the statutory amendment introduced in this clause. All day-counting tests, such as the non-statutory 91-day test, will follow the same principle that any day where the individual is in the UK at the end of the day will be included as a day of residence. The same exception from that general rule will apply where the individual is a passenger in transit and their activities whilst in the UK are not substantially unrelated to that travel.[7]

Whether an individual is present in the UK at the end of a day (presumably ending at midnight) is a straightforward question of fact. Individuals staying overnight and departing the next day will face detailed examination of minute and subtle fact relating to their presence as illustrated by HMRC examples.

Example 1

Peter works for the Jersey arm of HSBC and is travelling from Jersey to Frankfurt. He flies from Jersey to Gatwick and will catch his onward flight the next day to Frankfurt from London City airport. He travels from Gatwick to Canary Wharf for a meeting with several other HSBC colleagues before staying overnight in a nearby hotel. The meeting with colleagues is not an activity substantially related to completing travel to a foreign destination. The transit passenger provisions will not apply.

Example 2

John works for the Jersey arm of HSBC and is travelling from Jersey to Frankfurt via Gatwick and London City airport. In the lobby of his hotel near London City Airport, he unexpectedly spots another colleague who has just arrived from Paris. They have a couple of pints together and their conversation covers a number of business-related issues. Peter then travels to London City airport to catch his onward connection. This meeting was not planned and therefore it can be considered that John's activities in the UK substantially related to completing travel to a foreign destination. The transit passenger provisions will apply.

Example 3

Shirley lives in Guernsey and is travelling to New Zealand by way of Gatwick and Heathrow. She has planned to spend most of the day with her daughter and grandchildren, who live in Crawley and will also spend the night there before travelling to Heathrow for her onward flight. Her visit is not an activity substantially related to completing travel to a foreign destination. The transit passenger provisions will not apply.

Example 4

Phil lives in Guernsey and is travelling to New Zealand by way of Gatwick and Heathrow. His flight from Guernsey is delayed by fog and he arrives too late to make his onward connection to New Zealand that day. His son had already arranged to meet him at Gatwick and drive him to Heathrow; now he drives him to a hotel near Heathrow instead where Phil will stay overnight before catching his rearranged flight. At the hotel they have a snack together. These activities are substantially related to completing travel to a foreign destination – Phil would have eaten in the hotel even if he had been unaccompanied. The transit passenger provisions will apply.

Example 5

George lives in the Isle of Man and is flying to New York on business via Manchester. He has made an appointment with a consultant orthopaedic surgeon based in Manchester to carry out a number of tests. He will stay in the clinic overnight before travelling on to New York the following afternoon. The appointment is not an activity substantially related to completing travel to a foreign destination. The transit passenger provisions will not apply.

Example 6

George lives in Jersey and is travelling to Stavanger. He does not fly and travels to the UK by ferry before continuing to London by train. He stays overnight at a West End hotel, having prearranged dinner and a trip to the theatre with friends. The next day he travels to Newcastle by train, where he boards a ferry to Stavanger. His activities in the UK are not substantially related to completing travel to a foreign destination. The transit passenger provisions will not apply.

---

1 *Wilkie v IRC* (1951) 32 TC 495.
2 *Wilkie v IRC* (1951) 32 TC 495 at 508.
3 *Wilkie v IRC* (1951) 32 TC 495 at 511.
4 *Wilkie v IRC* (1951) 32 TC 495 at 511.
5 See IR20 (July 2008) para 1.2 and Ch 3 and in particular para 3.3. See also *Glyn v Revenue & Customs* [2013] UKFTT 645 (TC) at paras 168–172.
6 CCAB Notes (TR 508) on Taxation Anomalies and Practical Difficulties.
7 Explanatory Notes to Clause 22 of 2008 Finance Bill, para 17. See also the example in HMRC6 reproduced in Appendix 3 to this book.

5.10   The significance of 'the tax year'

ITA 2007 s 831 refers to actual residence of a total period equal to 183 days (or more) 'in the tax year in question' while s 832 refers to 'during the tax year in question'. It is perfectly possible, therefore, for a person to arrive in the UK on 5 October in one year and to leave on 5 October in the following year (4 October if that year is a leap year) and thus spend a full 12 months in the UK without reaching the threshold that would result in deemed residence in both tax years. Although 364 days will have been spent in the UK, only 182 days will have been spent in each of two consecutive but separate tax years. In the *Zorab* case,[1] Mr Zorab arrived in the UK on 1 November 1920 and departed on 3 October 1921 thus spending 337 consecutive days in the UK. Of those

337 days, only 156 were spent here in 1920–21 and only 181 were spent here in 1921–22 in consequence of which no challenge on 'six-month rule' grounds was raised against his non-resident status.

Any temporary visitor whose visits follow this pattern may, of course, find himself attributed with the status of residence. Although presence for 183 days of the tax year will ensure that he is treated as resident for the purposes of ITA 2007, ss 831 and 832, presence for less than 183 days will not ensure that he is *not* attributed with the quality of residence for those or any other purposes under the Taxes Acts.

---

1 *IRC v Zorab* (1926) 11 TC 289. See **5.05** above.

5.11 The capital gains tax test

The equivalent capital gains tax provisions raise their own questions of construction. TCGA 1992 s 2(1) provides that, subject to certain exceptions:

> '… a person shall be chargeable to capital gains tax in respect of chargeable gains accruing to him in a year of assessment during any part of which he is resident in the United Kingdom, or during which he is ordinarily resident in the UK.'

The meaning of residence is addressed in s 9, the relevant parts of which read:

> '(1) In this Act "resident" and "ordinarily resident" have the same meanings as in the Income Tax Acts.

> (3) Subject to sections 10(1) (non-residents with UK branch or agency) and 10A (temporary non-residents), an individual who is in the United Kingdom for some temporary purpose only and not with any view or intent to establish his residence in the United Kingdom shall be charged to capital gains tax on chargeable gains accruing in any year of assessment if and only if the individual spends (in total) at least 183 days in the United Kingdom.

> (4) The question whether for the purposes of subsection (3) above an individual is in the United Kingdom for some temporary purpose only and not with any view or intent to establish his residence there shall be decided without regard to any living accommodation available in the United Kingdom for his use.'

Finance Act 2008 s 24(6) amended the wording of s 9(3) of TCGA 1992 so that the former reference in that provision to 'six months' is replaced by a reference to '183 days'. It brings some consistency in this respect to the statutory language used in the relevant provisions in this respect for both capital gains tax and income tax purposes.

It seems beyond doubt that the terms 'temporary purpose', 'view or intent to establish his residence' and '183 days' fall to be construed in similar manner to that indicated at **5.05**, **5.06** and **5.09** above despite the use of the composite phrase 'view or intent to establish his residence' in the capital gains tax formulation of the rule. Similarly the modern language to determine presence in s 9(5) and (6) mirrors that found in the income tax provisions.

Only two subsections earlier TCGA 1992 s 9(1) states that 'resident' and 'ordinarily resident' have the same meanings as in the Income Tax Acts. In

Karim v HMRC,[1] the First-tier Tribunal decided that although s 9(3) and (4) track the wording of the predecessor to ITA 2007 s 831, the effect of s 9(1) is to incorporate into the TCGA the meanings applicable to the Taxes Act including the 'effect' of the predecessor to ITA 2007 s 829. This conclusion does not seem well founded under the predecessor legislation which charges non-residents meeting the requirements of the section as residents and in *Hankinson v HMRC* the First-tier Tribunal (Judges Avery Jones and Clark) (Judge Hellier) decided that it did not.[2] There may be more force in the argument under the present rewritten provisions which treat such non-residents as resident.

TCGA 1992 s 9(3) qualifies the charging provision in s 2(1) by simply stating that in the case of individuals who have come to the UK for some temporary purpose without any view or intent to establish UK residence, they cannot be charged to capital gains tax unless the total aggregate period in which the individual is in the UK is at least 183 days. TCGA 1992 s 9(3) is purely a relieving provision; and the words 'and only if' within the section affirm that that is so. By comparison ITA 2007 s 831 not only removes from the charge imposed under ITTOIA and ITEPA certain persons who would otherwise be chargeable, but also draws into the charge certain persons who would otherwise be beyond its reach. Although s 831 is, in part, a relieving section, it is, therefore, also, in part (and unlike TCGA 1992 s 9(3)), a charging section. As Lord Shand said in *Lloyd v Sulley*:[3]

> 'Although the provision ... is in the language of exemption ... it rather appears to me to be a section which is intended to impose liability,'[4]

and, as Sir R Webster A-G put it even more positively in *Colquhoun v Brooks*,[5] the section is

> '... not an exempting section in the proper sense of the word; it is a special charging section under limited circumstances.'

In short, ITA 2007 s 831 is saying (in this author's view) that, once a temporary visitor has been here for a total of 183 days, he must, if he is found not to possess residence status on general grounds, be attributed with quasi-residence status and charged to tax accordingly; while TCGA 1992 s 9(3) is saying (again, in this author's view) that if a temporary visitor has acquired residence status on general grounds and would therefore fall to be charged to capital gains tax, he must be excused from the charge provided he possesses that status for less than 183 days in the year.

Section 9(4) of TCGA 1992 provides that in determining whether for capital gains tax, as for income tax, a person is in the UK for some temporary purpose only and not with any view or intent to establish residence no regard shall be taken of any living accommodation available in the UK for that person's use.

---

1 *Karim v HMRC* [2009] UKFTT 368 (TC) at para 37.
2 *Hankinson v HMRC* [2009] UKFTT 384 (TC) at para 32. See generally **5.13** to **5.15**.
3 *Lloyd v Sulley* (1884) 2 TC 37.
4 *Lloyd v Sulley* (1884) 2 TC 37 at 44.
5 *Colquhoun v Brooks* (1899) 2 TC 490.

5.12   HMRC Guidance on coming to the UK

HMRC guidance for years starting from 6 April 2009 is contained in HMRC6. Part 7 is titled 'When someone becomes resident in the UK.' The presentation of HMRC views on when an individual coming to the UK is, in their view, resident, is commingled with comments on the consequences. The following is the author's extraction of the guidance on the question of residence. The examples set out in HMRC6 are reproduced at Appendix 2. In HMRC6, each section quoted below is prefaced by the following:

> 'Part 2 explains what we mean by resident in the UK while part 3 explains what we mean by ordinarily resident in the UK. You should read both parts.'

The guidance reads:

'7.2 When you have come to the UK permanently or to live or work for three years or more

If your home has been abroad and you have come to the UK to live here permanently you will be resident and ordinarily resident from the date you arrive. You will also be resident and ordinarily resident from the date you arrive if you have come to the UK to remain here for three years or more. By saying that you have come here permanently or for at least three years, you have made it clear that you are not simply visiting the UK.

Sidenote

When we say "remain" in the UK, we mean that you are here on a continuing basis – the only trips you make outside the UK are when you go abroad for holidays or short business trips.

7.4 When you have come to visit the UK for less than three years

If your home has been abroad and you have come to the UK but are not going to live here permanently or remain here for three years or more, you may be visiting the UK.

You are not simply visiting the UK if, when you arrive:

- you are going to be in the UK for 183 days or more during a tax year
- you have come to the UK for a purpose which means that you will be remaining here for at least two years – for example, an employment.

If either of these points apply, you will be resident in the UK from the day you arrive – see paragraph 7.2. Visitors to the UK are those people who are here for a temporary purpose and either of the above points indicates that your purpose for being here is not temporary.

If neither of the points made applies and you can genuinely say that you have come only to visit the UK, the following guidance will apply.

It is possible that after you first come to the UK to visit, or after you have made a number of visits here, your circumstances change and you become resident and ordinarily resident in the UK.

There are two main types of visitor to the UK:

- short term visitors – who are not going to remain in the UK for an extended period and will visit for limited periods in one or more tax years – see paragraph 7.5
- longer term visitors – who have not come to the UK permanently but have come here indefinitely or for an extended period which might cover several tax years – see paragraph 7.7.

It does not matter what type of visitor you are. If you are in the UK for 183 days or more in a tax year, you will be resident here in that year. But although you are resident you might be not ordinarily resident which will affect what UK tax you have to pay.

7.5 Short term visitors

Residence and Ordinary Residence

If you are making a single one-off visit to the UK and leave before you have been here for 183 days and do not intend to return, you will not be resident or ordinarily resident in the UK.

But, if you are going to make regular visits to the UK you need to consider if those visits will mean that you become resident and/or ordinarily resident here.

Even when you are not in the UK for 183 days during a tax year, if you are making several visits, you must also consider the average number of days that you spend here. If, when you first start to visit the UK, you do not know how long you will continue to visit and your visits average 91 days or more per tax year over a four year period, you will be resident and ordinarily resident from the fifth year if you continue to visit.

You might become resident and ordinarily resident in the UK before you have been visiting for four years if:

- you know, when you start visiting the UK, that your visits here are going to be for an average of 91 days or more, in which case you will be resident and ordinarily resident from 6 April of the tax year in which you first start making your visits.
- you realise after starting to visit the UK regularly that your visits are going to be for an average of 91 days or more – you will be resident and ordinarily resident from 6 April of that tax year.

7.6 How to calculate your average visits to the UK

If you need to calculate your annual average visits to the UK, you do so like this:

$$\frac{\text{Total days visiting the UK}}{\text{Tax years you have visited (in days)}} \times 365 = \text{annual average visits}$$

7.7 Longer term visitors

It is possible that you will become resident and ordinarily resident in the UK before you have been visiting for four years if:

- you know when you start visiting the UK that your visits here are going to be for an average of 91 days or more, you will be resident and ordinarily resident from 6 April of the tax year when you first start making your visits.

- you realise after starting to visit the UK regularly that your visits are going to be for an average of 91 days or more – you will be resident and ordinarily resident from 6 April of that tax year.

7.7.1 Longer term visitors – residence

You are a longer term visitor if you come to the UK but you are not going to remain here permanently or for three years or more (see 7.2). As a longer term visitor you will be resident in the UK from the day that you arrive if you have come here for at least two years.

You will also become resident in the UK if, during your visit you are here for 183 days or more in the tax year.'

These positions owe much to the predecessor practice contained in IR20. However, HMRC now states that the document merely reflects their interpretation of the law and is not their practice, Apart from the 183-day test which is connected with ITA 2007 ss 831 and 832 it is difficult to identify the legal rules or principles they purport to interpret.

Individuals leaving the UK

5.13 Residence of individuals temporarily abroad

Departure from the UK does not automatically bring with it an end to taxation of income on a worldwide basis. ITA 2007 s 829 states:

'(1) This section applies if –
  (a) an individual has left the United Kingdom for the purpose only of occasional residence abroad, and
  (b) at the time of leaving the individual was both UK resident and ordinarily UK resident.
(2) Treat the individual as UK resident for the purpose of determining the individual's liability for income tax for any tax year during the whole or a part of which the individual remains outside the United Kingdom for the purpose only of occasional residence abroad.'

Although this rule is aimed at individuals who leave the UK, the circumstances where it is brought into play compared with the rules relating to temporary presence in the UK in ITA 2007 ss 831 and 832 are not entirely obvious and several recent residence cases[1] examine both.

---

1 *Shepherd v Revenue & Customs Commissioners* [2006] EWHC 1512 (Ch); *Gaines-Cooper v HMRC* [2006] UKSPC SPC 568, *Barrett v Revenue & Customs* [2007] UKSPC SPC 639 and *Grace v Revenue & Customs Commissioners* [2008] EWHC 2708 (Ch).

5.14 Occasional residence

ITA 2007 s 829 is concerned with persons who are both resident and ordinarily resident in the UK. If any such person leaves the UK for the purpose 'only of occasional residence abroad' he is, despite his absence, to be treated as resident here. The words in quotation marks are of very great importance. Firstly, s 829(1)(a) permits the purpose in taking up residence abroad to be tested as is the purpose of individuals present in the UK. Secondly, the period within which an individual is to be treated as resident while remaining outside the UK is by reference to occasional residence abroad. Thus s 829(2) specifies that an individual is deemed UK resident for income tax during the whole or a part of any tax year in which the individual is outside the country only for the purpose of occasional residence abroad. 'Occasional residence abroad' was, in one of the earliest cases on the subject of residence, *Rogers v IRC*,[1] held to include a temporary absence which extended over an entire tax year. The case concerned the validity of a charge to tax within the context of the first part of ITA 1842 s 39 – one of the predecessors of ITA 2007 s 829 – which provided that:

> '... any subject of Her Majesty whose ordinary residence shall have been in Great Britain, and who shall have departed from Great Britain and gone into any parts beyond the seas, for the purpose only of occasional residence ... shall be deemed, notwithstanding such temporary absence, a person chargeable to the duties granted by this Act as a person actually residing in Great Britain.'

The case concerned a master mariner who, because he was absent from the UK throughout the whole of 1878–79, contended that his residence abroad was not merely 'occasional' and that he was, therefore, beyond the scope of s 39 and thus not liable to tax for that year. The Lord President Inglis did not agree:

> 'The circumstance that Captain Rogers has been absent from the country during the whole year to which the assessment applies does not seem to me to be a speciality of the least consequence. That is a mere accident. He is not a bit the less a resident of Great Britain because the exigencies of his business have happened to carry him away for a somewhat longer time than usual during this particular voyage.'[2]

Captain Rogers was a British subject, commanded a British ship, owned a house at Innerleven in the county of Fife in which his wife and children dwelt throughout the year in question, owned no house elsewhere, and was absent merely by reason of following his vocation of master mariner. Despite the fact that he was not physically present for even a single day in the tax year 1878–79, he was, therefore, qualitatively resident in the UK throughout that tax year.[3]

The principle – that occasional residence abroad may extend to absences in excess of an entire tax year – remained unchanged and, indeed, was reiterated a quarter of a century later in the Irish case of *Iveagh v Revenue Comrs*[4] when, in the course of expressing his opinion on the application of what had then become rule 3 of the General Rules applicable to Schedules A, B, C, D and E under ITA 1918, Hanna J declared:

> 'It may well be that under this rule a citizen absent through illness for a lengthy period, even two years, may be liable to tax ...'[5]

and when, in that same case, it was held that the Special Commissioners had not misdirected themselves in point of law in holding that

'... there must be personal presence ... at some time during the year of assessment, except in a case coming within the terms of Rule 3 of the General Rules.'[6]

Anyone who is 'resident in the United Kingdom for a year of assessment, but ... absent from the United Kingdom throughout that year' can clearly only be someone who has been attributed with the quality of residence in the UK for a particular tax year without ever having been physically present in the UK during any part of that year. This was noted by Nicholls J in *Reed v Clark*[7] who later confirmed that:

'There is nothing in the language or in my view the context of s 49 to show that regardless of the circumstances a person can never be said to have left for the purpose of occasional residence abroad if his residence abroad extends throughout an entire tax year. A man ordinarily resident here may go to live abroad in March intending to return some months later but through serious illness of himself or others or other unforeseen change of circumstances not return until the end of the following March. I can see no reason why, depending on all the facts, such a man may not fall within s 49. If that is right, it would be absurd that such a man should fall outside s 49 if the emergency which kept him abroad should chance to last for a week or two longer and not permit his return until after 5 April.'[8]

Cases where an individual absent for the whole year is resident are likely to be exceptional. It is plain that an individual who is not physically present in the UK throughout a tax year will be outside ss 831 and 832 and that s 829 will only apply to individuals who are resident and ordinarily resident immediately before they leave the UK. Some 100 years after Captain Rogers' voyage the Revenue again challenged the residence of an individual who was not physically present in the UK throughout a tax year, this time a musician who went to California in *Reed v Clark*[9] where Dave Clark's absence was admittedly motivated by tax avoidance considerations. In *IRC v Combe*,[10] Lord Clyde LP said that:

'..."occasional residence" is residence taken up or happening as passing opportunity requires, in one case, or admits in another, and contrasts with the residence, or ordinary residence, of a person who ... is "resident" or "ordinarily resident" in some place or country,'[11]

and in *Reed v Clark*[12] Nicholls J, commenting on s 49, said:

'In this section occasional residence is the converse of ordinary residence.'[13]

The duration of the physical absence from the UK in the context of an individual falling within ITA 2007 s 829 is of relevance, therefore, only to the extent to which it shows that the residence abroad is 'occasional' and thus bears on whether or not that person has, in fact, become ordinarily resident elsewhere. If an individual, having been resident and ordinarily resident in the UK at the time of leaving these shores, establishes ordinary residence overseas that residence will not be 'occasional'. Absence alone which extends over a whole tax year is, as the earlier cases show, not conclusive evidence in law of a purpose beyond occasional residence, and although even the courts have conceded that the attribution of residential status to a person who 'during a whole year, the year of assessment ... has never been in this country ... would require a pretty strong case indeed',[14] that is not to say that there are no circumstances in which such a case could be made by the Revenue – as *Reed v Clark*[15] plainly shows.

In *Shepherd v Revenue & Customs Comrs*[16] the taxpayer was an airline pilot who was domiciled in the UK. He bought a flat in Cyprus and from then on spent only 80 days a year in the UK. He therefore fell within the 90 days 'test' set out in HMRC's booklet IR20 at para 2.2. The rest of the year he was either living in Cyprus, working abroad or on holiday abroad. He had a home in the UK and stayed in it with his wife when here. The High Court upheld the Commissioners' decision that he was abroad only for the purpose of 'occasional residence' and therefore remained ordinarily resident in the UK. Lewison J upheld the decision of Special Commissioner Brice who found the absences of Captain Shepherd after October 1998 were temporary absences from the UK, as were his absences when flying in the course of his duties, and his absences when sailing, and his absences when visiting Europe.[17] The argument that what is now s 829 is not engaged by an individual who is in the UK for a temporary purpose only and thus within s 831 was dismissed without analysis of the relationship between the provisions.[18]

The Special Commissioners in *Gaines-Cooper v Revenue & Customs Comrs*[19] held that the taxpayer was also resident within the terms of what is now s 829. They did not regard him as a 'temporary resident', although those words are not contained in that provision. Since however they had held that he was not in the UK for some 'temporary purpose' within what is now s 831, they may have felt that he could not be said to have left the UK otherwise than for an 'occasional residence' – the actual words of s 829 – abroad. If therefore he was not a temporary resident here he could be nothing more than an occasional resident abroad. Again, there was no attempt to address the relationship between the provisions.

Some elements of the relationship between the provisions appeared in *Grace v Revenue & Customs Commissioners.*[20] It was common ground that the predecessor to s 829 did not assist HMRC either because (according to HMRC) the section did not apply because Mr Grace never 'left' the UK, or because (according to the taxpayer) although Mr Grace did leave the UK he did not do so for the sole purpose of occasional residence abroad. HMRC accepted that if Mr Grace had left the UK by reason of having set up home in Cape Town, he had left for more than occasional residence abroad. Accordingly, only the predecessor to s 831 was in issue.[21] At the re-hearing of *Grace* before the First-tier Tribunal, HMRC unsuccessfully attempted to argue that they were not bound by their concession in the High Court under the predecessor to ITA 2007 s 829.[22] Judge Mosedale commented in any event that their case on it was not made out. She found that Mr Grace's abode in Cape Town was adopted voluntarily and for a settled purpose as part of the regular order of his life. Although he always intended to return to the UK after each stay in South

Africa, he also intended to return to South Africa after each stay in the UK. It was therefore not an occasional residence and the predecessor to s 829 would not bite.[23]

---

1 *Rogers v IRC* (1879) 1 TC 225.
2 *Rogers v IRC* (1879) 1 TC 225 at 227.
3 It is unlikely that any present-day Captain Rogers would be regarded as resident in the circumstances described, but this would be because of the application of ITA 2007 s 830 – see **5.15** below – not because of any change in the judicial view of the meaning of 'occasional residence abroad'.
4 (1930) 1 ITC 316.
5 (1930) 1 ITC 316 at 349.
6 (1930) 1 ITC 316 at 356–357.
7 [1985] STC 323.
8 [1985] STC 323 at 344.
9 [1985] STC 323.
10 (1932) 17 TC 405.
11 (1932) 17 TC 405 at 410.
12 [1985] STC 323.
13 [1985] STC 323, at 345.
14 *Turnbull v Foster* (1904) 6 TC 206 at 209, per Clerk LJ.
15 [1985] STC 323.
16 *Shepherd v Revenue & Customs Commissioners* [2006] EWHC 1512 (Ch).
17 *Shepherd v Revenue & Customs Commissioners* [2006] EWHC 1512 (Ch) at para 12.
18 *Shepherd v Revenue & Customs Commissioners* [2006] EWHC 1512 (Ch) at para 15.
19 *Gaines-Cooper v HMRC* [2006] UKSPC SPC568.
20 *Grace v Revenue & Customs Commissioners* [2008] EWHC 2708 (Ch).
21 *Grace v Revenue & Customs Commissioners* [2008] EWHC 2708 (Ch) at para 6.
22 *Grace v Revenue & Customs* [2011] UKFTT 36 (TC) at para 8.
23 At para 183.

5.15　A distinct break

A person within the category prescribed by ITA 2007 s 829 *will* be deemed to be resident in accordance with that section unless there is evidence of 'a distinct break' with the UK, as the leading case, *Levene v IRC*,[1] concerning the application of ITA 1918 Sch 1, rule 3 of the General Rules applicable to Schedules A, B, C, D and E (the predecessor of ITA 2007 s 829), makes very plain.

Until March 1918, Mr Louis Levene, a British subject, leased a house in Curzon Street, London. On that date he surrendered the lease, sold his furniture and, until January 1925, was of no fixed abode but stayed at hotels either in the UK or abroad. Until December 1919, he stayed in England and was, on his own admission, resident and ordinarily resident in the UK until that date. In December 1919, however, he went abroad but returned to the UK in July 1920 and, from then until January 1925, spent between four and five months here in each tax year. The purpose of his annual visits to the UK was to obtain medical advice for himself and his wife, to visit relatives and the graves of his parents, to take part in certain Jewish religious observances and to deal with his tax affairs. In January 1925 he took a nine-year lease on a flat in Monaco.

Mr Levene contended that for the years 1920–21 to 1924–25 he was neither resident nor ordinarily resident in the UK and that, in consequence, he was entitled to exemption from tax on certain interest and dividends from securities. The Special Commissioners did not agree and the High Court, the Court of Appeal and finally the House of Lords upheld the Commissioners' decision. Key passages from Viscount Sumner's lucid judgment are given below.

> 'My Lords, early in 1918 Mr Levene, a British subject, formed the intention to "live abroad". He sold his house in Mayfair, sold such furniture as was not in settlement, and then lived in hotels in England for the best part of two years. I will assume that, but for passport difficulties and the condition of his wife's health, he would have gone abroad sooner. He left England in December, 1919.
>
> Accordingly on 6 April 1920, at the beginning of the five years of charge now in question, he was, in the words of Rule 3 of the General Rules, "a British subject, whose ordinary residence has been in the UK" and so he remained chargeable to tax notwithstanding, if he had left the United Kingdom for the purpose only of occasional residence abroad. Was that the only purpose of his leaving so far as residence is concerned?
>
> The Special Commissioners found that it was, and I think it is clear that they had evidence before them on which they could so find. His only declaration was that he meant to live abroad, not saying whether it was to be an occasional or a constant, a part time or a whole time sojourn. He was advised by his doctor to seek a better climate, which is consistent with returning to England when English weather mends. He had gone out of business in England and broken up his establishment, but he still had in England business interests connected with his Income Tax assessments, and ties of filial piety and religious observance, for his father was buried at Southampton and he was himself a member of the English community of Jews. What he actually did was to come back to England after an absence of about seven months, and he remained for nearly five. In the meantime he had not set up an establishment abroad but had lived in hotels. This, however, was only what he had done in England from March, 1918, to December, 1919. I think there was ample evidence before the Commissioners to show that a man, who left England to live abroad as he had been living here, and when warm weather came returned to his native country and to his permanent associations, had in 1919 "left the United Kingdom for the purposes of occasional residence only". If so, he remained chargeable.
>
> So much for the year of charge 1920–21. In the following years he was a bird of passage of almost mechanical regularity. No material change occurred in his way of living, for his enquiries for a permanent flat came to nothing until so late as not to affect his life and residence for the period in question … The evidence as a whole disclosed that Mr Levene continued to go to and fro during the years in question, leaving at the beginning of winter and coming back in summer, his home thus remaining as before. He changed his sky but not his home.[2] On this I see no error in law in saying of each year that his purpose in leaving the United Kingdom was occasional residence abroad only. The occasion was the approach of an English winter and when with the promise of summer here that occasion passed away, back came Mr Levene to attend the calls of interest, of friendship and of piety.[3]

Not until January 1925 was there evidence of a distinct break with Mr Levene's former residence in the UK and, accordingly, not until 1925 could his periods of residence abroad be anything other than occasional residence within the context of the predecessor of ITA 2007 s 829, despite the fact that for a period of five years Mr Levene had no fixed abode in this country and consistently spent the greater part of each year overseas.

The case of Mr Levene may usefully be compared and contrasted with that of Mr F L Brown.[4] Mr Brown was a British subject whose ordinary residence had been in the UK from 1893 until February 1918. On that date he, like Mr Levene, gave up his house in Folkestone, stored his furniture and, until October 1919, lived at hotels in various places in the UK. In October 1919, however, he departed for an hotel in Menton on the French Riviera where he had habitually stayed for two or three months every winter since 1906, and from October 1919 his ordinary and usual habit of life was to spend seven months of each year in the same suite of rooms in that hotel (ie practically the whole of the hotel's open season), two months in Switzerland or at the Italian lakes, and three months in the UK. Mr Brown had four sons living in the UK and his visits to the UK were to see them, other relations and friends, and for a change. Sometimes he stayed with friends or relatives, other times he stayed at hotels or boarding houses. He had no business ties in the UK but he had a banking account here into which dividends were paid. The Inland Revenue contended that Mr Brown, being a British subject whose ordinary residence had been in the UK, had gone abroad for the purpose of occasional residence only within the meaning of rule 3 of the General Rules, but the Special Commissioners did not agree. They held that 'there had been a definite break in his habit of life in February 1918, when the house in the UK was given up'.[5] In a remarkably brief judgment, Rowlatt J dismissed the Crown's appeal on the grounds that he could see no error of law in the Commissioners' finding and could not, therefore, interfere with it. Nevertheless, he made his reservations plain: Mr Brown 'had some furniture and a banking account and he had connections with England, and if the Commissioners had found the other way I should not have disturbed them'.[6] There was a break, but one which, clearly, was not as clean as Rowlatt J would have liked to find it. Because of that break, however, Mr Brown became non-resident from 6 April 1918 and his residence status for 1924–25, the tax year in question, was determined by the Commissioners under the statutory provisions now contained in ITA 2007 s 831 which relate to visitors in the UK.[7] Because the Commissioners considered that Mr Levene had made no such break prior to January 1925, however, his residence status for the years 1920–21 to 1924–25 could not be determined under those provisions. Hence the difference in outcome of what, on the face of them, were very similar cases.

The principle that once there is a 'distinct break' in a person's residence in the UK, the overseas residence that ensues will necessarily be more than 'occasional' residence, was emphasised some six years later by Lord Sands in *IRC v Combe*.[8] Captain Combe, a British subject, left the UK for America and there served an apprenticeship under a New York employer with a view to becoming that employer's European representative. During each of the three years following his departure, he made visits here on his employer's business but, having no place of abode in the UK, stayed in hotels. The Crown claimed that Captain Combe had remained resident in the UK throughout the three years in question as, within the terms of the predecessor of ITA 2007 s 829, he had left the UK for the purpose only of occasional residence abroad. This claim was, however, rejected by the Commissioners and, on appeal, by the Court of Session. Lord Sands, referring to the fact that Captain Combe had left the UK on 24 April 1926 and had not returned for a visit until 4 March 1927, said:

> 'There was a distinct break. Any residence in the first year in this country was what might have been accounted for by simply not very prolonged holidays.'[9]

It was that opinion on which, in part, Nicholls J based his judgment in *Reed v Clark*.[10] Dave Clark was a British subject whose ordinary residence had been in England until, on 3 April 1978, he left England to live and work in Los Angeles for 13 months. The 13 months intentionally spanned the tax year 1978–79 because Dave Clark had been advised that, by staying abroad throughout that year, he would avoid tax on $450,000 received in the previous year from the sale of Polydor Ltd – a German recording company – of the right to make and sell certain recordings of the 'Dave Clark Five' – a band which he had formed and which had enjoyed considerable success in the 1960s.

Mr Clark was unmarried and, before leaving for America, he lived with his mother in a house he had bought for her in North London. Upon returning to the UK on 2 May 1979 he resumed residence there. Throughout the period, Dave Clark (London) Ltd – a company of which Mr Clark was sole director – owned the lease of a flat in Mayfair and, until leaving for America, Mr Clark had an office and bedroom there. A firm of estate agents were instructed to sub-let the flat during the period of his absence but they were unable to do so. Mr Clark had, however, packed away his files and other belongings and the flat was in a state of readiness for a sub-tenant had one been found.

In contending that Mr Clark's residence in America was merely occasional residence abroad, the Crown stressed the fact that it was, from the outset, Mr Clark's intention to return to the UK after 13 months; the fact that during his absence his established domestic and business arrangements in this country were maintained to such a degree that, immediately upon his return, his ordinary pattern of life could be resumed without any significant disruption; and the fact that his absence was contrived for tax avoidance purposes.

Nicholls J was of the opinion that none of those facts brought Mr Clark's residence within the term 'occasional residence' as used in ICTA 1970 s 49. He said:

> 'In this case there was a distinct break in the pattern of the taxpayer's life which lasted (as from the outset he intended) for just over a year. He ceased living in London and for that year he lived in or near Los Angeles, mostly in one fixed place of abode, and he worked from there. For that year Los Angeles was his headquarters. He did not visit this country at all. On the whole I do not think he can be said to have left the UK for the purpose only of occasional residence abroad. In my judgment the conclusion of the commissioners on this was correct.'[11]

In *Barrett v Revenue & Customs*,[12] the taxpayers' contention that there was a distinct break was rejected on the basis that there was no change in his circumstances. Mr Barrett continued to be employed by the same employer under the same contract of employment and seemed to have been doing much what he was doing before. He was looking for a musical act or acts to manage through his employer and had worked abroad before for them. He did not establish a permanent home or 'HQ' abroad. His partner and family continued to be in the UK in the family home where they still live. He paid the UK bills from his UK accounts and made no special financial arrangement for his time abroad (such as bank account, credit card, medical insurance etc). No special arrangements seem to have been made as to his car, driving licence, residence permits, foreign identity card or similar matters. There was a lack of certainty as to when he went abroad, which the Special Commissioner found surprising if it was a distinct break in the pattern of his life. It was also surprising that there was no ticket or boarding pass stub or similar evidence if this was so different from what had gone on before so as to be a distinct break in the pattern of his life. If he went abroad for tax reasons to escape the UK tax net, having taken advice from well-known advisers, one would have expected him to have been advised of the importance of objective evidence to show this.

Lewison J commented on the use of the expression 'distinct break' in *Grace v Revenue & Customs Commissioners*[13] thus:

'The phrase "distinct break" does not feature in the Act. What it means is not therefore a question of statutory construction. It is an idea that has been developed in the application of section [829] and its predecessors, which requires determination of the questions whether the taxpayer has "left" the United Kingdom and, if he has, whether he has left for "occasional residence" abroad. It is not, therefore, profitable, to attempt to define what it means if used (as the Special Commissioner used it) as a tool to help decide whether Mr Grace was resident in the United Kingdom.'

Clearly, the individual is required to have 'left' the UK to engage s 829(1)(a) and this word requires interpretation. In addition, the time of 'leaving' within s 829(1)(b) must be identified because it is at that time the individual must be both resident and ordinarily resident in the UK. This is simple in obvious cases where an individual departs and, for example, does not return. The exigencies of life and the facility of modern travel mean that such cases will be few and far between.

Although the cases show that a distinct break is not essential to the common law meaning of residence, the waters in this area were muddied somewhat on the re-hearing of *Grace* before the First-tier Tribunal. Judge Mosedale said:

'[A]lthough ... it is not essential to show a distinct break, it must be difficult ... to show that UK residence has been lost unless a distinct break in the taxpayer's pattern of life has occurred. I can envisage a set of circumstances where a taxpayer gradually runs down his connections with and presence in the UK to the extent that ultimately he becomes non-resident without actually ever one year on another making a distinct break.'[14]

She found that the main change in Mr Grace's life in September 1997 was a distinct decrease in amount of time spent in UK and the creation of new ties in South Africa but did not consider this a 'sufficient break' with the UK.[15] Instead, she found that Mr Grace went from being a person resident in one country to being a person resident in two.

In *Glyn v Revenue & Customs*,[16] Judge Nowlan in the First-tier Tribunal elaborated on the expression thus:

'Since the Supreme Court's decision in *Gaines-Cooper* [2011] UKSC 47, we consider that the penultimate bullet point above considerably understates the significance of a "distinct break". A summary that better reflects the law after the Gaines-Cooper case is that in order to demonstrate that a UK resident person has ceased to be UK resident, it is virtually critical to demonstrate a "complete break", and that this requires it to be shown that the person has not necessarily severed family, social and business ties with the UK, but that at least there has been a "substantial loosening" of such ties.'[17]

The Tribunal found that Mr Glyn severed virtually every active business connection and, when all the properties for whose management he had been largely responsible, had actually been sold, and when any continuing UK business activities were either trivial or minor matters of 'tidying up'. He was found to have effected a very substantial loosening of ties with his and wife's friends in London. He saw a reasonable amount, but again materially less than in earlier years of their adult children. Visits were made for various different purposes, often two or more being combined, and virtually none were fundamentally required and were thus aptly described as 'visits'. Accordingly, it was held that Mr Glyn effected a 'distinct break' from his previous life in London.[18] On appeal, however, the Upper Tribunal[19] ruled that the First-tier Tribunal had taken into account irrelevant factors and they failed to have regard, or sufficient regard, to certain relevant factors. Assessing the duration of UK presence and the regularity and frequency of visits, the nature of the visits and connection with the UK are relevant, but what is irrelevant is whether they demonstrated any settled purpose. In addition, there is no basis in the authorities for considering the reasons for the retention of a house in the UK are relevant. Rather, the way and the regularity with which the house was used should have been considered. Speculation on what the individual might have done if his understanding of the relevant law had been better is not relevant. Similarly, in relation to the loosening of social ties, the purpose, or principal purpose of visits to the UK, but instead, whether, having regard to what he did while he was in London and where he did it, he had ceased to be UK resident. It was also irrelevant whether it would be necessary to abandon or artificially restrict an invariable Jewish tradition of Friday night family dinners in order to become non-UK resident.

---

1 *Levene v IRC* (1928) 13 TC 486.
2 Although Viscount Sumner is generally credited with the coining of this striking phrase, it seems that he, either consciously or unconsciously, had in mind the Latin poet Horace who centuries earlier had written 'caelum non animum mutant qui trans mare currunt' (Epist I.xi.27) – 'they change their sky but not their soul who speed across the sea'.
3 *Levene v IRC* (1928) 13 TC 486 at 501.
4 *IRC v Brown* (1926) 11 TC 292.
5 *IRC v Brown* (1926) 11 TC 292 at 295.
6 *IRC v Brown* (1926) 11 TC 292 at 296.
7 See **5.04** to **5.10** above.
8 (1932) 17 TC 405.
9 (1932) 17 TC 405 at 411.
10 [1985] STC 323.
11 [1985] STC 323 at 346.
12 [2007] UKSPC SPC639.
13 *Grace v Revenue & Customs Commissioners* [2008] EWHC 2708 (Ch) at para 43.
14 *Grace v Revenue & Customs* [2011] UKFTT 36 (TC) at para 37.
15 At para 176.

16 *Glyn v Revenue & Customs* [2013] UKFTT 645 (TC).
17 [2013] UKFTT 645 at para 117.
18 [2013] UKFTT 645 at para 174.
19 *HMRC v Glyn* [2015] UKUT 551 (TCC).

5.16 Residence of individuals working abroad

A different rule applies in the case of individuals who work abroad. The statutory provision concerning the residence of these individuals is that contained in ITA 2007 s 830:

'(1) This section applies for income tax purposes if an individual works full-time in one or both of –
    (a) a foreign trade, and
    (b) a foreign employment.
(2) In determining whether the individual is UK resident ignore any living accommodation available in the UK for the individual's use.
(3) A trade is foreign if no part of it is carried on in the UK.
(4) An employment is foreign if all of its duties are performed outside the UK.
(5) An employment is also foreign if in the tax year in question –
    (a) the duties of the employment are in substance performed outside the UK, and
    (b) the only duties of the employment performed in the UK are duties which are merely incidental to the duties of the employment performed outside the UK in the year.
(6) In this section –
'employment' includes an office, and
'trade' includes profession and vocation.'

By concession this is extended to determine the status of an individual accompanying or later joining a spouse who goes abroad for full-time employment.[1]

1 Extra-statutory Concession A 78.

5.17 Full-time work

ITA 2007 s 830 is of no application to anyone who does not work full-time in one, or more than one, trade, profession, vocation, office or employment. 'Full-time' is, however, a term which is undefined in the statute and which must, therefore, be given its ordinary, accepted meaning. This, according to *Chambers Dictionary*[1] is: 'occupied during or extending over the whole working day, week etc'. The words 'works full-time' appear in only one other place in the Taxes Acts and that is in relation to loans to participators by close companies.[2] In that context, it is Revenue practice to treat a director or employee as working full-time if his hours of work are equivalent to at least three-quarters of the company's normal working hours.

Even if we take s 830 as being directed, therefore, only at those who, apart from periods of holiday, leave, sickness etc, are occupied in their work throughout substantially the whole (ie at least 25 hours) of each working week, the term 'full-time' has not, however, been cleared of all its difficulties of construction. Although the term is clearly intended to contrast full-time work with part-time work, the words 'in one or more of the following, that is to say, a trade, profession, vocation, office or employment' do not, on a strict construction, exclude a person who, although working only part-time in relation to any one trade, profession, employment or the like, does so in relation to more than one trade, profession, employment or the like so that his various part-time occupations extend over the whole of each working week. The Revenue now appear to accept this view.[3] It has also been endorsed by the First-tier Tribunal in *Hankinson v HMRC*.[4]

ITA 2007 s 830 is silent as to whether the full-time occupation to which it refers must extend over an entire tax year in order that its provisions might be effective for that tax year but there would seem to be no strong argument in favour of such a construction.

The section does not grant a full-time overseas worker non-resident status. Section 832(2) merely says that residence status is to be decided without regard to any living accommodation that is available in the UK. Disregard of a person's living accommodation in the UK will, however, not prevent the attribution of residence status to a person whose period of full-time work abroad does not span an entire tax year if the various connecting factors described at **2.16** to **2.18** above imbue the person with residence status which will, in law, be attributed to him for the whole of the tax year in question.

Clearly, the timing of relatively short overseas assignments can assume great importance in the light of these considerations.

The application of the section is not limited to individuals who have been UK residents and thus applies to anyone working abroad. Unlike the parallel rule in s 831 for those in the UK for a temporary purpose only, it has no day counting test but the need for full-time work abroad will, in practice, have a similar effect.

---

1 1998 edition.

2 ICTA 1988 s 420(2)(b).

3 Revenue Interpretation, Tax Bulletin 40 (February) 1993. See also *Pamer v Maloney* [1999] STC 890 (CA).

4 *Hankinson v HMRC* [2009] UKFTT 384 (TC) at para 47.

5.18 Trades and professions

The fact that a person may so work full-time in a trade, profession or vocation employment is, however, not sufficient, on its own, to guarantee inclusion within ITA 2007 s 830. In the case of a person working full-time in a trade, profession or vocation, s 830(3) requires that no part of the trade, profession or vocation is carried on in the UK. If any part of it is carried on then the person is outside the scope of the section. The rule goes beyond the activities of the individual concerned and rests on the place where any part of the trade, profession or vocation as a whole is carried out. The question of whether the individual ever actually works in the UK is only relevant to the extent that such work would taint the trade with being carried on in the UK. The trade is, however, equally tainted by the activities of others that result in any part being carried out in the UK. In many cases, such as modern cross-border professional partnerships, whether the requirements of s 830 can be met, will be beyond the control of the individual concerned.

The test as to where a trade is carried on is a very broad one and necessitates a detailed examination of all the facts in any particular case, but a number of decided cases have given rise to certain general principles. The primary test is the place where the contract constituting the trade is made. Where contracts are actually made in the UK, by a person not resident here, he may, according to the decision in *Erichsen v Last*,[1] be regarded as trading in the UK, even though, for example, the fulfilment of the contracts made in the UK takes place overseas. The importance which the place of the making of sales contracts has assumed in these matters may be traced back to *Werle & Co v Colquhoun*[2] where Esher MR said:

'... the contract is the very foundation of the trade. It is the trade really ... If the trade consists in making contracts which are profitable contracts, if those contracts are made in England, then the trade is carried on in England, because the making of the contracts is the very substance and essence of the trade.'[3]

This formulation arose in the context of a case which concerned the merchanting of champagne. Even there, the place of delivery and the place of payment were held to be important matters for consideration. Where contracting is not the essential ingredient of the trade, the second test to determine where a trade is carried on was held in *Smidth & Co v Greenwood*[4] to be: 'Where do the operations take place from which the profits in substance arise?' As Atkin LJ said in that case:

'The contracts in this case were made abroad. But I am not prepared to hold that this test is decisive. I can imagine cases where the contract of re-sale is made abroad and yet the manufacture of the goods, some negotiation of the terms and complete execution of the contract take place here under such circumstances that the trade was in truth exercised here.'[5]

Certain preparatory or supporting activities do not constitute the trade. In *Sully v A-G*,[6] for instance, it was decided that merely contracting to purchase goods in the UK for subsequent resale abroad cannot constitute the carrying on of trade in the UK. Nor, according to the decision in *Grainger & Son v Gough*,[7] another champagne case, can the mere soliciting of sales orders which are then actually entered into overseas amount to trading in the UK. (In that case, the now-familiar distinction between trading *in* the UK and trading *with* the UK was drawn.) Similarly, in that case it was decided that assistance given in the UK in relation to the negotiation and execution of sales contracts concluded overseas did not amount to trading here.

The requirement in relation to a trade is strict. If the answer to the question is that the trade is carried on partly within and partly outside the UK, then ITA 2007 s 830 is of no application.

---

1 *Erichsen v Last* (1881) 1 TC 351.

2 *Werle & Co v Colquhoun* (1888) 2 TC 402.
3 *Werle & Co v Colquhoun* (1888) 2 TC 402 at 410–412.
4 *Smidth & Co v Greenwood* (1922) 8 TC 193.
5 *Smidth & Co v Greenwood* (1922) 8 TC 193 at 204, per Atkin LJ.
6 *Sully v A-G* (1860) 2 TC 149.
7 *Grainger & Son v Gough* (1896) 3 TC 311.

5.19   Employment

The condition which must be fulfilled before a person who works full-time in an office or employment will become entitled to have his residence status decided without regard to any living accommodation available in the UK is contained in ITA 2007 s 830(4) and is that 'all its duties are performed outside the UK'.

Unlike the rule for trades, the employment, however, is also foreign for this purpose if it meets the provisions of s 830(5), if the duties are in substance performed outside the UK and the only duties performed in the UK are incidental to the foreign duties. The exception for incidental duties only applies in a particular year if in that year the duties are in substance performed outside the UK and only incidental duties are performed in the UK. Furthermore, since it is only the employment of the individual whose residence is being tested, the extent to which the individual can meet the requirements of the section is under the control of that individual to a greater extent than in the case of a trade in which others are involved.

In *Robson v Dixon*,[1] Pennycuick V-C expressed doubt as to whether the requirement of substance had any meaning if viewed as anything but an adjunct to the question whether the duties were incidental:

> 'The words "in substance" are extremely vague in their import. Moreover, it is extremely difficult to see in what circumstances that requirement could be of any significance independently of the second requirement in the subsection. The Special Commissioners skated over the first requirement. I think they were quite right to do so, and I propose to follow their example. The sole question is whether the second requirement is performed.'[2]

It is suggested, however, that this opinion (and its last sentence in particular) should not be taken as an absolute dismissal of the term 'in substance' but merely as the Vice-Chancellor's own assessment of its relevance in the context of the *Robson* case, coloured as that case was by his own particular interpretation of the word 'incidental'.

1 (1972) 48 TC 527.
2 (1972) 48 TC 527 at 534.

5.20   Incidental duties

The discussion in the previous paragraph brings us to the words 'merely incidental' which are central in ITA 2007 s 830(5)(b). Unfortunately for the taxpayer, these words have been given a judicial definition which is not only exceedingly narrow but which may be at variance with the understanding of that term in the mind of 'the man on the Clapham omnibus':[1]

> 'The expression "merely incidental to" is a striking one, and effect must be given to the natural meaning of those words. The words "merely incidental to" are upon their ordinary use apt to denote an activity (here the performance of duties) which does not serve any independent purpose but is carried out in order to further some other purpose.'[2]

Although that definition must presently be adhered to, it is interesting to compare it with the definition of 'incidental' provided by *Chambers Dictionary*[3] – 'liable to occur: naturally attached: accompanying: concomitant: occasional, casual' – and to observe, as this discussion proceeds, that had any one of those meanings been adopted by Pennycuick V-C in the *Robson* case, its outcome would undoubtedly have been quite different.

Having said that, it must be admitted that Pennycuick V-C's understanding of the term does not actually invalidate the examples of 'incidental duties' offered by the Royal Commission on the Taxation of Profits and Income when, in 1955, it recommended that:

> '... there should be a saving qualification to the effect that work is not the less to be treated as performed wholly in one country because certain merely incidental duties such as returning for report, to collect samples, etc, are carried out in another'.[4]

In a parliamentary debate, however, it was said that:

> '... if a man were in this country, perhaps on leave, for a month during the year, and was called to the London office to give an opinion on something, or received instructions,'[5]

his performance of those duties could be regarded as incidental to the duties he performed abroad. That first example is surely beyond the narrow scope of the Vice-Chancellor's definition, for the giving of an opinion would surely serve a purpose independent of the purpose of the person's overseas duties.

It should also be noted that all the examples given concern occurrences of short *duration* which merely break briefly into the long-term pattern of overseas activity. This could be taken as indicating that Parliament, at least, understood the word 'incidental' to be expressive of temporariness, and it was this factor that was, Mr Robson argued, of paramount importance in deciding whether or not duties performed in the UK were merely incidental to duties performed abroad.

Mr Robson was a pilot employed by KLM, a Dutch airline, and was based at Schipol Airport in Amsterdam, although he and his wife and children had their home in Chorleywood, Hertfordshire. So far as his employment allowed him to do so, he commuted between Chorleywood and Schipol, travelling at preferential rates on passenger flights to and from Heathrow Airport. During the years 1961–62 to 1966–67 (for which he had been assessed to tax as a person resident in the UK), his regular duty was to fly aircraft on scheduled journeys between Amsterdam and various worldwide locations, in particular

North and South America. Of the 811 take-offs and landings which he made during the years in question, 38 landings took place in the UK, but none related to flights beginning here, and of the 38 landings 16 were on charter services which were outside his regular duties. Landings in the UK generally involved a wait of 45 to 60 minutes before taking-off again, though there would be a further hour or so delay if refuelling was necessary. In each of the relevant years, Mr Robson spent less than 60 days in the UK, excluding days on which he had landed here as described, and he contended, therefore, that his residence status should have been decided without regard to his home in Chorleywood. As he saw it, he worked full-time in an employment of which all the duties were performed outside the UK apart from duties which 'were of short duration by contrast with the substantial periods spent outside the UK'[6] and which were therefore merely incidental to the performance of his duties outside the UK. Accordingly, in his opinion, he came within the ambit of FA 1956 s 11 (now ITA 2007 s 830). Pennycuick V-C could not agree:

> 'With the best will in the world, I find it impossible to say that the activities carried on in or over England are merely incidental to the performance of the comparable duties carried on in or over Holland or in or over the ultimate destination in America. The activities are precisely co-ordinate, and I cannot see how it can properly be said that the activities in England are in some way incidental to the other activities. Going back to the words of the section, when one asks, 'What exactly are the other duties outside the United Kingdom to which the performance of the duties are incidental?' no satisfactory answer can be given. The other duties are simply co-ordinate duties.'[7]

If one were to take the dictionary definition of 'incidental' quoted earlier, one could retort, 'But co-ordinate duties *are* incidental duties; no satisfactory answer can be given to your question because of the particular way in which you have chosen to define the word "incidental"; and you are not "going back to the words of the section" but to the extremely narrow interpretation you have given to the words of the section.' It is, however, no part of the Inland Revenue's duties to dilute the strength of a favourable judicial decision, however open to criticism that decision might be, and, accordingly, it has merely taken-up and amplified the Vice-Chancellor's dicta in its guidance notes relating to this matter.[8]

Commenting on the construction of ICTA 1970 s 50(3) (now ITA 2007 s 830(5)) advanced by Mr Robson, the Vice-Chancellor said:

> 'I think it is impossible to construe subsection three ... as indicating merely relatively short periods of employment in the United Kingdom in relation to the period of employment outside the United Kingdom. It would have been quite simple for the section so to provide; and it may well be that if the condition were imported only by the expression 'in substance' that would be the result. But the second requirement is expressed in quite different terms and cannot, I think, be treated as referring merely to what has been described as a quantitative, in contradistinction to a qualitative, basis.'[9]

Again it must be said that, had the Vice-Chancellor attached a more usual meaning to the word 'incidental', there would have been no divergence between the words of the first and second requirements and Mr Robson's contention could have been upheld. As matters now stand, however, the amount of time occupied by duties performed in the UK must be regarded as being of no significance for the purpose of deciding whether or not those duties are 'merely incidental', and, in consequence, great care will need to be taken by anyone who works full-time abroad to ensure that he does not inadvertently place himself beyond the ambit of ITA 2007 s 830 by allowing his normal duties to bring him, however fleetingly, into the UK. Having said that, it must, however, be added that an isolated performance of duties in the UK which are qualitatively no different from the duties performed overseas will not always preclude the operation of the section. In the *Robson* case, the Vice-Chancellor made it clear that, so far as a pilot is concerned,

'... it is accepted on behalf of the Crown that a landing in the United Kingdom by reason of some emergency, such as weather conditions or mechanical trouble, might be regarded as incidental to the performance of duties outside the United Kingdom,'[10]

and he not only thought that was right but outlined other situations which, though he could express no view on them, clearly commended themselves to him as cases for leniency:

'... the position of *de minimis* – a single landing ... the position if a pilot's normal route did not touch on the United Kingdom but on one or two occasions he had landed in the United Kingdom while acting as a substitute for some other pilot who was ill. Those might well be borderline questions.'[11]

In the event, the Crown accepted that the *de minimis* principle[12] should be applied as regards 1961–62, a year in which Mr Robson made only one landing and take-off in the UK, and, three years after the *Robson* case, it was confirmed in an answer to a parliamentary question concerning airline pilots that:

'In practice, where only a single take-off and landing in this country occurred in a year, the Inland Revenue would normally disregard this on *de minimis* grounds in considering whether any duties were performed in this country.'[13]

Although the circumstances in the *Robson* case served to highlight the particular problems which airline pilots may encounter in attempting to fulfil the 'incidental duties' requirement, there would seem to be no obvious argument which HMRC could advance were the *de minimis* principle to be pleaded in relation to a single transgression of the rules by a member of any other class of overseas employee.

---

1 An expression coined by Lord Devlin.
2 *Robson v Dixon* (1972) 48 TC 527 at 534, per Pennycuick V-C.
3 1998 edition.
4 Final Report, 1955, Cmd 9474, para 300.
5 *Hansard*, 7 June 1956, col 1456.
6 *Robson v Dixon* (1972) 48 TC 527 at 530.
7 *Robson v Dixon* (1972) 48 TC 527 at 534.
8 IR20 (July 2008), paras 5.7, 5.8 and 5.5.

9 *Robson v Dixon* (1972) 48 TC 527 at 535.
10 *Robson v Dixon* (1972) 48 TC 527 at 535.
11 *Robson v Dixon* (1972) 48 TC 527 at 535.
12 *De minimis non curat lex*: the law does not concern itself with trifles.
13 *Hansard*, 28 October 1975, vol 898, no 187, col 431. Contained in Statement of Practice A10.

5.21 HMRC Guidance on departing from the UK

Part 8 of HMRC6 is headed: 'When someone stops being resident in the UK.' Observations made in relation to HMRC guidance on becoming resident in para 4.12 above are equally applicable to the following extracts from the guidance on the question of ceasing residence.

'If you emigrate from the UK you will stop being resident here. This would mean that you leave, set up home elsewhere, and substantially cut your ties to the UK.

If you leave for shorter periods, for occasional residence abroad, or with no settled purpose abroad, it is likely that you will remain resident in the UK – even if you become resident in another country under that country's rules.

8.1 Leaving the UK permanently or indefinitely

If you are leaving the UK permanently or indefinitely, either to work or for another reason, you must tell us by contacting your tax office. We will give you form P85 to complete so that you can get any tax refund you are owed. We will also tell you if you will need to complete a UK tax return after you have left the country.

Leaving the UK "permanently" means that you are leaving the country to live abroad and will not return here to live. Leaving "indefinitely" means that you are leaving to live abroad for a long time (at least three years) but you think that you might eventually return to live here, although you do not currently have plans to do so.

The act of leaving the UK does not necessarily make you not resident and not ordinarily resident. You must also make a definite break from the UK and any remaining ties you have with the UK must be consistent with not being resident here. If you say that you are no longer resident and ordinarily resident in the UK, we might ask you to give some evidence to show that you have left the UK permanently or indefinitely and that there has been a clear change in the pattern of your life. For example, we would expect you to show that when you left the UK you had acquired accommodation abroad to live in as a permanent home. If you still have property in the UK which you can use after you leave, we might want you to explain how retaining that property is consistent with leaving the UK.

You will not cease to be resident in the UK simply because you become resident elsewhere. You can become resident in another country and remain resident in the UK.

If you are leaving the UK permanently or indefinitely you will become not resident and not ordinarily resident from the day after the day of your departure.

8.1.1 The year you leave

Although the normal rule in law is that you are taxed as a resident for the whole of the tax year in which you are UK resident, there is an extra-statutory concession (ESC A11) that allows the tax year to be split. The effect of this concession is that you have to pay UK tax as a resident only for the part of the tax year before you finally leave.

ESC A11 has particular conditions; it does not apply in all cases. If you were ordinarily resident in the UK before your date of departure you have to cease to be ordinarily resident here in order to benefit from the concession. Part 3 explains what we mean by ordinarily resident in the UK. ESC A11 will never apply if your date of departure and date of return fall in successive tax years.

You will always need to be not resident for at least a whole tax year for it to apply.

An extra-statutory concession will not be given in any case where an attempt is made to use it for tax avoidance.

8.2 Leaving the UK for shorter periods of time

You will still be treated as resident in the UK if any periods of time you spend outside the UK are for occasional residence abroad only. Occasional residence means you have no settled purpose for a continuing absence from the UK.

"Occasional" does not mean that your absence must be isolated or of short duration. A series of business trips abroad is an example of periods of occasional residence abroad.

If you normally live in the UK and go abroad regularly, for example on extended holidays, you will continue to be resident here. This type of absence does not stop you being resident and ordinarily resident in the UK, because you have not made a definite break from the UK.

8.2.1 Evidence of a definite break

If you do not make a definite break and cut your UK ties then you remain resident in the UK. You could also be dual resident – that is resident in the UK and another country.

You might not have evidence of a definite break from the UK for some time after you leave the UK. In this situation you will need to review your residence status later to confirm whether you have become not resident, and when this happened.

For example, if you have travelled in and out of the UK fairly frequently, the exact timing of the end of your residence here could be difficult to establish. You should therefore keep evidence relating to your lifestyle before and after the date on which you think you ceased to be resident.

If the circumstances of your life change gradually, then you will become not resident only when you have sufficiently reduced your ties to the UK and are more than occasionally resident abroad.

The evidence that you will be able to show that you have made a definite break will depend on the extent of your UK ties initially. If you had few initial connections with the UK you will have less evidence to show you have made a definite break.

In those circumstances strong ties to another country, including a home and settled purpose for your presence there throughout a complete tax year, would be more of a factor in deciding if you have left the UK permanently or indefinitely.

8.3 Complete absence from the UK

Residence is connected to physical presence. If you live outside the UK for a complete tax year and do not set foot in the UK you will not be resident in the UK for that tax year, unless your absence from the UK is for the purpose of occasional residence abroad only. For example, if your absence was for a one-off year long holiday after which your residence in the UK resumed its previous pattern, you would remain UK resident during your absence.

If you became not resident simply because of a complete absence from the UK, it is unlikely that your presence in the UK on your return is for a temporary purpose only if any of your UK ties remained throughout your period of absence. You would most likely become resident again on your return.

Even when you are absent for a whole tax year and so become not resident, you might remain ordinarily resident in the UK. You will need to consider the pattern of your residence over a number of years and the purpose and pattern of any ordinary residence abroad.

8.4 Special rules for certain employees and offices

There are special rules for some employees who work abroad or hold certain offices. These are explained in brief below with links to further guidance where applicable. Some groups of employees are dealt with in specialist tax offices and where this is the case the office is shown in part 13 Contacting HMRC.

Where no specialist office is shown individuals should contact their own tax office.

Crown employees

A Crown employee is someone who holds an office or employment under the Crown such as a member of the UK armed forces, a civil servant or a diplomat.

It does not include all public servants such as doctors and nurses, who work for their local NHS Trust, or teachers who work for the Local Education Authority. Nor does it include employees of government agencies and non-departmental public bodies.

Crown employees are always taxed in the UK in full on their Crown employment income whether the duties of the employment are carried out in the UK or overseas. As a result residence is irrelevant in determining their tax liability on their Crown employment income.

UK merchant navy seafarers

Seafarers working on UK ships, who usually live in the UK when they are not at sea, are resident in the UK. But while they are working as seafarers wholly or partly outside the UK, they may be entitled to the "Seafarer's Earnings Deduction" which can reduce the tax they have to pay. Full details can be found at www.hmrc.gov.uk/cnr/seafarerstax.htm

Certain oil and gas workers

Where an individual works in the oil or gas exploration/extraction industry within the UK's territorial waters, or other designated areas, they are taxed in full in the UK on those earnings irrespective of their residence status. Different rules can apply for those working outside the designated areas or those working for non-UK employers. Further guidance can be found at www.hmrc.gov.uk/manuals/eimanual/EIM40208.htm

Entertainers and sportspeople

Entertainers or sports people who are not resident in the UK but perform or compete in the UK are still taxable in the UK on any payments received in connection with that UK work. Normally the person paying the entertainer or sportsperson will withhold tax from the payments.

Students

The UK has entered into Double Taxation Agreements with many countries that provide special rules for students who come to the UK to study, or go from the UK to study abroad. Under these rules certain income is not taxable in the country of study if it is used only for the maintenance and education of the student. Further general guidance for students can be found at www.hmrc.gov.uk/students/

People seconded to work in the UK by their employer

If you are seconded to work in the UK by your employer, and continue to undertake duties abroad, you should keep records of work done in the UK and abroad, covering both the nature of the work and its extent. In recording working days, part days are included for these purposes, not just those days where you are in the UK at midnight.

Employees of the European Union

If someone from one Member State goes to live in another Member State to work for the European Union their residence status does not change and they will retain the residence status of the last state they were resident in.

So if Mr Adams was resident and ordinarily resident in the UK and went to Luxembourg to work for the European Union he would remain resident and ordinarily resident in the UK.

Members of the UK Parliament and House of Lords

Members of the House of Commons ("MPs") and House of Lords ("Peers") are resident, ordinarily resident and domiciled in the UK for Income Tax, Inheritance Tax and Capital Gains Tax. This will apply to the whole of each tax year in which a person is a member of either House, starting in 2010–11. This applies even if that person is a member for only part of the tax year and regardless of whether or not they are on a leave of absence. It does not apply to the Lords Spiritual or Peers who are disqualified from sitting and voting as a result of becoming a Member of the European Parliament or a judge.

8.5 Leaving the UK to work abroad as an employee

If you are leaving the UK to work abroad full-time, you will only become not resident and not ordinarily resident from the day after the day of your departure, as long as:

- you are leaving to work abroad under a contract of employment for at least a whole tax year
- you have actually physically left the UK to begin your employment abroad and not, for example, to have a holiday until you begin your employment
- you will be absent from the UK for at least a whole tax year
- your visits to the UK after you have left to begin your overseas employment will
  - total less than 183 days in any tax year, and
  - average less than 91 days a tax year. This average is taken over the period of absence up to a maximum of four years.

To calculate your annual average visits to the UK:

$$\frac{\text{Total days visiting UK}}{\text{Tax years you have visited (in days)}} \times 365 = \text{annual average visits}$$

Example

This is for illustrative purposes and any calculation you make would be based upon your own circumstances – the day that you actually left the UK and the days that you have visited the UK in the period.

If you were to leave the UK on 20 May 2008 to work full-time abroad and you visit the UK for:

79 days in the tax year 2008–09 (320 days in the remainder of the tax year)

91 days in the tax year 2009–10 (365 days in the tax year)

98 days in the tax year 2010–11 (365 days in the tax year)

79 days in the tax year 2011–12 (366 days in the tax year)

The average of your visits would be:

2008–09 – $79 \div 320 \times 365 = 90.1$ therefore treated as not resident from 21 May 2008

(subject to split year treatment applying)

2009–10 – $(79 + 91) \div (320 + 365) \times 365 = 90.6$ therefore not resident

2010–11 – $(79 + 91 + 98) \div (320 + 365 + 365) \times 365 = 93.2$ therefore resident

2011–12 – $(79 + 91 + 98 + 79) \div (320 + 365 + 365 + 366) \times 365 = 89.4$ therefore not resident

The calculation of average visits for the year 2012–13 will not include the visits or relevant days for the year of departure. The rolling period of four years is maintained by excluding the oldest year at each annual review.

Any days you spend in the UK because of exceptional circumstances beyond your control, for example an illness which prevents you from travelling, are not normally counted for this purpose.

If you do not meet all of these conditions, you will remain resident and ordinarily resident in the UK unless paragraph 8.1 applies to you.

If your employment comes to an end and you do not return to the UK it will be necessary to consider if you continue to be not resident and not ordinarily resident in the UK.

Sidenote

What we mean by full-time employment: UK tax law does not give a definition of full-time employment. The decision on whether or not you are employed abroad full-time will depend on the particular circumstances of your case.

If you say that you are working abroad full-time, we would expect you to be able to show that your employment:

- has a standard pattern of hours which can be compared to a typical UK working week or
- if your employment does not have a formal structure or fixed number of working days, it can, by looking at the local conditions and practices of the particular occupation, be compared to similar full-time employment in the country where you are working.

8.6 Returning to the UK after working abroad

If you were not resident and not ordinarily resident when you were working abroad and you return to the UK when your employment ends, you will be not resident and not ordinarily resident in the UK until the day before you return to the UK. You will become resident and ordinarily resident on the day you return to the UK unless you can show that your return was simply a short visit to the UK between two periods of full-time employment abroad.

However, if you have previously been resident in the UK and are returning to become resident here again after a period of residence abroad, you might need to consider whether your absence from the UK was a period of "temporary non-residence". If you were temporarily non-resident in the UK, this may affect your liability to UK tax when you return to become resident in the UK again.

8.7 Changes to your employment when abroad

If your circumstances change while you are abroad, for example there is a break in full-time employment, you might no longer meet the requirements of paragraph 8.5 and so remain resident and ordinarily resident in the UK. You must tell us about such changes by contacting your tax office.

You must also tell us when you return to the UK at the end of an overseas employment, even if you are planning to go abroad again to work under a new contract of employment. You must do this even though you see your return to the UK as temporary and for a very short period. You should tell us this information by contacting your tax office.

8.8 Leaving the UK to become self-employed abroad

If you are leaving the UK to work abroad for yourself in a trade, profession or vocation, then as long as your working circumstances are similar to those outlined in paragraph 8.5, you will be taxed in the same way.

8.9 Leaving the UK with your spouse or partner

When your husband, wife or civil partner leaves the UK to work abroad within the terms of paragraphs 8.5 or 8.8, you are able to receive the same tax treatment if you accompany or later join them abroad. This treatment is by concession (extra-statutory concession A78) and means that even when you yourself are not in full-time employment abroad, you will also be not resident and not ordinarily resident in the UK from the day after your departure. This treatment will apply as long as:

- you will be absent from the UK for at least a whole tax year, and
- your visits to the UK after you have left
  - total less than 183 days in any tax year, and
  - average less than 91 days a tax year.

This average is taken over the period of absence up to a maximum of four years – see 8.5 which will show you how to work out this average. Any days you spend in the UK because of exceptional circumstances beyond your control, for example an illness which prevents you from travelling, are not normally counted for this purpose).

You will remain not resident and not ordinarily resident in the UK until the day before you return to the UK. You become resident and ordinarily resident on the day you return to the UK.'

CHAPTER 6

Residence of trusts and estates

6.01 Introduction

A trust is, in law, a relationship rather than a person. It is the equitable obligation which is created when one person (the settlor) transfers assets (the trust property) to another person (the trustee) who is to hold, control and deal with those assets for the benefit of third parties (the beneficiaries) of whom the trustee himself may be one and any one of whom may enforce the obligation. If the trust is created by the settlor *inter vivos* it is usually referred to as a settlement and the trust property is known as settled property.

Residence, on the other hand, is a personal attribute – a quality that a person attracts to himself by virtue of the strength of his association with a particular place or country. The liability to tax in relation to trusts is by reference to the persons concerned as a result. In the case of the trustees, their personal residence will thus determine their fiscal affiliation as the representative owners of the trust property.

Prior to Finance Act 2006 the position was unsystematic and problematic where there were resident and non-resident trustees. Different rules applied for income tax and capital gains tax. In relation to income tax, in *Dawson v IRC*[1] the House of Lords ruled that, where the general administration of the trust was ordinarily carried on outside the UK and a majority of the trustees were non-resident, a UK-resident trustee was not assessable under Schedule D in respect of income derived from sources outside the UK. It was held that the trust income did not accrue to an individual trustee in his personal capacity and that he had no right of control over it except, in conjunction with his co-trustees, to see that it was applied in accordance with the terms of the trust.[2]

Finance Act 2006[3] aimed at a structured and systematic treatment of the subject. For the first time it made the tests to be applied to determine the residence status of the trustees of a settlement identical for income tax and capital gains tax. The present rules in ITA 2007 ss 474–476 for income tax are effective from 5 April 2007 and follow the latest efforts of the Tax Law Rewrite Project, replacing the wording in FA 2006. The capital gains tax equivalent provisions are TCGA 1992 s 69(1) and (2).

The Finance Act 2006 also provided that the trustees of a settlement are to be treated as a single person for the purposes of the Taxes Act unless the context requires otherwise. Also, the meaning of 'settled property' and, for most purposes, of 'settlement' and 'settlor' are now identical for the two taxes.

1 [1989] STC 473.
2 [1989] STC 473 at 479, per Lord Keith.
3 Sch 13 (income tax) and Pt 1 of Sch 12 (capital gains tax).

Trusts

6.02 Residence

The new rules start by bestowing a collective legal personality on the trustees. Thus, the trustees of a settlement are to be treated as a single 'deemed person' for the purposes of the Taxes Act unless the context requires otherwise.[1] If different parts of the settled property in relation to a settlement are vested in different bodies of trustees, the residence rules still apply in relation to the different bodies as if they were all one body.[2] As part of the process of rationalisation and simplification, the meaning of 'settled property' and, for most purposes, of 'settlement' and 'settlor', are also identical for the two taxes.

1 ITA 2007 s 474(1).
2 ITA 2007 s 474(2)).

6.03 Single residence trustees

Where all the trustees are resident in the UK, the position is straightforward. The trustees (ie the 'deemed person') is treated for income tax and capital gains tax purposes as resident and ordinarily resident in the UK. Where all the trustees are not resident in the UK, then conversely the trustees are neither resident nor ordinarily resident in the UK.

6.04 Mixed residence trustees

Where there are trustees who are resident and trustees who are non-resident in the UK, then the residence of the persons who comprise the deemed person does not determine the residence of that deemed person. The focus of attention shifts to the settlor. This is the case where at least one trustee is resident in the UK and at least one is not. If there is at least one of each, then it does not matter how many more trustees may be resident or non-resident. Thus, a majority of non-resident trustees does not make the deemed person non-resident, and neither does a majority of resident trustees make for a resident trust.

Instead, the residence and ordinary residence of the deemed person is decided by whether the settlor was resident, ordinarily resident, or domiciled in the UK at the 'relevant time'.[1] If, at a time when the settlor made the settlement (or is treated for income tax or capital gains tax purposes as making the settlement) he was UK resident, ordinarily UK resident or domiciled in the UK, then the trustees are resident and ordinarily resident in the UK from the time the settlement is made.[2]

A transfer of property between settlements can affect the residence of the trustees. Thus, if there is a transfer of property between settlements, and a settlor is treated as a settlor in relation to the transferee settlement[3] as a result, and immediately before the transfer, that settlor meets the residence, ordinary residence or domicile condition as a settlor in relation to the transferring settlement then he also meets that condition as a settlor in relation to the transferee settlement from the time he becomes such a settlor until he ceases to be such a settlor.[4]

Trusts taking effect on death require a determination of the settlor's status at that time. If the settlement arose on the settlor's death, whether by will or intestacy or in any other way, and immediately before the settlor's death, he was UK resident, ordinarily UK resident or domiciled in the UK, then the trustees are resident and ordinarily resident in the UK from the date of death of the settlor.[5]

The trustees will be neither resident nor ordinarily resident in the UK in cases where the settlor is not UK resident, ordinarily UK resident or domiciled in the UK at the relevant time. Furthermore, where the settlor has met these conditions at the relevant time, the trustees will cease to be resident and ordinarily resident when the settlor ceases to be treated as a settlor in relation to the settlement.

It will be apparent that these statutory provisions, in effect, abolish the possibility of a distinction between residence and ordinary residence for trustees. The residence *simpliciter* of the trustees and the status of the settlor determine the residence and ordinary residence of the trustees at a single stroke.

---

1 'Condition C' see ITA 2007 s 476.
2 ITA 2007 s 476(3).
3 Under ITA 2007 s 470.
4 ITA 2007 s 476(4).
5 ITA 2007 s 476(2).

6.05   Non-resident trustees with a UK permanent establishment

As has been seen, the residence of the single deemed person constituting the trustees is in part determined by examining the residence of the trustees who make up that deemed person. The residence of each trustee is determined by reference to the rules applicable in the case of individual trustees in Chapters 2 and 3 and in the case of corporate trustees in Chapter 7. An exception is made in the case of non-resident trustees operating in the UK. ITA 2007 s 475(6) reads:

'475(6) If at a time a person ("T") who is a trustee of the settlement acts as trustee in the course of a business which T carries on in the United Kingdom through a branch, agency or permanent establishment there, then for the purposes of subsections (4) and (5) assume that T is UK resident at that time.'

The expression 'branch or agency' is now used only in relation to income tax to determine the extent of any UK representative's liability in respect of a trade carried on in the UK by a non-resident individual,[1] as well as the limit on liability to income tax of non-UK residents[2] and capital gains tax.[3]

Permanent establishment is the equivalent expression in relation to non-resident companies carrying on a trade in the UK[4] introduced by Finance Act 2003 s 148. In general:

'148(1) For the purposes of the Tax Acts a company has a permanent establishment in a territory if, and only if–
    (a)   it has a fixed place of business there through which the business of the company is wholly or partly carried on, or
    (b)   an agent acting on behalf of the company has and habitually exercises there authority to do business on behalf of the company.'

The consequence of a non-resident trustee acting as such in the course of a business is that such trustee is treated as resident in the UK for the purpose of determining the residence and ordinary residence of the single deemed person.

HMRC accept that for trustees the 'branch' and 'agency' tests apply to non-corporate trustees and the 'permanent establishment' test to corporate trustees.[5] Although in most cases the analysis will be similar, features particular to the permanent establishment concept are applicable to corporate trustees only.[6] In their view, the first step is to ask whether the trustee is carrying on a business in the UK, and, if so, is it carrying on that business through a branch, agent, or permanent establishment in the UK? In each case, the business in question is that of providing professional trustee services for a fee. This question does not relate to the business of a particular trust that might be conducted by the trustee. It is only if both questions are answered in the positive that the examination then turns to the activity of being a trustee of a particular trust whose residence is tested.[7]

A trustee is 'carrying on the function of being a trustee' in the context activities of being a trustee of a particular trust when it performs the core activities of a trustee and not those activities which are auxiliary or preparatory. This applies equally to non-corporate trustees.[8] A trustee is the person who has a legal duty to manage the assets of that trust in the best interests of the beneficiary or beneficiaries. The trustee manages, employs and disposes of the trust assets in accordance with both the terms of the trust and the duties and responsibilities which the law places upon trustees. The core activities of a trustee are regarded by HMRC as including:

1   the general administration of the trusts;
2   the over-arching investment strategy;
3   monitoring the performance of those investments; and
4   decisions on how trust income will be dealt with and whether distributions should be made.[9]

Preparatory or auxiliary activities can include information gathering meetings, including meetings with independent agents or with beneficiaries but, as mentioned below, each case will have to be considered individually.[10] However, rather more contentiously, HMRC also take the view that the frequency as well as the nature or significance of the individual activities and meetings go to whether the non-UK resident corporate trustee was acting as a trustee through that permanent establishment. This they say arises where, in relation to a particular trust, there is considerable administrative work – such as meetings with investment managers or beneficiaries – being carried on in the UK through a permanent establishment, so that such meetings have become a major element of the trustee's activities in relation to that trust, and no longer preparatory or auxiliary.[11]

The activity of providing services to a non-UK resident trustee, whether by a connected person or not, does not of itself create a dependent agency permanent establishment under Finance Act 2003 s 148(1)(b). In the view of HMRC it is necessary to consider the capacity in which the person provides the services to the trust on behalf of the non-UK resident trustee. Where the services are only those that the person is contractually obliged to provide under their agreement with the non-UK resident trustee and are remunerated at arm's length, then they regard this as unlikely to create a dependent agency permanent establishment.[12] HMRC views on the application on the existence or otherwise of a permanent establishment of a non-resident trustee and whether the trustee acts as such in the course of a business carried on through a permanent establishment in the UK in specified circumstances are set out in a Guidance note agreed by HMRC with certain professional bodies.[13]

1 FA 1995 s 126(8).
2 ITA 2007 s 811.
3 TCGA 1992 s 9.
4 ICTA 1988 s 11(1).
5 HMRC Guidance Note, 3 August 2009: Trustee Residence Guidance, Version 1 July 2009, paragraph 5.
6 Paragraph 7.
7 Paragraph 8.
8 Paragraph 9.
9 Paragraph10.
10 Paragraph 11.
11 Paragraph 12.
12 Paragraph 3.2.
13 Trustee Residence Taxguide 06/15 agreed by HMRC, reissued August 2015 by the Tax Faculty of the Institute of Chartered Accountants in England and Wales, the Chartered Institute of Taxation and the Society of Trust and Estate Practitioners.

6.06   Individual trustees with split-year treatment

Individuals who become or cease to be UK resident part way through a tax year may be accorded split-year treatment.[1] They are, however, deemed to be resident throughout the year.[2] Thus the residence of the settlement during the overseas part of a split year of a trustee is determined on the basis that the trustee is resident even during that overseas part. A narrow exception applies to an individual who becomes or ceases to be a trustee of a settlement during a tax year. If the individual is a trustee of the settlement only during the overseas part of the year, then the individual is treated as if he had been non-UK resident for the year and consequently for the part of the year when he was a trustee of the settlement.[3]

This exception does not apply to a trustee who acts as such in the course of a business which he carries on in the UK through a branch, agency or permanent establishment there. Such trustees are always UK resident.[4]

---

1 See **2.30**.
2 See **2.31**.
3 ITA 2007 s 475(7) and (8) for income tax and TCGA 1992 s 69 (2DA) for capital gains tax. Inserted by FA 2013 Sch 45, paras 102 and 103 respectively.
4 ITA 2007 s 475(9) for income tax and TCGA 1992 s 69 (2DB) for capital gains tax. Inserted by FA 2013 Sch 45, paras 102 and 103 respectively.

6.07   Residence for tax treaties

As is the case with any other person, the trustees may be treated as resident in the UK under its laws but at the same time treated as a resident in another country for the purposes of its tax laws. Qualification as a person and a resident will normally bring with it access to treaty benefits under treaties patterned on the OECD Model:

> '4(1) For the purposes of this Convention, the term "resident of a Contracting State" means any person who, under the laws of that State, is liable to tax therein by reason of his domicile, residence, place of management or any other criterion of a similar nature, and also includes that State and any political subdivision or local authority thereof. This term, however, does not include any person who is liable to tax in that State in respect only of income from sources in that State or capital situated therein.'

Where a tax treaty is in place, such dual residence may be resolved for the purposes of the treaty by the following mechanism:

> '4(3) Where by reason of the provisions of paragraph 1 a person other than an individual is a resident of both Contracting States, then it shall be deemed to be a resident only of the State in which its place of effective management is situated.'

The commentary to the OECD Model does not directly consider the position of trusts. However, the Special Commissioners have considered the meaning of the expression 'place of effective management' in two decisions. In *Trustees of Wensleydale's Settlement v IR Commrs*[1] the success or failure simple of a capital gains tax avoidance scheme turned entirely upon whether in fact the trustees of a settlement were deemed to be a resident of the Republic of Ireland for the reason that they, being 'a person other than an individual' and a resident of both the Republic of Ireland and of the UK, 'its place of effective management was situated' in the Republic. In the absence of much guidance the Special Commissioner considered that 'effective' implies realistic, positive management. On the evidence he found that she was a trustee in name rather than in reality, signing all the documents placed before her and on this basis held that the place of effective management of the trust was not in the Republic of Ireland.

A similar conclusion was reached in *Trevor Smallwood Trust v R & C Commrs*[2] which also concerned a not dissimilar tax avoidance scheme where a trust moved from the UK to Mauritius. The Special Commissioners believed 'effective' should be understood in the sense of the French *effective (siège de direction effective)* which connotes real, French being the other official version of the OECD Model. Having regard to the ordinary meaning of the words in their context and in the light of their object and purpose, the place of effective management depended on where the real top-level management (or the realistic, positive management) of the trustee, as trustee, was to be found. They accepted that the administration of the trust moved to Mauritius, but in their view the 'key' decisions were made in the UK and consequently, the trust's 'place of effective management' was in the UK.

The Court of Appeal,[3] however, divided on where the place of effective management was and how it was to be determined. Patten LJ, with whom Ward LJ agreed, was of the view that although the Mauritius trustees were appointed as part of a pre-existing scheme and they accepted the trusteeship on the basis that the shares would be sold as part of that exercise and that the shares were indeed sold in accordance with the scheme, they retained their right and duties as trustees to consider the matter at the time of alienation and did not agree merely to act on the instructions which they received from the accountants who advised on the scheme. Thus it was not open to say that effective management was exercised by anyone other than the trustees in Mauritius. Hughes LJ, dissenting, considered that because first, the trustees are treated as a single and continuing body of persons, the place of effective management of the trust is that of the trustees as a continuing body; and secondly, the scheme was devised and orchestrated throughout from the UK, which included that the trust should be exported to Mauritius for a brief temporary period and then returned, within the fiscal year, to the UK, there was a scheme of management which went above and beyond the day-to-day management exercised by the trustees for the time being, and the control of it was in the UK. The majority view of the court is to be preferred. The dissent of Hughes LJ seems to be unduly influenced by the existence of a tax avoidance scheme to articulate any principle of general application and appears to rely on blending both past and present trustees together.

Dual resident trusts and estates will be affected by OECD proposals made pursuant to the OECD/G20 Base Erosion and Profit Shifting Project to change the treaty rule for resolving dual residence cases aimed at corporate tax avoidance, discussed at **7.6**.

---

1 (1996) Sp C 73.

2 *Trevor Smallwood & Mary Caroline Smallwood Trustees of the Trevor Smallwood Trust v R & C Commrs; Trevor Smallwood Settlor of the Trevor Smallwood Trust v R & C Commrs* [2008] UKSPC 669. In the High Court ([2009] EWHC 777 (Ch)), Mann J ruled that the question of dual residence did not arise and consequently Art 4(3) of the treaty was not engaged.

3 *HMRC v Smallwood & Anor* [2010] EWCA Civ 778. See generally Jonathan Schwarz, *Schwarz on Tax Treaties* (CCH, 2013) Ch 6 on treaty residence.

6.08 Residence of estates

Unlike the residence of trustees, the residence of personal representatives of deceased estates was not comprehensively reformed by the Finance Act 2006. Legislation only addresses the case of mixed personal representatives. HMRC take the position that the personal representatives are deemed to have the same residence and domicile status as the deceased had at the date of death.[1]

The statutory treatment of personal representatives of a deceased person is somewhat similar in the case of mixed residence personal representatives to that of trustees. For income tax purposes, if the personal representatives of a deceased person include one or more persons who are UK resident and one or more persons who are non-UK resident, then if the deceased died resident or domiciled in the UK, the UK-resident persons are treated, in their capacity as personal representatives, as UK resident. In contrast then if the deceased died not resident or domiciled in the UK, the UK-resident persons are treated, in their capacity as personal representatives, as not UK resident.[2] For capital gains tax purposes, 'resident' has the same meaning in TCGA 1992 as in the Income Tax Acts.[3] No mitigation is available to personal representatives who come to or leave the UK and qualify for split-year treatment. They are resident even during the overseas part of a split year.

---

1 HMRC Capital Gains Manual CG30650.
2 ITA 2007 s 834.
3 TCGA 1992 s 9(1).

CHAPTER 7

Residence of companies

A Company Limited? What may that be?
The term, I rather think, is new to me.

Sir W S Gilbert, Utopia Limited (Finale)

7.01 Introduction

A corporation is a legal entity. It is, under the law, an artificial person, separate and distinct from its members and endowed with an existence independent of their existence.[1]

Although a corporation's personality is artificial, it is not fictitious. Since 1889 the word 'person' in any Act of Parliament has included 'a body of persons corporate' unless the contrary intention appears,[2] and a corporation may, accordingly, be fined for contempt of court,[3] be convicted of an offence involving a fraudulent intent,[4] and be a 'respectable and responsible person' to whom to assign a lease.[5] This chapter examines the residence of companies. Corporation tax has undergone the rewrite process and its fruits are to be found in the Corporation Tax Act 2009 which generally has effect for accounting periods ending on or after 1 April 2009 and the Corporation Tax Act 2010 which generally has effect for accounting periods ending on or after 1 April 2010. The term 'company' is not, of course, descriptive only of a limited company but, under CTA 2010 s 1121, must be taken to mean, in this context, 'any body corporate or unincorporated association' excluding 'a partnership, a local authority or a local authority association'. More to the point, it may possess the status of residence and ordinary residence:

> 'Now the definition of the word "residence" is founded upon the habits and relations of the natural man and is therefore inapplicable to the artificial and legal person whom we call a corporation. But for the purpose of giving effect to the words of the Legislature an artificial residence must be assigned to this artificial person, and one formed on the analogy of natural persons.'[6]

The territorial basis of taxation applies to companies who are chargeable to corporation tax on their profits.[7] Profits for this purpose means income and chargeable gains.[8] A UK-resident company is chargeable to corporation tax on all its profits wherever arising,[9] but a company not resident in the UK is not within the charge to corporation tax unless it carries on a trade in the UK through a permanent establishment there.[10] Where it does so, it is chargeable to corporation tax only on profits attributable to the permanent establishment and on trading income and chargeable gains relating to assets used or held by or for the permanent establishment.[11] A company that is not resident in the UK may also be liable to income tax on certain income from sources within the UK not attributable to a permanent establishment.[12]

Until 1988 there was no statutory definition of residence for companies. The statutory definitions are now conveniently gathered in CTA 2009 Pt 2 Ch 3. In terms, these statutory provisions apply for the purposes of the Corporation Tax Acts.[13] The predecessor legislation applied these statutory provisions for the purposes of the Taxes Acts.[14] The rewrite has approached this extension by incorporating CTA 2009 Pt 2 Ch 3 by reference into specific enactments.[15]

Although HMRC has long-standing published practice in this area (principally Statement of Practice SP 1/90 and the more thoughtful International Tax Manual, Chapter 3), the application of this practice has not given rise to the same difficulties faced in the individual residence area. Updated guidance in the International Manual INTM120000 and following now includes helpful examples of when HMRC will question the residence of companies and those circumstances in which they will normally not review residence. As will be explained,[16] the courts have been required to interpret the expression and a substantial body of case law has resulted.

---

1 *Salomon v Salomon & Co* [1897] AC 22.
2 Interpretation Act 1978 s 5 and Sch 1.
3 *R v J G Hammond & Co* [1914] 2 KB 866.
4 *R v ICR Haulage Ltd* [1944] KB 551.
5 *Ideal Film Renting Co v Nielson* [1921] 1 Ch 575.
6 *Calcutta Jute Mills Co Ltd v Nicholson* (1876) 1 TC 83 at 103, per Huddleston B.
7 CTA 2009 s 5.
8 CTA 2009 s 2(2).
9 CTA 2009 s 5(1).
10 CTA 2009 s 5(2).
11 CTA 2009 Pt 2 Ch 4.
12 ITA 2007 s 815.
13 See ICTA 1988 s 831(1)(a): 'the Corporation Tax Acts' means the enactments relating to the taxation of the income and chargeable gains of companies and of company distributions (including provisions relating also to income tax).
14 Effectively extending the provisions to income tax and capital gains tax. See TMA 1970 s 118(1), 'Taxes Acts' and related provisions.
15 See TMA 1970 s 109A; TCGA 1992 s 286A; ITA 2007 s 835A.
16 **7.03** and following.

7.02   UK incorporated companies

The residence of companies is now addressed in CTA 2009 Pt 2 Ch 3. Any company incorporated in the UK is deemed to be resident in the UK for the purposes of the Corporation Tax Acts.[1] Any other rule determining residence is excluded.[2] The case law which determined the test of residence on the basis of the location of a company's central control and management is of no relevance to any company which is incorporated in the UK. Although the term residence continues to be applied to such companies, the ordinary meaning of the term has been suspended in favour of a formal test. Thus the tax liability of companies incorporated in the UK is determined by the place of incorporation and not any factual enquiry as to where or how it conducts its business.

There are two limited exceptions to the incorporation rule by way of transitional relief from the time of adoption of the rule in 1988.[3] The first operates if the company was non-resident before 14 March 1988 and had become so before then, pursuant to a general or a specific Treasury consent[4] obtained under what was ICTA 1988 s 765 or its predecessors.[5]

If the consent was a specific consent, and if the company does not cease to carry on business, the company can remain non-resident regardless of where it is based, and it only becomes UK resident if it in fact becomes resident under the central management and control test.[6]

If the consent was a general consent, a further condition has to be satisfied, namely that the company was taxable in a foreign territory.[7] By 'taxable' is meant being liable to tax on income by reason of domicile, residence or place of management.[8] The second application of the exception is for companies which commenced business before 15 March 1988 and become non-resident on or after 15 March 1988 but before 1 April 2009, pursuant to a specific consent applied for before 15 March 1988.[9] If it ceases to carry on business, or becomes resident under the central management and control test, the exception will cease to apply.[10]

---

1 CTA 2009 s 14(1). See **7.03** below.
2 CTA 2009 s 14(2).
3 CTA 2009 Sch 2 Pt 5.
4 CTA 2009 Sch 2 Pt 5 para 13(1). It must also have remained non-resident to 1 April 2009.
5 See CTA 2009 Sch 2 Pt 5 para 15(2). ICTA 1988 s 765 was repealed by FA 2009.
6 CTA 2009 Sch 2 Pt 5 para 13(2).
7 CTA 2009 Sch 2 Pt 5 para 13(2)(c).
8 CTA 2009 Sch 2 Pt 5 para 15(1).
9 CTA 2009 Sch 2 Pt 5 para 14(1).
10 CTA 2009 Sch 2 Pt 5 para 14(2).

7.03   Residence under case law

Wisely, the Tax Law Rewrite Committee refrained from attempting to put the case law test of residence into statutory form. The test of central control and management is now only in most cases applicable to foreign incorporated companies. Thus, a foreign incorporated company will be resident in the UK if the central management and control of the company is exercised in the UK.

The phrase 'central management and control' was coined not by Parliament but by Lord Loreburn in one of the earliest of all the cases concerning company residence, *De Beers Consolidated Mines v Howe*,[1] at the beginning of the 20th century. The head office was formally at Kimberley, and the general meetings were held there. Profits were made out of diamonds raised in South Africa, and sold under annual contracts for delivery in South Africa. Further, some of the directors and Life Governors lived in South Africa, and there were directors' meetings at Kimberley as well as in London. But the majority of directors and Life Governors lived in England. The directors' meetings in London were the meetings where the real control was always exercised in practically all the important business of the company, except the mining operations. London always controlled the negotiation of the contracts with the syndicates to whom the diamonds were sold, determined policy in the disposal of diamonds and other assets, the working and development of mines, the application of profits, and the appointment of directors. London also always controlled matters that required to be determined by the majority of all the directors, which included all questions of expenditure except wages, materials, and such like at the mines, and a limited sum which might be spent by the directors at Kimberley. In finding the company resident in the UK, Lord Loreburn formulated the principle as:

> 'A company resides, for the purposes of Income Tax, where its real business is carried on ... I regard that as the true rule; and the real business is carried on where the central management and control actually abides'.

In *Bullock v Unit Construction Co Ltd*,[2] Lord Radcliffe summarised the position as it existed in 1959 as:[3]

> '... the necessity of establishing some common standard for the treatment of different taxpayers meant that the Courts of Law were bound in course of time to produce and apply some general principle of their own to form an acceptable test of residence ... [T]he principle was adopted that a company is resident where its central management and control abide: words which, according to the decision of the House of Lords that finally propounded the test, *De Beers Consolidated Mines Ltd v Howe*,[4] are equivalent to saying that a company's residence is where its "real business" is carried on ... .
>
> ... as precise and unequivocal as a positive statutory injunction ... I do not know of any other test which has either been substituted for that of central management and control, or has been defined with sufficient precision to be regarded as an acceptable alternative to it. To me ... it seems impossible to read Lord Loreburn's words without seeing that he regarded the formula he was propounding as constituting the test of residence.'

---

1 *De Beers Consolidated Mines Ltd v Howe* (1906) 5 TC 198 at 213.
2 (1959) 38 TC 712.
3 (1959) 38 TC 712, per Lord Radcliffe at 738.
4 (1906) 5 TC 198.

7.04   The *Untelrab* synthesis

From a practical perspective, a brief statement of principles is most desirable. In *Untelrab Ltd & Ors v McGregor* (HMIT),[1] the first published decision of the Special Commissioners dealing with company residence, an attempt was made to synthesise the principles developed in a large number of cases over more than a century as follows:

'From these authorities we have identified the following principles:

– that the residence of a company is where the directors meet and transact their business and exercise the powers conferred upon them;

– that if the directors meet in two places then the company's residence is where its real business is carried on and the real business is carried on where the central management and control actually abides;

– that a determination as to whether a case falls within that rule is a pure question of fact to be determined by a scrutiny of the course of business and trading;

– that the actual place of management, and not the place where a company ought to be managed, fixes the place of residence of a company;

– that it is an exceptional case for a parent company to usurp control from its subsidiaries; a parent company usually operates through the boards of its subsidiaries;

– that although a board might do what it was told to do it did not follow that the control and management of the company lay with another, so long as the board exercised their discretion when coming to their decisions and would have refused to carry out an improper or unwise transaction; and

– that when deciding the issue of residence one should stand back from the detail and make up one's mind from the picture which the whole of the evidence presents.'[2]

The case is one that represents two modern circumstances where arguments between companies and the Revenue have been most acute. The first, as in *Untelrab*, is where a company forms part of an international group of companies and the operations of group members are affected to a greater or lesser extent by group policies led from the parent company. The second is in relation to privately owned companies where it claimed that the power of a dominant shareholder prevails. Very often these are special purpose vehicles set up to perform a specific function within a corporate group or in organising an individual's affairs.

Untelrab concerned subsidiaries of a UK-resident public company incorporated in the Channel Islands and Bermuda. Their directors were lawyers and accountants resident in those territories. Board meetings were held there and the day-to-day management of the companies undertaken there. Although managed overseas, in certain respects, they adopted group policy as formulated by the parent company. The Special Commissioners found that the board of Untelrab met in Bermuda and transacted the company's business there. At board meetings proposals were discussed and decisions were made by the directors in the best interests of the company. They would have refused to carry out any proposal which was improper or unreasonable. The UK-resident parent company did not control the board in the exercise of their powers. It could have taken steps to remove the directors but could not control them in their conduct of Untelrab's business.[3] The decision was not appealed. It was, however, endorsed by Park J in the High Court in *Wood v Holden*.[4]

1 (1995) SpC 55.
2 *Untelrab Ltd & Ors v McGregor* (HMIT) (1995) SpC 55 at para 74.
3 *Untelrab Ltd & Ors v McGregor* (HMIT) (1995) SpC 55 at para 73.
4 [2005] EWHC 547 (Ch) at para 26.

7.05 A question of fact

In relation to the application of the central management and control test, Lord Loreburn, having formulated the rule,[1] continued in *De Beers*:

'It remains to be considered whether the present case falls within that rule. This is a pure question of fact, to be determined, not according to the construction of this or that regulation or byelaw, but upon a scrutiny of the course of business and trading.'[2]

Although the enquiry into exercise of central management and control is a factual enquiry, special considerations apply in the context of a legal person. Early case law proceeded by analogy with individuals. Thus, in the seminal decision in *De Beers*, Lord Loreburn said:

'In applying the conception of residence to a Company, we ought, I think, to proceed as nearly as we can upon the analogy of an individual. A Company cannot eat or sleep, but it can keep house and do business. We ought, therefore, to see whether it really keeps house and does business. An individual may be of foreign nationality, and yet reside in the United Kingdom. So may a Company.'[3]

While the habits and lifestyle of an individual form the obvious fact base, in the case of companies, the question as to which facts ought to be examined is less obvious and has been controversial. Case law and administrative practice has focused on identifying, what is meant by 'central management and control', who exercises it and where that exercise takes place. These elements are interrelated but may be considered individually for ease of analysis.

Because the residence of a company is to be determined by the location of its central management and control, and because that location is a question of fact, a finding by the Commissioners that a company is resident in this place or that will be unassailable provided the Commissioners have before them evidence from which their finding can be made and providing they do not misdirect themselves in law.[4] The court's approach is well-illustrated by Lord Loreburn's conclusion in the *De Beers* case:[5]

'The Commissioners, after sifting the evidence, arrived at the two following conclusions, viz: ... (2) That the head and seat and directing power of the affairs of the Appellant Company were at the office in London, from whence the chief operations of the Company, both in the United Kingdom and elsewhere, were, in fact, controlled, managed and directed. That conclusion of fact cannot be impugned, and it follows that this Company was resident within the United Kingdom for the purposes of Income Tax.'[6]

1 See **7.03**.
2 *De Beers Consolidated Mines v Howe* (1906) 5 TC 198 at 213.

3 *De Beers Consolidated Mines v Howe* (1906) 5 TC 198 at 212.
4 See **3.03** above.
5 *De Beers Consolidated Mines v Howe* (1906) 5 TC 198.
6 *De Beers Consolidated Mines v Howe* (1906) 5 TC 198 at 213–214.

7.06   Who exercises central management and control?

Bullock v Unit Construction Co Ltd[1] has for many years formed the basis
of a very broad approach to the factual enquiry by the Revenue. There, Unit
Construction Company Ltd, a UK-resident subsidiary of Alfred Booth & Co
Ltd, a UK-resident parent company, made subvention payments to three of
its fellow subsidiary companies in Kenya and claimed that those payments
were, under FA 1953 s 20, permissible deductions in arriving at its profits for
tax purposes. This would have been so only if the three Kenyan subsidiaries
also were resident in the UK, but the Inland Revenue contended that they were
not. The three subsidiaries had been incorporated in Kenya and their articles
of association expressly placed their management and control in the hands of
their directors and required directors' meetings to be held outside the UK. That
being so, the three Kenyan subsidiaries must, said the Revenue, be resident
outside the UK. The Commissioners found as a *fact*, however, that, due to
trading difficulties which the subsidiaries had encountered,

> '... at the material times ... the boards of directors of the African subsidiaries ...
> were standing aside in all matters of real importance and in many matters of minor
> importance affecting the central management and control, and ... the real control
> and management was being exercised by the board of directors of Alfred Booth &
> Co Ltd in London.'[2]

Accordingly, the Commissioners found that each of the African subsidiaries
was resident in the UK, and their finding was ultimately upheld in the House
of Lords. Referring to the reversals the decision had suffered at the hands of the
High Court and the Court of Appeal, Viscount Simonds said:

> '... the contention of learned Counsel for the Crown which has so far found favour
> with the courts is no less than this, that if by the constitution of the company, that
> is, by its memorandum and articles of association interpreted in the light of the
> relevant law, that is, in this case the law of Kenya, the management of the company's
> business is contemplated as being exercised, and ought therefore to be exercised, in
> Kenya or at any rate outside the United Kingdom, then for the purpose of British
> Income Tax law the facts are to be disregarded and the control and management
> which as a fact are found to abide in the United Kingdom are to be regarded as
> abiding outside it. There is no doubt, I think, that the management of the African
> subsidiaries, which were incorporated in Kenya under the Kenya Companies
> Ordinance and registered in Nairobi, was placed in the hands of their directors and
> that their articles of association expressly provided that directors' meetings might
> be held anywhere outside the United Kingdom. Nor can there be any doubt – for this
> is the unchallengeable finding of the Commissioners – that the management of the
> business of the companies was not exercised in the manner contemplated. Whence
> it follows that the business was conducted in a manner irregular, unauthorised and
> perhaps unlawful ...

'My Lords, I should certainly be prepared to admit that the many Judges who in the past have pronounced upon this question had not in mind such a case as this. But, with great respect to those who take a different view, the present case does not seem to lie outside the principle underlying their judgment. Nothing can be more factual and concrete than the acts of management which enable a Court to find as a fact that central management and control is exercised in one country or another. It does not in any way alter their character that in greater or less degree they are irregular or unauthorised or unlawful. The business is not the less managed in London because it ought to be managed in Kenya. Its residence is determined by the solid facts, not by the terms of its constitution, however imperative. If indeed I must disregard the facts as they are, because they are irregular, I find a company without any central management at all. For, though I may disregard existing facts, I cannot invent facts which do not exist and say that the company's business is managed in Kenya. Yet it is the place of central management which, however much or little weight ought to be given to other factors, essentially determines its residence. I come, therefore, to the conclusion … that it is the actual place of management, not the place in which it ought to be managed, which fixes the residence of a company.'[3]

The broad approach is highlighted in the HMRC Statement of Practice on company residence:

'In some cases … central management and control is exercised by a single individual. This may happen when a chairman or managing director exercises powers formally conferred by the company's Articles and the other board members are little more than cyphers, or by reason of a dominant shareholding or for some other reason. In those cases the residence of the company is where the controlling individual exercises his powers.[4]

Generally, however, where doubts arise about a particular company's residence status, the Inland Revenue adopt the following approach:

(i)   They first try to ascertain whether the directors of the company in fact exercise central management and control.

(ii)   If so, they seek to determine where the directors exercise this central management and control (which is not necessarily where they meet).

(iii)   In cases where the directors apparently do not exercise central management and control of the company, the Revenue then look to establish where and by whom it is exercised.'[5]

The full extent to which this approach is considered to apply is illustrated in *Wood v Holden (Inspector of Taxes)*[6] where the Court of Appeal affirmed the decision of the High Court judge who had overruled the conclusion of Special Commissioners Wallace and Brice that a Netherlands company was resident in the UK.

The case arose from a scheme to avoid capital gains tax on the sale of trading companies by two UK-resident individuals. The scheme had been designed by a firm of accountants who also attended to its implementation. The shares in the trading companies came to be held by a Netherlands-incorporated company itself owned by a British Virgin Islands company which was in turn owned by trustees of offshore family trusts. The sole director of the Netherlands company was a Dutch trust company. HMRC argued that the company registered in the Netherlands (but surprisingly, not the BVI company) was nevertheless resident in the UK. The HMRC case was that the Dutch corporate director did not in fact take the decisions but did what it was told to do by Mr Wood or by the firm of UK-based chartered accountants acting on his behalf. This contention was upheld by the Special Commissioners[7] but not by the High Court or the Court of Appeal. The House of Lords refused leave to appeal. In the Court of Appeal Chadwick LJ said at para 27:

> 'In my view the judge was correct in his analysis of the law. In seeking to determine where "central management and control" of a company incorporated outside the United Kingdom lies, it is essential to recognise the distinction between cases where management and control of the company is exercised through its own constitutional organs (the board of directors or the general meeting) and cases where the functions of those constitutional organs are "usurped" – in the sense that management and control is exercised independently of, or without regard to, those constitutional organs. And, in cases which fall within the former class, it is essential to recognise the distinction (in concept, at least) between the role of an "outsider" in proposing, advising and influencing the decisions which the constitutional organs take in fulfilling their functions and the role of an outsider who dictates the decisions which are to be taken. In that context an "outsider" is a person who is not, himself, a participant in the formal process (a board meeting or a general meeting) through which the relevant constitutional organ fulfils its function.'

The Netherlands company's directors had not been bypassed and they had not stood aside. They had also decided to accept the agreement proposed by the accountants and had made the decision to sign and execute the documents. Theirs was an effective decision by a constitutional organ, exercising management and control.

This reveals two categories of management pattern to consider. The first category is where management and control of the company is exercised by its own constitutional organs. The second category concerns where the functions of those constitutional organs are 'usurped'. Where it is determined that management and control is exercised by the company's constitutional organs, it is necessary to examine what those organs do and where they are. Where management and control is usurped, the place and nature of the usurper's action must be the focus of attention.

Constitutional organs cannot be comprised of 'fake' directors. In *Bywater Investments Limited & Ors v Commissioner of Taxation*,[8] the Australian High Court ruled that, where it was intended from the outset that an Australian resident, who had disguised his ownership and control of non-Australian companies, would make all the decisions for those companies, and that a husband and wife resident in Switzerland appointed as directors, whose only role would be to implement the Australian's decisions, the Australian resident exercised central management and control. The Swiss directors' role was a 'fake'. In that case, the constitutional organs of the company did not, and were not intended to, exercise central management and control of the companies.[9]

---

1 (1959) 38 TC 712.
2 (1959) 38 TC 712 at 721–722.
3 (1959) 38 TC 712 at 735–736.
4 SP 1/90, para 13.
5 SP 1/90 para 15.

6 2006 STC 443.
7 *Sub nom R & Anor v Holden (HM Inspector of Taxes)* [2004] UK SPC422.
8 *Bywater Investments Limited & Ors v Commissioner of Taxation* [2016] HCA 45.
9 *Bywater Investments Limited & Ors v Commissioner of Taxation* [2016] HCA 45 at paras 75
   to 77.

7.07 Delegated management and control

Delegated management and control and *central* management and control
are mutually exclusive concepts. Indeed delegation is itself an exercise of
management and control.

In *Calcutta Jute Mills v Nicholson*,[1] Huddleston B held that the central
management and control of the Calcutta Jute Mills, though ostensibly exercised
by a director in India, was actually exercised from the company's office in
London where the board of directors met:

> 'From that office would issue all the orders to the managing director in Calcutta.
> No doubt, until he received orders to the contrary, he would have full power and
> discretion to do what he liked in Calcutta; but at any moment, from this head office,
> they might have revoked his authority, or altered any arrangement which he had
> made connected with the working of the company.'[2]

The director in Calcutta was, for all his powers, a mere delegate and one had,
therefore, to look beyond him to the delegators from whom his powers had
been derived and by whom they were being sustained.

In *American Thread Company v Joyce*[3] the delegation of powers to the
American Thread Co Ltd was ostensibly managed and controlled by an
executive committee of directors in New York. The Master of the Rolls was,
however, quite clear that central management and control lay in Manchester,
England:

> 'Now the current business the daily purchasing and selling of raw materials and
> making them into thread is, no doubt, carried out by the executive committee in New
> York, the executive committee of three. Who appoint them? The English board. It
> must be done by the English board where the majority of the directors, four out of
> seven, reside. They are appointed by them, their salary is fixed by them, in fact the
> whole control of the machine, so to say, is kept and carefully kept at Manchester.'[4]

In *News Datacom Ltd & News Data Security Products Ltd v Revenue &
Customs*,[5] an executive committee of the board of directors existed as permitted
by the articles of association. It was concerned with day-to-day operational
matters and seven of its nine meetings were in the UK. HMRC argued that it,
rather than the board, exercised central management and control. The Special
Commissioners found that the executive committee exercised no part in the
'controlling brain' of the company.

What all these cases illustrate, therefore, is that, in determining the location
of a company's central management and control, it is necessary to ask of those
who appear to be exercising such control, 'To whom do you look over your
shoulder? From whom do you derive your powers and who is able to modify

or withdraw them?' If the answer is, 'No one. We derive our powers from the shareholders who appointed us and, short of the shareholders removing us from office, no-one can interfere with our powers', identification of those who exercise central management and control will have been made.[6] If the answer is otherwise it will provide a pointer either to those who truly exercise central management and control or to a person or persons who are one step nearer to the centre than those to whom the question was addressed.

---

1 (1876) 1 TC 83.
2 (1876) 1 TC 83 at 107.
3 (1913) 6 TC 163.
4 (1913) 6 TC 163.
5 [2006] UKSPC SPC561.
6 The distinction between shareholder control and central management and control is discussed at **7.08** below.

7.08   Shareholder control

It must be stressed that the test of corporate residence involves the identification of the place of central management *and* (not *or*) control. In other words, the control in question is that which relates to the highest level of management of a company's business and must not, therefore, be confused with the control which vests in a company's shareholders *per se*. The distinction was stressed by Moulton LJ in *Stanley v Gramophone and Typewriter Ltd*[1] when he said:

'... the individual corporator does not carry on the business of the corporation; he is only entitled to the profits of that business to a certain extent, fixed and ascertained in a certain way, depending upon the constitution of the corporation and his holding in it. This legal proposition ... is not weakened by the fact that the extent of his interest in it entitles him to exercise a greater or lesser amount of control over the manner in which the business is carried on. Such control is inseparable from his position as a corporator, and is a wholly different thing both in fact and in law from carrying on the business himself. The Directors and employees of the corporation are not his agents, and he has no power of giving directions to them which they must obey. It has been decided by this court in the *Automatic Self-cleaning Filter Syndicate Co Ltd v Cunninghame*[2] that in an English Company by whose Articles of Association certain powers were placed in the hands of the Directors the shareholders could not interfere with the exercise of those powers by the Directors even by a majority in General Meeting. Their course is to obtain the requisite majority to remove the Directors and put persons in their place who agree to their policy. This shows that the control of individual corporators is something wholly different from the management of the business itself. Nor is this principle less true when the holding of the individual corporator is so large that he is able to override the wishes of the other corporators in matters relating to the control of the business of the Company. The extent but not the nature of his power is changed by the magnitude of his holding.'[3]

It follows, therefore, that a company whose business is, in fact, managed and controlled by a board of directors in, say, London, will none the less be resident in England even if, say, 98% of its shares are owned by an individual resident in France. This proposition was specifically approved by the Court of Appeal in *Bullock v Unit Construction Co Ltd*[4] and still stands. The Court of Appeal also assented to the proposition, however, that:

'... a shareholder who holds sufficient in a company can *de facto* control its affairs by his ability to remove directors who disagree with his policy and to vote others into their places.'[5]

The significance of a shareholder's power was given detailed consideration in *American Thread Co v Joyce*.[6] There, the Crown contended that the operations of the American company were controlled from Manchester not merely because a majority of directors met there but also because the English parent company owned the entire share capital of the American company.

In the Court of Appeal, Buckley LJ went to some lengths to emphasise that it was not shareholder control on which the finding that the American company was resident in the UK rested:

'The shareholders can, no doubt, by virtue of their votes control the corporation; they can compel directors ... to do their will, but it does not follow that the corporators are managing the corporation. The contrary is the truth; they are not. It is the directors who are managing the affairs of the corporation ... [T]he executive committee in New York were in fact controlled ... on this side in extraordinary sessions of the Board which were held once a fortnight, and the real control, the head and seat and directing power of the affairs of the Company were here. It was in that sense that the control was here ... .'[7]

Before leaving the question of shareholder control, attention must – for the sake of completeness – be drawn to *Apthorpe v Peter Schoenhoffen Brewing Co Ltd*[8] which concerned the wholly owned American brewing subsidiary of an English company. The directors of the English company had full power of management and control of the affairs of the American company but they delegated these powers to a committee of management in Chicago. The Commissioners found that:

'... the head and seat and directing power of the [English] Company were at the [English] Company's registered office in the City of London, and that if the business at Chicago and the profits made thereby were technically the business and profits of the American company the American company was for such purpose the agent of the [English] Company.'[9]

In its statement of practice, the Revenue declares its position on wholly owned subsidiaries to be as follows:

'It is particularly difficult to apply the "central management and control" test in the situation where a subsidiary company and its parent operate in different territories. In this situation, the parent will normally influence, to a greater or lesser extent, the actions of the subsidiary. Where that influence is exerted by the parent exercising the powers which a sole or majority shareholder has in general meetings of the subsidiary, for example to appoint or dismiss members of the board of the subsidiary and to initiate or approve alterations to its financial structure, the Revenue would not seek to argue that central control and management of the subsidiary is located where the parent company is resident. However, in cases where the parent usurps the functions of the board of the subsidiary (such as *Unit Construction* itself) or where that board merely rubber stamps the parent company's decisions without giving them any independent consideration of its own, the Revenue draw the conclusion that the subsidiary has the same residence for tax purposes as its parent.[10]

This may reflect the case law described in this chapter if it is read as going no further than *Untelrab* and *Wood v Holden*. However, the statement then goes on to say that:

'The Revenue recognise that there may be many cases where a company is a member of a group having its ultimate holding company in another country which will not fall readily into either of the categories referred to above. In considering whether the board of such a subsidiary company exercises central management and control of the subsidiary's business, they have regard to the degree of autonomy which those directors have in conducting the company's business. Matters (among others) that may be taken into account are the extent to which the directors of the subsidiary take decisions on their own authority as to investment, production, marketing and procurement without reference to the parent.'[11]

This is plainly at odds with the current state of the law but remains unamended. Nonetheless, the application of the law to particular circumstances, especially where tax planned schemes are implemented by foreign subsidiaries, may be challenging, given the intensely factual nature of the enquiry.

Development Securities (No 9) Ltd & Ors v Revenue and Customs,[12] also involved the residence of non-UK incorporated companies for a limited and specific purpose. As was the case in *Untelrab Ltd v McGregor*,[13] subsidiaries were formed in Jersey in order to undertake specific transactions as part of a tax planning arrangement. The directors of the subsidiaries were Jersey resident directors provided by a Jersey law firm and the company secretary of the UK resident parent company, who was a UK resident. Judge Harriet Morgan noted that it does not necessarily follow that central management and control of an overseas group company, which has been formed for a specific purpose is UK resident simply because it follows the parent company's plan and does what is expected, if proper consideration is given to the proposal and the directors are in fact exercising their discretion.[14] She considered that the case was unusual because the Jersey companies were set up only to acquire assets for an amount substantially in excess of their market value. This single transaction that they were to undertake was inherently uncommercial from their perspective. Consequently, the transaction could only be valid as a matter of corporate law if the UK parent company specifically approved the transaction and the Jersey companies were adequately funded such that there was no prejudice to creditors. In addition, the companies were to become UK tax resident six weeks after acquiring the assets.[15]

Although the directors were serious in their concern to check the legality of the proposed actions and regarded it as their responsibility to ensure that the Jersey companies and they themselves were not acting unlawfully, she regarded checking that there were no legal impediments as insufficient to constitute taking the decision about the proposed action. Judge Morgan concluded that the strategic decision, that is, whether it was a good plan for the

Jersey companies to acquire the assets at a price in excess of their value, was not made by the board of directors in Jersey.[16]

These circumstances were distinguished from *Wood v Holden*, where the board considered a proposal and, having taken appropriate advice, decided that it was in the best interests of the companies to enter into the transaction. Since the transaction was not in the interests of the Jersey companies and could only take place with parent company approval, 'the inescapable conclusion is that the board was simply doing what the parent ... in effect instructed it to do. In the circumstances, the line was crossed from the parent influencing and giving strategic or policy direction to the parent giving an instruction.'[17]

The decision is not easy to square with *Wood v Holden* because the company's directors did not stand aside but decided, as a constitutional organ, to accept the proposal of the parent company in accordance with the company's corporate requirements. It does however indicate the difficulty in drawing the dividing line between on the one hand, directors who sign documents 'mindlessly, without even thinking what the documents are', and an effective decision of a constitutional organ on the other. The finding in *Development Securities* that the directors simply agreed to take the formal actions required as the final part of what they were engaged to do from the outset, sits on the boundary. Discrepancies and lack of credibility in the taxpayer's evidence will also play a part.

---

1 (1908) 5 TC 358.
2 [1906] 2 Ch 34.
3 (1908) 5 TC 358 at 376.
4 (1959) 38 TC 712 at 729–730, per Romer LJ.
5 (1959) 38 TC 712 at 730.
6 (1913) 6 TC 163.
7 (1913) 6 TC 163.
8 (1899) 4 TC 41.
9 (1899) 4 TC 41 at 46.
10 SP 1/90, para 16.
11 SP 1/90, para 17.
12 *Development Securities (No 9) Ltd & Ors v Revenue and Customs* [2017] UKFTT 565 (TC).
13 *Untelrab Ltd v McGregor* [1996] STC (SCD) [see **7.4.**].
14 *Development Securities (No 9) Ltd & Ors v Revenue and Customs* [2017] UKFTT 565 (TC), at para 401.
15 [2017] UKFTT 565 (TC), at para 402.
16 [2017] UKFTT 565 (TC), at paras 416 and 417.
17 [2017] UKFTT 565 (TC), at para 426.

7.09 Elements of central management and control

In the two cases in which the test was first established,[1] all business activities of the companies concerned were carried out, and largely controlled, overseas. Calcutta Jute Mills Co manufactured and sold jute in India and the Cesena Sulphur Co manufactured and sold sulphur in Italy. All Calcutta's property was situated in India – indeed the directors of Calcutta did not have even an office in the UK but met in that belonging to one of their number! – and Cesena's main books, accounts and banking accounts were maintained in Italy. Yet, on the basis of the 'real business' test, the court held that both companies were resident in the UK. Clearly, therefore, it cannot have been the day-to-day management and control of the business activities of those companies which Kelly CB and Huddleston B had in mind when they decided that the 'real business' of those companies was carried on, not overseas, but in the UK.

The clue as to what they did have in mind is provided by Kelly CB who said that:

'... the answer to the question, Where does a joint stock company reside? is, ... where its governing body is to be met with and found, and where its governing body exercises the powers conferred upon it by the Act of Parliament, and by the Articles of Association, where it meets and is in bodily and personal presence for the purposes of the concern.'[2]

The 'real business' of Calcutta Jute Mills Ltd and of Cesena Sulphur Co Ltd was, in other words, carried on, not in India or Italy, but in the place from which the decision to carry out operations in India or Italy had emanated. As Huddleston B said of the Cesena Sulphur Co Ltd's business:

'No doubt the manufacturing part may be done and was done in Italy; so supposing that in another part of the world they found sulphur and carried on their business there, the manufacturing part of the business would be carried on there, no doubt; but the administrative part of the business would be carried on at the place from which all the orders came, from which all the directions flowed, and where the appointments were made, where the appointments of the officers were revoked, where the agents were nominated, where their powers were recalled, where the money was received (whatever may have been sent), where the dividends were payable, and where the dividends were declared. We find that all these Acts are performed in London. I cannot help thinking that the main place of business of the Company is in England ... .'[3]

The place of central management and control is, then, not necessarily the place in which a company's manufacturing or trading activities take place but the place in which the parameters governing those activities are set and the place in which the fundamental policies to be implemented in the UK or elsewhere are adopted.

The activities that make up management and control of a closely held, entrepreneurially run company were examined in *Laerstate BV v HMRC*.[4] Laerstate BV a Netherlands incorporated company was the vehicle for taking control of Lonrho Plc, a UK-based multinational company quoted on the London Stock Exchange by a German entrepreneur Mr Dieter Bock. On 9 December 1992, Mr Bock became the sole shareholder of Laerstate and was appointed a director in addition to the existing director Mr Edward Trapman, a business associate of Mr Bock. On 9 December 1992, the Laerstate participation in Lonrho was secured by subscription for new shares, a purchase of existing shares and associated put and call options over further shares from a company ultimately owned by Mr Tiny Rowland, who then controlled Lonrho, and financed by a loan from a German bank. Mr Bock became joint managing director and CEO of Lonrho in London on 10 February 1993. Although he remained a German resident, Mr Bock spent significant periods of time in the UK including staying in a family flat from April 1994 and thus became

UK resident. During 1996 the sale of the shares in Lonrho were negotiated. Mr Bock resigned as a director on 30 August 1996 and the sale took place in November of that year. The complexity of the arrangements for the purchase, ownership and sale of the Lonrho shares were such that more or less continuous management activity was required.

Laerstate argued that acts of central management and control can be identified as board resolutions where this precedes the signing of a document, or the signing of the document itself where there is no resolution which in each case were outside the UK. First-tier Tribunal Judges Avery Jones and Berner considered that:

> '[the] test does not confine itself to a consideration of particular actions of the company, such as the signing of documents or the making of certain board resolutions outside the UK if, in a given case, a more general overview of the course of business and trading demonstrates that as a matter of fact central management and control abides in the UK.'[5]

In their view:

> 'In relation to the actions taken by the Appellant and the Appellant's board, it is clear that the mere physical acts of signing resolutions or documents do not suffice for actual management.'[6]

The Tribunal found that in the period Mr Bock was a director, under the constitution of the company independently authorised to represent the appellant at law and otherwise. Both at the times when board meetings were held and during the period when there were no such meetings, Mr Bock himself conducted the business of Laerstate. They accepted that on occasion he did so with the assistance, cooperation and concurrence of Mr Trapman and that acts of management took place in various locations, including in the Netherlands and Germany, but throughout the period during which Mr Bock was a director they found that he carried out activities of a strategic and policy nature and managed the business of Laerstate, and that he did so to a substantial extent in the UK. Although Mr Trapman was a director, the evidence shows that his involvement was very much secondary to that of Mr Bock, who was responsible for all the negotiation and strategic decisions on matters at these times. For a considerable time there were no board meetings even though there were significant management activities taking place. Those management activities were undertaken by Mr Bock, substantially in the UK.[7] They suspected that he had concluded that he should not be a director at the time of disposal of the shares in Lonrho[8] and found that the company had been run in the same way as when Mr Bock was a director.

In contrast, the UK resident director of a Jersey incorporated company who was also secretary of the UK resident parent company in *Development Securities (No 9) Ltd & Ors v Revenue and Customs*[9] did not himself make strategic and management decisions. His function was mostly administrative as a communicator, co-ordinator and facilitator.

---

1 *Calcutta Jute Mills Co Ltd v Nicholson* (1876) 1 TC 83 and *Cesena Sulphur Co Ltd v Nicholson* (1876) 1 TC 88.

2 (1876) 1 TC 83 at 95.
3 (1876) 1 TC 88 at 107.
4 *Laerstate BV v HMRC* [2009] UKFTT 209 (TC).
5 At para 28.
6 At para 33.
7 At para 16.
8 At para 18.
9 *Development Securities (No 9) Ltd & Ors v Revenue and Customs* [2017] UKFTT 565 (TC) at paras 431 and 432. [See **7.8**].

7.10 Finance as a key element

If, as has been demonstrated at **7.09** above, policy-making is the primary expression of central management and control, the raising and allocation of the funds without which a company's policies could not be implemented must be an almost equally important manifestation of such management and control.

In *American Thread Co v Joyce*,[1] for instance, the Master of the Rolls noted that the business of the New York company was one in which seasonable purchases of cotton had to be made, and commented:

> 'Those purchases of cotton necessarily involve considerable financing. The whole policy depends really upon aye or no, shall we finance to the extent of, I think in one case it appears, £300,000. The New York people cannot do that at all. The whole purse-strings in the sense of money coming in by borrowing are kept most zealously at Manchester, and by means of those purse strings they are able to control and do control the policy of the Company and the mode in which they carry on their business of buying and selling.'[2]

Similarly, in *De Beers Consolidated Mines Ltd v Howe*,[3] the Lord Chancellor took as evidence that the company was resident in the UK the fact that:

> 'London has ... always controlled ... all questions of expenditure except wages, materials, and such like at the mines, and a limited sum which may be spent by the Directors at Kimberley.'[4]

A further factor to be considered – though one which alone is not, it seems, determinative of central management and control[5] – is the declaration of dividends. In *Calcutta Jute Mills Co Ltd v Nicholson*,[6] it was asserted (in support of the proposition that the company was resident in India) that the activities of the company in England were minimal, consisting of little more than the dividing between the English shareholders of the amount, less expenses, remitted to this country from India. Huddleston B refuted such a contention by pointing out that:

> 'The operation of the Company in London was, not to divide the amount sent among the shareholders, but it was to "declare" the amount; and I apprehend that, within the meaning of that clause, the directors in London, who had full power, might say, "Well, we do not approve of this system upon which the division has been made, and we shall require a different dividend for the future", or something of that kind, – showing plainly that they exercise the authority, and that they are the persons who are the principal body ... .'[7]

Similarly, in the *American Thread Company* case,[8] one of the factors which led Hamilton J to uphold the finding of the Commissioners that the central management and control of the American company rested with the English directors was that:

'In each year the directors, sitting in extraordinary session in England, recommend what the dividend on the common stock should be … But in the year 1904, when the dividend was 16 per cent, though the Board by resolution recommended that rate, the gentleman who sent the cablegram to the American directors said that the Board had decided that the dividend should be 16 per cent, and went on to say: "Arrange for usual formal resolutions as regards dividends on preferred shares and common stock without delay". Accordingly, the 16 per cent was announced … .'[9]

These words of Hamilton J make it clear that, so far as dividends are concerned, the person or group of persons who actually decides upon the quantum of the dividend, that is the directors and not the persons who formally resolve to pay it or give their formal approval to its declaration, that is, the shareholders.

---

1 (1913) 6 TC 163.
2 (1913) 6 TC 163.
3 (1906) 5 TC 198.
4 (1906) 5 TC 198 at 213.
5 In *Egyptian Hotels Ltd v Mitchell* (1914) 6 TC 542 at 552 Lord Sumner said that 'The mere declaration and payment of a dividend here out of profits earned in a business otherwise wholly carried on abroad, does not prevent the business in which the profits have already been earned from having been wholly carried on abroad. To say that part of a Company's business is to pay dividends, if it has earned them, seems to me to be a play upon words.'
6 (1876) 1 TC 83.
7 (1876) 1 TC 83 at 107.
8 (1913) 6 TC 163.
9 (1913) 6 TC 163.

7.11 Degree of activity

The degree of activity does not form part of the test and must be put in context. In *Wood v Holden (Inspector of Taxes)*[1] in the Court of Appeal Chadwick LJ[2] adopted the analysis of Park J in the High Court as compelling where he said:

'[64] … The making of the board resolutions and the signing and execution of documents which the Commissioners say were the only acts of management and control of Eulalia all took place in the Netherlands. A company is resident where its central management and control are situated. How, therefore, can Eulalia have been resident in the United Kingdom? How can it have been resident anywhere other than the Netherlands?

[65] … What [the Commissioners] seem really to be saying is that, although the only acts of control and management took place outside the United Kingdom, there was not much involved in them. But the test of a company's residence is still the central control and management test: it is not the law that that test is superseded by some different test if the business of a company is such that not a great deal is required for central control and management of its business to be carried out.

[66] … If directors of an overseas company sign documents mindlessly, without even thinking what the documents are, I accept that it would be difficult to say that the national jurisdiction in which the directors do that is the jurisdiction of residence of the company. But if they apply their minds to whether or not to sign the documents, the authorities … indicate that it is a very different matter … .'

Park J also rejected the notion that 'effective decisions … require some minimum level of information' with the implication that decisions taken by a director that were not informed somehow did not count.

1 [2006] EWCA Civ 26.
2 At paras [35] and [36].

7.12 Administrative functions

The undertaking of activities to comply with company law such as those of a company secretary are not indications of residence.[1] More recently in *News Datacom*,[2] the Special Commissioners concluded that a single meeting in the UK was concerned only with ministerial matters and matters of good housekeeping. The meeting was not concerned with policy, strategic, or management matters relating to the conduct of the business of the company. It did not reflect a manifestation of the controlling brain or where the business of the company was really carried on. It was not an exercise of central management and control. It was the tidying up operation, conducted by alternate directors. The circumstances are unusual and the extent to which any principle is established is questionable.

1 *Todd v Egyptian Delta Land and Investment Co Ltd* (1929) 14 TC 119, contrary to *Swedish Central Railway Co Ltd v Thompson* (1925) 9 TC 342.
2 *News Datacom Ltd & News Data Security Products Ltd v Revenue & Customs* [2006] UKSPC SPC561.

7.13 Influence compared with management and control

Influencing of company policy by persons who are not authorised to make decisions as part of the constitutional organs of the company is not an exercise of central management and control, at least in cases where the functions of those organs have not been 'usurped'. As Chadwick LJ said at para 27 in *Wood v Holden*:

'[I]t is essential to recognise the distinction (in concept, at least) between the role of an "outsider" in proposing, advising and influencing the decisions which the constitutional organs take in fulfilling their functions and the role of an outsider who dictates the decisions which are to be taken. In that context an "outsider" is a person who is not, himself, a participant in the formal process (a board meeting or a general meeting) through which the relevant constitutional organ fulfils its function.'

Thus the design and superintending of the transaction by the accountants on behalf of their client did not constitute an exercise of central management and control.

7.14 Location of central management and control

Identification of the person or group of persons who exercise *de facto* central management and control of a company does not, of course, conclude the question of a company's residence. There remains the final step of identifying the place from which they exercise that central management and control.

Where, as will usually be the case, full powers of management and control are vested in the directors of a company and those powers are exercised by the directors or delegated to others under their control,[1] the place where the directors habitually meet to make their decisions on policy, finance and related matters will be the place of central management and control. This is stressed in case after case.

In *Calcutta Jute Mills Co v Nicholson*,[2] for example, Kelly CB says that a company resides

'… where its governing body is to be met with and found, and where its governing body exercises the powers conferred upon it … where it meets and is in bodily and personal presence for the purposes of the concern … at the office or place of dwelling … where the directors meet.'[3]

Similarly, in *De Beers Consolidated Mines Ltd v Howe*,[4] the Lord Chancellor said:

'… it is clearly established … that the Directors' Meetings in London are the meetings where the real control is exercised in practically all the important business of the Company… .'[5]

This recurrent emphasis on the place of directors' meetings must not, however, lead one to suppose that the location of directors' meetings is *the* test of company residence. As Lord Radcliffe pointed out in *Bullock v Unit Construction Co Ltd*:[6]

'… the necessity of establishing some common standard for the treatment of different tax payers meant that the Courts of Law were bound in course of time to produce and apply some general principles of their own to form an acceptable test of residence. No doubt it might have taken a variety of forms … the site of meetings of the directors' board [was a] possible candidate … for selection as the criterion. In fact, as we know, the principle was adopted that a company is resident where its central control and management abide … .'[7]

Even if central management and control is in the hands of the directors because their role has not been usurped, their place of meeting may not determine the company's place of residence if their meetings there are merely a matter of form. The Revenue Statement of Practice[8] puts it as follows:

'In general the place of directors' meetings is significant only in so far as those meetings constitute the medium through which central management and control is exercised. If, for example, the directors of a company were engaged together actively in the United Kingdom in the complete running of a business which was wholly in the United Kingdom, the company would not be regarded as resident outside the

United Kingdom merely because the directors held formal board meetings outside the United Kingdom.'[9]

This statement is now mostly limited to those extreme cases where the directors as a matter of proper exercise of their functions have already made the decisions that constitute central management and control in the UK but hold meetings pretending that the decisions are made elsewhere. In *Wood v Holden*, Park J said,[10] 'that the principle almost always followed is that a company is resident in the jurisdiction where its board of directors meets. In the previous sentence I have said "almost always" because it is possible for a company to be resident in one territory even if it does not hold directors' meetings there' (where the board's function is usurped).

Such judicial statements have not deterred HMRC from pressing the point. The HMRC position was argued in *News Datacorp* thus:

'129. Mr Brennan QC submitted that the test of corporate residence is the *De Beers* test. This required the questions to be asked where is the real business of the company carried on and where does central management and control actually abide?

130. These questions were to be answered in all cases by reference to the course of business and trading.

131. The test of central management and control is not to be treated as a test which depends solely on the location where the directors meet. The search is for the principal seat of business – it is there where the central management and control actually abides (see the *Calcutta Jute* case at page 96). This carries with it connotations of continuity because of the use of phrases such as "actually abides", "carries on business", "keeping house". It is not sufficient, therefore, to look simply at the period during July 1992 when the relevant transactions were carried out: instead it is necessary to consider the overall pattern of conduct established over a period of time – residence does not change on every occasion where there is short-term change in the location of board meetings.

132. The location of directors' meetings could have been but was not chosen as the test for corporate residence (see Lord Radcliffe in *Unit Construction* [1960] AC 351 at 365).'

The correct approach now in the case of legal persons is to pay attention to the legal framework and constitution that gives them life. There have thus far been no cases concerning companies where the board does not function through meetings but via written resolutions or where meetings are held by telephone or video conference.

The residence of a company is where the directors perform the functions that constitute central management and control, not where they reside. In *John Hood & Co Ltd v Magee*,[11] for instance, Mr Hood was the sole director of a company incorporated in Belfast and registered in New York. The Commissioners found that, although the company traded in both Ireland and America, it kept house and did its real business in Belfast where Mr Hood held the majority of his board 'meetings'. Kenny J said: 'It is a mere accident that Mr Hood resides in New York.'[12]

Gibson, J put it thus:

> 'The residence of the company cannot be determined by Mr Hood's choice of his own residence. No doubt, wherever he went, he carried his functions with him ... All the same, he was not the company, it owned his brain and capacity as well as the business. The tap-root of the fruit-bearing tree was at Belfast.'[13]

Clearly, the residence of individual directors may be of some significance from an evidentiary perspective.

---

1 See **7.07** above.
2 (1876) 1 TC 83.
3 (1876) 1 TC 83 at 95–96.
4 (1906) 5 TC 198.
5 (1906) 5 TC 198 at 213.
6 (1959) 38 TC 712.
7 (1959) 38 TC 712 at 738.
8 SP 1/90.
9 SP 1/90 para 14.
10 SP 1/90 para 21.
11 (1918) 7 TC 327.
12 (1918) 7 TC 327 at 358.
13 (1918) 7 TC 327 at p 350.

7.15 Dual or multiple residence

In this chapter the quest hitherto has been that, no matter how complex the affairs of a company or how dispersed over the face of the earth its activities might be, it may be possible to find the place of central management and control exercised in the UK. Exceptionally, that place may not be the UK exclusively. As Lord Radcliffe says in *Bullock v Unit Construction Co Ltd*:[1]

> '... the facts of individual cases have not always so arranged themselves as to make it possible to identify any one country as the seat of central management and control at all. Though such instances must be rare, the management and control may be divided or even, at any rate in theory, peripatetic. Situations of this kind do not arise just to tease the minds of Judges: they are the product of some peculiar necessity, political or otherwise.'[2]

Such a division of management and control will necessitate a finding of dual residence, and, although the first such finding was not made until 1925, the possibility of such a finding had been admitted earlier.

In 1915, *Mitchell v Egyptian Hotels Ltd*[3] came before the court and, in an oblique way, the matter was moved forward a stage. Egyptian Hotels Ltd had admitted to being resident in the UK and its residence status was, therefore, not in question. It was held, however, that the company was managed and controlled in Egypt so as to be liable to tax on its profits under Schedule D, Case V. Viscount Cave saw this decision as being a tacit acceptance of the principle of dual residence:

> '... the facts ... were sufficient ... to establish residence in Egypt, so that, if a company can have but one residence – namely, the place where its control and

management abides, it must have been held that the company being resident in Egypt was not resident here, and accordingly was not taxable at all; but no such suggestion was made either by counsel or by any member of the tribunals by which the decision was given and upheld. This being so, while the case does not expressly decide that a company may have two residences for income tax purposes, the decision appears to be inconsistent with any other view.'[4]

This opinion was expressed by Viscount Cave LC in the context of his judgment in *Swedish Central Rly Co Ltd v Thompson*,[5] the first case in which an actual finding of dual residence was made and upheld. The decision in that case was, however, later described as 'unfortunate ... having regard to the course of authority both before and after its date',[6] and the facts reveal why. The company concerned had been incorporated in England for the purpose of constructing, maintaining and leasing a railway between Frovi and Ludvika in Sweden. During the period with which the case was concerned the company had fulfilled all these objectives and was merely drawing an annual rental under a lease granted to a Swedish traffic company. The registered office of the company was maintained in London and there the company seal was kept, formal administrative business was dealt with by a committee of three directors, transfers of shares were made and registered, and the accounts were drawn up and audited. All directors' and shareholders' meetings were, however, held in Stockholm and there the minimal business activity of the company (the receipt of rents) was carried on. It was found as a fact by the Special Commissioners that the central control and management was in Sweden but that the company was also resident in the UK, and their findings were upheld in the House of Lords. In another part of the speech from which the earlier quotation is taken, Viscount Cave LC said that:

'... when the central management and control of a company abides in a particular place the company is held for the purposes of income tax to have a residence in that place; but it does not follow that it cannot have a residence elsewhere. An individual may clearly have more than one residence (see *Cooper v Cadwalader*[7]); and in principle there appears to be no reason why a company should not be in the same position. The central management and control may be divided and it may "keep house and do business" in more than one place; and if so it may have more than one residence.'[8]

The finding of the Commissioners, however, had been not that central management and control was divided, but that it lay in Sweden. Once upheld by the House of Lords, therefore, the case began to be regarded as an authority for the proposition that, while central management and control was one test of corporate residence, there was another test also: that of the location of administrative control. This was the approach taken by the Crown in *Egyptian Delta Land and Investment Co Ltd v Todd*,[9] but, there, in the House of Lords, Viscount Sumner went to great lengths to stamp out the idea and to forestall any endorsement of it by his brethren:

'All that was decided in the *Swedish Central Railway* case was that the company could have two residences, one in England as well as one in Sweden. Your Lordships were not asked to decide more. It is true that by admission the controlling power over the business was in Sweden, but other business was done in London the character and importance of which, though set out in the Case, was not discussed at the Bar. It was a matter of degree on the facts and your Lordships cannot be deemed to have come to some unexpressed conclusion on that ground merely because you did not for yourselves declare … that there was no evidence of business carried on in England … Nor is it decisive of the point to say now that the business done in England was only administrative. It was in fact a good deal more, and in the static condition of the company's affairs it was not much less important than the Swedish part. If new questions arose the Swedish directors could settle them, but as things were little had to be done anywhere except "administration" … and that was fairly divided between the two countries.'[10]

In other words, the question whether the Swedish Central Railway Co Ltd had more than one residence had been a question of fact for the Commissioners to determine, and the House of Lords, having held that there was some evidence on which the Commissioners' finding of dual residence could have been made, had felt itself unable to interfere with that finding. That did not mean, however, that the control of administrative duties (which was the only control the London board appeared to exercise) was an alternative test of residence. It was not, and the Law Lords had never said it was. Central control and management remained the only test and one must reconcile that with the Commissioners' decision by assuming a finding of divided central management and control.

Viscount Sumner's speech was a skilful piece of oratory – verbally shoring-up the meagre facts until they were able (if only just) to carry the weighty conclusion the Commissioners had placed on them – and it was much needed, for the facts in the *Egyptian Delta* case[11] then before the House of Lords, though not, on the face of it, dissimilar from the facts in the *Swedish Railway* case,[12] had led the Commissioners to find that Egyptian Delta Land and Investment Co Ltd was resident in Egypt only!

Viscount Sumner contrived a distinction between the two findings by declaring that such management and control as there was in the *Swedish Railway* case[13] was almost equally divided between London and Stockholm while, in the *Egyptian Delta* case,[14] the whole of the central management and control was situated in Cairo. This method of reconciling the apparently irreconcilable found such favour with Lord Radcliffe that, in *Bullock v Unit Construction Co Ltd*,[15] he declared:

'I am myself of the opinion that the best way of treating the matter is to regard the *Swedish Central Railway Company* and the *Egyptian Delta Land Company* decisions as if they were in effect one decision of the House and the speech of Viscount Sumner in the later case as affording an authoritative commentary on the significance of the earlier. He was party to both of them. If this is done much of the difficulty disappears; for it is clear that Lord Sumner wished it to be understood that the Swedish Central Railway Company's business and administration were of such a nature that what managing and controlling had to be done was in fact done as much on English as on Swedish soil. He regarded the key of the earlier decision as being contained in the words of Lord Cave: "The central management and control of a company may be divided, and it may 'keep house and do business' in more than one place; and if so it may have more than one residence".[16] On this basis the 1925 decision of the House is … a decision on that special class of case[17] … where the facts themselves are genuinely such as to not to admit of a finding that central management and control are exercised in or from any one country.'[18]

The second case in which a finding of dual residence was made was *Union Corpn Ltd v IRC*.[19] The case concerned a company which had been incorporated in South Africa but which carried on its activities partly in London and partly in South Africa. Management and control at the highest level was divided between the directors in the UK and those in South Africa but final and supreme authority lay with the directors in London. On those facts, therefore, the Commissioners found that the company was resident in the UK. That finding was rejected by the Court of Appeal as being wrong in law.

Sir Raymond Evershed MR found himself in difficulties but derived assistance from the Australian case of *Koitaki Para Rubber Estates Ltd v Federal Comr of Taxation*[20] in which Dixon J had said:

'... a finding that a company is a resident of more than one country ought not to be made unless the control of the general affairs of the company is not centred in one country but is divided or distributed among two or more countries. The matter must always be one of degree and residence may be constituted by a combination of various factors, but one factor to be looked for is the existence in the place claimed as a residence of some part of the superior or directing authority by means of which the affairs of the company are controlled.'[21]

In the light of this judgment, and of the English authorities, Sir Raymond Evershed MR rejected the Special Commissioners' view and arrived at the conclusion that:

'... there must, in order to constitute residence, be not only some substantial business operations in any given country but also present some part of the superior and directing authority ... [T]he question of the extent of the superior or directing authority required (as well as of the business operations being performed) is one of fact to be determined by the Special Commissioners.'[22]

In other words, final and supreme arbitrating authority is not the same thing as central management and control and if the latter is found to be divided to a significant degree between two or more territories a finding of multiple residence must be made – even if in one of those territories is a person or group of persons with the power of ultimate arbitrament.

It is important to understand that the decision in *Union Corpn Ltd v IRC*[23] has not established a new or modified test of residence but has merely provided a basis for decision where *the* test of residence ('Where does the central control and management of this company abide?') will not admit of the single-territory answer which the word 'central' in the test question demands. Sir Raymond Evershed's solution was to 'fragment' the principle underlying the test of residence and to 'establish a residence for tax purposes wherever the exercise of some portion of controlling power and authority can be identified'.[24] Lord Radcliffe suggested this solution might still be open to question,[25] but the remainder of his dicta in *Bullock v Unit Construction Co Ltd*[26] make it clear that any basis for decision which involved a concept other than central management and control could never be countenanced.

---

1 (1959) 38 TC 712.
2 (1959) 38 TC 712 at 739.

3 (1915) 6 TC 542.
4 (1925) 9 TC 342 at 374.
5 (1925) 9 TC 342 at 374.
6 *Bullock v Unit Construction Co Ltd* (1959) 38 TC 712 at 740, per Lord Radcliffe.
7 (1904) 5 TC 101. See **3.08** above.
8 *Swedish Central Rly Co Ltd v Thompson* (1925) 9 TC 342 at 372.
9 (1929) 14 TC 119.
10 (1929) 14 TC 119 at 143.
11 (1929) 14 TC 119.
12 (1925) 9 TC 342.
13 (1925) 9 TC 342.
14 (1929) 14 TC 119.
15 (1959) 38 TC 712.
16 *Swedish Central Rly Co Ltd v Thompson* (1925) 9 TC 342 at 372.
17 *Swedish Central Rly Co Ltd v Thompson* (1925) 9 TC 342 at 372.
18 *Bullock v Unit Construction Co Ltd* (1959) 38 TC 712 at 740.
19 (1952) 34 TC 207.
20 (1940) 64 CLR 15.
21 (1952) 34 TC 207 at 241.
22 (1952) 34 TC 207 at 275.
23 (1952) 34 TC 207 at 275.
24 *Bullock v Unit Construction Co Ltd* (1959) 38 TC 712 at 739, per Lord Radcliffe.
25 *Bullock v Unit Construction Co Ltd* (1959) 38 TC 712 at 739, per Lord Radcliffe.
26 (1959) 38 TC 712.

7.16   Residence for tax treaty purposes

The purpose and effect of double taxation treaties has already been described at **2.45** above. In relation to companies, Art 4(1) of the OECD Model provides:

> '4(1) For the purposes of this Convention, the term "resident of a Contracting State" means any person who, under the laws of that State, is liable to tax therein by reason of his domicile, residence, place of management or any other criterion of a similar nature, and also includes that State and any political subdivision or local authority thereof. This term, however, does not include any person who is liable to tax in that State in respect only of income from sources in that State or capital situated therein.'

Thus a company may be treated as a resident under domestic law on the basis of the place of incorporation (domicile). 'Residence or place of management' will generally suffice to cover the place where central management and control are exercised. Thus, prima facie, a company incorporated in the UK or one whose central management and control is exercised there will be a resident of a contracting state, that is the UK, for treaty purposes. Where a tax treaty is in place, such dual residence may be resolved for the purposes of the treaty by the following mechanism:

> '4(3) Where by reason of the provisions of paragraph 1 a person other than an individual is a resident of both Contracting States, then it shall be deemed to be a resident only of the State in which its place of effective management is situated.'

Whether the company is also at the same time resident of the other contracting state will depend on the domestic tax law of that state. Thus a finding of dual residence as described at **7.15** above will not itself entail dual residence for treaty purposes.

There has been little consensus internationally on the meaning of 'place of effective management' and recent attempts by the English courts to interpret and apply it to companies have not been entirely satisfactory.

The OECD Commentary on Art 4(3) has itself been controversial. Its latest version found in the 2008 OECD Model treaty reads:

'24.1 An entity may have more than one place of management, but it can have only one place of effective management at any one time.

24.2 The place of effective management is the place where the key management and commercial decisions that are necessary for the conduct of the entity's business are in substance made, *i.e.* the place where the actions to be taken by the entity as a whole are, *in fact*, determined and all. *All the* relevant facts and circumstances must be examined to determine the place of effective management.

24.3 The place of effective management will ordinarily be the place where the most senior person or group of persons (for example a board of directors) makes its decisions, which normally corresponds to where it meets. There are cases, however, where the key management and commercial decisions necessary for the conduct of the entity's business are in substance made in one place somewhere by a person or group of persons but are formally finalized somewhere else by it or by another person or group of persons. In such cases, it will be necessary to consider other factors. Depending on the circumstances, these other factors could include:

– Where a board of directors formally finalizes key management and commercial decisions necessary for the conduct of the entity's business at meetings held in one State but these decisions are in substance made in another State, the place of effective management will be in the latter State.
– If there is a person such as a controlling interest holder (e.g. a parent company or associated enterprise) that effectively makes the key management and commercial decisions that are necessary for the conduct of the entity's business, the place of effective management will be where that person makes these key decisions. For that to be the case, however, the key decisions made by that person must go beyond decisions related to the normal management and policy formulation of a group's activities (e.g. the type of decisions that a parent company of a multinational group would be expected to take as regards the direction, co-ordination and supervision of the activities of each part of the group).
– Where a board of directors routinely approves the commercial and strategic decisions made by the executive officers, the place where the executive officers perform their functions would be important in determining the place of effective management of the entity. In distinguishing between a place where a decision is made as opposed to where it is merely approved, one should consider the place where advice on recommendations or options relating to the decisions were considered and where the decisions were ultimately developed.'

Indofood International Finance Ltd v JP Morgan Chase Bank NA[1] involved the Indonesia-Netherlands tax treaty in a commercial dispute governed by English law. The court was asked to deal with what an Indonesian court would have decided was the place of effective management of a hypothetical Dutch company. Two judges in the Court of Appeal declined to decide the case on this point but Sir Andrew Morritt, the Chancellor expressed the following views:

> 'As counsel for the issuer pointed out the test, as elaborated by the OECD commentary, refers to the place where "key" decisions are taken. The provisions of the trust deed and, more particularly, of the note conditions show clearly that they must be taken by the parent guarantor. Whilst I do not doubt that the board of directors of Newco would be permitted to determine what to do with the handling charges and equity capital and would be responsible for complying with the requirements of Dutch law, those are hardly the "key" decisions. Let it be assumed that the issuer and Newco are otherwise resident in Holland and the question arose whether to interpose Newco it is, in my view, plain beyond doubt that such a decision and the terms of any interposition would not be left to the issuer or Newco but would be decided by the board of the parent guarantor. In particular it would not be left to the board of the issuer or of Newco to decide whether to assign or to accept the benefit of the loan agreement between the parent guarantor and the issuer and if so on what terms. Questions in relation to any subsequent migration, substitution or interposition of another company between the parent guarantor and Newco or between Newco and the issuer would be decided by the board of the parent guarantor. In my view it is plain that the place of effective management of the issuer is Indonesia and that the place of effective management of Newco, if interposed between the parent guarantor and the issuer, would be Indonesia too.'[2]

These comments cast little light on the expression as the key decisions referred to are shareholder issues rather than those relating to the management of the hypothetical company.

In *Wood v Holden* the Commissioners accepted the HMRC submission that in the present context there is no difference between central management and control and the place of effective management.[3] Park J said: 'Article 4(3) requires there to be identified a "place" of effective management, and it has to be a place situated in one of the two States'[4] and 'when it comes to applying the detailed wording of article 4(3) what was the "place ... situated" in the United Kingdom which was Eulalia's "place of effective management"?'[5] The Court of Appeal[6] did not address the issue.

In *Trevor Smallwood Trust v R & C Comrs*[7] the Special Commissioners reviewed this case and the OECD commentary as it applies to companies but ultimately merely concluded that 'having regard to the ordinary meaning of the words in their context and in the light of their object and purpose, we should approach the issue of POEM as considering in which state the real top level management is found'.[8] When the matter came before the Court of Appeal, it ruled that on the basis of *Wood v Holden*, since the directors of the trust company in Mauritius were in place and exercised their powers as such, the fact that they might agree to act in accordance with the instructions they received from accountants in the UK did not permit a conclusion that the POEM was in the UK.[9]

Where a company incorporated in one contracting state has its central management and control entirely in the other contracting state, then the place of effective management cannot be in the state of incorporation by reason of formal connection there. Similarly, if a director's role in a contracting state is merely a 'fake' or a 'façade', then place of effective management cannot be in that state.[10]

Exceptionally, UK tax treaties may depart from the OECD model in resolving dual residence problems by reference to the place of effective management of the taxpayer. These treaties do not adopt any rule but, instead, require such dual residence and to be resolved by agreement between the competent authorities of the contracting states.[11] Historically, such treaties were rare. They are, however, becoming common in UK tax treaties. The absence of any rule means that taxpayers are unable to determine their tax liabilities, which is left to the discretion of tax administrations. Dissatisfied taxpayers will need to look to administrative law remedies such as judicial review, rather than by way of appeal to the tribunal's and courts.

This approach may become the norm as a result of Actions 2 and 6 of the OECD/G20 Base Erosion and Profit Shifting (BEPS) Project.[12] The final reports have resulted in a change to Art 4(3) of the OECD model, by providing that cases of dual treaty residence of persons other than individuals would be solved on a case-by-case basis by the competent authorities, rather than the current legal rule based on place of effective management. The new version envisages that where a person other than an individual is a resident of both states, the competent authorities of the states must endeavour to determine, by mutual agreement, which state such a person is resident for the purposes of the treaty, having regard to its place of effective management, the place where it is incorporated or otherwise constituted and any other relevant factors. In the absence of such agreement, such a person will not be entitled to any treaty relief or exemption except to the extent and in such manner as may be agreed by the competent authorities. This radical approach plainly overshoots the stated objective to ensure that dual resident entities are not used to obtain the benefits of treaties unduly. This revised approach is included in Art 4(1) of the Multilateral Convention to Implement Tax Treaty Related Measures to Prevent Base Erosion and Profit Shifting which includes all treaty-related BEPS proposals.[13,14] In ratifying the Convention, the United Kingdom has chosen to apply this rule to all its tax treaties covered by the Convention.

---

1 [2006] EWCA Civ 158.

2 At para 57.

3 At para 146.

4 [2005] EWHC 547 (Ch) para 77.

5 At para 78.

6 [2006] EWCA Civ 26.

7 *Trevor Smallwood & Mary Caroline Smallwood Trustees of the Trevor Smallwood Trust v R & C Comrs; Trevor Smallwood Settlor of the Trevor Smallwood Trust v R & C Comrs*, [2008] UKSPC 669.

8 At para 130. On appeal to the High Court ([2009] EWHC 777 (Ch)), Mann J ruled that the question of dual residence did not arise and consequently art 4(3) of the treaty was not engaged.

9 *HMRC v Smallwood & Anor* [2010] EWCA Civ 778 at para 63. See **7.06** above and generally Jonathan Schwarz, *Schwarz on Tax Treaties* (Croner-i, 2018) Ch 5 on treaty residence.

10 *Bywater Investments Limited & Ors v Commissioner of Taxation* [2016] HCA 45 per Gordon, J, at paras 171 and 184.

11 See, for example, Convention between the Government of the United Kingdom of Great Britain and Northern Ireland and the Government of Canada for the Avoidance of Double Taxation and the Prevention of Fiscal Evasion with Respect to Taxes on Income and Capital Gains of 8 September 1978 (SI 1980/709) as amended by Protocol of 15 April 1980 (SI 1980/1528), Protocol of 16 October 1985 (SI 1985/1996) and Protocol of 7 May 2003 (SI 2003/2619), Art 4(3).

12 OECD, *Neutralising the Effects of Hybrid Mismatch Arrangements*, Action 2 – 2015 Final Report; *Preventing the Granting of Treaty Benefits in Inappropriate Circumstances*, Action 6 – 2015 Final Report, OECD/G20 Base Erosion and Profit Shifting Project (OECD Publishing, Paris, 2015).
13 OECD, *Multilateral Convention to Implement Tax Treaty Related Measures to Prevent Base Erosion and Profit Shifting* signed at Paris on 7 June 2017.
14 United Kingdom Reservations and Notifications, Notification of Existing Provisions in Listed Agreements Pursuant to Art 3(6).

7.17   Transfer of residence abroad

Following the decision of the courts that the place of a company's central management and control was the sole determinant of its place of residence, it became commonplace for companies engaged extensively in overseas activities to amend their articles of association and to transfer their central management and control abroad once the burden of UK taxation became significantly greater than that which would be imposed were they to be resident overseas. Of the companies involved in the cases discussed in this chapter, two, at least, changed their place of residence in this way: The Cesena Sulphur Company became resident in Italy and The American Thread Company became resident in America,[1] and, in 1928, when the validity of The Egyptian Delta Land and Investment Co Ltd's change of residence was being challenged, Viscount Sumner was able to affirm that:

> 'Many companies have, at the cost of some trouble and expense, transferred their control and management abroad on the faith of decisions, or if you will, *dicta*, to the effect that by so doing they could legitimately reduce the burden of their taxation.'[2]

A company incorporated outside the UK may cease to be resident there by moving its central management and control outside the territory. A company incorporated in the UK will only cease to be resident if it is able to benefit from tax treaty under which it is treated as resident in the other contracting state by application of the tie-breaker in Art 4(3) or equivalent provisions.

1 See paras 3 and 4 of the case stated in *Bradbury v English Sewing Cotton Co Ltd* (1923) 8 TC 481 at 482.
2 *Egyptian Delta Land and Investment Co Ltd v Todd* (1929) 14 TC 119 at 156.

7.18   Treaty non-resident companies

Under CTA 2009 s 18, a company which would otherwise be regarded as resident in the UK and is regarded for the purpose of any double taxation relief arrangements as resident in a territory outside the UK and not resident in the UK is treated as non-resident.

7.19 European Companies

The European Company Regulation[1] came into force on 8 October 2004. The Regulation permitted the formation of a European Company (SE), which would be subject to the tax law of the country within the EU in which it was resident. Under the company laws applicable in the UK, it is not possible for a company incorporated in the UK to transfer its registered office out of the UK and likewise, there is no company law mechanism to accept the transfer into the UK of the registered office of a foreign incorporated company. However, an SE is permitted to transfer its registered office between Member States of the European Union and one which transfers its registered office to the UK, in accordance with Art 8 of the Council Regulation, upon registration there is regarded for the purposes of the Taxes Acts as resident in the UK; the central management and control test is displaced by registration.[2] However, an SE does not cease to be regarded as resident in the UK by reason only of the subsequent transfer from the UK of its registered office.[3] This would suggest that a transfer out of the registration must be accompanied by the exercise of central management and control outside the UK. The same rules[4] apply to a European Cooperative Society (SCE) under the Statute for a European Cooperative Society.[5]

1 Council Regulation (EC) 2157/2001 on the Statute for a European Company (Societas Europaea).
2 CTA 2009 s 16(2) and (3).
3 CTA 2009 s 16(4).
4 CTA 2009 s 17.
5 EC Council Regulation No 1435/2003 on the Statute for a European Cooperative Society (SCE).

7.20 Residence for special statutory purposes

For most corporation tax purposes, a single question is posed: is the company a resident of the UK or not? If it is not, then the corporation tax system does not care where its residence may be found.[1] This indifference is replaced with specific statutory measures in relation to three elements of the corporation tax system, namely group relief, controlled foreign companies and transfer pricing. Each of these has its own mechanism for identifying the territory of residence of a non-UK resident company. In the case of the controlled foreign companies and transfer pricing rules, the mechanisms include determining which of two or more foreign territories the company in question is resident in for those purposes.

1 *News Datacom Ltd v Atkinson* (HMIT) [2006] UKSPC 561 para 123.

7.21 Group relief

Losses and certain other amounts incurred in one member of a group of UK-resident companies may be set off by way of group relief against profits in other UK-resident companies.[1] If, in the material accounting period of the company which would otherwise be the surrendering company, that company is a 'dual resident investing company', no such losses or other amounts may be surrendered by it.[2] Dual resident company is referred to in CTA 2010 as follows:

'109(1) This section applies if in the surrender period the surrendering company is UK resident and is also within a charge to non-UK tax under the law of a territory because–

(a)   it derives its status as a company from that law,

(b)   its place of management is in that territory, or

(c)   it is for some other reason treated under that law as resident in that territory for the purposes of that tax.'

In the case of dual resident investing companies the inability to surrender group relief occurs if the company is liable to tax in another territory under foreign law. The language of s 109 borrows from Art 4(1) of the OECD Model treaty in specifying that if the company is within the foreign tax charge by reason of its place of incorporation or place of management, then it is treated as a dual resident. The same is true if the territory applies some other residence test. A place of management in this sense is likely not limited to the UK 'central management and control' test. It is, however, insufficient that the company be regarded as dual resident for UK corporation tax purposes. A company is only dual resident for this purpose if it is also a resident of another territory under the tax laws of that territory. It does not matter for these purposes if the company is resident in more than one foreign territory under more than one foreign law.

---

1 CTA 2010, Pt 5, Ch 2.
2 CTA 2010 s 109(2).

7.22   Controlled Foreign Companies

If a company is not resident in the UK, and is controlled by a UK-resident person or persons, then it is a CFC and the Controlled Foreign Companies provisions apply. The CFC charge is imposed in relation to a CFC's accounting period if the CFC has chargeable profits for that period and none of the entity level exemptions set out in TIOPA 2010 Pt 9A, Chs 10 to 14 applies for that period. In such a case, the chargeable profits of that CFC and its creditable tax (if any) for that period are apportioned among its shareholders and taxed in the hands of UK-resident corporate shareholders with at least a 25% interest in that company.[1]

For this purpose, the question whether a company is non-UK resident is determined by reference to the normal rules of company residence described in this chapter. The residence of a CFC in a particular territory will determine whether it qualifies for certain exemptions. TIOPA 2010 s 371TA sets out a hierarchy of tests to determine the particular territory in which a CFC is resident for these purposes.

As is the case with dual resident companies, the prime residence test borrows heavily from Art 4(1) of the OECD Model:

> '371TB (1) The CFC is taken to be resident in the territory under the law of which, at all times during the relevant accounting period, the CFC is liable to tax by reason of domicile, residence or place of management.'

Thus the residence of a CFC is determined in the first instance by local tax law of the territory in question. Resolution of the foreign dual or multiple residence is addressed through a series of sub-tests. Reference to the tax law of a foreign territory must be taken to include a reference to applicable tax treaties and therefore any treaty rules to resolve dual residence must be applied to decide if the company is dual resident before applying these tests.

Dual or multiple foreign residence is resolved, first, in favour of the place of effective management of the company.[2] The legislation thus adopts the language of Art 4(3) of the OECD Model Double Taxation Convention.[3] The draftsperson, however, misunderstood the meaning of 'place of effective management' in Art 4(3), as is demonstrated by the second rule which addresses the case where the place of effective management is in two or more territories.[4] In such a case, it is said that the company is resident in the territory where more than 50% of its assets are situated. The territory where more than 50% of its assets are situated is likewise deemed to be where the company is resident if its place of effective management is in none of the territories under whose laws it is resident.[5]

If none of these results in a single territory of residence, the third rule specifies that a company may elect to be treated as resident in a particular territory.[6] Where an election has not been made within the statutory time limit, an officer of HM Revenue & Customs may designate the territory of residence on a just and reasonable basis.[7]

A company with no territory of residence under the prime test is normally treated as resident in the territory where it is incorporated.[8] This could be the case for example, because it is only in a country with no system of corporate taxation or one which imposes tax on companies not by reference to domicile, residence or place of management, However, where the CFC is incorporated in the UK but resident in another territory under the tie-breaker provisions of a tax treaty with that territory and non-UK resident under CTA 2009, s 18, the CFC will be resident in that other territory.[9]

---

1 See generally: Part 9A of TIOPA 2010 inserted by Schedule 20 FA 2012.
2 TIOPA 2010 s 371TB(2).
3 See **7.16** above.
4 TIOPA 2010 s 371TB(6). A company can have only one place of effective management: *Trevor Smallwood & Mary Caroline Smallwood Trustees of the Trevor Smallwood Trust v R & C Comrs; Trevor Smallwood Settlor of the Trevor Smallwood Trust v R & C Comrs*, [2008] UKSPC 669 at para 127.
5 TIOPA 2010 s 371TB(7).
6 TIOPA 2010 s 371TB(8).
7 TIOPA 2010 s 371TB(9).
8 TIOPA 2010 s 371TA(1)(b)(ii).
9 TIOPA 2010 s 371TA(2).

7.23 Transfer pricing – exemption for small or medium-sized enterprises

Profits of persons where there is common participation in the management control or capital fall to be adjusted in relation to transactions between them that are not on arm's-length terms.[1] This rule does not apply generally to small enterprises and is modified in the case of medium-sized enterprises.[2] These exceptions do not apply to transactions with persons resident in a 'non-qualifying territory'.[3] The exception applies whether or not that person is also a resident of a qualifying territory. For this purpose 'resident', in relation to a territory,

(a)   means a person who, under the laws of that territory, is liable to tax there by reason of his domicile, residence or place of management; but

(b)   does not include a person who is liable to tax in that territory in respect only of income from sources in that territory or capital situated there.[4]

1 Taxation (International and Other Provisions) Act 2010 (TIOPA 2010), Pt 4.
2 TIOPA 2010 Pt 4 Ch 3.
3 TIOPA 2010 s 167.
4 TIOPA 2010 s 167(5).

7.24 Foreign dividends received by small companies

Dividends or other distributions received by a small company may be exempt from corporation tax if, among other requirements, the payer is a resident of (and only of) a qualifying territory at the time that the distribution is received.[1] For this purpose of CTA 2009 s 930, a company is a resident of a territory if, under the laws of the territory, the company is liable to tax there:

(a)   by reason of its domicile, residence or place of management; but

(b)   not in respect only of income from sources in that territory or capital situated there.[2]

1 CTA 2009 s 930B(a).
2 CTA 2009 s 930C.

7.25 Company liquidations and business cessations

The appointment of a liquidator with a view to the winding up of a company places the liquidator in control of the company's affairs and generally removes the powers of the directors and shareholders. In the case of a company incorporated outside the UK, it the liquidator would typically be appointed under the law of the place of incorporation. Where such a company was resident in the UK prior to the liquidators' appointment by reason of its central management and control having been exercised in the UK, CTA 2009 s 15 preserves the UK residence of the company, and HMRC view UK residence as continuing until the company ceases to exist.[1] The same rule applies to a company that ceases to carry on business.[2] HMRC state that the company will remain resident unless and until it starts business again and its central management and control is then outside the UK.[3]

---

1 HMRC International Manual INTM120100.
2 CTA 2009 s 1592(b).
3 HMRC International Manual INTM120100.

CHAPTER 8

Residence of partnerships

One likes to do business with a British firm. One knows where one is, if you see what I mean.

Graham Greene *Our Man in Havana*, Ch 1

8.01   Introduction

As the foregoing chapters have made clear, residence is a personal attribute – a quality which attracts to a person by virtue of the strength of the association with a particular place or country. Partnership is the relationship which subsists between persons carrying on a business in common with a view of profit.[1] In England and Wales, a partnership has no existence independent of its constituent members but, in Scotland, it is 'a legal person distinct from the partners of whom it is composed'.[2] The characterisation of a foreign legal entity as a partnership is by analogy to partnerships in the UK applied to the rights, legal rights and obligations under the governing foreign law.[3] Thus in principle any partnership that does not have legal personality under its governing law cannot have the quality of residence attributed to it. The direct tax treatment of partnerships is consistent with this approach by treating each partner as individually carrying on a notional trade in respect of the partnership trade actually carried on in common.[4] Residence or an analogous quality is, however, imputed by statute in the case of firms with a foreign element for limited purposes. First, the remittance basis is made applicable to the foreign profits of a trade carried on in partnership where the control and management of the partnership's trade is outside the UK.[5] Secondly, tax treaty protection from UK tax on the trading profits of partnerships resident outside the UK or whose trade is controlled and managed outside the UK is overridden in the case of UK-resident partners.[6]

---

1 Partnership Act 1890 s 1.
2 Partnership Act 1890 s 4(2).
3 *Memec Plc v IRC* [1998] STC 754 (CA).
4 See generally, ITTOIA 2005 Pt 9.
5 ITTOIA 2005 s 857.
6 ITTIOA 2005 s 858.

8.02 Control and management

Although a partnership, lacking in legal personality, cannot, in principle, have a residence, the Court of Appeal in *Padmore v Inland Revenue Commissioners*[1] observed that under the predecessor to ITTOIA 2005 Pt 9 a residence is ascribed in the legislation to some partnerships. This residence is by reference to a test of control or management of the trade or business. Under the predecessor legislation, the partnership, rather than each partner, was assessed to income tax on its trading profits. Fox LJ also observed that the test for partnerships was statutory, unlike the judge-made test for companies.[2] Despite the different origins of the corporate and partnership tests, there has been little disagreement that the same analysis applies to question whether the control and management of a partnership carried on outside the UK as that which the courts have formulated for ascertaining the residence status of companies.

In *Padmore* the partnership was governed by the laws of Jersey. The overwhelming majority of the partners were resident in the UK. The business of the partnership was carried on from its offices in St Helier, Jersey; and its day-to-day business is dealt with by two managing partners who were Jersey residents. General meetings of the partners were held in Jersey or Guernsey (but nowhere else) four times a year, or more frequently as occasion demanded. At those meetings policy matters were discussed and the decisions taken were thereafter implemented by the Jersey resident managing partners. On those facts, it was common ground that the control and management of the business of the partnership was situated abroad.

Similarly in *Newstead (HM Inspector of Taxes) v Frost*,[3] a Bahamian partnership established to exploit the services and intellectual property of the entertainer David Frost, a UK resident, outside the UK was found by the Special Commissioners as a fact, without analysis of the legal principles, to be controlled and managed abroad on the basis that the partnership meetings and all the activities of the partnership took place outside the UK.[4]

Specific examination of the relationship between the partnership and corporate principles by the First-tier Tribunal in *Mark Higgins Rallying (a firm) v Revenue & Customs*[5] resulted in the conclusion that:

> '[T]he appropriate test for the location of control and management of the business of a partnership is that adopted by the courts in relation to residence of companies. We note the same conclusion was reached by HMRC and stated in their Manual; also that it was the one argued for before us by the Partnership.'[6]

In October 1991 Mr Dixon and Mr Higgins, both Manxmen resident in the Isle of Man, entered into a partnership to combine Mr Dixon's management and commercial experience with Mr Higgins' driving skills. Mr Higgins relocated to the UK in 1993. No records were kept of any partners' meetings. The partners reconstructed a diary of partnership meetings from 1991 to 2006. Mr Dixon, a solicitor, was very aware of the need to maintain control and management of the partnership outside the UK. Mr Higgins was rather perplexed at the rules that Mr Dixon laid down, but bowed to Mr Dixon's professional knowledge in these matters. While in the UK, Mr Higgins did not discuss with Mr Dixon or make any decisions and would travel back to the Isle of Man, when he requested, for meetings to discuss major decisions and to sign contracts.

ITTIOA 2005 s 858(1)(a)(i) applies to partnerships resident outside the UK in addition to those whose trade is controlled and managed outside the UK. The meaning of residence in this provision has yet to be judicially construed, but it would seem unlikely to add much to the analysis.

1 *Padmore v Inland Revenue Commissioners* [1989] STC 493 (CA).
2 At p 499. See Chapter 7 on the residence of companies.
3 *Newstead (HM Inspector of Taxes) v Frost* (1975–1981) 53 TC 525.
4 At p 533.
5 *Mark Higgins Rallying (a firm) v Revenue & Customs* [2011] UKFTT 340 (TC).
6 At para 51.

CHAPTER 9

Domicile

If I should die, think only this of me:
That there's some corner of a foreign field
That is forever England ...

Rupert Brooke, The Soldier

9.01 Introduction

The purpose of this chapter is to explore the concept of domicile as a determinant of liability to inheritance tax and as a modifying factor in relation to other taxes, and to explain how a person's domicile may be identified.

Since publication of the decisions of the Special Commissioners started in 1995, several cases have been reported concerning the domicile of individuals.[1] Only one[2] has been appealed by a taxpayer (unsuccessfully) to the High Court or the Upper Tribunal, and none have grappled with the essential elements of the law of domicile which has shown much stability. In *Gaines-Cooper* it was argued that the Special Commissioners made an error of law if their conclusion was not the only true and reasonable conclusion on the basis of the facts found *and the unchallenged evidence*. This was not found to be the case. Arguments on the law of domicile advanced by the taxpayer were likewise rejected. All have turned on the facts and surrounding circumstances examined in great detail by the Commissioners. They all make interesting reading, but a comparison of the facts of one domicile case with the facts of another domicile case is of limited assistance in deciding the domicile of any particular person.[3]

---

1 *Anderson (executor of Anderson dec'd) v IRC* (1997) Sp C 147; *F & Anor (as personal representatives of F deceased) v Commissioners of Inland Revenue* (1999) Sp C 219; *Civil Engineer v IRC* (2001) Sp C 299; *Surveyor v IRC* (2002) Sp C 339; *Executors of Moore dec'd v IRC* [2002] UKSC SPC335; *Executors of Winifred Johnson Dec'd v HMRC* (2005) Sp C 481; *Gaines-Cooper v HMRC* [2006] UKSPC SPC568.
2 *Gaines-Cooper v HMRC* [2007] EWHC 2617 (Ch).
3 Cf Lord Justice Mummery in *Agulian & Anor v Cyganik* [2006] EWCA Civ 129 para 49.

The nature of domicile

9.02 Historical background

The concept of domicile (or domicil, as some prefer to call it) originated in the Roman Empire when, following the downfall of the Republic, Italy was divided into a number of individual townships known as *municipia* and the Empire was fragmented into numerous provinces. Each province and *municipium* possessed its own jurisdiction and, to a large extent, its own divergent internal law which was administered and enforced by magistrates. Most inhabitants of the Empire were connected by citizenship with one or more of these provincial or municipal communities and/or with Rome itself.

The link of citizenship could arise in various ways – by *origo* (the place within the Empire to which a person's father or, if he was illegitimate, his mother belonged), by adoption, by election or by manumission – and that presented three possibilities. A person might be a citizen of one place, a citizen of more than one place[1] or a citizen of none. This inevitably created difficulties. Given that, as stated, each province or *municipium* had its own system of law, to which system should a man in each of those situations be subject? The answer supplied by Rome was, in the first situation, the law of the man's place of citizenship, and, in the second situation, the law of his *origo*. In the third situation, however, a different determinant was needed and the determinant created was 'domicile' – the place in which a person had made his permanent home.

That concept of domicile was one of the concepts of Roman law, which, in the thirteenth century, was enthusiastically revived by the 'post-glossators' jurists who were attached to the Italian universities and who were engaged in developing the Roman law to meet the nation's changing needs.[2] Italy had by then emerged from the barbarism and feudalism into which the civilised world had been plunged following the fall of the Roman Empire in the fifth century and had become a land of independent, cosmopolitan cities – Bologna, Florence, Genoa, Milan, Padua, Pisa, etc – all of which were subject generally to Roman law, but each of which had diverse laws of its own which gave rise to conflict as commercial intercourse between the cities increased. As a basis for the resolution of such conflicts, the post-glossators developed a set of principles, known to legal historians as 'statute theory', and it was into these that the revived concept of domicile was introduced.

A 'statute' in the terminology of the post-glossators was any legislative or customary local law which was found to be contrary to Roman law in general; and the statute theory proceeded from the premise that all such laws were either 'real', 'personal' or 'mixed'. A law which concerned things other than moveables was 'real',[3] a law which concerned persons and moveables was 'personal', and a law which concerned acts (such as the making of a contract) was 'mixed' as it generally concerned both persons and things. Real statutes were seen as essentially territorial and as having no application beyond the territorial bounds of the locality in which they were found. Mixed statutes were seen as partially territorial in that they applied to all acts done within the territorial bounds of the locality in which they were found but could give rise to litigation elsewhere. Personal statutes, on the other hand, were seen as non-territorial and as applicable to any person *domiciled* within the locality in which the laws were found, wherever that person might be. Thus a Bologna-born merchant whose permanent home was in Florence would remain subject to Florentine personal laws while visiting, say, Padua, and neither Bolognan nor Paduan personal laws would apply to him.

The statute theory – the basis of today's 'private international law' or 'conflict of laws' as it is often called – was neither as simple nor as effective as it might appear and it was much refined by French jurists in the sixteenth century and Dutch jurists in the seventeenth century. Its subsequent development is beyond the scope of this work and it is sufficient to say that, despite all the changes which have taken place and despite the English and Scottish developments of the conflict of laws in the nineteenth century, the concept of domicile, and its use as the determinant of the system of personal law to which a person should be subject wherever he might be, has remained intact to the present day in the common law jurisdictions of the UK, the Commonwealth and the United States of America. To such nations, possessing as they do within their territorial boundaries a number of diverse legal systems, domicile still presents, as it once presented to Italy, the best determinant of the relevant personal law. Ironically, in the nineteenth century, Italy itself and most other countries in Europe rejected the test of domicile in favour of the test of nationality, and Japan and many South American states followed suit.

---

1 St Paul, for example, was a citizen of Tarsus in Cilicia and a citizen of Rome (Acts 21: 39; 22: 27).

2 In the eleventh century the jurists of Italy had taken the *Corpus Juris* – the Justinian code of Roman law – and added to it *glossae* – explanatory notes. The jurists themselves came to be known as the 'glossators' and the revived and expanded Roman law became the general law throughout Italy and the legal code on which the post-glossators then worked.

3 From late Latin *realis* (Latin *res*), a thing.

9.03   The two roles of domicile

The brief picture of domicile's origins given at **9.02** above should have sufficed to show that domicile is essentially a conflict of laws concept employed in determining the system of personal law which should be applied where a person has connections with more than one jurisdiction. Personal law is that part of law which, to some degree, governs the validity of marriage, the effect of marriage on the proprietary rights of husband and wife, divorce and nullity of marriage, legitimacy, legitimation and adoption, wills of moveables and intestate succession to moveables. It follows, therefore, that, whenever a question arises in the English courts concerning any of these matters, it must be determined according to the law of the domicile of the person concerned and not (unless English law happens to be the law of his domicile) according to English law, the law of the territory in which he happens to be, or the law of the nation of which the person is a citizen.

Example

Alan, a citizen of Eriador (where wills require the attestation of three witnesses), dies on holiday in Mordor (where wills require the attestation of four witnesses) but, at the time of his death, is domiciled in Gondor under whose laws he has made a will attested by only one witness as is permitted under Gondorian law. His will is contested in the English courts on the grounds that two witnesses are required under English law or, alternatively, that three are required under Eriadorian law or, alternatively, that four are required under Mordorian law. The suit fails.[1]

The rationale for this lies in the fact that (conceptually, at any rate) domicile, at any given moment in a person's life or at the moment of his death, singles out, from among all the territories in the world, the one territory in which – irrespective of where that person happens to be or happens to reside or ordinarily reside – that person has their real home; and, once that person's real home has been identified, the law of that territory, and of no other, is the law which should be applied in all matters which relate to them as a person.

One of those matters is the transfer of capital to another – dispositions which reduce the value of a person's estate upon death or, in certain circumstances, during lifetime – and it is upon such transfers of value that, under UK revenue law, inheritance tax is charged. It is entirely appropriate, therefore, that – except as regards any part of a person's estate which is situated in the UK – the determinant of liability to tax on capital transfers should be the same as the determinant of the personal law governing those transfers (ie domicile).

There is, however, a second and more cogent reason why a person's domicile is a more appropriate determinant of liability to inheritance tax than residence. Inheritance tax is a cumulative charge on transfers of value made by a person upon death *and* during the previous seven years, and there is also a seven-year cumulation period in respect of lifetime chargeable transfers.[2] The effectiveness of the inheritance tax system depends, therefore, on a link of the greatest possible strength being used to attach a person to the UK, and domicile is just such a link. Residence may more easily be snapped, ordinary residence is only a little stronger, but the bonds of domicile are very difficult to break – and, as is explained later.[3] The confinement of UK taxation of income and capital gains to the taxation of remittances in the case of income and gains generated overseas by a person who is not domiciled in the UK is further parliamentary recognition of the strength of the link between person and territory which domicile represents.

---

1 The territories used in this example are some of the fictitious territories created by J R R Tolkien as a setting for *The Lord of the Rings*.
2 IHTA 1984 s 7 as amended by FA 1986.
3 At **9.16** below.

9.04   The five principles of domicile

Domicile, being a common law concept, is not defined in the Taxes Acts. In 1858, however, Lord Cranworth said: 'By domicile we mean home, the permanent home,'[1] and, ever since, that has been regarded as a basic (if deceptively simple) definition of the term. Although the idea of a permanent home is indeed central to the concept of domicile, the meaning of 'permanent home' in this context is not necessarily the meaning which the "man on the Clapham omnibus" would give to the term. There are, as will be shown, instances in which the courts will decide that a person's permanent home is in some faraway territory in which the person has never set foot and with which there may be no direct personal connection. This is because domicile, though founded on fact, is not merely a finding of fact but a conclusion of law which is reached by application of a set of legal principles.

The principles referred to are five in number, and the first is that no one shall, at any time, be without a domicile.[2] The necessity for this becomes apparent once we remind ourselves that domicile is, in English law, the sole determinant of the personal law to which a person is to be subject. Indeed, it is one of the weaknesses of legal systems which have opted for nationality as a determinant of the personal law that a person may be stateless and may thus not possess the required connecting link. This is not to say, of course, that assigning a domicile to every person never presents difficulties: it frequently does, but the courts have developed additional principles to overcome these problems.

The second principle is that no one can simultaneously have more than one operative domicile.[3] The justification for this is that domicile, being the sole determinant of the personal law, must, by its very nature, be exclusive, otherwise a further determinant will be needed. This exposes another weakness in systems which have taken nationality as the determinant of the personal law, for many persons have dual nationality. The adjective 'operative' has been introduced into the above statement of principle because, as will be explained,[4] there are three kinds of domicile and one of these, domicile of origin, will, if displaced by either of the others, become dormant but will, in the event of either of the others being lost, instantly revive. It should be noted that, in English law, domicile is regarded as a purely objective concept which remains unaffected by the subject matter of the point at issue.[5] In theory, therefore, there should be no question, in English law, of a person having one domicile for taxation purposes and another for, say, the purposes of divorce. As explained below, however, there are certain situations in which that may be possible – though not through any abandonment of the objective approach.

The third principle is said to be that domicile must relate to a territory subject to a single system of law, whether or not the limits of that territory coincide with national boundaries. This, so far as the UK is concerned, would mean that a domicile could arise only in Northern Ireland, Scotland or England and Wales.

However, the Taxes Acts speak not of domicile in Northern Ireland or Scotland or England and Wales but of domicile 'in the United Kingdom'.[6]

The fourth principle is that a change of domicile may never be presumed.[7] As Jenkins LJ has said:

'Change of domicile, particularly where the change is from the domicile of origin to a domicile of choice (as distinct from a change from one domicile of choice to another) has always been regarded as a serious step which is only to be imputed to a person upon clear and unequivocal evidence.'[8]

In other words, a change of domicile will always have to be proved and, as Lord Chelmsford has said:

'… the burden of proof unquestionably lies upon the party who asserts the change.'[9]

The question of the degree of proof required is considered at **7.15** below.

The fifth principle is that domicile must be determined according to the English concept of domicile. As Lindley MR said in *Re Martin*:[10]

'The domicil … must be determined by the English Court … according to those legal principles applicable to domicil which are recognised in this country and are part of its law.'[11]

The significance of this rule lies in the fact that 'domicile' does not have a precise and universally accepted meaning. Not all jurisdictions accept the objective approach to domicile, others (such as Australia, New Zealand and the United States) do not accept English doctrines such as that of the revival of the domicile of origin,[12] and under some international conventions domicile is equated with habitual residence.[13]

---

1 *Whicker v Hume* (1858) 7 HL Cas 124 at 160.
2 *Udny v Udny* (1869) Lr 1 Sc & Div 441 at 457, per Lord Westbury.
3 *IRC v Bullock* [1976] STC 409 at 414, per Buckley LJ.
4 See **9.06** below.
5 It is understood that a subjective or 'multiple concept' view of domicile is increasingly being adopted in the United States.
6 Eg, ICTA 1988 ss 65(4), 192 and 207 and TCGA 1992 s 12(1).
7 See *Moorhouse v Lord* (1863) 10 HL Cas 272 at 286, per Lord Chelmsford.
8 *Travers v Holley* [1953] P 246 at 252.
9 *Moorhouse v Lord* (1863) 10 HL Cas 272 at 286.
10 [1900] P 211.
11 [1900] P 211 at 227.
12 See **9.06** below.
13 Article 5 of the 1955 Hague Convention to Regulate Conflicts between the Law of Nationality and the Law of Domicile attributes domicile with this meaning.

Domicile of origin

9.05 Acquisition

English law recognises three kinds of domicile: domicile of origin; domicile of dependence; and domicile of choice. Every person will possess the first of these, and may, at different times, possess either of the others. *Henderson & Ors v Revenue and Customs*[1] graphically illustrates the interaction of all three kinds of domicile. The case concerned a claim by four individuals to have a domicile of origin in Brazil through a domicile of choice acquired by their grandfather as a result of a move from England to Brazil which was in place when their father was born. For the individuals to succeed, the grandfather would also need to not have abandoned that domicile of choice before their father turned 16 (which would have revived the grandfather's English domicile of origin and given their father an English domicile of dependence). In addition, if their father had a Brazilian domicile, he would need to have not acquired a domicile of choice in England before the four individuals were born. The taxpayers failed but the case usefully reveals the application of the rules to a peripatetic family of English origin: The grandfather, Ian was born in 1930 and went to Brazil in 1960 for work and married a Brazilian. The father, Nicholas, was born in Brazil in 1963. Ian and his wife, whose parents were of New Zealand origin, moved permanently to London in 1966. Nicholas spent a gap year in Brazil but lived primarily in England with army postings elsewhere. The First-tier Tribunal concluded that Ian never acquired a domicile of choice in Brazil and Nicholas consequently only ever had a domicile of origin in England. The reasons will be apparent from the discussion that follows.

The domicile of origin is the form of domicile which is imposed on every person at the moment of their birth. It is a link, forged by the law, which attaches a person to a particular system of law and which remains throughout life. Should a domicile of dependence or a domicile of choice be acquired, the link will be removed, but not destroyed; rather it will be held at readiness to reattach the person instantly to the original system of law should the domicile of dependence cease or the domicile of choice be abandoned.

Except in the case of a foundling (when the domicile of origin imposed is that of the place where the child is found), the basis of imposition of a domicile of origin is parentage. If a child is born legitimate and during the father's lifetime, the domicile of origin imposed is that of the father at the time of the child's birth.[2] If a child is born illegitimate,[3] or born legitimate but after the father's death,[4] the domicile of origin imposed is that of the mother.

One problem which could arise in this connection springs from the fact that the question of legitimacy is itself a matter of personal law. As the determinant of the appropriate person law is the child's domicile and as the child's domicile cannot be determined until the question of its legitimacy has been settled, it can be seen that, unless both parents are of the same domicile, an endless legal loop is created. Various solutions to the problem have been proposed[5] but there is no authority on the question in English law.

It seems clear that in the event of an illegitimate child being legitimated the child's domicile of origin will remain unaffected since, under the Legitimacy Acts, legitimation does not operate retrospectively.[6] In the event of a child becoming adopted, however, it would appear that a new domicile of origin will be acquired since adoption involves the complete severance of the legal relationship between parent and child and the establishment of a new one between child and the adoptive parent.[7]

The Law Commission and the Scottish Law Commission have recommended that the domicile of origin be abolished and that, in future, a child's domicile should be determined from the outset under revised domicile of dependence rules.[8]

---

1 *Henderson & Ors v Revenue and Customs* [2017] UKFTT 556 (TC).
2 *Udny v Udny* (1869) LR 1 Sc & Div 441 at 457, per Lord Westbury.
3 *Udny v Udny* (1869) LR 1 Sc & Div 441 at 457, per Lord Westbury.
4 This is apparently unsupported by any English authority.
5 Eg, by R H Graveson in *Private International Law* (Sweet and Maxwell, 7th edn) at pp 195–196.
6 See **9.08** below for the domicile of dependence which legitimation creates.

7 Lowe and Douglas, *Bromley's Family Law* 10th edn (Oxford University Press, 2006) p 408.
8 The Law Commission Working Paper No 88 and the Scottish Law Commission Consultative Memorandum No 63, 'Private International Law, The Law of Domicile' (1985), para 4.22. See **9.08** below.

9.06 Displacement and revival

A domicile of origin, being a domicile imposed by operation of law independently of a person's will, can never be extinguished by an act of will or by mere abandonment. It will continue to be operative, whether its possessor wishes it to be operative or not, until it is displaced by the acquisition of either a domicile of dependency or a domicile of choice. This is well illustrated by the leading case of *Bell v Kennedy*.[1]

Mr Bell was born in 1802 of Scottish parents who were domiciled by choice in the island of Jamaica. Accordingly, he possessed a Jamaican domicile of origin. Following the death of his mother, Bell, at the age of two, was sent to Scotland to be cared for and educated. When he was ten years old his father died and left him his Jamaican estate. Mr Bell completed his education in Scotland, travelled for a while in Europe, then, shortly after reaching his majority, returned to Jamaica to cultivate the estate that had been left to him. The estate prospered and Mr Bell became a wealthy and important personage, attaining membership of the island's Legislative Assembly. He married and fathered three children. In 1834, however, the law was changed with regard to slavery and the change was to culminate in the complete emancipation of slaves in 1838. Mr Bell strongly disapproved of the change and that, coupled with his failing health, decided him upon a permanent return to the UK. Accordingly, in 1837, he sold the estate and left the island for good. Initially, he and his immediate family resided with his mother-in-law in Edinburgh and Mr Bell set about finding a suitable estate, preferably in Scotland but possibly across the border, in England, which he could purchase and in which he and his family could settle down. Before he had succeeded in this, however, his wife died. At that time, a woman acquired the domicile of her husband upon marriage and, accordingly, in order to resolve a dispute which had arisen concerning Mr and Mrs Bell's daughter's succession to Mrs Bell's share in goods held in common between Mr and Mrs Bell at the date of Mrs Bell's death, it became necessary to determine Mr Bell's domicile at the date of his wife's death. The court held that his domicile was his domicile of origin (ie Jamaica). Lord Cairns said:

'The birth-domicile of [Bell] in Jamaica continued, at all events till 1837, and the onus lies upon those who desire to shew that there was a change in this domicile ... to prove that that change took place. The law is, beyond all doubt, clear with regard to the domicile of birth, that the personal status indicated by that term clings and adheres to the subject of it until an actual change is made by which the personal status of another domicile is acquired ... It appears to me ... that so far from [Mr and Mrs Bell's daughter and her husband] having discharged the onus which lies upon them to prove the adoption of a Scottish domicile, they have entirely failed in discharging that burden of proof, and that the evidence leads quite in the opposite direction. There is nothing in it to shew that [Bell's] personal status of domicile as a native and inhabitant of Jamaica has been changed on coming here by that which alone could change it, his assumption of domicile in another country.'[2]

Lord Colonsay had this to say:

'I think it is very clear that Mr Bell left Jamaica with the intention of never returning ... But I do not think that his having sailed from Jamaica with that intent extinguished his Jamaica domicile ... He could not so displace the effect which law gives to the domicile of origin, and which continues to attach until a new domicile is acquired *animo et facto*.'[3]

Once a person has, however, *animo et facto* or through the act of the person on whom they are dependent, acquired a new domicile, the domicile of origin, though displaced, still does not die. It lives on dormant but ready to awake and come back into operation in the instant any other domicile is voluntarily abandoned. As Lord Westbury has said in *Udny v Udny*:[4]

'When another domicile is put on, the domicile of origin is for that purpose relinquished, and remains in abeyance during the continuance of the domicile of choice; but as the domicile of origin is the creature of law, and independent of the will of the party, it would be inconsistent with the principles on which it is by law created and ascribed to suppose that it is capable of being by the act of the party entirely obliterated and extinguished.'[5]

Colonel Udny acquired a domicile of origin in Scotland when he was born there of Scottish parents in 1779. His childhood was spent in Scotland but, after serving as an officer in the Guards, in 1812, he married and settled in London. There he resided for the next 32 years. In 1844, however, the Colonel 'having been involved for some time in pecuniary difficulties (owing chiefly to his connection with the turf) was compelled to leave England in order to avoid his creditors'.[6] He first went to Scotland and from there he arranged for the sale of the lease of the London house and 'everything that was in the house, including what had belonged to his mother, his sister, and his ... wife';[7] he then fled to Boulogne. It was in Boulogne that he formed the illicit attachment that resulted in the birth of a child whose legitimation was in question.

Some doubt was expressed by the court whether Colonel Udny had ever, in fact, acquired an English domicile of choice. Nevertheless, the Lord Chancellor was of the opinion that:

'... the English domicil of Colonel Udny, if it were ever acquired, was formally and completely abandoned in 1844 when he sold his house and broke up his English establishment with the intention never to return. And, indeed, his return to that country was barred against him by the continued threat of process by his creditors. I think that on such abandonment his domicil of origin revived. It is clear that by our law a man must have some domicil, and must have a single domicil. It is clear, on the evidence, that the Colonel did not contemplate residing in France ... Why should not the domicil of origin cast on him by no choice of his own, and changed for a time, be the state to which he naturally falls back when his first choice has been abandoned *animo et facto*, and whilst he is deliberating before he makes a second choice.'[8]

Both the Private International Law Committee[9] and now the Law Commission and the Scottish Law Commission[10] have recommended that the principle of revival be discarded and that an existing domicile should continue until a new domicile is acquired. This is the rule in the United States,[11] New Zealand[12] and Australia.[13]

The question of the precise point at which the domicile of origin will revive upon a domicile of choice being abandoned is fully discussed at **9.15** below.

---

1 *Bell v Kennedy* (1868) LR 1 Sc & Div 307.
2 *Bell v Kennedy* (1868) LR 1 Sc & Div 307 at 310, 316–317.
3 *Bell v Kennedy* (1868) LR 1 Sc & Div 307 at 323.
4 (1869) LR 1 Sc & Div 441.
5 (1869) LR 1 Sc & Div 441 at 458.
6 (1869) LR 1 Sc & Div 441 at 445.
7 (1869) LR 1 Sc & Div 441 at 445.
8 (1869) LR 1 Sc & Div 441 at 448.
9 First Report (1954) Cmd 9068, para 14.
10 The Law Commission Working Paper No 88 and the Scottish Law Commission Consultative Memorandum No 63, 'Private International Law, The Law of Domicile' (1985, HMSO), para 5.22.
11 *Re Jones' Estate* 192 Iowa 78, 182 NW 227 (1921).
12 Domicile Act 1976 s 11 (New Zealand).
13 Domicile Act 1982 s 7 (Australia).

Domicile of dependence

9.07 Married women

Until 1 January 1974 there were three classes of persons who could or would acquire a domicile of dependence: children, mentally disordered persons and married women. Now, only the first two classes remain, for, by the Domicile and Matrimonial Proceedings Act 1973 s 1, the rule at common law that every woman acquired from her husband his domicile immediately upon her marriage was swept away.[1] The Act provides that the domicile of a married woman as at any time on or after 1 January 1974:

> '... shall, instead of being the same as her husband's by virtue only of marriage, be ascertained by reference to the same factors as in the case of any other individual capable of having an independent domicile.'[2]

So far as any woman who married on, or has married since, 1 January 1974 is concerned, the position is quite straightforward. As the subsection quoted makes plain, the woman has the same capacity as her husband or any other non-dependent person for acquiring a domicile of choice. It will, of course, usually be the case that the domicile of a husband and his wife will normally be the same, but this will now merely be because of their independent choice to live together permanently in the same place. Such a choice is not always made at the time of the marriage, or if made then, may not be implemented by residence until later. In that event, each may, under the Act, retain different domiciles.

Example

Marie-Louise is domiciled in Belgium. While attending art college in Manchester in 1985 she marries a fellow student, Henri, who is domiciled in France. Upon the completion of their respective courses they are resolved to settle permanently in Monaco. Until that decision is implemented by residence in Monaco, Marie-Louise will retain her Belgian domicile and Henri will retain his French domicile. Thereafter they will each acquire a Monagesque domicile of choice. Had they married before 1 January 1974, Marie-Louise would, upon her marriage, have acquired a French domicile of dependence and then, when they settled in Monaco, a Monagesque domicile of dependence.

The position of a woman who married before 1 January 1974 is set out in subsection (2) of the Act:

> 'Where immediately before [1 January 1974] a woman was married and then had her husband's domicile by dependence, she is to be treated as retaining that domicile (as a domicile of choice, if it is not also her domicile of origin) unless and until it is changed by acquisition or revival of another domicile on or after [1 January 1974].'[3]

The principal difficulty to which this provision gives rise was dealt with in *IRC v Duchess of Portland*.[4] In 1948, the taxpayer, a Canadian citizen with a domicile of origin in Quebec, married Lord William Cavendish-Bentinck (subsequently the Duke of Portland) in England and became Lady William Cavendish-Bentinck (subsequently the Duchess of Portland). Thereupon she acquired from her husband an English domicile of dependence which displaced her Quebec domicile of origin, but she was resolved to return to live in Canada should her husband predecease her and she hoped to persuade him to live in Canada on his retirement. Throughout her marriage, the Duchess of Portland maintained her links with Canada, returning there to visit friends and relatives for between ten and 12 weeks each year and (since about 1964) owning and maintaining there at her own expense her family home in Metis Beach, Quebec. The Duchess of Portland's first visit to Canada following the enactment of the Domicile and Matrimonial Proceedings Act 1973 was in July 1974, and following that visit she claimed that, under s 1(2) of the Act, her domicile of dependence had been changed by the revival of her Quebec domicile of origin. Had her claim succeeded she would have become exempt under ICTA 1970 s 122(2)(a) from liability to tax on income accruing to her in Canada but not remitted to the UK.

The basis of the Duchess of Portland's claim was that the domicile of choice which, under DMPA 1973 s 1(2), she acquired on 1 January 1974 was merely a *deemed* domicile of choice and that the strict test applicable to the abandonment of a true domicile of choice should not be applied in deciding whether or not her deemed domicile of choice had been abandoned. Instead, she claimed, the more lenient test applicable to the abandonment of a domicile of dependency was appropriate. Nourse J agreed that DMPA 1973 s 1(2) was a deeming provision but said:

> '... that which is deemed in a case where the domicile of dependency is not the same as the domicile of origin is the retention of the domicile of dependency as a domicile of choice. I think that that must mean that the effect of the subsection is

to reimpose the domicile of dependency as a domicile of choice. The concept of an imposed domicile of choice is not one which it is very easy to grasp, but the force of the subsection requires me to do the best I can. It requires me to treat the taxpayer as if she had acquired an English domicile of choice, even though the facts found by the commissioners tell me that that would have been an impossibility in the real world. In my judgment it necessarily follows that the question whether, after 1 January 1974, the taxpayer abandoned her deemed English domicile of choice must be determined by reference to the test appropriate to the abandonment of a domicile of choice and not by reference to the more lenient test appropriate to the abandonment of one of dependency.'[5]

It was pointed out in *IRC v Duchess of Portland* that, if the Duke and Duchess had married on or after 1 January 1974 the effect of DMPA 1973 s 1(1) would have been to preserve the Duchess's domicile of origin. Nourse J admitted that it was so and said:

'It seems clear that a woman living in England with her husband who was married before 1 January 1974 can only free herself from the shackles of dependency by choosing to leave her husband for permanent residence in another country. That is a very limited freedom and it is less than that available under s 1(1) to those who marry on or after 1 January 1974. Be that as it may, Parliament did not, as it might have done, provide that a woman who was married before 1 January 1974 was to be treated as if she had never acquired her domicile of dependency. Section 1(2) having taken the form which it has, by treating the married woman as retaining her domicile of dependency as a domicile of choice, I regret that I have no choice but to attach to it all the consequences which the law has long recognised the latter domicile to have.'[6]

A second difficulty which arises in relation to DMPA 1973 s 1(2) concerns the position after 1 January 1974 of a woman who, having married before that date, had left or had been abandoned by her husband before that date and had settled permanently in some country other than that of her domicile of dependence. In the absence of some new act on her part on or after 1 January 1974, does the woman retain her domicile of dependence as her domicile of choice or does she immediately acquire as her domicile of choice the country in which she settled permanently during her domicile of dependency? This question was also answered, albeit *obiter*, in *IRC v Duchess of Portland*. The problem, said Nourse J, is to be resolved 'consistently with the rule which would have applied if the husband had died before 1 January 1974' [7] The rule he referred to was established in *Re Cooke's Trustees*[8] and *Re Scullard,*[9] and is that where a husband and wife have been living apart, the intent and act of the wife in permanently making her home elsewhere creates a domicile of choice upon the death of her husband without the need for any additional act on her part, or, if the country in which she has settled is her domicile of origin, revives her domicile of origin without the need for any such act. The application of the rule is straightforward.

Example

In 1952, Tom, who was, and continued to be, domiciled in England, married Ingrid, who had a domicile of origin in Germany. In 1968 Ingrid left Tom and made her permanent home in Switzerland. Upon her marriage, Ingrid acquired an English domicile of dependence. This endured until 1 January 1974, but, on that date, in accordance with the rule in *Re Scullard's Estate*,[10] she automatically acquired a domicile of choice in Switzerland. Had Ingrid, upon leaving Tom, made her permanent home in Germany rather than Switzerland, her domicile of origin would have automatically revived on 1 January 1974.

Nourse J summed up as follows the procedure that DMPA 1973 s 1(2) requires one to adopt in determining the domicile of a woman who was married before 1 January 1974:

'... first ... look at the state of affairs prevailing on 1 January 1974 to see whether there has been any automatic change on that date [as in the above example]. If there has not ... look at events after that date in order to see whether any change has occurred subsequently.'[11]

---

1 The author's view is that domicile of dependence is, in any event, inconsistent with Art 14 (prohibition of discrimination) read with Art 1 (protection of property) to the First Protocol of the European Convention on Human Rights. See Irish Supreme Court in *W v W* 1993 IR 476, a case under the non-discrimination provisions of the Irish Constitution.
2 DMPA 1973 s 1(1).
3 DMPA 1973 s 1(2).
4 [1982] STC 149.
5 [1982] STC 149 at 154.
6 [1982] STC 149 at 156.
7 [1982] STC 149 at 155.
8 (1887) 56 LT 737.
9 [1956] 3 All ER 898.
10 [1956] 3 All ER 898.
11 *IRC v Duchess of Portland* [1982] STC 149 at 155.

9.08 Children

Until 1 January 1974, it was the rule at common law that a minor, whether married or not, was totally incapable of acquiring by their own act an independent domicile of choice.[1] A female child who, before then, married before attaining her majority acquired her husband's domicile as a domicile of dependence and, if widowed before that date, reacquired the domicile she had immediately before her marriage.[2]

On 1 January 1974, however, the Domicile and Matrimonial Proceedings Act 1973 came into effect and, with application only to England and Wales and Northern Ireland,[3] confined this rule to unmarried children under the age of 16.[4] Since then, any child reaching the age of 16 or marrying under that age, has been capable of acquiring an independent domicile of choice; and the same applied to any child who, at that date, was already over the age of 16 or, if then still under the age of 16, was then already married.[5]

The present position is, then, that every child acquires at birth a domicile of origin[6] and cannot, so long as they remain unmarried and below the age of 16, displace that domicile of origin by a domicile of choice acquired by their own act of will. There is, however, nothing to prevent their domicile of origin being displaced by an act of will on the part of one of their parents, and if this occurs the new domicile they acquire will be a domicile of dependence.

The primary rule is that, upon any change in the domicile of a child's father after the child's birth, a legitimate or adopted child will acquire their father's new domicile as a domicile of dependence unless their parents[7] are living apart and they either have then a home with their mother and not with their father or having had a home with their mother have not since then had a home with their father.[8] This is because, upon a separation, a child acquires a domicile of dependence from the parent with whom they make their home and, should they subsequently make their home with the other parent, they will (subject to a mother's right *not* to communicate her domicile to a child who is dependent upon her – see next paragraph) acquire a new domicile of dependence from that parent, but, should they cease to have a home with either parent, their last-acquired domicile of dependence will continue. A legitimate, legitimated or adopted child who shares their time between the homes of both parents will acquire and retain throughout the arrangement the domicile of their father.

Where a child is illegitimate or was born after the death of their father, they will prima facie acquire as a domicile of dependence any new domicile acquired by their mother whether they have a home with her or not,[9] unless the mother elects, bona fide and in the interests of the child, that the child's domicile shall not change with her domicile.[10]

Where one or both of a child's parents die during a child's period of dependency, the rules are as follows.

Where a legitimate or adopted child's father dies after the child is born, the child acquires (if they have not acquired it already[11]) the domicile of their mother as a domicile of dependence[12] which will then change as her domicile changes – subject, as explained above, to her right to elect that it shall not be so. The same will be true of an illegitimate child who, before their father's death, has been legitimated, for such a child will, upon legitimation, have received their father's domicile as a domicile of dependence. The death of the father of an illegitimate child who has not been legitimated will have no effect.

Where a child's mother dies, the death will have no effect on the child's domicile unless the child was either born illegitimate and has never been legitimated or has (or last had) a home with their mother following a separation of their parents. In either event, the child will continue to have their dead mother's domicile as a domicile of dependence unless and until, in the case of a legitimate or legitimated or adopted child only, they make a home with their father.[13]

Where a child's parents both die, the domicile of dependence which the child possessed at the date of their deaths will continue; though a child's guardian has no capacity to change the domicile of their ward.[14]

A domicile of dependence will continue until *animo et facto* they abandon the country of that domicile. Thereupon their domicile of origin will revive until it is displaced by a domicile of choice.[15]

Example

Susan is born of an English domiciled father and thus acquires an English domicile of origin by operation of law. When she is eight years old she and her parents move to Denmark and her father acquires there a domicile of choice which is then automatically communicated to Susan as a domicile of dependence. Susan continues to live with her parents until she is 24 when she marries a Norwegian and moves to Oslo where she intends to spend the rest of her life. Her Danish domicile of dependence will endure until she leaves Danish territorial waters, whereupon her English domicile of origin will revive. Upon arriving in Norway, however, her domicile of origin will be displaced by her Norwegian domicile of choice.

It should be noted that it is usually easier to establish the abandonment of a domicile of dependence than to establish the abandonment of a domicile of choice.[16]

The Law Commission and the Scottish Law Commission have proposed that the domicile of any person under the age of 16 should be determined according to where the child has their home. If their home is with both parents, their domicile, they say, should be the same as, and change with, that of their parents if their domiciles are the same, or with that of their mother if their domiciles are different. If their home is with only one parent, their domicile, they say, should be the same as, and change with, the domicile of that parent. And in any other case, the child's domicile should, they say, be the country with which they are, for the time being, most closely connected.[17]

---

1 *Forbes v Forbes* (1854) Kay 341; *Harrison v Harrison* [1953] 1 WLR 865.

2 *Shekleton v Shekleton* [1972] 2 NSWR 675.

3 Not Scotland. Under Scottish law the relevant respective ages are 14 in the case of a boy, 12 in the case of a girl.

4 DMPA 1973 s 3.

5 Because no English domiciled child has the capacity to marry below that age, however, the parts of the rule which relate to persons who are married under the age of 16 is of application only to foreign domiciled children whose marriages are recognised by the courts in this country – as, for example in *Mohamed v Knott* [1968] 2 All ER 563.

6 See **9.05** above.

7 Adoptive parents in the case of an adopted child (Children Act 1975 Sch 1, para 3 as repealed and re-enacted in the Adoption Act 1976 s 39(1) and the Adoption (Scotland) Act 1978 s 39(1)).

8 *D'Etchegoyen v D'Etchegoyen* (1888) 13 PD 132, DMPA 1973 s 4(1)–(2).

9 DMPA 1973 s 4(4) and *Johnstone v Beattie* (1843) 10 Cl & Fin 42.

10 In *Re Beaumont* [1893] 3 Ch 490 at 496, Stirling J said, 'Change in the domicile of an infant which ... may follow from a change of domicile on the part of the mother, is not to be regarded as the necessary consequence of a change of the mother's domicile, but as the result of the exercise by her of a power vested in her for the welfare of the infants, which in their interest she may abstain from exercising, even when she changes her own domicile.' Where, however, a mother exercises her power in her own interest (eg to take advantage of a law of succession more beneficial to herself), such an exercise of her power will be ineffective (*Potinger v Wightman* (1817) 3 Mer 67).

11 The child might already have acquired their mother's domicile as a domicile of dependence if their parents had separated before their father's death and if the child had, upon the separation, made their home with their mother.

12 *Potinger v Wightman* (1817) 3 Mer 67.

13 DMPA 1973 s 4(3).

14 See Dicey and Morris, *The Conflict of Laws* (13th edn, Sweet & Maxwell), Vol 1, p 141.

15 *Re Macreight, Paxton v Macreight* (1885) 30 ChD 165.

16 *Harrison v Harrison* [1953] 1 WLR 865.
17 The Law Commission Working Paper No 88 and the Scottish Law Commission Consultative Memorandum No 63, 'Private International Law, The Law of Domicile' (1985, HMSO), para 4.18.

9.09 Persons suffering from mental disorder

The position of a person suffering from mental disorder is lacking in direct authority so far as the question of their domicile is concerned. Until a child reaches the age of 16 or marries under that age, the rules governing their domicile will be those already discussed at **9.05** and **9.08** above. If, however, a child becomes insane and their insanity continues beyond their 16th[1] birthday, the law would appear to be that their domicile will continue to change with the parent from whom they last acquired a domicile of dependence, but that where they become of unsound mind after they have attained the age of 16 or married under that age, they will permanently retain whatever domicile they then possessed and that domicile will be incapable of change either by their own act or by that of those who are entrusted with their care.[2] The degree of mental unsoundness which is required before these rules will have effect is not settled, but it is arguable that the test to be applied should be whether or not the person is capable of forming the necessary intention to bring about a change in domicile.[3]

The Law Commission and the Scottish Law Commission have recommended that the domicile of an adult *incapax* should not be frozen at the onset of their incapacity but should be changed as necessary so that their domicile is always that of the country with which they are at any time most closely connected.[4]

1 In Scotland, 14 in the case of a boy, 12 in the case of a girl.
2 *Sharpe v Crispin* (1869) LR 1 P & D 611 at 615, per Sir J P Wilde.
3 See **9.12** below.
4 The Law Commission Working Paper No 88 and the Scottish Law Commission Consultative Memorandum No 63, 'Private International Law, The Law of Domicile' (1985, HMSO), para 6.9.

Domicile of choice

9.10 Acquisition

As has been explained at **9.07** to **9.09** above, a domicile of choice can be acquired only by a person who is not incapacitated either by age or by unsoundness of mind. There are no formal steps to be taken for a person of full age and capacity to acquire a domicile of choice. As the former HMRC guidance put it:

'To do so, you must broadly leave your current country of domicile and settle in another country. You need to provide strong evidence that you intend to live there permanently or indefinitely.'[1]

In *Udny v Udny*,[2] Lord Westbury described a domicile of choice as:

> '... a conclusion or inference which the law derives from the fact of a man fixing voluntarily his sole or chief residence in a particular place, with the intention of continuing to reside there for an unlimited time.'[3]

Both elements must be present. As Lord Chelmsford put it in *Bell v Kennedy*:[4]

> '... a new domicile is not acquired until there is not only a fixed intention of establishing a permanent residence in some other country, but until also this intention has been carried out by actual residence there.'[5]

These two elements are known, respectively, as the *animus manendi* (the intention to remain) and the *factum* (the fact of residence) and, as foregoing dicta make clear, both are essential. Before considering each element individually, however, one point must be made. The 'country' to which both the *animus* and the *factum* relate must, for the purpose of determining whether a domicile of choice has been acquired under common law, be 'a territory subject to a distinctive legal system.'[6]

This follows from the third principle of domicile discussed at **9.04** above but, as explained there, the problem which arises when discussing domicile in the context of UK taxation is that, under the Taxes Acts, the question to be determined is whether a person is domiciled 'in the UK' (ie a territory which is *not* subject to a distinctive legal system). It is important to refer to the earlier discussion, therefore, and to bear in mind that where a reference is made to a 'country' or 'territory' in the following paragraphs, it is possible that, for the purposes of this work, the country or territory referred to may be the UK collectively and not necessarily Northern Ireland, Scotland or England and Wales individually.

---

1 HMRC6 (April 2009), para 4.3.2.
2 (1869) LR 1 Sc & Div 441.
3 (1869) LR 1 Sc & Div 441 at 458.
4 (1868) LR 1 Sc & Div 307.
5 (1868) LR 1 Sc & Div 307 at 319.
6 *Re Fuld's Estate (No 3)* [1968] P 675 at 684, per Scarman J reiterating the formula in *Henderson v Henderson* [1967] P 77 at 79.

9.11 Residence

The meaning of the term 'residence' has already been explored at some depth in the earlier chapters of this work but here a distinction must be drawn between residence as a connecting factor in its own right for the purposes of UK taxation and residence in the context of the acquisition of the connecting factor of domicile. In *IRC v Duchess of Portland*,[1] Nourse J said:

> 'Residence in a country for the purposes of the law of domicile is physical presence in that country as an inhabitant of it ... [I]n a case where the domiciliary divides his physical presence between two countries at a time ... it is necessary to look at all the facts in order to decide which of the two countries is the one he inhabits.'[2]

The Duchess of Portland had claimed that, by spending some 10 to 12 weeks each year in Quebec visiting relatives and maintaining her links with Canada (the land of her birth and the country to which she hoped eventually to return), she had acquired a domicile of choice in Canada. She spent the rest of her time living with her husband in England. Nourse J said:

> 'On those facts it appears clear to me that since 1948 the taxpayer has been physically present in this country as an inhabitant of it. Her physical presence in Quebec has been for periods of limited duration and for the purpose of maintaining her links with the country to which it is her intention ultimately to return. That is not enough to have made her an inhabitant of Quebec. In my judgment it is clear that she was resident in England on 1 January 1974 and that that residence was not displaced when she went to Canada in July 1974 or at any other time during the material period.'[3]

It has been shown that residence for tax purposes (ie as a territorial connecting link *per se*), is a quality of the person which – despite judicial asseverations to the contrary – may be attributed to a person not according to its ordinary meaning in the speech of plain men but according to a special, forensic meaning derived from case law precedents and Revenue practice. It will be recalled, for instance, that the celebrated Mr Lysaght, who had a settled place of residence in Ireland, was attributed with UK residence status merely by reason of his regular monthly business trips to the UK during the course of which he stayed with his brother or at the Spa Hotel in Bath.[4] It has also been demonstrated that, because residence in its taxation context is a qualitative attribute, a person may (as in the case of Lysaght) be resident in two or more countries at the same time.[5] It is clear from the judgment of Nourse J, however, that neither of these possibilities is open so far as residence in the context of the acquisition of a domicile of choice is concerned. A person *may* be resident in a particular country for both taxation purposes *and* domicile purposes, but he will not necessarily be so. Residence for domicile purposes involves actual inhabitance of a country,[6] dwelling within its borders rather than merely paying it visits, however extensive and regular those visits might be: and where a person inhabits two different countries, the only one in which he will be regarded as resident for domicile purposes is the one in which, on the balance of the facts, he is shown to have his 'chief residence'.[7]

The length of a person's residence in a particular country may be of great importance in determining whether or not a person has acquired a domicile of choice in that country, but it is not in itself determinative of the matter. As Lord Chelmsford said in *Bell v Kennedy*:[8]

> 'It may be conceded that if the intention of permanently residing in a place exists, a residence in pursuance of that intention, however short, will establish domicile.'[9]

This principle was reiterated (with the insertion of an interesting additional clause) by Nourse J in *Re Clore (No 2)*:[10]

> '... if the evidence [of intention] is there, particularly perhaps where the motive is the avoidance of taxes, the necessary intention will not be held to be missing merely because the period of actual residence is a short one.'[11]

The fact of residence does, however, raise a presumption of domicile in the country of residence[12] and this presumption grows with the length of the period of residence so that, in some instances, it will be sufficient to override declarations of contrary intention[13] and will require a person's actual removal elsewhere if it is to be rebutted.[14] In *Udny v Udny*,[15] Lord Chelmsford said:

> 'Time is always a material element in questions of domicil; and if there is nothing to counteract its effect, it may be conclusive upon the subject.'[16]

Anderson v Laneuville[17] provides an interesting illustration of the point. The case concerned Anderson, a person born in 1768 with an Irish domicile of origin who, at the age of 67 (by which time he had acquired an English domicile of choice) traced, and thereafter until his death some 24 years later, cohabited with, in France, a widow, Madame Laneuville, who, some 46 years earlier, had risked her life in helping him to escape the Terror of the revolution in France where he was then being educated. Anderson had, it seems, expressed some intention of returning to England should Madame Laneuville have predeceased him, but on appeal from the Prerogative Court of Canterbury, that one fact was held to carry insufficient weight to counteract the effect of the length of Anderson's residence in France, and that long period of residence was held to lead inevitably to the conclusion that Anderson had died domiciled in France.

Thus it was in the more recent case of *Re Furse, Furse v IRC*.[18] William King Furse was born in Rhode Island in 1883 and had a Rhode Island domicile of origin. At the age of four, he was brought to England by his father but, after completing his education here, he returned to America, married and remained in employment there until 1916. He then left America to serve in the British army in the 1914–18 war. Upon demobilisation in 1919 he returned to New York where his wife had purchased a house and he found employment there. In 1923 Furse and his wife and children moved to England and bought a farm in West Hoathly. There Furse lived until his death 40 years later. From time to time between 1923 and the early 1950s, Furse and his wife contemplated a return to America and in the 1940s actually inspected a farm in Maryland. In the early 1950s Furse decided, however, that he would not return to America unless he became incapable of leading an active life on his farm in England. Fox J, declaring that Furse died domiciled in England, said:

> '... the facts ... show a man deeply settled in England. He came to England at the age of four; he died in England at the age of 80. Of the intervening 76 years he spent 58 in England (in the sense that England was his normal place of abode in those years) and three or four in the British army ... [He] was wholly integrated into the English community in which he lived. There is no doubt at all, as I see it, that the life which he was living in England was the life he wanted to go on living to the end of his life ... In my view, by the time of his death, the balance of probabilities is that he can have had no real intention of leaving; a fact which is emphasised by the vagueness of his expressed intentions.'[19]

There was, to use Lord Chelmsford's words, nothing (or nothing sufficiently concrete in the way of intention or surrounding circumstances) to counteract the effect of time, and time was, therefore, conclusive on the subject. This is not to say, however, that residence of long duration will alone suffice to establish domicile. It will not. As the previous HMRC guidance correctly pointed out:

> 'Living in another country for a long time, although an important factor, is not enough in itself to prove you have acquired a new domicile.'[20]

This follows from what Cottenham LC said in *Munro v Munro*:[21]

> 'Residence alone has no effect, per se, though it may be most important as a ground from which to infer intention.'[22]

In both *Anderson v Laneuville*[23] and *Re Furse, Furse v IRC*,[24] that was where the significance of the long residence of Anderson and Furse lay. All the evidence suggested that, despite their vague assertions of a possible return to their native lands, Anderson and Furse would have remained where they were, however long they had lived; and the courts, therefore, permitted the *animus* of true intention to be inferred from the *factum* of residence.

Where, however, there is evidence to the contrary – something sufficiently concrete to counteract the effect of the duration of residence – the duration of residence will not be conclusive upon the subject as *Ramsay v Liverpool Royal Infirmary*[25] illustrates. George Bowie (the validity of whose will was in question) was born in Glasgow in 1845 and acquired from his father a Scottish domicile of origin. Upon reaching the age of 37 he gave up his employment as a commercial traveller and steadfastly refused to work again throughout the remainder of his life. For ten years he 'lived on the bounty' of his mother and sisters in Glasgow, then, in 1892, he moved to lodgings in Liverpool and for the next 21 years sponged instead on his brother. Upon his brother's death, Bowie moved into his brother's house and for the next eight years sponged on his sister until she died in 1920. He remained at his brother's house and died in Liverpool (where he had arranged to be buried) seven years later. Bowie boasted of being a Glasgow man but during the 36 years he lived in England he refused to return to Scotland, even for his mother's funeral. He left England only twice, once to visit America and once to holiday in the Isle of Man. On those facts, the House of Lords held unanimously that Bowie had *not* acquired a domicile of choice in England but that his Scottish domicile of origin was still operative at the date of his death. Their lordships were convinced that declarations by Bowie to the effect that he would never return to Scotland were mere posturing and that, had Bowie's source of funds dried up, he would, in fact, have gone back there. That, plus the fact that there was no evidence to show that Bowie had made his permanent home in England was, in their view, sufficient to quash the inference of intention to which Bowie's 36 years of residence in England would otherwise have given rise. Lord Macmillan said:

> 'Prolonged actual residence is an important item of evidence of ... volition, but it must be supplemented by other facts and circumstances indicative of intention. The residence must answer a qualitative as well as a quantitative test.'[26]

IRC v Bullock[27] provides a modern (and much more convincing) illustration of the application of this principle. Group Captain Bullock had a domicile of origin in Nova Scotia but came to England in 1932 and joined the Royal Air Force. He intended to return to Canada on completing his service but, in 1946, he married an Englishwoman some three years his junior. Between then and 1960, Bullock and his wife made several trips to Canada and, upon leaving the RAF in 1959, Bullock would have liked them to move there permanently. His wife did not wish to do so, however, so Bullock took up civilian employment in England until 1961 when an inheritance enabled him to retire completely. Until 1966, Bullock continued to try to persuade his wife to move with him to Canada, but thereafter resigned himself to the fact that she would never do so. In that year, however, he made a will under Nova Scotia law in which he declared that his domicile was and would continue to be the Province of Nova Scotia and that he would return and remain there upon his wife's death. Bullock retained his Canadian nationality and passport, never acquired British nationality or a British passport, refused to vote in local or parliamentary elections, maintained close contact with Canadian relatives and friends, and was a regular reader of a Toronto newspaper. On these facts the Commissioners found that Bullock was not domiciled in England and the Court of Appeal (reversing Brightman J's judgment in the High Court) upheld the Commissioners' finding. Bullock's residence in England, though over 40 years in duration, was accompanied at all times by a clear and definite intention to return to Canada upon the substantial possibility of his wife predeceasing him, and that was sufficient to counteract the effect of the element of time.

---

1 [1982] STC 149.
2 [1982] STC 149 at 155.
3 [1982] STC 149 at 155–156.
4 See **3.12** above.
5 See **3.21** above.
6 *IRC v Duchess of Portland* [1982] STC 149 at 155, per Nourse J.
7 *Re Fuld's Estate (No 3)* [1968] P 675 at 682, per Scarman J.
8 (1868) LR 1 Sc & Div 307.
9 (1868) LR 1 Sc & Div 307 at 319.
10 [1984] STC 609.
11 [1984] STC 609 at 615.
12 *Bruce v Bruce* (1790) 2 Bos & P 229; *Bempde v Johnstone* (1796) 3 Ves 198.
13 *Stanley v Bernes* (1830) 3 Hagg Ecc 373; *Re Marrett, Chalmers v Wingfield* (1887) 36 Ch D 400.
14 *Hodgson v De Beauchesne* (1858) 12 Moo PC 285.
15 (1869) LR 1 Sc & Div 441.
16 (1869) LR 1 Sc & Div 441 at 455.
17 (1854) 9 Moo PC 325.
18 [1980] STC 596.
19 [1980] STC 596 at 606.
20 IR20 (July 2008), para 4.5.
21 (1840) 7 Cl & Fin 842.
22 (1840) 7 Cl & Fin 842 at 877.
23 (1854) 9 Moo PC 325.
24 [1980] STC 596.
25 [1930] AC 588.
26 [1930] AC 588 at 598.
27 [1976] STC 409. See also *IRC v Cohen* (1937) 21 TC 301 where a person with an English domicile of origin who went to Australia at the age of 18 and did not return to England until 32 years later was nonetheless held to have retained his English domicile of origin throughout. Overturning the Commissioners' finding that Henry Cohen had acquired an Australian

domicile of choice and never abandoned it, Finlay J held (at 315) that the true inference from the facts was that Henry Cohen 'intended to reside and to reside for a long time in Australia, but ... he intended to reside there so long only as his business made that necessary, and his business connection with Australia ceased in 1911'.

9.12   Intention

The acquisition of a domicile of choice requires not only residence (in the sense of actual habitation of the chosen territory) but also an intention to make that territory 'the permanent home'.[1] The problem of what is meant by 'permanent' has lain at the root of many a case concerning domicile. Lord Chelmsford took a strict view of the matter. In *Moorhouse v Lord*[2] he said:

'The present intention of making a place a person's permanent home can exist only where he has no other idea than to continue there without looking forward to any event, certain or uncertain, which might induce him to change his residence. If he has in contemplation some event upon the happening of which residence will cease, it is not correct to call this even a present intention of making it a permanent home. It is rather a present intention of making it a temporary home, though for a period indefinite and contingent.'[3]

But others thought that far too strict. In *A-G v Pottinger*,[4] Bramwell B said:

'There is not a man who has not contingent intentions to do something that would be very much to his benefit if the occasion arises. But if every such intention or expression of intention prevented a man having a fixed domicil, no man would ever have a domicil at all, except his domicil of origin.'[5]

The less absolute view of the nature of the necessary intention may be discerned in Lord Westbury's statement in *Udny v Udny*[6] that the residence which is the other necessary element in the acquisition of a domicile of choice:

'... must be a residence not for a limited period or particular purpose, but general and indefinite in its future contemplation.'[7]

It emerged even more openly when, in *Gulbenkian v Gulbenkian*,[8] Langton J said:

'The intention must be a present intention to reside permanently, but it does not mean that such intention must be irrevocable. It must be an intention unlimited in period, but not irrevocable in character.'[9]

And it is clearly discernible in the two widely-approved propositions concerning the acquisition of a domicile of choice made by Scarman J in *Re Fuld's Estate (No 3)*:[10]

'... a domicile of choice is acquired when a man fixes voluntarily his sole or chief residence in a particular place with an intention of continuing to reside there for an unlimited time.'[11]

'A domicile of choice is acquired only if it be affirmatively shown that the *propositus* is resident within a territory subject to a distinctive legal system with the intention, formed independently of external pressures, of residing there indefinitely.'[12]

'Permanent', it will be noted, has become 'indefinite' or 'unlimited' and the difference that brings about may clearly be seen by comparing the dictum of Lord Cairns in *Bell v Kennedy*[13] and that of Buckley LJ in *IRC v Bullock*.[14] Lord Cairns said:

'The question ... is ... Whether [Bell] ... had determined to make, and had made, Scotland his home, with the intention of establishing himself and his family there, and ending his days in that country.'[15]

Buckley LJ said:

'I do not think that it is necessary to show that the intention to make a home in the new country is irrevocable or that the person whose intention is under consideration believes that for reasons of health or otherwise he will have no opportunity to change his mind. In my judgment, the true test is whether he intends to make his home in the new country until the end of his days *unless and until something happens to make him change his mind*.'[16]

Buckley LJ had not only the authority of Bramwell B to rely on in adding those final 11 words. In *Aikman v Aikman*,[17] Campbell LC (another nineteenth-century judge) had said that a mere intention to return to a man's native country on a doubtful contingency would not prevent residence in a foreign country putting an end to his domicile of origin.

Given that Scarman J and Buckley J have accurately stated the current judicial view of intention for domicile of choice purposes, however, the question then arises: what constitutes a 'doubtful contingency'; what is the 'something' which a person might have in contemplation without the necessary intention of indefinite or unlimited residence being found lacking? Scarman J has answered the question thus:

'If a man intends to return to the land of his birth upon a clearly foreseen and reasonably anticipated contingency, eg the end of his job, the intention required by law is lacking: but if he has in mind only a vague possibility, such as making a fortune (a modern example might be winning a football pool) or some sentiment about dying in the land of his fathers, such a state of mind is consistent with the intention required by law. But no clear line can be drawn; the ultimate decision in each case is one of fact.'[18]

And Buckley LJ has answered it in a similar manner:

'No doubt, if a man who has made his home in a country other than his domicile of origin has expressed an intention to return to his domicile of origin or to remove to some third country on an event or condition of an indefinite kind (for example 'if I make a fortune' or 'when I've had enough of it'), it might be hard, if not impossible, to conclude that he retained any real intention of so returning or removing. Such a man, in the graphic language of James LJ in *Doucet v Geoghegan*,[19] is like a man who expects to reach the horizon; he finds it at last no nearer than it was at the beginning of his journey.'[20]

In both these passages, however, the contingency contemplated is of a 'pipe dream' character. What if the contingency contemplated is something more specific? In the event, said Buckley LJ, the question to be asked is:

'... is there a sufficiently substantial possibility of the contingency happening to justify regarding the intention to return as a real determination to do so on the contingency occurring rather than a vague hope or aspiration?'[21]

The facts of the case of *IRC v Bullock*[22] in which that test was propounded, have already been set out at **9.11** above and it is clear from those facts that the single contingency upon which Group Captain Bullock intended to return to Canada was the death of his wife. It was only his wife's refusal to live in Canada which was keeping the Group Captain here, and, as his wife was only two or three years his junior, there was a substantial possibility that she would predecease him. Accordingly, Buckley LJ held that his test question could be answered affirmatively: Group Captain Bullock did not have the necessary intention to make England his domicile of choice. When applied to the facts in *Re Furse, Furse v IRC*[23] (also set out at **9.11** above), however, Buckley LJ's test produced the opposite answer. William Furse was happy and content in England and the only contingency upon which he intended to return to America was his becoming physically incapable of taking an active interest in his farm. Fox J said:

'It seems to me that the intention of [Furse] was indeed to continue to reside in England for an unlimited period. His intention was to continue to live here for the rest of his life, save on the contingency which he expressed. That contingency is so vague that I do not think it can be regarded as imposing any clear limitation on the period of his residence. I do not believe that he was ever prepared to face up to such a limitation. The contingency is of the sort which Simon P in *Qureshi v Qureshi*[24] described as 'open-ended' ... I think that, when [Furse] died in his 81st year, still in England and still with no arrangements made for leaving England, one could not realistically regard his permanent home as other than in England. He intended to live out his days here, save on a contingency so vaguely expressed that I do not think, against the history of his life, it could be regarded for practical purposes as limiting that intention.'[25]

It will have been noted that in many of the extracts from judgments given in this section the words 'present intention' are used. The force of the adjective 'present' emphasises that what must be considered is the state of a person's mind at the time when the acquisition of a domicile of choice is alleged to have taken place. Subsequent variations in that intention are irrelevant[26] unless accompanied or followed by appropriate action.[27]

It should not be overlooked, however, that evidence of a subsequent change of mind might, in some instances, lead the court to infer that the original intention to remain indefinitely in the country of choice was not as settled as the evidence of that original intention indicated.

Although actual residence and the intention to reside indefinitely must concur before a domicile of choice can be created, the intention may precede or succeed the commencement of residence. The person who decides to emigrate to Quebec will possess the intention which is one element in the creation of a Quebec domicile of choice before he establishes the residence which is the other essential element. The refugee escaping persecution may, on the other hand, establish residence before acquiring the intention to remain indefinitely in the land of current residence.

The only remaining point to be made concerning intention is that it is only the intention to remain indefinitely in a country which is relevant to the acquisition of a domicile of choice. If a person has that intention and there comes a time when the intention coincides with actual residence, a domicile of choice is acquired whether it was also the person's intention to acquire a domicile of choice or not. Thus, in *Re Steer*,[28] Mr Steer, an Englishman who established his permanent home in Hamburg and died there 50 years later, was held to have died domiciled in Germany even though, on one of his temporary visits to England, he had made a will in which he declared that although he was returning to Hamburg he had no intention of renouncing his English domicile of origin. The principle governing this matter was succinctly stated over a century ago:

'If the intention [to reside indefinitely in a particular country] exists and if it is sufficiently carried into effect certain legal consequences follow from it, whether such consequences are intended or not and perhaps even though the person in question may have intended the exact opposite.'[29]

---

1 *Whicker v Hume* (1858) 7 HL Cas 124 at 160, per Lord Cranworth.
2 (1863) 10 HL Cas 272.
3 (1863) 10 HL Cas 272 at 285–286.
4 (1861) 30 LJ Ex 284.
5 (1861) 30 LJ Ex 284 at 292.
6 (1869) LR 1 Sc & Div 441.
7 (1869) LR 1 Sc & Div 441 at 458.
8 [1937] 4 All ER 618.
9 [1937] 4 All ER 618 at 627.
10 [1968] P 675.
11 [1968] P 675 at 682.
12 [1968] P 675 at 684.
13 (1868) LR 1 Sc & Div 307.
14 [1976] STC 409.
15 *Bell v Kennedy* (1868) LR 1 Sc & Div 307 at 311.
16 *IRC v Bullock* [1976] STC 409 at 415. [Author's italics.]
17 (1861) 4 LT 374 at 376.
18 *Re Fuld's Estate (No 3)* [1968] P 675 at 685, per Scarman J.
19 (1878) 9 Ch D 441 at 457.
20 *IRC v Bullock* [1976] STC 409 at 416.
21 *IRC v Bullock* [1976] STC 409 at 416.
22 [1976] STC 409.
23 [1980] STC 596.
24 [1971] 1 All ER 325 at 340.
25 *Re Furse, Furse v IRC* [1980] STC 596 at 606.
26 *Re Marrett, Chalmers v Wingfield* (1887) 36 Ch D 400.
27 See **9.15** below.

28 (1858) 3 H & N 594. See also *Re Lawton* discussed at **9.14** below.
29 *Douglas v Douglas* (1871) LR 12 Eq 617 at 644–645.

9.13 Motive as evidence of intention

It will have been noted that the first of Scarman J's two propositions concerning the acquisition of a domicile of choice, quoted at **9.12** above contains the words 'fixes *voluntarily* his sole or chief residence', and that the second contains the words 'with the intention, *formed independently of external pressures*, of residing'. Those words draw attention to the fact that the acquisition of a domicile of choice presupposes a freedom of choice. As Lord Westbury put it in *Udny v Udny*:[1]

> 'There must be a residence freely chosen, and not prescribed or dictated by any external necessity … .'[2]

If it can be shown that a person resides where they do, not by choice but by constraint, the necessary intention will be lacking and no change of domicile will be imputed to the involuntary exile.

The most obvious example of residence by constraint rather than through choice is imprisonment in some country other than that of the existing domicile. No prisoner, during a term of imprisonment, will acquire a new domicile in the country of imprisonment, even if the imprisonment is for a very long term, for this residence is not a matter of choice.[3]

Another example of constraint is the persecution which may impel a person to flee his existing country of domicile for some other country. Although the residence in the country of refuge will be a matter of free choice, the inference at law will be that the refugee will return to their homeland upon it being safe to do so and they will, therefore, prima facie lack the intention to reside permanently in the country of refuge which would be necessary in order to acquire a domicile of choice in that country. It might be, of course, that a refugee will acquire such an intention during the course of their exile.[4]

A fugitive from justice is in much the same position as the refugee except that, if the crime is such that the fugitive will always (or for a very long time) be liable to proceedings in the country from which they have fled, there will be a presumption at law that the country of refuge has been selected with the intention of residing there indefinitely.[5] The departure will have been a matter of constraint but the establishment of residence elsewhere will have been a matter of free choice.

'The demands of creditors' was one of Lord Westbury's examples of an external necessity which might result in a person residing where they would not otherwise reside.[6] So it was with Colonel Udny and his residence in France. But the fact that a person has fled the country to escape creditors will not necessarily mean that a domicile of choice cannot be acquired in the country to which the debtor has fled. It will depend on circumstances: the size of the debts, the likelihood of them ultimately being met, how long their discharge is likely to take, and the imminence of recovery proceedings.

The invalid who, although in no immediate danger of untimely death, settles for health reasons in a country other than the country of their existing domicile is regarded at law as doing so out of choice rather than out of constraint. In the case of *Hoskins v Matthews*,[7] for example, Turner LJ said that Mr Matthews, an Englishman who, at the age of 60, had gone to Florence suffering from a spinal injury and had died there 12 years later, was not, when he first took up residence in Florence,

> '... in any immediate danger or apprehension. He was, no doubt, out of health, and he went abroad for the purpose of trying the effect of other remedies and other climates. That he would have preferred settling in England I have little doubt, but I think he was not driven to settle in Italy by any cogent necessity. I think that in settling there he was exercising a preference, and not acting upon a necessity, and I cannot venture to hold that in such a case the domicil cannot be changed.'[8]

If, however, the change of environment is a matter of life or death, or if, death being imminent and inevitable, the change of climate will alleviate suffering, there will, it seems, be no presumption of a change in domicile.[9]

The 'tax exile' who, in order to escape the incidence of taxation in the country of existing domicile, settles in a country with a less harsh tax regime, will, it seems, be presumed to intend to remain in the new country permanently. In *Re Clore (No 2)*,[10] Nourse J said that even a short period of residence would be sufficient to establish a domicile of choice 'if the evidence is there, particularly perhaps where the motive is the avoidance of taxes'.[11]

In the *Clore* case, there were, according to Nourse J, three areas where the evidence supported Sir Charles Clore's acquisition of a domicile of choice in Monaco. One was the severance of the more important of his connections with England where Sir Charles had his domicile of origin. Another was the establishment of connections with Monaco including residence there. But the most important, in Nourse J's eyes, was that:

> '... the professional advice which Sir Charles received was given not solely with the immediate object of his acquiring a non-resident status for income and capital gains tax purposes, but with the long-term objective of his acquiring a foreign domicile. Further, unless the operation was to be at least partially counter-productive, it was essential that the new country should be one where no tax was payable. Monaco was chosen because it was the only tax haven with which Sir Charles was familiar and the only one which could have been acceptable to him.'[12]

Against the evidence in those three areas, however, was the evidence of four of his close friends who were unanimous in their testimony that Sir Charles was unhappy in Monaco and had never, in his heart of hearts, abandoned England. All his actions from mid-1978 until his death in London on 26 July 1979 were tentative and, right up to the time of his death, he was showing an interest in acquiring residential properties in France and Israel. Accordingly, Nourse J held that Sir Charles died domiciled in England. That decision must not, however, be allowed to obscure the fact that, because Sir Charles had resided in Monaco and his motive for residing there was tax avoidance, Nourse J accepted that there was a presumption at law that a domicile of choice had been acquired in Monaco. As with any presumption at law, however, the presumption to which a tax avoidance motive will give rise may be rebutted by other evidence, and in the *Clore* case it was rebutted by the evidence of parol declarations made by Sir Charles in his final years and testified to by his four friends.

It must finally be pointed out that the residence of a person in a country other than the country of their existing domicile will give rise to no presumption that a domicile of choice has been acquired in the new country if the person is there in pursuit of what Lord Westbury called 'the duties of office'.[13] These have been held to include the duties of a consul,[14] chief justice,[15] embassy attaché,[16] naval officer,[17] and army officer.[18] Such a negative presumption may, of course, be rebutted by evidence to the contrary.[19]

1 (1869) LR 1 Sc & Div 441.
2 (1869) LR 1 Sc & Div 441 at 458.
3 *Re the late Emperor Napoleon Bonaparte* (1853) 2 Rob Eccl 606.
4 *De Bonneval v De Bonneval* (1838) 1 Curt 856. See also *Steiner v IRC* (1973) 49 TC 13 where a refugee from the Nazi persecution of Jews made his home in England in 1939 but was held not to have acquired an English domicile of choice here until about 1950 when the facts were such as to indicate that he had formed the intention of remaining permanently in England.
5 *Re Martin, Loustalan v Loustalan* [1900] P 211.
6 *Udny v Udny* (1869) LR 1 Sc & Div 441 at 458.
7 (1856) 8 De GM & G 13.
8 (1856) 8 De GM & G 13 at 28–29.
9 See Lord Kingsdown's comments in *Moorhouse v Lord* (1863) 10 HL Cas 272 at 292.
10 [1984] STC 609.
11 [1984] STC 609 at 615.
12 [1984] STC 609 at 614.
13 *Udny v Udny* (1869) LR 1 Sc & Div 441 at 458.
14 *Sharpe v Crispin* (1869) LR 1 P & D 611.
15 *A-G v Lady Rowe* (1862) 1 H & C 31.
16 *A-G v Kent* (1862) 31 LJ Ex 391.
17 *Re Patten's Goods* (1860) 6 Jur NS 151.
18 *Firebrace v Firebrace* (1878) 4 PD 63.
19 *Donaldson v Donaldson* [1949] P 363.

9.14 Proof of intention

As Scarman J said in *Re Fuld's Estate (No 3)*:[1]

'It is beyond doubt that the burden of proving the abandonment of a domicile of origin and the acquisition of a domicile of choice is upon the party asserting the change. But it is not so clear what is the standard of proof: is it to be proved beyond reasonable doubt or upon the balance of probabilities, or does the standard vary according to whether one seeks to establish abandonment of domicile of origin or merely a switch from one domicile of choice to another? Or is there some other standard? ... The formula of proof beyond reasonable doubt is not frequently used in probate cases and I do not propose to give it currency. It is enough that the authorities emphasise that the conscience of the court ... must be satisfied by the evidence. The weight to be attached to evidence, the inferences to be drawn, the facts justifying the exclusion of doubt and the expression of satisfaction will vary according to the nature of the case. Two things are clear – first, that unless the judicial conscience is satisfied by evidence of change, the domicile of origin persists: and secondly, that the acquisition of a domicile of choice is a serious matter not to be lightly inferred from slight indications or casual words.'[2]

Those statements were later endorsed by Orr LJ who, in *Buswell v IRC*,[3] said:

'I ... accept the statements as accurate and would only add that in referring to the judicial conscience I am satisfied that Scarman J was not recognising the existence of some general standard of proof intermediate between the criminal and civil standards but was merely emphasising that in the application of the civil standard the degree of proof required will vary with the subject-matter of the case.'[4]

The approach to assessing evidence of intention was neatly expressed by Mummery LJ in *Agulian & Anor v Cyganik*:[5]

'(1)   Although it is helpful to trace ... life events chronologically and to halt on the journey from time to time to take stock, this question cannot be decided in stages. [T]he court must look back at the whole of the deceased's life, at what he had done with his life, at what life had done to him and at what were his inferred intentions in order to decide whether he had acquired a domicile of choice in England by the date of his death. Soren Kierkegaard's aphorism that "Life must be lived forwards, but can only be understood backwards" resonates in the biographical data of domicile disputes.

(2)   Secondly, special care must be taken in the analysis of the evidence about isolating individual factors from all the other factors present over time and treating a particular factor as decisive.'

If the judicial conscience is to be satisfied that a change in domicile has taken place, the courts must subject every department of a person's life to the most searching scrutiny. The length and nature of residence in the country in which it is asserted that the person has acquired a domicile will, of course, be a factor of particular interest since, as has been explained,[6] residence gives rise at law to a presumption of domicile, and intention may be inferred from residence if the residence is of sufficient length and there is other evidence to support such an inference. Motives too must be examined for, as has been explained at **9.13** above, a person's motive in taking up residence in a country other than that of their existing domicile may give rise to an inference of, or against, a change in domicile. But the court's concern is never confined merely to residence and the motive for residence. As Lord Atkinson said of *Winans v A-G*[7] in *Casdagli v Casdagli*:[8]

'... the tastes, habits, conduct, actions, ambitions, health, hopes, and projects of Mr Winans deceased were all considered as keys to his intention to make a home in England.'[9]

It is often said that if a person wishes to ensure that a change of domicile will withstand the scrutiny of the courts the person must not only take up residence in the country of choice but should purchase a property there and dispose of any property in the country that has been abandoned, apply for citizenship of the new country, obtain a passport in the new country and relinquish an existing passport, close all bank accounts in the abandoned country and open new accounts in the country of choice, relinquish credit cards and obtain new ones in the country of choice, resign any directorships in the abandoned country and acquire business interests in the country of choice, sever membership of clubs, societies, religious organisations etc in the abandoned country and join clubs etc in the country of choice, vote in the new country's elections,[10] become involved in its politics and socially integrated into its life, educate children in its schools, have a will drawn up under its laws and make arrangements to be buried or cremated there. Such a checklist has a certain value, being a list of factors to which particular significance has been attached in cases which have come before the courts at different times. But the approach is wrong. A person who has genuinely made a 'permanent home' in a new country will, in those and many other ways, manifest the reality of their intention to live out their days as an inhabitant of the land to which they have gone; but the person who is engaged in nothing more than a cosmetic exercise designed to conceal the fact that 'in spite of all temptations to belong to other nations, he remains an Englishman'[11] is likely to betray his lack of genuine intention no matter how scrupulously he adheres to a list of 'dos and don'ts'. No one factor will, in itself, be decisive, and even a factor which seems of supreme significance when viewed in isolation may carry little weight when set against all other factors. Thus, for example, in *Wahl v A-G*,[12] the fact that a person with a German domicile of origin and German nationality had become a naturalised British subject was not regarded as being at all conclusive:

> 'I am far from saying that an application for naturalisation is not a matter to be carefully considered as part of the evidence in a case of domicile, but it must be regarded as one of the totality of facts and it cannot assume the dominant importance attached to it in the judgment of the trial judge ... It is not the law either that a change of domicile is a condition of naturalisation, or that naturalisation involves necessarily a change of domicile.'[13]

In making his application for naturalisation, Wahl had made a statutory declaration to the effect that he intended to continue to reside permanently within the UK. That too formed part of the evidence of his intention and, since such declarations are frequently made by persons changing their domicile, their value must now be considered. In *F v IRC*[14] the executor of F, a former Iranian national who had died in 1993, appealed against the determination of the Revenue that he had been domiciled in the UK for the years of assessment 1986–87 to 1992–93 inclusive. F had operated an accountancy business in Iran. He had bought land with a view to developing it, owned three houses and had constructed a large family home. At the time of the Iranian revolution he had sent his wife and children to live in the UK while remaining himself in Iran. At the time of the US hostage crisis F had decided to remain outside Iran at the same time he had been placed on an exit barred list due to alleged outstanding tax liabilities. In 1980 he had been granted indefinite leave to remain in the UK. He had subsequently applied for naturalisation, falsely claiming that he had left Iran to escape religious persecution. Up until the time of his death, F had made efforts at getting the exit bar removed. He had continued to consider Iran as his home. The Court in allowing the appeal held that the Revenue had not discharged the burden of proof to demonstrate that F had not abandoned his Iranian domicile. Having regard to the evidence, it had always been F's intention to return to Iran permanently during the relevant years for assessment. His acquisition of British citizenship and a British passport had not affected his domicile of origin in Iran, and so *Wahl v A-G* applied. He had been keen to gain the necessary documentation that would enable him to continue to travel freely in the furtherance of his business interests and had been willing to lie in order to gain such documentation. His return to Iran had been precluded by the exit bar. Such external pressures had prevented F from forming a free intention to acquire another domicile.

An example of the difficulties to which a written declaration might give rise is found in *Buswell v IRC*.[15] Leslie Buswell had a Transvaal domicile of origin acquired from his father who had a Transvaal domicile of choice. In 1928, when Buswell was seven years old, he and his parents moved to England so that Buswell could be educated here. Following his education and a brief period which Buswell spent as a teacher in Tenbury Wells, he was called up in 1941 and served in the Royal Indian Navy. Upon demobilisation in 1945, he took employment in India and remained there until 1952 when he returned to England where his father was living in a poor state of health. Once in England, he took employment with a publishing firm for six months, then obtained a position with British Olivetti Ltd which he held until 1963. In 1955, Buswell obtained a South African passport and elected for South African nationality when South Africa left the Commonwealth, and, in 1958, wrote to a cousin in South Africa saying he intended to return there one day. In 1961, he married an Englishwoman of means who was agreeable to settling eventually in South Africa, and, by her, had children who were educated in England but were registered as South African nationals. In 1968, Buswell and his wife visited South Africa (Buswell's first visit there for 40 years) and bought a property in which they thereafter spent some three months of each year. Buswell claimed that, for the years 1961–62 to 1967–68, he was 'not domiciled in the UK' for the purposes of ITA 1952 s 132 (now ITTOIA s 832)). That claim was resisted by the Inland Revenue on the grounds that, on 11 November 1952, Buswell had completed a Revenue questionnaire (Form P86) by answering 'Yes' to the question 'Do you propose to remain permanently in the UK?' and inserting a dash in answer to the next question: 'If not, how long do you expect to remain in this country?' The Commissioners attached great weight to those replies and accordingly found that Buswell had acquired an English domicile of choice. The High Court upheld the Commissioners' finding on appeal, but the Court of Appeal reversed it. Orr LJ said.

'The crucial question … is … whether the Commissioners, in coming to their conclusion, attributed to the answers on Form P86 a weight which in all the circumstances they could not reasonably bear. For this purpose it is necessary to consider both the terms of the questions asked on the form and the circumstances in which it may reasonably be supposed that [Buswell] answered them … [T]he form was not intended by the Revenue to ascertain domicile and it nowhere used that word … A person faced with … mutually exclusive questions, would, I think, be very likely to consider that he was not expected to say "I do not know" in answer to the second question, an answer which would have to be given if he said "No" to the first … I find … that, in attributing a decisive importance to [Buswell's] answers on the Form P86, given at a time when he had been back in this country for less than five months after an absence of ten years, and against the background to which I have referred, the Commissioners acted "upon a view of the facts which could not reasonably be entertained".'[16]

Often a written declaration of intention will appear in a person's will, taking a form similar to that appearing in the will of Frank Lawton in *Re Lawton*:[17]

> 'Inasmuch as I am a British subject having my original domicile in England (which domicile I have never relinquished or abandoned) it is my wish and intention that this my will … shall be construed and operate so far as the case admits as if I were now and remained until my death domiciled in England.'[18]

The value of such a declaration was assessed by Romer LJ in *A-G v Yule and Mercantile Bank of India*[19] as follows:

> 'For myself, I am not prepared to attach any importance to a declaration by a man as to his domicile unless there is some evidence to show that the man knew what "domicile" means. A declaration by a man made orally or in writing that he intends to remain in a certain country will, if not inconsistent with the facts, be of assistance in determining the question whether he has become domiciled there. Domicile is, however, a legal conception on which the views of a layman are not of much assistance.'[20]

Lawton had, in fact, left England before he had attained the age of 21 and, having lived and worked in Argentina and Spain, retired to France where he died some 63 years later. Upjohn J held that, despite the declaration in his will, Lawton died domiciled in France.

Where the assertion of intention as to residence has been made orally, the testimony of the person to whom it was made is admissible as evidence of intention but, if made long after the assertion itself was made, will be treated with caution:

> 'To entitle such declarations to any weight, the court must be satisfied not only of the veracity of the witnesses who depose to such declarations, but of the accuracy of their memory, and that the declarations contain a real expression of the intention of the deceased.'[21]

Where the assertion is actually made by the person whose domicile is being determined during the court proceedings at which the determination of domicile is to be made, the assertion will, of course, carry very little weight indeed. In *Bell v Kennedy*[22] the Lord Chancellor said of Bell's own testimony:

> '… it is to be accepted with very considerable reserve. An Appellant has naturally, on an issue like the present, a very strong bias calculated to influence his mind, and he is, moreover, speaking of what was his intention some twenty-five years ago.'[23]

---

1 [1968] P 675.
2 [1968] P 675 at 685–686.
3 [1974] STC 266.
4 [1974] STC 266 at 273.
5 [2006] EWCA Civ 129 at para 49.
6 See **9.11** above.
7 [1904] AC 287.
8 [1919] AC 145.
9 [1919] AC 145 at 178.

10 The fact that an individual is registered on the UK electoral roll as an overseas voter does not affect his domicile unless the individual wishes it to be taken into account: ITA 2007 s 835B.
11 W S Gilbert, *HMS Pinafore*, Act II.
12 (1932) 147 LT 382.
13 (1932) 147 LT 382 at 385, per Lord Atkin.
14 [2000] 1 WTLR 505.
15 (1974) 49 TC 334.
16 (1974) 49 TC 334 at 362–363.
17 (1958) 37 ATC 216. See also *Re Steer* discussed at **9.12** above.
18 (1958) 37 ATC 216 at 218.
19 (1931) 145 LT 9.
20 (1931) 145 LT 9 at 17.
21 *Hodgson v De Beauchesne* (1858) 12 Moo PC 285 at 325.
22 (1868) LR 1 Sc & Div 307.
23 (1868) LR 1 Sc & Div 307 at 313.

9.15   Change of domicile of choice

It should by now have become clear that the courts will not easily be satisfied that a domicile of origin has been replaced by a domicile of choice. The presumption of a domicile of origin's continuance is of the utmost strength and, compared with a domicile of choice:

'… its character is more enduring, its hold stronger and less easily shaken off.'[1]

This is because a domicile of origin is conferred on a person by operation of law whereas, as has been explained,[2] a domicile of choice is acquired merely *animo et facto*. Once acquired, however, a domicile of choice may be extinguished *animo et facto* also (ie by an intention and an act). The act is the leaving of the country of the domicile of choice and the intention is the intention not to resume permanent residence there. This last is technically referred to as an *animus non revertendi*. Such an *animus* does not, it should be noted, include within it a decision to reside permanently elsewhere. In *Udny v Udny*,[3] the Lord Chancellor summed up the whole matter as follows:

'… if the choice of a new abode and actual settlement there constitute a change of the original domicil, then the exact converse of such a procedure, viz the intention to abandon the new domicil, and an actual abandonment of it, ought to be equally effective to destroy the new domicil. That which may be acquired may surely be abandoned, and though a man cannot, for civil reasons, be left without a domicil, no such difficulty arises if it be simply held that the original domicil revives. That original domicil depended not on choice but attached itself to its subject on his birth, and it seems to be consonant both to convenience and to the currency of the whole law of domicil to hold that the man born with a domicil may shift and vary it as often as he pleases, indicating each change by intention and act, whether in its acquisition or abandonment; and, further, to hold that every acquired domicil is capable of simple abandonment *animo et facto* the process by which it was acquired, without its being necessary that a new one should be at the same time chosen, otherwise one is driven to the absurdity of asserting a person to be domiciled in a country which he has resolutely forsaken and cast off, simply because he may (perhaps for years) be deliberating before he settles himself elsewhere.'[4]

Just as a domicile of choice cannot be acquired *animo solo*, however, a domicile of choice cannot be abandoned unless the intention to leave the territory of the existing domicile of choice for good is accompanied by an actual departure from that territory. As Cotton LJ said in *Re Marrett*:[5]

'... in order to lose the domicil of choice once acquired, it is not only necessary that a man should be dissatisfied with his domicil of choice, and form an intention to leave it, but he must have left it, with the intention of leaving it permanently.'[6]

The application of this principle is to be found in *Zanelli v Zanelli*.[7] The case concerned an Italian who, having married an Englishwoman and lived with her in England, deserted her and returned to Italy. The wife petitioned for divorce in England claiming that the English courts had jurisdiction because immediately before deserting her, her husband was domiciled in England within the terms of the Matrimonial Causes Act 1973 s 13. The question before the court was whether that was so. It was accepted that, following the marriage, the woman's husband had acquired a domicile of choice in England and it was accepted also that, by the time of his desertion, he had formed the intention to return permanently to Italy. But did that bring about a loss of domicile of choice? Lord du Parcq decided that no, it did not:

'... although the husband may have given up an intention to reside here, he certainly had not given up residence here. The *factum* had not occurred.'[8]

Accordingly, the woman's petition was granted and her divorce (which would not have been permitted under Italian law) was granted under English law.

The question when the *factum* of departure does occur is not always an easy question to answer as *Re Raffenel's Goods*[9] illustrates. Madame Raffenel had a domicile of origin in England but, upon marrying a French naval officer, had acquired a French domicile of dependence. Following her husband's death, she decided to return permanently to England. She boarded ship at Calais with her children and baggage, having closed down her establishment in Dunkirk, but, before the ship left the harbour, became so ill that she had to disembark. She returned to Dunkirk where she later died. Sir Cresswell Cresswell said:

'I cannot think that the French domicil was abandoned so long as the deceased remained in the territory of France. It must be admitted that she never left France, and that intention alone is not sufficient.'[10]

Although that case was concerned with abandonment of a domicile of dependence, Lord du Parcq, in the case of *Zanelli v Zanelli*[11] which (as explained above) concerned the abandonment of a domicile of choice, expressly approved the decision in *Re Raffenel's Goods*[12] and drew no distinction between the two types of domicile in this connection. Speaking of Zanelli's desertion of his wife he said:

'... he cannot be said to have lost his domicile of choice even at the moment when he stepped into the train with his ticket in his pocket. Having regard to what was decided ... in *Re Raffenel's Goods* ... I do not think that, even when he stepped on board the ship which was to carry him to the Continent, he had yet lost his domicile of choice.'[13]

It should be noted, however, that in that case, Asquith LJ went even further:

> 'To change an English domicile of choice there must be both *animus* and *factum*, the *animus* being the formation of the intention, and the *factum* consisting in some outward and visible act evincing it such as leaving this country or, *perhaps more accurately, arriving in another.*'[14]

And on the strength of that dictum, Baker J held, in *Leon v Leon*,[15] that a person who had displaced his domicile of origin in British Guiana (now Guyana) by a domicile of choice in England but had then left England for good and returned to British Guiana, had:

> '... kept his English domicile until he reverted to his domicile of origin on his arrival in British Guiana in August 1964.'[16]

This, it is suggested, was stretching Sir Cresswell Cresswell's dicta in *Re Raffenel's Goods*[17] too far. Surely, the domicile of origin of both Zanelli and Leon revived as soon as their respective ships left the territorial waters of the UK, not when they docked on the shores of their respective homelands.

It was said at the outset of this section that the *animus* required to effect the abandonment of a domicile of choice is an *animus non revertendi* (ie an intention not to return). It must now be emphasised that (despite recent indications of some relaxation in this view)[18] such an *animus* does *not* cover a case of mere irresolution (*sine animo revertendi*). A person who leaves the country of their existing domicile of choice in a state of indecision as to whether or not to return there retains their existing domicile of choice until such time as the indecision hardens into a decision never to return. This is illustrated by *Fielden v IRC*.[19] Fielden had an English domicile of origin but, in or about 1935, this was displaced by a Michigan domicile of choice when he married a Michigan resident and settled in that state of America with the intention of remaining there permanently. In 1943, Fielden and his wife moved to Burnley in Lancashire with the intention of helping in his father's ailing business, and they bought a house there. In 1947, Fielden became a director of his father's company and later became chairman and managing director. It seems that he then decided that he owed it to his father to remain in England until he was satisfied the business could continue successfully without him, but he asserted that, upon his retirement, he would return to America, though not necessarily to Michigan. At the time the case was heard, however, he was still living in Burnley, 22 years after leaving America. The Commissioners decided that, by 1954–55, the first of the years for which his domicile was in question, Fielden's English domicile of origin had revived, but they also found that his Michigan domicile of choice had been retained for some years after his return to England, probably until 1947. This was, it is suggested, because for those years he was merely *sine animo revertendi* to Michigan, not *animo non revertendi* to Michigan. Later, however, his intention to return to America in general became too vague to prevent him being regarded as *animo non revertendi* and thereupon his domicile of origin revived. The Commissioners' findings were upheld by Cross J who said:

'... it is not necessary, in order to retain a domicile of choice after a change of residence, to have an unwavering intention of returning to live in the place of domicile in all circumstances ... When [Fielden] came to England in 1943, he came under the stress of circumstances. He wanted to help his country and his father in the war; and the Commissioners have found – I think quite rightly found – that he did not there and then lose his Michigan domicile of choice. It would not, I think, matter for this purpose whether he then had an intention to go back as soon as possible to Michigan after the war, or simply to go back to some place in the United States after the war. But then one finds that after the war he buys a house here, that when he goes to the United States it is only for a short stay, and that he remains here continuously until the present time ... [H]e re-acquired his English domicile of origin about 1947 ... because ... such intention as he may thereafter have had of going to live somewhere in the United States after his retirement was really too vague and uncertain to prevent the re-acquisition of his English domicile of origin.'[20]

If a person leaves a domicile of choice *animo revertendi* but subsequently abandons the intention to return, the domicile of origin will, of course, thereupon revive.[21]

Finally, it should be noted that where a person *animo et facto* abandons one domicile of choice and *animo et facto* acquires another, the domicile of origin will revive for the duration of the interval, however brief, between the abandonment and the acquisition.[22]

---

1 *Winans v A-G* [1904] AC 287 at 290, per Lord Macnaghten; *F (F's Personal Representatives v IRC)* [2000] STC (SCD) 1.
2 See **9.10** above.
3 (1869) LR 1 Sc & Div 441.
4 (1869) LR 1 Sc & Div 441 at 450.
5 (1887) 36 Ch D 400.
6 (1887) 36 Ch D 400 at 407.
7 (1948) 64 TLR 556.
8 (1948) 64 TLR 556.
9 (1863) 3 Sw & Tr 49.
10 (1863) 3 Sw & Tr 49.
11 (1948) 64 TLR 556.
12 (1863) 3 Sw & Tr 49.
13 (1948) 64 TLR 556.
14 (1948) 64 TLR 556 at 557. [Author's italics.]
15 [1967] P 275.
16 [1967] P 275 at 282. These words must not be taken as some sort of authority for the proposition that presence in the domicile of origin is necessary for that domicile's revival. As *Tee v Tee* [1974] 1 WLR 213 clearly shows, it is not.
17 (1863) 3 Sw & Tr 49.
18 In *Re Flynn* [1968] 1 WLR 103 Megarry J said (*obiter* at 113) that 'mere negative absence of any intention' to resume residence, rather than a positive intention not to return, would suffice to bring a domicile of choice to an end, and this was approved in *Qureshi v Qureshi* [1971] 2 WLR 518 at 530; but see *Executors of Winifred Johnson Dec'd v HMRC* [2005] UKSPC 481.
19 (1965) 42 TC 501.
20 (1965) 42 TC 501 at 507–508.
21 *Tee v Tee* [1973] 3 All ER 1105.

22 *Harrison v Harrison* [1953] 1 WLR 865. The proposal of The Law Commission and the Scottish Law Commission is that this should cease to be so and that an abandoned domicile of choice should continue until a new domicile is acquired (Working Paper No 88 and Consultative Memorandum No 63, para 5.22).

9.16 Deemed domicile to 5 April 2017

In introducing the capital transfer tax (which was renamed 'inheritance tax'), the Finance Act 1975 s 45 provided that, under any of three sets of circumstances a person who was not domiciled in the UK under the common law rules described in this chapter was nevertheless to be treated as domiciled in the UK for most purposes of the tax. The provision relating to one of those three sets of circumstances was repealed by Finance (No 2) Act 1983 s 12 and the provisions describing the remaining two sets of circumstances were substantially re-enacted as the Inheritance Tax Act 1984 s 267(1)(a) and (b).

Section 267(1)(a) and (3) provided that a person not domiciled in the UK at the time of a transfer of value etc ('the relevant time') is to be treated as domiciled in the UK at that time if he was domiciled in the UK on or after 10 December 1974 and within the three years immediately preceding the relevant time.

In the absence of statutory definition to the contrary, 'year' means a period of 12 calendar months consisting of 365 days or 366 days in a leap year.[1]

The effect of this provision is to postpone (for inheritance tax purposes only) a person's acquisition of a domicile in some country outside the UK to a date three years after the date on which, according to common law rules, the acquisition of the new domicile actually took place. Thus, any transfer of value made by the person within the three years immediately following his acquisition of an overseas domicile will remain potentially subject to inheritance tax regardless of the *situs* of the asset.

This rule has no rational basis and is transparently directed at keeping within the inheritance tax net for a period of time anyone who leaves the UK permanently. Superficially, it parallels a Revenue practice regarding the residence status of a person who leaves the UK for permanent residence abroad, ie that a decision on that person's claim to have become non-resident and not ordinarily resident in the UK will be postponed for three years and that during those three years the person's tax liabilities will be calculated on the basis that he remains a UK resident; but, in the case of residence, a decision at the end of three years that the person had become non-resident on his departure is then applied retrospectively to the date of departure and all assessments are revised accordingly. There is, however, nothing similarly provisional about the three-year postponement of non-domiciled status.

Unlike s 267(1)(a), s 267(1)(b) is a more rational piece of legislation which was designed to place a non-domiciled person who has lived in the UK for a specified number of years on an equal footing with the UK-domiciled taxpayer.[2] It (and s 267(3)) provided that a person not domiciled in the UK at the time a transfer of value etc. takes place ('the relevant time') is to be treated as domiciled in the UK at that time if the individual was resident in the UK on or after 10 December 1974 and in not less than 17 of the 20 years of assessment ending with the year of assessment in which the relevant time falls. It should be noted, however, that, for the purposes of this provision:

'... the question of whether a person was resident in the UK in any year of assessment shall be determined as for the purposes of income tax.'[3]

Chapters 3 and 5 should, therefore, be studied in this context in relation to years up to 5 April 2013, and Chapter 2 for years thereafter. In deciding whether an individual is deemed domiciled under s 267, any election to be treated as domiciled in the UK under ss 267ZA and 267ZB is ignored.[4]

The provision itself has two effects. The first is to bring persons who have never been domiciled in the UK into the inheritance tax net. The second (and often overlooked) effect is, unless the change of domicile takes place on 6 April, to keep a person who has been, but is no longer, domiciled in the UK within the inheritance tax net for up to almost a year longer than s 267(1)(a) will keep that person there.

Members of the House of Commons (Members of Parliament) and House of Lords (Peers) are deemed domiciled in the UK for the purposes of income tax, inheritance tax and capital gains tax.[5]

---

1 *IRC v Hobhouse* [1956] 1 WLR 1393.
2 See Official Report, Standing Committee A, 13 February 1975, cols 1645–1646.
3 IHTA 1984 s 267(4).
4 IHTA 1984 s 267(5). See **9.17**.
5 Constitutional Reform and Governance Act 2010 s 41(1)–(3). See also Chapter 2, at **2.27**.

9.17 Deemed domicile from 6 April 2017

Finance (No 2) Act 2017 comprehensively reformed the tax treatment of individuals who are not domiciled in any part of the UK at common law. A major extension of the deemed domicile legislation was proposed in Summer Budget of July 2015 and the consultation that followed.[1] Two targets of this reform were identified: first, non-domiciled individuals who have been resident in the UK for 15 out of the preceding 20 years, and, secondly, individuals who were born in the UK, who have a UK domicile of origin but have acquired a foreign domicile and are resident in the UK. Broadly, both categories of individuals who are not domiciled in any part of the UK will no longer qualify as such for UK tax purposes. Individuals who cease to be domiciled in the UK continue to remain UK domiciled for three years after giving up a UK domicile for inheritance tax purposes.[2] Similarly Members of the House of Commons (Members of Parliament) and House of Lords (Peers) continue to be deemed domiciled in the UK for the purposes of income tax, inheritance tax and capital gains tax.[3]

The deemed domicile provisions apply to income tax, capital gains tax[4] and inheritance tax.[5] The rules are to similar effect in each case but there are notable differences for income tax, capital gains tax purposes on the one hand, and for inheritance tax purposes on the other. The rationale of reducing the time that non-UK domiciled residents may continue to reside in the UK before being put in the same tax position as UK domiciled residents will produce haphazard outcomes for individuals in its interaction with both the case law and statutory residence tests. A close study of Chapters 2, 3 and 5 will indicate that individuals with relatively modest connections to the UK may become resident. Such individuals will inevitably also have substantial residential connections with other countries. The prospects of double taxation are significantly increased as a result.

Income tax and capital gains tax

An individual not domiciled in the UK at common law at a time in a tax year, is treated as domiciled in the United Kingdom for income tax and capital gains tax purposes at that time if that individual has been UK resident for at least 15 of the 20 tax years immediately preceding the relevant tax year.[6] Thus individuals who cease to be resident from 6 April 2018 will continue to be treated as UK domiciled unless and until they are non-UK resident for at least six tax years in the 20 tax years before the relevant tax year. A transitional rule permits individuals who have not been UK resident in any tax year from 6 April 2017 and including the year when their domicile is to be determined (a 'relevant tax year'), to be not UK domiciled for this purpose.[7]

An individual not domiciled in the UK at common law at a time in a tax year, is also treated as domiciled in the United Kingdom for income tax and capital gains tax purposes at that time if (a) the individual was born in the United Kingdom, (b) the individual's domicile of origin was in the United Kingdom, and (c) the individual is UK resident for the relevant tax year.[8] Consequently, a UK born individual who originally had a domicile of origin in any part of the UK but who subsequently acquired a foreign domicile (of choice or dependence) will be deemed to be UK domiciled in any tax year when they are UK resident. This rule will apply, for example, to a child born in England of English parents who emigrate from the UK to Australia as a family and remain there permanently. If in adulthood, that child returns to the UK, for example for a one-year short-term work assignment, that child will be deemed domiciled during that tax year of UK residence.

The consequence of deemed domicile status is essentially the loss of access to the remittance basis for foreign income and gains. Some complexities of such a loss of status are addressed in F(No 2) A 2017, Sch 8.

Inheritance tax

An individual not domiciled in the UK at common law at a time in a tax year, is treated as domiciled in the United Kingdom for inheritance tax purposes at that time if the individual was resident in the United Kingdom for at least 15 of the 20 tax years immediately preceding the relevant tax year, and for at least one of the four tax years ending with the relevant tax year.[9] This differs from the income tax and capital gains tax test in that an individual person who would otherwise satisfy the 15 of 20 tax years test will not be deemed domiciled if they are non UK resident in that tax year and have been non-resident for the previous three consecutive tax years.

An individual not domiciled in the UK at common law at a time in a tax year, is treated as domiciled in the United Kingdom for inheritance tax purposes at that time if the individual is a 'formerly domiciled resident' for the tax year.[10] A 'formerly domiciled resident' is an individual (a) who was born in the United Kingdom,(b) whose domicile of origin was in the United Kingdom, (c) who was resident in the United Kingdom for the relevant tax year, and (d) who was resident in the United Kingdom for at least one of the two tax years immediately preceding the relevant tax year.[11] Thus the difference between deemed domicile of UK born individuals is that for inheritance tax purposes, the individual must be UK resident in at least two tax years. Income tax and capital gains tax require residence in only one year. Thus in the example of a child born in England of English parents who emigrate from the UK to Australia as a family and remain there permanently, if in adulthood, that child returns to the UK, for example for a one-year short-term work assignment, that child will not be deemed domiciled during a single tax year of UK residence. However, a one-year short-term work assignment to the UK that straddles two tax years, making the individual resident in both,[12] will result in deemed domicile for inheritance tax in the second year of residence.

A transitional rule permits individuals who have not been UK resident in any tax year from 6 April 2017 and including the year when their domicile is to be determined (a 'relevant tax year'), to be not UK domiciled for this purpose.[13] As a result, individuals who are not UK domiciled at common law and who ceased to be resident from the 2017/18 tax year and who do not again become UK resident will not be domiciled in the UK for inheritance tax from 6 April 2017. Such individuals who cease to be resident after 5 April 2018 will need to wait until they no longer have been resident for 15 of the 20 preceding tax years to cease to be deemed domiciled.

The broad effect of deemed domicile is that property situated outside the UK will no longer qualify for exclusion from inheritance tax. This is subject to detailed rules in F(No 2)A 2017, s 30.

Deemed domicile and the statutory residence test

The question whether an individual was UK resident in any given tax year will be answered by reference to the law in that year. Thus, for years up to 5 April 2013 the case law tests discussed in Chapters 3 and 5 will apply. FA 2013, Sch 45, para 1(4) makes clear that the Statutory Residence Test, discussed in Chapter 2 applies thereafter.

One consequence of the residence rules is that residence at any time in a tax year, no matter how short, will make the individual resident for that year.

An individual who qualifies for split year treatment under FA 2013, Sch 45, Pt 3, in a given tax year, will likewise be resident for the whole of that tax year for purposes of the deemed domicile rules.[14] Depending on the time of arrival and departure from the UK, it may be possible to become deemed domiciled with a little over 12 years actual living in the UK.

---

1 HMRC Technical Note, Technical briefing on foreign domiciled persons changes announced at Summer Budget 2015 (8 July 2015); HM Treasury Consultation document, Reforms to the taxation of non-domiciles; further consultation (19 August 2015); HM Treasury Consultation document, Reforms to the taxation of non-domiciles (30 September 2015).
2 IHTA 1984, s 267(1)(a).
3 Constitutional Reform and Governance Act 2010, s 41(1)–(3). See also Chapter 2, at **2.27**.
4 ITA 2007, s 835BA(1), inserted by F(No 2) A 2017, s 29(1).
5 IHTA 1984, s 267(1), amended by F(No 2) A 2017, s 30(1).
6 ITA 2007, s 835BA(2) and (4) ('Condition B').
7 ITA 2007, s 835BA(5).
8 ITA 2007, s 835BA(2) and (3) ('Condition A').
9 IHTA 1984, s 267(1)(b).
10 IHTA 1984, s 267(1)(aa).
11 IHTA 1984, s 272.
12 See 'Fulltime work in the UK', discussed in Chapter 2 at **2.14**.
13 F(No 2) A 2017, s 30(10).
14 See Chapter 2, at **2.31**.

9.18   Elective UK domicile for spouses and civil partners

On 24 October 2012 the EU Commission requested the UK to review inheritance taxation of transfer between spouses. The Commission noted that UK legislation provides that transfers between domiciled spouses or civil partners are exempt from inheritance tax. However, transfers between domiciled and non-domiciled spouses or civil partners are not exempt from inheritance tax. Furthermore, in the latter case the rules on the nil rate band applicable to subsequent transfers differ and may result globally in a higher taxation. In the Commission's view, this difference in tax treatment is discriminatory and contrary to EU law (Article 18 TFEU).[1]

FA 2013 provides a legislative response in the form of an election by the non-domiciled spouse or civil partner of a UK-domiciled individual to choose to be treated as UK domiciled for the purposes of the IHTA 1984.[2] In determining whether a person making an election under this section is or was UK domiciled, the deemed domicile rules in s 267 are ignored.[3] An election may be made in writing to HMRC in two circumstances:

Firstly, a lifetime election may be made to be treated as UK domiciled by an individual, if at any time from 6 April 2013 and during the period of seven years ending with the date on which the election is made, he or she had a spouse or civil partner who was UK domiciled.[4] A lifetime election takes effect on the date specified in the notice of election which must be on or after 6 April 2013 and within the period of seven years of the date of election. On the effective date, the individual making the election must have been married to, or in a civil partnership with, the spouse or civil partner who was then domiciled in the United Kingdom.[5]

Secondly, a death election may be made if at any time from 6 April 2013 an individual dies, and within the period of seven years ending with the date of death the deceased was: (a) domiciled in the United Kingdom; and (b) the spouse or civil partner of the person who would, by virtue of the election, be treated as domiciled in the United Kingdom.[6] This election may be made by the deceased person's personal representatives.[7] A death election may only be made within two years of the death of the deceased or such longer period as an officer of Revenue and Customs may allow.[8] A death election takes effect on a date specified in the notice, which must be on or after 6 April 2013 and within the period of seven years ending with the date of death of the deceased. On the effective date, the person who is to be treated as UK domiciled by virtue of the election must have been married to, or in a civil partnership with, the deceased who was then UK domiciled.[9]

Any such election is irrevocable.[10] It does not affect the application of a tax treaty,[11] and it does not affect a person's domicile for the purposes of ss 6(2) or (3) or 48(4).[12] Thus the individual does not become liable to inheritance tax in respect of excluded property situated outside the UK.

Although the election is irrevocable, it ceases to have effect if the electing person is resident outside the UK for more than four full consecutive tax years.[13] As part of the proposed extension of deemed domicile for tax purposes discussed in **9.16**, one proposed consequence of deemed domicile resulting from UK residence for 15 out of 20 years, is that the period of non-residence before the election ceased to have effect be amended to six years.

---

1 EU Commission MEMO/12/794 Case No 2010/2111. See Chapter 10 on the EU fundamental freedoms.
2 FA 2013 s 177, inserting s 267ZA and s 267ZB.
3 IHTA 1984 s 267ZA(8).
4 IHTA 1984 s 267ZA(1) and (3).
5 IHTA 1984 s 267ZB(3), (4) and (5).
6 IHTA 1984 s 267ZA(1) and (4).
7 IHTA 1984 s 267ZA(2).
8 IHTA 1984 s 267ZB (6).
9 IHTA 1984 s 267ZB(3), (4) and (5).
10 IHTA 1984 s 267ZB(9).
11 IHTA 1984 s 267ZA(6)–(8). See **9.18**.
12 IHTA 1984 s 267ZA(5).
13 IHTA 1984 s 267ZA(8).

9.19 Domicile for tax treaty purposes

Where (whether under these deemed domicile rules or not) a person is regarded under UK law as domiciled in the UK but is regarded under the law of a foreign state with which the UK has a double tax treaty covering estate and inheritance taxes as domiciled in that foreign state, the provisions of the treaty will apply so as to ensure that the person is treated by both the UK and the foreign state as being domiciled only in one of the territories for the purpose of that treaty. In this context, the meaning of domicile in such treaties only refers to common law domicile and not to statutory deemed domicile.[1] Article 4(2) of the OECD 1982 draft double taxation convention on estates and inheritances provides for this to be achieved by a series of tests identical to those applied to determine fiscal residence as described at **2.45** above. A number of these treaties are, however, old and contain a variety of provisions addressing fiscal domicile quite differently from the OECD Model.

1 IHTA 1984 ss 158 and 267(2).

CHAPTER 10

Residence, nationality and discrimination in the European Union

10.01 Introduction

The Treaty on the Functioning of the European Union (TFEU)[1] grants important rights to citizens of the Member States and the European Union and to businesses established in the EU. These are:

'Article 18

Within the scope of application of this Treaty, and without prejudice to any special provisions contained therein, any discrimination on grounds of nationality shall be prohibited.'

'Article 21

(1) Every citizen of the Union shall have the right to move and reside freely within the territory of the Member States, subject to the limitations and conditions laid down in this Treaty and by the measures adopted to give it effect.'[2]

'Article 45

(1) Freedom of movement for workers shall be secured within the Union.
(2) Such freedom of movement shall entail the abolition of any discrimination based on nationality between workers of the Member States as regards employment, remuneration and other conditions of work and employment.
(3) It shall entail the right, subject to limitations justified on grounds of public policy, public security or public health:
  (a) to accept offers of employment actually made;
  (b) to move freely within the territory of Member States for this purpose;
  (c) to stay in a Member State for the purpose of employment in accordance with the provisions governing the employment of nationals of that State laid down by law, regulation or administrative action; ...'

'Article 49

Within the framework of the provisions set out below, restrictions on the freedom of establishment of nationals of a Member State in the territory of another Member State shall be prohibited. Such prohibition shall also apply to restrictions on the setting up of agencies, branches or subsidiaries by nationals of any Member State established in the territory of any Member State.

Freedom of establishment shall include the right to take up and pursue activities as self-employed persons and to set up and manage undertakings, in particular companies or firms within the meaning of the second paragraph of article 54, under the conditions laid down for its own nationals by the law of the country where such establishment is effected subject to the provisions of the chapter relating to capital.'

'Article 54

Companies or firms formed in accordance with the law of a Member State and having their registered office, central administration or principal place of business within the Union shall, for the purposes of this Chapter, be treated in the same way as natural persons who are nationals of Member States.

"Companies or firms" means companies or firms constituted under civil or commercial law, including co-operative societies, and other legal persons governed by public or private law, save for those which are non-profit-making.'

'Article 56

Within the framework of the provisions set out below, restrictions on freedom to provide services within the Union shall be prohibited in respect of nationals of Member States who are established in a Member State other than that of the person for whom the services are intended.'

'Article 63

(1) Within the framework of the provisions set out in this Chapter, all restrictions on the movement of capital between Member States and between Member States and third countries shall be prohibited.

(2) Within the framework of the provisions set out in this Chapter, all restrictions on payments between Member States and between Member States and third countries shall be prohibited.'

'Article 65

(1) The provisions of Article 63 shall be without prejudice to the right of Member States:
  (a) to apply the relevant provisions of their tax law which distinguish between taxpayers who are not in the same situation with regard to their place of residence or with regard to the place where their capital is invested;
  (b) to take all requisite measures to prevent infringements of national law and regulations, in particular in the field of taxation and the prudential supervision of financial institutions, or to lay down procedures for the declaration of capital movements for purposes of administrative or statistical information, or to take measures which are justified on grounds of public policy or public security.

(2) The provisions of this Chapter shall be without prejudice to the applicability of restrictions on the right of establishment which are compatible with this Treaty.

(3) The measures and procedures referred to in paragraphs 1 and 2 shall not constitute a means of arbitrary discrimination or a disguised restriction on the free movement of capital and payments as defined in Article 63.'

Direct taxation does not at present fall within the purview of the European Union, but the powers over direct taxation which are retained by Member States must be exercised consistently with the TFEU.

Since the mid-1980s the European Court of Justice (ECJ) has increasingly been called upon to hear cases where taxpayers have argued that the national tax laws of Member States infringe the rights granted by European law.

TFEU rights are not, in principle, determined by reference to residence. The general prohibition against discrimination is on the basis of nationality.[3] The freedom of establishment and to provide cross-border services are also guaranteed to nationals of Member States.[4] In the case of freedom of movement for workers, this entails the abolition of all discrimination based on nationality.[5] The concept of residence makes an appearance in the broad right of free movement for citizens of the European Union. The right to move feely and *reside* in the territory of Member States is a key right of European citizens.[6]

On the other hand, the prohibition on the free movement of capital is, in principle, granted not by reference to persons but in respect of the capital itself.[7] This prohibition is not absolute and Member States may, in certain circumstances, apply the relevant provisions of their tax law which distinguish between taxpayers who are not in the same situation with regard to their place of residence.[8]

The UK, in common with other Member States has not adopted nationality as a significant connecting factor for tax purposes. Despite the lack of direct reference to residence, the central territorial connecting factor in taxation, in the enumeration of EC Treaty rights, there have been over 100 direct tax cases in which the ECJ has examined differences in Member State treatment, many based on residence. The vast majority have been found to infringe Community rights.

---

1 Treaty of Lisbon, signed on 13 December 2007 [2008] OJ C115/47 (9 May 2008) (Consolidated Version). Article numbers have been changed from earlier treaties establishing the European Community.
2 European citizenship is granted to citizens of Member States.
3 Art 18.
4 Arts 49 and 54.
5 Art 45.
6 Art 21.
7 Art 63.
8 Art 65(1)(a).

10.02   Individual nationality and tax residence

In *Giovanni Maria Sotgiu v Deutsche Bundespost*[1] the Court was asked to consider the relationship between residence and nationality in this context. In other words, whether the non-discrimination article was to be interpreted as containing a prohibition not only against treating a worker differently because he is a national of another Member State, but also against treating him differently because he is resident in another Member State. The ECJ ruled that regarding equality of treatment in the treaty, not only overt discrimination by reason of nationality was forbidden, but also all covert forms of discrimination which, by the application of other criteria of differentiation, lead in fact to the same result. This interpretation, which is necessary to ensure the effective working of one of the fundamental principles of the community which requires that equality of treatment of workers shall be ensured 'in fact and in law'. Therefore, criteria such as residence of a worker may, according to circumstances, be tantamount, as regards their practical effect, to discrimination on the grounds of nationality, such as is prohibited by the treaty. The rules regarding equality of treatment forbid not only overt discrimination by reason of nationality but also all covert forms of discrimination which, by the application of other criteria of differentiation, lead in fact to the same result. The approach in *Sotgiu* was adopted by the court in *Finanzamt Köln-Altstadt v Roland Schumacker*[2] and has been consistently applied since then. Thus, where there is no objective difference between the situations of such a non-resident and a resident engaged in comparable activity such as to justify different treatment, this is regarded as an unacceptable restriction on the fundamental freedoms granted to nationals of Member States. The non-resident taxpayer must be subject to an overall tax burden greater than that placed on resident taxpayers and on persons in a similar situation whose circumstances are comparable to those of non-resident taxpayers for such rights to be infringed.[3]

---

1 *Giovanni Maria Sotgiu v Deutsche Bundespost* (152–73) [1974] ECR 153.
2 *Finanzant v Schumacher* (C-279/93) [1995] STC 306 at 314.
3 *Skatteverket v Hilkka Hirvonen* (C-632/13).

10.03 Corporate nationality and tax residence

The residence of companies, as legal persons, is not identical to that of individuals. Article 54 of the TFEU provides for companies or firms formed in accordance with the law of a Member State and having their registered office, central administration or principal place of business within the Community to be treated in the same way as natural persons who are nationals of Member States for the purpose of the right of establishment. The adoption of the place of incorporation test in CTA 2009 s 14[1] has the effect of granting UK incorporated companies notional nationality for these purposes.

In *EC Commission v France*,[2] with regard to the right of establishment of companies, the court noted in the context of Art 54 that it is their 'seat' that serves as the connecting factor within the legal system of a particular state, like nationality in the case of natural persons. In the same judgment the court held that acceptance of the proposition that the Member State in which a company seeks to establish itself may freely apply to it different treatment solely by reason of the fact that its seat is situated in another Member State would deprive the provision of all meaning.

In *R v Inland Revenue Commissioners, ex parte Commerzbank AG*[3] the court considered the impact of tax residence explicitly in relation to indirect discrimination on grounds of nationality. Commerzbank AG was a company incorporated under German law with its registered office in Germany. It had a branch in the UK through which it granted loans to a number of US companies and it paid tax in the UK on the interest received from those companies. It was discovered that because of a provision in the UK/US Double Taxation Convention the interest was not properly taxable since Commerzbank was not resident in the UK. The tax was accordingly repaid to it.

Commerzbank then claimed a 'repayment supplement' under ICTA 1988 s 825. That section enabled resident companies to recover interest on tax overpaid and the Revenue refused the claim accordingly. Commerzbank argued successfully in the ECJ that the residence requirement infringed the right of establishment. In following the *Sotgiu* judgment the ECJ ruled that equality of treatment forbids not only overt discrimination by reason of nationality or, in the case of a company, its seat, but all covert forms of discrimination which, by the application of other criteria of differentiation, lead in fact to the same result. The issue of tax residence was addressed thus:

'Although it applies independently of a company's seat, the use of the criterion of fiscal residence within national territory for the purpose of granting repayment supplement on overpaid tax is liable to work more particularly to the disadvantage of companies having their seat in other Member States. Indeed, it is most often those companies which are resident for tax purposes outside the territory of the Member State in question.'[4]

The court does not as a result seek to apply a residence test but rather tests the Member State laws including where appropriate, tax residence for compliance with Community law.

1 See **7.02** above.
2 Case C-270/83 [1987] 1 CMLR 401.
3 Case C-330/91 [1993] ECR I-4017.
4 At para 15.

10.04   Change of residence and exit taxes

Taxable events that are triggered by a change in residence implicitly run counter to the principles of free movement and the right of establishment enshrined in the TFEU. The European Court has considered the question on several occasions, including as a result of infringement proceedings initiated by the Commission both in relation to individuals and companies.

In *Hughes de Lasteyrie du Saillant v Ministère de l'Economie, des Finances et de l'Industrie,*[1] Mr de Lasteyrie left France to settle in Belgium for the purpose of carrying on his profession there. He was deemed to dispose of shares in a family-owned company at market value on the date of departure under French law.

The ECJ ruled that a taxpayer wishing to transfer his tax residence in exercise of the right of freedom of establishment is subjected to disadvantageous treatment in comparison with a person who maintains his residence in that state where he becomes liable, simply by reason of such a transfer, to tax on unrealised gains, whereas, if he remained in that state, increases in value would become taxable only when, and to the extent that, they were actually realised.

Thus, the court held that what is now Art 49 TFEU must be interpreted as precluding a Member State from taxing latent, unrealised, increases in value of company shares, where a taxpayer transfers his tax residence outside that state. The difference in treatment cannot be justified (as the French government argued) by the aim of preventing tax avoidance, since tax avoidance or evasion cannot be inferred generally from the fact that the tax residence of a physical person has been transferred to another Member State.

Similarly, in *N v Inspecteur van de Belastingdienst Oost/kantoor Almelo*,[2] by reference not only to the right of establishment in what is now Art 49 but also the right of free movement for European citizens in what is now Art 21, the court ruled that the Netherlands regime for individuals who ceased to be resident infringed EU rights. The infringing system taxed increases in the value of shares in a company at the time of transfer of residence outside that of the Netherlands. The court concluded that although this made moving to another Member State less attractive, it was a legitimate exercise of taxing rights to tax appreciation to the date of departure. Under the Netherlands exit tax, deferment of the payment of the liability until the time of actual disposal was available, conditional on the provision of guarantees. Furthermore, in computing the gain, no account was taken of reductions in value after the transfer of residence and up to the time of actual disposal. The court decided that these provisions went beyond what is strictly necessary to ensure the functioning and effectiveness of a tax system based on the principle of fiscal territoriality.

In *European Commission v Kingdom of Spain*,[3] the Spanish law in question did not treat ceasing to be resident as a taxable event. Instead, persons ceasing to be resident were required to pay immediately and in full the tax on income which has been realised but not yet charged, solely on account of the transfer of residence. This, the court held, obstructs the exercise of the freedoms of movement and establishment. As was the case in *N*, the restrictions went beyond what was necessary to ensure the effectiveness of fiscal supervision and the prevention of tax avoidance and thus could not be justified.

Although not strictly a case on exit taxes, *R v HM Treasury and Commissioners of Inland Revenue, ex parte Daily Mail and General Trust Plc*[4] concerned the right of a legal person to leave its Member State of origin.

At that time, Treasury consent was a prerequisite for a company resident in the UK to cease to be resident.[5] As a company incorporated under English law and having its registered office in the UK it could establish its central management and control outside the UK and cease to be resident for tax purposes without losing legal personality or ceasing to be a company incorporated in the UK.

The company applied for consent to transfer its central management and control to the Netherlands. The principal reason for the proposed transfer of central management and control was to enable the company to sell a significant part of its assets and to use the proceeds of that sale to buy its own shares, without having to pay the UK tax on these transactions. The company would be subject to Netherlands corporation tax, but the transactions envisaged would be taxed only on the basis of capital gains on increases in value accrued after the transfer of its residence for tax purposes. The Treasury, in negotiations with the company, proposed that it should sell at least part of the assets before transferring its residence out of the UK. This would have defeated the object of the exercise.

The court concluded that the state of Community law at that time conferred no right on a company incorporated under the legislation of a Member State and having its registered office there to transfer its central management and control to another Member State. This was based on the then Art 220 of the EC Treaty which provided for the conclusion of agreements between Member States with a view to securing, *inter alia*, the retention of legal personality in the event of transfer of the registered office of companies from one country to another.

In *National Grid Indus BV v Inspecteur van de Belastingdienst*,[6] the Netherlands corporate exit tax was examined by the Court. National Grid Indus was incorporated under Netherlands law as a limited liability company. Until 15 December 2000 its place of effective management was in the Netherlands. On that date it transferred its place of effective management to the UK. As a result, it became UK resident and, by virtue of Art 4(3) of the Netherlands-UK tax treaty, no longer liable to Netherlands tax on worldwide income as a Dutch resident. Under Netherlands law, it was deemed to have disposed of its only asset, a Sterling loan to its UK-resident parent company, at the time it ceased to be Dutch resident. The Court affirmed that Member States thus have the power to define both the connecting factor required of a company if it is to be regarded as incorporated under its national law and as such capable of enjoying the right of establishment, and that required if the company is to be able subsequently to maintain that status. A Member State is therefore able, in the case of a company, to make a company incorporated under its law's right to retain its legal personality under the law of that state subject to restrictions on the transfer abroad of the company's place of effective management. However, the transfer by National Grid Indus of its place of effective management to the UK did not affect its status as a company incorporated under Netherlands law, in accordance with that law. In such circumstances, the company could rely on the right of establishment when moving its place of effective management to another Member State. The Court ruled that the deemed disposal on exit was a restriction on that right but that the restriction was justified in that the territoriality principle requires that a Member State is entitled to tax the economic value generated by an unrealised capital gain accrued while the company is resident in its territory, even if the gain has not yet actually been realised. Unlike the departure of an individual, considered in the *N* case, the TFEU offers no guarantee to a company that transferring its place of effective management to another Member State will be neutral as regards taxation and accordingly there was no obligation to take any subsequent decrease in value into account. Consistent with its rulings relating to individuals the Court held that requiring immediate payment of the tax upon exit was unjustified and disproportionate.

Following this, and in light of the decision in *de Lasteyrie du Saillant*, the European Commission in its communication *Exit taxation and the need for co-ordination of Member States' tax policies*[7] expressed the view that corporate exit taxes infringe EU law. This was followed by requests to several Member States to change restrictive exit tax provisions for companies. Five have resulted in infringement proceedings before the Court.[8] The Advocate-General's opinion in *European Commission v Portuguese Republic*[9] identified the possibility that the outcome in cases of corporate migration might depend on the corporate law of the Member State of origin. Advocate General Mengozzi observed that while the Netherlands applies the incorporation theory by which it recognises without qualification the possibility of transferring the effective management of a Netherlands company without altering its legal personality by keeping its registered office in the Netherlands, Portugal does not. The Portuguese Commercial Companies Code authorises companies governed by Portuguese law to transfer their effective centre of management to another country whilst retaining their legal personality, provided this is permitted by the legislation of that other country. The court ruled that this situation is indistinguishable from that in *National Grid Indus* and that the Portuguese deemed disposal on exit infringed the right of establishment.

The Court of Justice has, however, ruled that the UK exit charge on trusts ceasing to be UK resident under TCGA 1992, s 80, infringes the right of establishment. In *Trustees of the P Panayi Accumulation & Maintenance Settlements v Commissioners for Her Majesty's Revenue and Customs*,[10] Mr Panayi, a Cypriot national resident in the UK established trusts in 1992 for the benefit of his children and other family members. The trustees were Mr and Mrs Panayi and a UK resident trust company. Mr and Mrs Panayi decided to leave the United Kingdom to return to Cyprus permanently. Before their departure, on 19 August 2004, the trustees resigned and three Cyprus resident trustees were appointed. The Court held that although the restriction on the right of establishment may be justified by the need to preserve the allocation of powers of taxation between the Member States, in this case the gain on trust property did not escape UK tax entirely because trust gains would be taxable in the hands of UK resident beneficiaries who receive capital payments under TCGA 1992, s 87. By the same token, the gain may well not be within the UK tax charge in some cases so that the restriction on the right of establishment was justified. The UK law was however not proportionate to the achievement of that justification and thus incompatible with EU law. This was because there was no provision for the taxpayer to defer payment of the tax, in line with the decision in *National Grid Indus*.

A radical reappraisal by the Commission of its views on corporate exit charges has meant that all Member States will be required to impose an exit tax on companies from 1 January 2019.[11]

---

1 *Hughes de Lasteyrie du Saillant v Ministère de l'Economie, des Finances et de l'Industrie* (C-9/02) [2004] ECR I-2409.

2 *N v Inspecteur van de Belastingdienst Oost/kantoor Almelo* (C-470/04) [2006] ECR I-7409.

3 *European Commission v Kingdom of Spain* (C-269/09).

4 *R v HM Treasury and Commissioners of Inland Revenue, ex parte Daily Mail and General Trust Plc* (81/87) [1988] ECR 273.

5 ICTA 1970 s 482(1)(a).

6 *National Grid Indus BV v Inspecteur van de Belastingdienst Rijnmond/kantoor Rotterdam* (C-371/10).

7 COM (2006) 825.

8 *European Commission v Portuguese Republic* (C-38/10) [2013] 1 CMLR 8. See also *European Commission v Spain* (C-64/11), *European Commission v Denmark* (C-261/11), and *European Commission v Netherlands* (C-301/11).

9 *European Commission v Portuguese Republic* (C-38/10) [2013] 1 CMLR 8.

10 *Trustees of the P Panayi Accumulation & Maintenance Settlements v Commissioners for Her Majesty's Revenue and Customs* (Case C-646/15).

11 Council Directive (EU) 2016/1164 of 12 July 2016 laying down rules against tax avoidance practices that directly affect the functioning of the internal market, Art 5.

10.05   Brexit

On 23 June 2016, in a legally non-binding referendum, a small majority of voters favoured the UK leaving the EU. The mechanism to terminate EU membership is set out in Article 50 of the Treaty on European Union.

Under Article 50(1), any Member State may decide to withdraw from the EU in accordance with its own constitutional requirements. The Supreme Court ruled in *Miller & Anor, R (on the application of) v Secretary of State for Exiting the European Union*,[1] that notice of withdrawal from the EU treaties could only be given with the prior approval of Parliament.

If a Member State so decided to withdraw, Article 50(2) requires that it must notify the European Council of its intention to withdraw. On 29 March 2017, the UK Government gave notice to withdraw from the EU pursuant to Art 50(2). As a result, the EU must negotiate and conclude an agreement with the withdrawing state, which sets out the arrangements for the withdrawal, taking account of the framework for its future relationship with the EU. Article 50(2) specifies that a single negotiation with the EU as a whole is required. Since the negotiation becomes a matter of foreign relations for the EU, the Commission normally makes recommendations to the Council, which adopts a decision authorising the opening of negotiations and, nominating the EU negotiator or the head of the Union's negotiating team. Any resulting agreement requires a qualified majority of the Council, after obtaining the consent of the European Parliament. Article 50(3) specifies that EU law then ceases to apply to the withdrawing state from the date the withdrawal agreement enters into force. If there is no agreement two years after notification of withdrawal is given, EU law ceases to apply automatically at that time, unless the Council unanimously decides to extend this period with the agreement of the withdrawing state. At the time of writing, no such agreement has been concluded.

British subjects will automatically cease to be European citizens under TFEU Article 20(1) and no longer benefit from the rights that European citizenship offers, particularly to move and reside freely within the territory of other Member States and to diplomatic and consular protection when outside the EU.

British citizens resident in other EU Member States and other EU nationals resident in the UK, shorn of their EU rights, may well find themselves compelled to move either because of the impact of the loss of EU rights or in search of employment and business opportunities in a changed economic environment.

Residence of individuals

The Statutory Residence Test, discussed in Chapter 2, can produce a straightforward outcome for individuals who are able to organise their lives around the test's mechanical rules. Individuals who don't have control over their arrival and departure times or who need to work in two states during the transition, or who have difficulty selling their homes, or have children who need to finish a school year will find the rules more challenging to navigate. More cases of dual residence are likely, with an increased need to look to

Article 4 of the UK's tax treaties with other Member States to resolve the problem. See **2.45**.

Domicile

Domicile of individuals, discussed in Chapter 9, will be influenced by Brexit. Questions of domicile where only limited immigration rights are available are likely to become more common. For example, it may be difficult to maintain an intention to remain in a state that is sufficient for a domicile of choice where restrictive immigration rules that make residence precarious are imposed. Returning British citizens may well revert to a domicile of origin in the UK where the loss of EU citizenship rights makes their intended return to other Member States unrealistic. The changes to the deemed domicile rules for tax purposes from April 2017 will in any event exclude them from treatment as not UK domiciled while UK resident if they were born in the UK. See **9.16**.

Social security

EU law on social security distinguishes between 'residence' (the place where a person habitually resides) and 'stay' (temporary residence) both for purposes of contributions and benefits. Cross-border workers post-Brexit will not benefit from the EU Social Security Directive to prevent double contributions and will need to look to the UK domestic law which applies the common law concepts of residence[2] and ordinary residence to determine their UK National Insurance Contributions liability. Ordinary residence has been abolished for tax purposes but will apply to NICs.[3]

Benefits too will be impacted. For example, the basic UK state pension depends on the level of NICs, and, for the purpose of making voluntary contributions which increase the amount of the pension, periods of residence in another Member State may count as UK residence.[4] This will no longer be the case post-Brexit.

Residence of companies

Corporate migration is likely to become more challenging where UK incorporated companies no longer benefit from the EU fundamental freedoms. UK tax treaties increasingly authorise the competent authorities to resolve dual residence by agreement rather than by a rule of law.[5] This approach gives greater power to HMRC to decide whether companies have successfully changed residence to or from the UK, which, post-Brexit will be unfettered by the constraints of EU free movement and establishment rights.

Exit taxes on companies and trusts

When a company or a trust ceases to be UK resident, it is deemed to dispose of its fixed assets at market value. This charge is the subject of scrutiny by the

CJEU for compliance with EU free movement and establishment rights.[6] In the case of companies, the obligation to impose an exit tax required for all Member States from 1 January 2019 may not apply to an early withdrawal from the EU.

---

1 *R (on the application of Miller and another) v Secretary of State for Exiting the European Union* [2017] UKSC 5.
2 See Chapter 3.
3 See Chapter 4.
4 *Garland v HMRC* [2015] UKFTT 417 (TC).
5 See Chapter 7, especially **7.16**.
6 See **10.4**.

CHAPTER 11

Compliance and appeals

'The bell', said Noggs, as though in explanation; 'at home?'
'Yes.'
'To anybody?'
'Yes.'
'To the tax-gatherer?'
'No! Let him call again.'

Charles Dickens *Nicholas Nickleby*, Ch 2

11.01 Introduction

Absence from the territory of the UK does not relieve compliance obligations or provide a defence against proceedings in the UK for the recovery of tax payable under an assessment. Any person chargeable to income tax or capital gains tax for a year of assessment and who has not received a notice requiring a return for that year of his total income and gains, must give to an officer of HMRC notice that he is so chargeable within six months from the end of that year.[1] Notice is not required in respect of certain classes of income where tax is deducted at source.[2] In *Whitney v IRC*,[3] Lord Wrenbury considered the obligation which ITA 1918 s 7(3) imposed on every person chargeable with supertax (a form of income taxation which no longer exists) to give notice that he was so chargeable, and said of Mr Whitney, an American citizen and a resident of New York who had received dividends in respect of shares in a UK corporation:

> If ... I am right in thinking that the non-resident alien is chargeable in respect of property in the UK, it was his duty to give that notice.[4]

In *IRC v Huni*,[5] for example, a Swiss national who was not resident in the UK argued that a notice to make a return for supertax purposes served on him at his Paris address was invalid since it had been served outside the territory of the UK. It followed, he said, that he could not have failed to make a return within the terms of the legislation (FA 1910 in relation to supertax) and that the Commissioners had, therefore, no jurisdiction to make an assessment to the best of their judgment. Furthermore, he contended, irrespective of the validity of the assessment, the notice of assessment (also served on him at his Paris address) was as invalid (on the same grounds) as had been the notice requiring him to make a return. Rowlatt J did not agree. He said:

> 'A great deal has been said in the course of this argument about a non-resident and about an alien, but I think I am confronted with the question as to the operation of this Statute without the realm ... In the words of the Statute there is no distinction drawn between aliens or residents or non-residents or anything of that sort; the question really is as to whether the Statute is to be cut down so as not to serve notices abroad. Now the principle involved here is the principle that Acts of Parliament are prima facie not to be construed so as to assume jurisdiction without the realm – extra-territorial jurisdiction – so as to make the jurisdiction extra-territorial. And of course where it comes to the case of creating a duty abroad or creating an offence abroad – both of which of course can be done by Parliament – ... the Courts are bound to look narrowly at the Statute to see whether that is what is meant. But I apprehend there is no difficulty of that sort in the way if what the Statute really directs is the mere service of a notice, and that is all it is. There is no international difficulty in serving a notice abroad ... It may have consequences, but it is a mere notice ... I think there is involved in this machinery the mere giving of a notice as a preliminary to the Commissioners proceeding to do something which they are entitled to do ... and that I ought not to limit the words of this Section so as to make this notice as a mere notice null and void.'[6]

That being so, the assessment which followed Mr Huni's failure to make the return required of him was valid. Accordingly Rowlatt J turned to the question of the notice of assessment:

> 'The Respondent says that the notice of assessment is bad too, because it was served on him abroad. That I cannot think is bad. If a man has been validly assessed in England, what principle of international law is to be invoked by way of reflection to limit the words of the Statute which says that he may be told he has been assessed, I cannot conceive.'[7]

This judgment was approved by the House of Lords in the *Whitney* case[8] where Mr Whitney had advanced arguments against his assessability similar to those which had been advanced by Mr Huni. Lord Wrenbury said:

> 'There was sent to the Appellant by post addressed to him in the United States a notice under Section 7(2) requiring him to make a return. It is contended that there was no right to send him a notice so addressed. The case, it is contended, is similar to the case of service of a writ out of the jurisdiction. I do not agree ... It is not a step in a judicial proceeding, but a step which will create *inter partes* a state of things in which judicial proceedings can subsequently be taken in default of compliance. I think the notice was duly served. In my opinion *IRC v Huni* was rightly decided.'[9]

If notice is to be served validly under the Taxes Acts, therefore, all that is required is that it be served at the 'usual or last known place of residence' of the person on whom it is served, whether that place of residence be in the UK or an address overseas.[10]

The provisions described above relate to income tax and capital gains tax, but similar provisions exist in relation to corporation tax and inheritance tax.

---

1 TMA 1970 s 7.
2 TMA 1970 s 7(3).
3 (1924) 10 TC 88.
4 (1924) 10 TC 88 at 114.
5 (1923) 8 TC 466.
6 (1923) 8 TC 466 at 474.
7 (1923) 8 TC 466 at 474.
8 (1924) 10 TC 88.
9 (1924) 10 TC 88 at 113.
10 TMA 1970 s 115.

11.02   Assessment of non-residents

Notwithstanding the above, the UK adopts two domestic law mechanisms of ensuring compliance with its direct tax laws in the international context by imposing obligations on persons other than the taxpayer. Firstly, in the case of non-residents, a UK representative may be jointly liable with the non-resident in relation to trade income.[1] Secondly, the system of deduction of tax at source by the payer of certain items of income is extended to persons whose 'usual place of abode' is outside the UK which often, but not always, coincides with non-residence.

---

1 ITA 2007 Pt 14, Chs 2B and 2C; TCGA 1992 Pt 7A for non-corporates and CTA 2010 Pt 22, Ch 6 for companies.

11.03   Deduction of tax at source – 'usual place of abode'

ITA 2007 imposes obligations on payers to deduct tax at source on certain amounts paid to persons whose 'usual place of abode is outside the UK'. This includes certain yearly interest[1], royalties, or sums payable periodically, in respect of a relevant intellectual property right,[2] and 'non-resident landlord income'.[3] The expression is not defined in the legislation and, like its counterpart expressions, residence, ordinary residence and domicile requires interpretation.

HMRC practice in this area is somewhat imprecise with slightly different expositions of their practice in different parts of their published guidance.

HMRC International Tax Manual explains that '[th]e term 'usual place of abode' is used in the legislation because the purpose of the legislation is to provide an effective way of collecting tax due from someone who is usually outside the UK and/or does not have a taxable presence in the UK.[4] Usual place of abode, it says, 'means principal place of business or the place where the person is normally to be found. It is not the same as tax residence'. The HMRC Property Income Manual suggests: 'Usual place of abode' is not identical in meaning to residence, or ordinary residence, but a person who is not resident in the UK should normally be treated as having their usual place of abode outside the UK'.[5]

One HMRC explanation of the usual place of abode in the context of 'non-resident' landlords in the Property Income Manual[6] reads:

'1) Individuals have a usual place of abode outside the UK if they usually live outside the UK. You should still regard the term as applying to them even if in a particular year they are resident in the UK for tax purposes, as long as the usual place of abode is outside the UK. (For example the individual may count as resident in the UK in a particular year because of a six months' visit, or a visit of a shorter time when he has a place of abode available in the UK). Do not treat someone as having their usual place of abode outside the UK if they are only temporarily living outside the UK, say for six months or less.

2) Companies that have their main office or other place of business outside the UK, and companies incorporated outside the UK, will normally have a usual place of abode outside the UK. However if the company is treated as resident in the UK for tax purposes, do not treat it as having a usual place of abode outside the UK.

3) Trustees have a usual place of abode outside the UK if all the trustees have a usual place of abode outside the UK.'

In relation to interest payments, the HMRC Savings Income Manual comments in relation to trustees:

'Trustees, including personal representatives, have a usual place of abode abroad if each trustee, considered as an individual or a company as the case may be, has a usual place of abode there. So if one trustee does not have a usual place of abode abroad, neither does the trust.'[7]

While it may have been true under the case law test that a person whose usual place of abode was in the UK was resident in the UK, it did not follow that a person whose usual place of abode was outside the UK was *not* resident in the UK.[8] The effect of the statutory residence test[9] is to disconnect the two connecting factors entirely from each other. In imposing a test of 'usual place of abode' (rather than a test of residence) in this context, it may be observed that a person on whom it places the onus of applying the test (ie any person making payment) will rarely be in possession of such facts as are required for the determination of the residence status of the person to whom payment is being made, whereas the determination of such a person's usual place of abode may arguably be capable of determination by mere enquiry and observation.

In *Haslope v Thorne*,[10] Lord Ellenborough CJ considered the term 'place of abode' in the context of a rule of court which required the place of abode of the deponent of an affidavit to be inserted in the affidavit and came to the conclusion that it meant 'the place where the deponent was most usually to be found'.[11] Thus, the place where a man 'lives with his family and sleeps at night' will always be 'his place of abode in the full sense of that expression'.[12] That does not presuppose, however, that the living and sleeping will take place in a house or flat or even an hotel room: a yacht,[13] a caravan,[14] a tent or bender,[15] and even a car[16] may constitute a person's place of abode!

1 ITA 2007 s 874.
2 ITA 2007 s 906.
3 ITA 2007 s 971.
4 INTM505020.
5 PIM4810 with PIM4800.
6 PIM4810 with PIM4800. Cf the International Manual INTM370060. Also see Savings Income Manual re interest SAIM9080.
7 SAIM9080.
8 See Chapter 3.
9 See Chapter 2.
10 (1813) 1 M & S 103.
11 (1813) 1 M & S 103 at 104. In accordance with that principle, the usual place of abode of a company will presumably be its principal place of business.
12 *R v Hammond* (1852) 17 QB 772 at 780, 781, per Lord Campbell CJ.
13 In *Bayard Brown v Burt* (1911) 5 TC 667, it was accepted that an ocean-going yacht anchored in territorial waters was the place of abode of Mr Bayard Brown, its owner and occupier.
14 In *Makins v Elson* [1977] STC 46, it was held that a wheeled caravan jacked up and resting on bricks, with water, electricity and telephone services installed, was a dwelling house.
15 In *Hipperson v Electoral Registration Officer for the District of Newbury* [1985] 2 All ER 456, Sir John Donaldson MR (at 462) rejected the submission that women living in tents, vehicles and benders (a form of tent) on Greenham Common in furtherance of their protest concerning cruise missiles could not be said to have a home in the camp: 'It may be unusual to make one's home in a tent, bender or vehicle, but we can see no reason in law why it should be impossible.'
16 In *R v Bundy* [1977] 2 All ER 382, the motor car in which a certain Mr Bundy had been living rough was held to be his place of abode when sited but not while in transit. The court held, at 384, that the term '"place of abode" ... connotes, first of all, a site. That is the ordinary meaning of the word "place". It is a site at which the occupier intends to abide. So there are two elements in the phrase "place of abode", the element of site and the element of intention. When the appellant took the motor car to a site with the intention of abiding there, then his motor car on that site could be said to be his "place of abode", but when he took it from that site to move it to another site where he intended to abide, the motor car could not be said to be his "place of abode" during transit.'

11.04   Claiming non-resident, treaty non-resident or non-domiciled status

For income and capital gains tax purposes, following the Finance Act 2008 it is normally necessary for an individual who is resident but not domiciled in the UK to claim such status (ITA 2007 s 809B). Where such individuals are liable to notify chargeability to tax, they will in consequence normally be required to complete a self-assessment tax return. Where a return is to be filed, the claim must be made in the return.[1] Provision for the making of such claims is made in the 'non-residence' pages of the return. Whether a claim to treaty non-residence is necessary is obscure.[2] Despite this legal obscurity, the non-resident pages of the return provide the same mechanism for treaty non-residence as for non-residence under domestic law or not domiciled status to be claimed or asserted.

Taxpayers have always needed to maintain records to demonstrate their status. The formulaic nature of the statutory residence test and the many numerical thresholds place a premium on accurate, detailed records to substantiate the contents of tax returns. HMRC views on record keeping for this purpose are set out in Appendix 2.

11.05   Administration of residence and domicile status of individuals

The administration of the residence and domicile status has moved closer to a pure self-assessment approach as a result of operational changes announced by HMRC on 25 March 2009.[1] HMRC will no longer accept initial non-domicile claims on form DOM 1 (domicile questionnaire) or form P86 (arrival form). Form DOM 1 has been withdrawn completely. From that date, until the Form P86 was withdrawn on 1 June 2010, individuals did not need to fill in boxes 12 to 17 which ask questions about domicile on the P86 when submitting it. If individuals chose to fill in those boxes HMRC will ignore the content when processing the form. Any DOM 1 forms received by HMRC by close of business 25 March 2009 will still be processed but any received after that date will be returned unexamined.

Consequently, individuals will be required to self-assess their residence and domicile for income tax and capital gains tax purposes each year and questions about domicile status will be dealt with by way of enquiry into a claim to non-domicile status either as a stand-alone enquiry, or as part of a wider enquiry.

Where an individual has already submitted a form DOM 1 or P86 and obtained an initial view from HMRC about their domicile status they say it will be unusual for them to open an enquiry into domicile status in the few years after that, unless new information becomes available that indicates their initial view was incorrect or there has been a change in circumstances. They also indicate that initial views from HMRC can become less and less useful as an indicator of domicile status with the passage of time, circumstances and intentions change.

On 11 April 2013, HMRC published a revised form P85 (departure form) for use by taxpayers leaving the UK who wish to claim tax relief or a repayment of tax. The revised form takes into account elements of the statutory residence test.

11.06   Inheritance tax accounts

HMRC indicate that an individual setting up a non-resident trust who considers they are non-UK domiciled is not obliged to submit an inheritance tax account to HMRC. If the settlor is non-UK domiciled then no inheritance tax is due. But if an inheritance tax account is submitted in these circumstances, HMRC will continue its existing practice and only open an enquiry into that return if the amounts of inheritance tax at stake make such an enquiry cost effective to carry out. At present that limit is £10,000.

As was previously the case, where HMRC has expressed an opinion on the domicile status of a settlor for inheritance tax purposes they will not normally seek to reconsider that opinion unless new information becomes available that indicates their initial opinion was incorrect or there has been a material change in the circumstances of the settlor. They warn that when they make a decision it applies only to the date of the transaction concerned. So if circumstances change, that individual's domicile may need to be considered again at another point in time.

11.07 Domicile enquiries

For 2008–09 and later years, in order to make a valid claim to the remittance basis individuals will be required to state on their self-assessment tax return the grounds for their entitlement by stating either that they are not domiciled in the UK or that they are not ordinarily resident in the UK (or both). If HMRC decide to enquire into an individual's domicile status this will be by way of a TMA 1970 s 9A enquiry into their self-assessment tax return. (Alternatively in appropriate cases HMRC may enquire into an individual's domicile status by way of an IHTA 1984 Pt VIII enquiry into an inheritance tax return.) Where a claim to the remittance basis is not challenged for that year it does not mean HMRC necessarily accept the individual's domicile is outside the UK and does not prevent HMRC from later opening an enquiry to consider the domicile status of the individual in relation to that, or any earlier year.

Enquiries aimed at establishing an individual's domicile are, by their very nature, examinations of an individual's background, lifestyle, habits and intentions, possibly over the course of a lifetime. Consequently, any such enquiries conducted by HMRC will, where necessary, extend to areas of individuals' and their families' affairs that may not normally be regarded as relevant to their UK tax position. New domicile guidance includes a section starting at para 49600 which explains the nature of a domicile enquiry and the sorts of questions an individual will need to answer as part of that enquiry.

Where HMRC have expressed a view on an individual's domicile status for income tax or capital gains tax purposes, as a result of an enquiry, then that view will also apply for inheritance tax purposes at that time. Likewise an HMRC view expressed for inheritance tax purposes, following an IHTA 1984 Pt VIII enquiry, will also apply for income tax and capital gains purposes at that time only.

Gulliver v Revenue and Customs,[1] concerned an application for a closure notice relating to a domicile enquiry. TMA 1970, s 28A allows a taxpayer to apply to the Tribunal for a direction that HMRC issue a closure notice, which the Tribunal must give unless it is satisfied that there are reasonable grounds for not issuing the notice. HMRC had opened an enquiry into Mr Gulliver's tax return for the 2013/14 tax year, for which the only outstanding issue was his domicile for that year. Mr Gulliver, the Group Chief Executive of HSBC plc, and a UK national with a UK domicile of origin, had an international business career with significant amounts of time living in the Far East. In 2002, he established a discretionary trust for the benefit of his family. At the time, his permanent home and the centre of his business and social life was Hong Kong. HSBC had asked him to undertake a specific assignment in London that was expected to last for two years after which he would return home to Hong Kong. In 2003 the then Inland Revenue agreed that Mr Gulliver, in funding the trust, had not made a transfer of value for inheritance tax purposes. This agreement implied recognition that he was not domiciled in the UK at the time, based on information provided.

In refusing the application, the First-tier Tribunal rejected the argument that, having determined that Mr Gulliver acquired a domicile of choice in Hong Kong, HMRC were stuck with the consequences. The presumption that his domicile of choice continued meant that HMRC bore the burden of showing that he abandoned that domicile of choice which was not supported by the evidence he had provided. The Tribunal ruled that the previous agreement was no impediment to HMRC enquiring, in relation to 2013/14, that Mr Gulliver never acquired a Hong Kong domicile of choice. The Tribunal noted that in 2003, a 'risk based approach' was taken to requests for confirmation of the inheritance tax treatment of lifetime transfers that took into account the amount of tax potentially in issue, and the chance of the taxpayer concerned being UK domiciled on the basis of the information provided. The amount of tax in issue was only £4,735 and there was not a high risk of Mr Gulliver being UK domiciled, based on the information provided.

The decision also highlights the onerous nature of domicile enquiries. HMRC requested large amounts of information and documents by way of notice under FA 2008, Sch 36. Answers to 123 questions and the provision of 33 categories of document were not limited to matters arising after the date of the Inland Revenue confirmation in 2003 and involved a searching examination of a number of aspects of his personal and professional life dating back to 1981.

---

1 *Gulliver v Revenue and Customs* [2017] UKFTT 222 (TC).

11.08   ITEPA s 690 directions

Employers of employees who are not UK resident or, if resident but not domiciled, work outside the UK and have foreign earnings when the remittance basis applies within ITEPA s 26A, are able to ask for a direction pursuant to ITEPA 2003 s 690 which permits them not to apply PAYE to certain employment income of those employees. An HMRC officer is permitted to treat the remittance basis as applicable even if no claim has been made by an employee.[1] This is necessary to permit such directions to be made as under the self-assessment system, claims are made after the relevant tax year has ended and is a minor modification to an otherwise complete self-assessment system.

---

1 ITEPA 2003 s 690(2A).

11.09   Certificates of residence

Where a UK resident is entitled to relief from foreign taxes by operation of a tax treaty, the foreign tax authority will usually require HMRC to certify that the person is a UK resident within the meaning of the treaty. Some fiscal authorities may also require HMRC to confirm that the person fulfils other conditions. HMRC practice is set out in their International Manual. They will issue a certificate of residence in most cases. Requests are normally only be refused if there is no doubt that customer would not be entitled to benefits. HMRC may decide to make a spontaneous exchange of information with the foreign tax authority where such entitlement is questioned.[1]

HMRC may also, on request, issue a 'letter of confirmation' instead of a certificate of residence that they regard a person as UK resident for purposes other than claiming relief from foreign taxes under a treaty such as relief from foreign taxes under the domestic law of the foreign state or EU law (such as under the EU Interest and Royalties Directive).[2]

HMRC officers will not carry out a detailed review of residence when they receive a request for a certificate of residence. The officer will usually be able to certify residence, as long as they can see that the customer is (or was for the period requested) liable to UK tax by virtue of their residence (eg by checking the customer's tax returns or, if no such returns have been submitted yet, the information provided with the request). If HMRC do not have enough information to determine whether a customer is liable to UK tax by virtue of their residence or, despite the self-assessments made by the customer, there are reasonable grounds for believing that the customer may not in fact be a resident of the UK, the request may be refused if sufficient doubt remains even after correspondence on the issue. A certificate of residence is not a formal determination of UK residence. It is simply confirmation that, to the best of HMRC's knowledge, the person is, or was for the period in question, liable to tax by virtue of UK residence. HMRC still have the right to enquire into a customer's self-assessment tax return when it is received.[3] Individuals may apply online for a certificate.[4] Other persons generally need to apply in writing.

---

1 HMRC International Manual, para INTM162010.
2 HMRC International Manual, para INTM162140.
3 HMRC International Manual, para INTM162040.
4 www.gov.uk/government/publications/apply-for-a-certificate-of-residence-in-the-uk.

11.10 Appeals

Up to the tax year 2007–08, a special procedure for dealing with disputes as to domicile or ordinary residence[1] required the Commissioners of Revenue & Customs to determine such disputed domicile or ordinary residence. Their decision was then subject to appeal to the Special Commissioners. This procedure has been repealed.[2] For the tax years 2008–09 and thereafter, appeals in relation to these issues will be dealt with under normal self-assessment provisions and appeal.

The Special and General Commissioners were abolished and replaced by the First-tier Tribunal and the new Upper Tribunal of the Tax Chamber with effect from 1 April 2009.[3] In addition, an internal review by HMRC is available. If a taxpayer gives notice of appeal to HMRC, the taxpayer may either require HMRC to review the matter or take it directly to the First-tier Tribunal. HMRC may also offer an internal review.[4] A decision of the First-tier Tribunal may be appealed to the Upper Tribunal but only with the permission of either the First-tier or Upper Tribunal.[5] In addition, the Tribunal may review its own decisions and in doing so may correct or set them aside.[6]

---

1 ITEPA 2003 Pt 2 and Ch 6, TCGA 1992 s 9(2).
2 FA 2008 Sch 7, paras 23, 54 and 77.
3 See generally Transfer of Tribunal Functions and Revenue & Customs Appeals Order, SI 2009/56.
4 TMA 1970 s 49B.
5 TCEA 2007 s 11(1) and Tribunal Procedure (First-tier) (Tax Chamber Rules) 2009, SI 2009/273, reg 39.
6 TCEA 2007 s 10 and Tribunal Procedure (First-tier) (Tax Chamber Rules) 2009, SI 2009/273, regs 37, 38 and 41.

11.11 Evidential burden on appeal

As early as 1876, in *Cesena Sulphur Co Ltd v Nicholson*[1] the court held that the burden of proof to show that a company was resident in the UK was on the Revenue and said, at p 105:

'I admit that the onus of proving residence lies upon the Crown ... and if the Crown fails to satisfy the Court that the place of residence is within the jurisdiction, or within the area of taxation, you cannot say that the company should be taxed.'

Several recent cases have involved a consideration of the evidential burden. The Revenue have unsuccessfully argued that the burden of proof simply lies with the taxpayer, relying on s 50(6) of the Taxes Management Act 1970 which provides:

'56(6) If, on an appeal, it appears to the majority of the Commissioners present at the hearing, by examination of the appellant on oath or affirmation, or by other lawful evidence, that the appellant is overcharged by any assessment, the assessment shall be reduced accordingly, but otherwise every such assessment shall stand good.'

Firstly, in *Untelrab Ltd & Ors v McGregor (HMIT)*[2] the Special Commissioners, on the authority of *Cesena* concluded that the burden of proving residence lies on the Crown. In their view s 50(6) was not relevant in the context of that appeal because it was not a case where the appellants were saying that they had been overcharged by an assessment but where they are saying that the Revenue had no jurisdiction to assess them at all.[3]

Secondly, in *Wood v Holden*[4] the Court of Appeal upheld Park J in the High Court in relation to shifts in the evidentiary burden even where TMA 1970 s 50(6) applies. Once the taxpayer, on appeal has 'done enough to raise a case that [the company] is not resident in the UK', the burden must then pass to the Revenue to produce some material to show that, despite what appears from everything which the taxpayer has produced, the company is actually resident in the UK. Chadwick LJ said this:[5]

'It is a feature of tax litigation – not least where the litigation arises from a tax avoidance scheme – that, in the first instance, the facts are likely to be known only to the taxpayer and his advisers. The revenue will not have been party to the transaction; and will know only those facts which have been disclosed by the taxpayer or others; following, perhaps, the exercise of the Revenue's investigatory powers. I have no doubt that there are cases in which the evidence before the special commissioners is so unsatisfactory that the only just course for them to take is to hold that the taxpayer has not discharged the burden of proof which section 50(6) of TMA 1970 has placed upon him. But, equally, I have no doubt that the judge was correct, for the reasons which he gave, to hold that the present case was not one of those cases. There was no reason to think that the material facts had not been disclosed; and the commissioners did not hold that it was for that reason that they were unable to decide the question of residence.'

In *News Datacom Ltd v Atkinson (HMIT)*[6] the Special Commissioners followed the guidance of Chadwick LJ in *Wood v Holden* and accordingly, proceeded on the basis that it was for the appellants there to show that the assessments had been wrongly made. They accepted that the evidential burden can shift to HMRC but did not reach a decision purely on grounds relating to the burden of proof in the *Wood v Holden* sense. They held the company to be not resident in the UK without a failure to discharge the evidential burden.[7]

The position is the same in for individuals. In *Daniel v HMRC*,[8] the burden of proving that he was non-resident, having previously been UK resident, generally lay with the taxpayer. The decision in *Daniel* is also a salutary reminder of the kind of evidence needed to discharge this burden. His claim to non-residence was largely on the basis that he was working full time abroad. The Tribunal found that Mr Daniel's evidence was mainly generalisations of having worked full time or anything approaching it, more about what 'he could have done [by way of work], not what he actually did'. His claimed pattern of work – essentially, none done when in London, but every available hour worked when elsewhere was not credible. More importantly, every piece of objective evidence in this case, such as fax and email correspondence, presentations, letters, and of computers, was unavailable. There was no documentary evidence available of the work he did and where it was undertaken, his frequent travel, or of living in his holiday home in the south of France.

The same fate befell Mr and Mrs Rumbelow who contended that they ceased to be UK resident for five tax years when they rented an apartment in Belgium and subsequently owned a house in Portugal.[9] They asserted that they left the UK in April 2001 for a settled purpose, namely, to live permanently overseas for Mrs Rumbelow 's health, to retire and improve quality of life. Distinct changes to pattern of life, they said, amounted to a distinct break and when returning to the UK they did so as visitors. The Tribunal found that there was no evidence of residence in Belgium or Portugal or absence from the UK. They had no contemporaneous record or documentary evidence of their movements. The rough schedule they produced was at odds with records kept by their solicitors in relation to transactions they had undertaken. Accordingly, they failed to demonstrate an intention of anything more than extended holidays abroad.

Individuals are likely to find the record-keeping requirements even more onerous under the statutory residence test. The very detailed statutory rules impose strict boundaries and call for records that may not necessarily be produced or maintained under normal living or working patterns. HMRC views on what it is required are set out in Appendix 2.

1 (1876) 1 TC 88.
2 (1995) Sp C 55.
3 At para 68.
4 [2006] EWCA Civ 26.
5 [2006] EWCA Civ 26, at para 33.
6 (2006) Sp C 561.
7 See para 155.
8 *Daniel v Revenue & Customs* [2014] UKFTT 173 (TC) at para 120.
9 *Rumbelow & Anor v Revenue & Customs* [2013] UKFTT 637 (TC).

11.12 Discovery assessments

Taxpayers claiming to be non-resident on their self-assessment returns need to carefully consider their status in making such a claim. An officer or the Board may make an assessment to recover the lost tax, if an officer of the Board, or the Board, 'discovers' that: (1) assessable income or chargeable gains have not been assessed to tax; (2) an assessment to tax has become insufficient; or (3) excessive relief has been given.[1]

Where a tax return has been filed, discovery assessments can only be made if either the loss of tax is because of the careless or deliberate behaviour (previously, fraudulent or negligent conduct) of the taxpayer or his agent; or, at the time HMRC ceased to be entitled to enquire into the return (or completed such an enquiry), the officer could not reasonably have been expected, on the basis of the information then available to him, to have been aware of the loss of tax.[2] Careless or deliberate behaviour also affects the ability of HMRC to make such assessments beyond the normal four-year time limit.

In *Daniel v HMRC*[3] one of the central questions was whether Mr Daniel's claim to non-resident status on his tax return was 'negligent conduct'. The test is whether a reasonable man filing his tax return, and applying the right legal test, would have claimed non-UK residence when reviewing the facts.[4] His claim to non-resident status was primarily that he was employed 'full-time abroad' within paragraphs 2.2 and 2.3 of IR20. While the burden of proof that he was non-resident lay with Mr Daniel, the burden of proof regarding whether he was negligent in doing so was on HMRC. HMRC would not discharge this burden if: (a) Mr Daniel had an honest and tenable basis for making this claim; or (b) he had sought to act on IR20 guidance(as he had done), and had a tenable claim to have satisfied the IR20 criteria.

The Tribunal accepted that the 'full-time working abroad' test in IR20 was a difficult one, in the sense that it involved a slightly vague definition that must be applied in different ways in different circumstances, with the result that there is inevitably an element of difficulty. The test, was not so difficult that no taxpayer could be expected to apply the test properly.[5]

The relevant facts 'unquestionably' involved 'the reality that there were countless weeks' during the period in question when 'plainly the Appellant had not worked full-time abroad'. Furthermore, He must have been aware that his role had been intermittent. The Tribunal 'simply [did] not accept that his evidence that he read documentation relating to a large transaction on which he worked for over 14 solid weeks can have been realistic or that he can have believed it himself'.[6] Although Mr Daniel may not have been given the very clearest of advice by his accountants, the Tribunal concluded that he must have known that his work had to be 'full-time' in a reasonably conventional sense. The Tribunal noted that he appeared to concentrate on the 91-day UK presence test, and did not appraise his work pattern.

1 TMA 1970, s 29(1); FA 1998, Sch 18, para 41.
2 TMA 1970, s 29(3), (4) and (5); FA 1998, Sch 18, paras 42, 43 and 44.
3 *Daniel v Revenue & Customs* [2014] UKFTT 173 (TC).
4 *Daniel v Revenue & Customs* [2014] UKFTT 173 (TC at para 155).
5 *Daniel v Revenue & Customs* [2014] UKFTT 173 (TC at para 157).
6 *Daniel v Revenue & Customs* [2014] UKFTT 173 (TC at para 155).

11.13   Requirement to correct historic offshore non-compliance

Finance (No 2) Act 2017, s. 67 and Sch 18 introduced draconian measures to require any past 'offshore tax non-compliance' existing on 5 April 2017. Offshore tax non-compliance means tax non-compliance involving under declared income tax, capital gains tax or inheritance tax that relates to income arising outside the UK, assets situated or held outside the UK, activities carried on outside the UK, or anything having a similar effect.[1] Failure to correct by 30 September 2018 will result in penalties of up to 200% of the under-declared tax plus 10% of the value of an offshore asset.[2] In addition, HMRC may publish the personal details of any person subject to a penalty, including, name, address, place of business and amount of penalty.[3]

HMRC guidance indicates that non-compliance may result from incorrect decisions about residence or domicile.[4]

1 F(No 2) A 2017, Sch 18, Pt 1.
2 F(No 2) A 2017, Sch 18, Pt 2.
3 F(No 2) A 2017, Sch 18, para 30.
4 https://www.gov.uk/guidance/requirement-to-correct-tax-due-on-offshore-assets#the-scope-of-the-rtc-rule, accessed 16 February 2018.

11.14   Judicial review

Judicial review is the process whereby the courts supervise public bodies to determine the lawfulness of a decision, action or a failure to act in relation to the exercise of a public function. Civil procedure rules Part 54 rule 54.1(2)(a)(ii). In the context of this work, the primary ground for judicial review is that HMRC published practice has created a legitimate expectation that a person would be entitled to a particular treatment and it would amount to an abuse of power for HMRC to act in a way so as to breach that expectation.[1]

The First-tier Tribunal, on a statutory appeal, cannot give effect to these public law principles. As a result, jurisdiction rests exclusively with the High Court. The effect is that where a taxpayer relies on HMRC practice, there are, in effect two tracks of legal remedy that may be pursued. One is a statutory appeal to the First-tier Tribunal, which has jurisdiction to consider the question of residence as a matter of law, and the other is an application to the High Court for judicial review, which has jurisdiction to consider whether HMRC may be compelled to apply their published practice to the taxpayer. This means that taxpayers disputing HMRC views will need to initiate both procedures. Although applications for permission to seek judicial review are made to the Administrative Court, powers given by s 31A of the Senior Courts Act 1981 permit the transfer of judicial review proceedings to the Tax and Chancery Chamber of the Upper Tribunal.

There is no set rule for determining whether the appeal to the First-tier Tribunal or the judicial review application should be heard first. In *Daniel v Revenue & Customs Comrs*,[2] it was Mr Daniel's position that he left the UK on 5 March 1999 in order to take up full-time employment abroad followed by a sale of shares in the following tax year. HMRC issued to the appellant a determination to the effect that he had been resident and ordinarily resident in the UK during the relevant year and a discovery assessment to tax on the gain resulting from the sale. The Court of Appeal confirmed that there is no hard and fast rule and that the appropriate course must inevitably be determined on a case-by-case basis.[3] The guiding principle is which route permits the matter to be resolved more quickly and cheaply.[4] In Daniel's case there was an underlying factual dispute between the taxpayer and HMRC which could only be conclusively resolved by the First-tier Tribunal. Resolution of the judicial review claim in such a case would not dispose of the dispute. If the taxpayer loses his judicial review claim, he will then have to pursue his statutory appeal. If the taxpayer wins his judicial review claim, HRMC will have to make its determination afresh, possibly with the guidance of the court as to how HMRC practice is to be applied. If such determinations are adverse to the taxpayer, he will again have to appeal. The statutory appeal had the potential finally to resolve the dispute concerning the taxpayer's residence. For these reasons, the Court of Appeal ruled that it is appropriate that the judicial review claim should be stayed whilst the statutory appeal proceeds to a determination.[5]

The same approach was adopted by the High Court in *R (on the application of Hankinson) v Revenue & Customs Commissioners*.[6] In contrast, the position will be different where judicial review requires no resolution of disputed facts and has the potential finally to dispose of the question. In *R (Davies) and Gaines-Cooper v Revenue & Customs Commissioners*,[7] Lord Wilson observed that, had Mr Gaines-Cooper's contention in his claim for judicial review prevailed, to the effect that he had only to show that he had kept his day count in the UK below 91 days, the 10-day hearing of his appeal before the Special Commissioners (now the First-tier Tribunal) would have been unnecessary.

---

1 *R v Inland Revenue Commissioners (ex parte Preston)* [1985] AC 835.
2 *Daniel v Revenue & Customs Comrs* [2012] EWCA Civ 1741.
3 At para 12.
4 At para 19.
5 At para 22.

6 *R (on the application of Hankinson) v Revenue & Customs Commissioners* [2009] EWHC 1774. See also **1.26**.
7 In *R (Davies) and Gaines-Cooper v Revenue & Customs Commissioners* [2011] UKSC 47, at para 6. See also **1.26**.

11.15   Role of Upper Tribunal or Court of Appeal

Residence and domicile are essentially factual in nature. The right of appeal from a decision of the First-tier Tribunal to the Upper Tribunal is on points of law only.[1] Only one reported decision of the Special Commissioners on domicile[2] has been appealed. In *Agulian & Anor v Cyganik*[3] the Court of Appeal was faced with the contention that the appeal was essentially against a finding or findings of fact by the court below and that it was not entitled to substitute its own assessment of the evidence for that of the deputy judge, who heard and saw the witnesses, preferred the evidence of his client and made a finding corroborated by independent evidence. Mummery LJ explained the normal role of the appellate court as follows:

> 'Further, this was not an appeal against the exercise of a discretion by the lower court nor was it a case in which the lower court was applying a fairly flexible and imprecise standard involving an evaluation of all the facts. ... In those cases the appellate court is more reluctant to interfere with the trial judge's decision than in the case of a finding of primary fact or an inference from primary facts. This is an appeal contesting the correctness of an inference as to Andreas's relevant intentions between 1995 and 1999. The function of the appellate court is to decide whether the inference is wrong, making proper allowances for any advantages that the trial judge would have had and an appellate court would not have and not interfering with inferences which the judge could reasonably have made.'[4]

In appeals from the First-tier Tribunal, by contrast, the appellate tribunal or court has no such power. It must be satisfied not that the Tribunal's evaluation of the facts was wrong, but that they made an error of law.[5]

Such a re-evaluation of the facts on appeal is only possible where there is a question of mixed fact and law as in *Edwards v Bairstow*[6] in which Lord Radcliffe said:

> 'If the case contains anything ex facie which is bad law and which bears upon the determination, it is, obviously, erroneous in point of law. But, without any such misconception appearing ex facie, it may be that the facts found are such that no person acting judicially and properly instructed as to the relevant law could have come to the determination under appeal. In those circumstances, too, the court must intervene. It has no option but to assume that there has been some misconception of the law and that, this has been responsible for the determination. So there, too, there has been error in point of law. I do not think that it much matters whether this state of affairs is described as one in which there is no evidence to support the determination or as one in which the evidence is inconsistent with and contradictory of the determination, or as one in which the true and only reasonable conclusion contradicts the determination. Rightly understood, each phrase propounds the same test. For my part, I prefer the last of the three, since I think that it is rather misleading to speak of there being no evidence to support a conclusion when in cases such as

these many of the facts are likely to be neutral in themselves, and only to take their colour from the combination of circumstances in which they are found to occur.'

In *Gaines-Cooper*, the fact that the Special Commissioners did not accept some of Mr Gaines-Cooper's evidence, or that 'in one short paragraph they utterly fail to do justice' to the evidence of witnesses as well as a number of other factual criticisms, was held on appeal to reveal no error of law. A general assertion that the tribunal's conclusion was against the weight of the evidence and was therefore wrong was held impermissible in an appeal restricted to questions of law. In *Grace*, the Court of Appeal was careful to restrict its decision to questions of law. In remitting the case to be re-determined by the First-tier Tribunal on the basis of his legal rulings, Lloyd LJ noted:

'Respectfully, I part company from the judge on that. I agree that a finding of residence is a possible conclusion, and perhaps a likely one, but it does not seem to me that it would be right for the court to pre-empt the decision of the Special Commissioner on that issue. The responsibility of the Special Commissioner to make such decisions, having found the primary facts, is stated and repeated in many of the cases … . Of course there are cases in which, on a correct view of the law, only one conclusion is possible, but it seems to me that the courts ought to be particularly cautious in substituting their own view on this.'[7]

A distinction, he said, had to be drawn between whether Mr Grace's presence in the UK to perform his tasks as a BA long-haul pilot, with whatever regularity and length of stay that is involved, using the house which he retained, is not such as to qualify as presence 'for some temporary purpose only', so as to come within s 831, which could be decided by an appellate court. However, it was not for the appellate court to decide on the balance stands between factors connecting the taxpayer with the UK on the one hand, and his connections with South Africa on the other hand, in terms of satisfying the non-statutory tests for residence and ordinary residence.[8]

---

1 TCEA 2007 s 11(1).
2 See **9.01** above.
3 [2006] EWCA Civ 129.
4 At para 12.
5 *Gaines-Cooper v Revenue & Customs Commissioners* [2007] EWHC 2617 (Ch) at para 27.
6 [1956] AC 14; 36 TC 207.
7 *Grace v HMRC* [2009] EWCA Civ 1082 at para 38.
8 At para 40.

HMRC Guidance Note: Statutory Residence Test (SRT): Annex A

Annex A: Home and accommodation

A1 The statutory residence test concept of 'home'

This guidance provides information about how HMRC interprets the term 'home' in the context of applying the SRT to an individual's circumstances. It must be read in conjunction with the draft statutory residence test legislation, which forms Schedule 43 to the Finance (No.2) Bill 2013 particularly paragraph 25 of the Schedule, to gain a comprehensive understanding.

A2 How do I know if I have to read this annex?

This guidance is intended primarily to help individuals apply the second automatic UK test (in paragraph 8 of the Schedule containing the SRT legislation) to establish their UK residence position. However, this guidance applies to the term 'home' used throughout the SRT.

A3 As the meaning of 'home' can vary according to its context it is not possible for this guidance to provide an absolute definition of the term. What this guidance does is to give indicators outlining the characteristics that a home will generally have. We give some general examples of what a home may or may not be; whether a place is or is not a home will always be dependent on the facts and circumstances of its use by the individual. HMRC may choose to enquire into those facts and circumstances.

A4 For the purpose of the SRT we consider that a person's home is a place that a reasonable onlooker with knowledge of the material facts would regard as that person's home.

A5 The concept of home as described in this guidance relates only to the SRT. The guidance does not apply for the purpose of applying the residence

Article under a double taxation arrangement. Double taxation agreements have additional qualifiers that are not included as part of the SRT and so the two terms do not have the same meaning.

A6 It is possible to have more than one home, either in the same country or in more than one country.

A7 The vast majority of people will have only one place where they live and this will be their home. If an individual has more than one place to live then each of those places may be a home. In this situation, whether or not either place is a home will be determined by the facts.

A8   Why the meaning of 'home' matters for SRT

An individual may be resident under the second automatic UK test if they have a home in the UK. Also:

- An individual will get Case 2 split year treatment only if they have no home in the UK at any time, or have homes in both the UK and overseas but spend the greater part of the time living in the overseas home.
- An individual will get Case 3 split year treatment only if they no longer have any home in the UK.
- An individual will get Case 4 split year treatment on the basis of coming to live in the UK only if they cease to have any home overseas.
- An individual will get Case 8 split year treatment only if they have no home in the UK at the start of the tax year but then acquire a home and continue to have a home in the UK.
- The definition of an accommodation tie includes having a home in the UK.

Home takes the same meaning in all these places.

A9   The principles and characteristics of a home for the purpose of the statutory residence test

A home can be a building (or part of a building), a vehicle, vessel or structure of any kind which is used as a home by an individual. It will be somewhere which an individual uses with a sufficient degree of permanence or stability to count as a home.

Example A1

Jim lives in a mobile home with his wife. They travel extensively throughout the UK to wherever Jim can find work. They keep their personal belongings in the mobile home, take their meals there, and with the exception of their annual holiday abroad, sleep in it every night. It's where Jim and his wife spend most of their time when Jim is not working. It is their home.

Example A2

Mary comes back to the UK to take up employment after spending three years studying abroad. She has given up the tenancy on the flat she occupied abroad and moves into her parents' house. Her parents' house is her home.

A10   A home will remain an individual's home until such a time as it stops being used as such by them.

Example A3

William has business interests in both Switzerland and the UK. He flies to Switzerland each Monday returning to the UK every Thursday. In Switzerland he lives in a rented flat. When in the UK he lives with his family at the family home which he has owned for many years. In this situation both properties are his homes.

William subsequently decides he does not need to spend so much time in Switzerland and starts to travel there less frequently. He sub-lets his flat in Switzerland retaining no rights to use it, choosing instead to stay in whatever hotel can accommodate him. He now has only one home, which is in the UK.

A11   A place can still be a home even if an individual does not stay there continuously. If, for example they move out temporarily but their spouse and children continue to live there, then it is still likely to be their home.

Example A4

Elizabeth is seconded to New York for two months by her UK employer. She stays in a hotel when she is there. Prior to her secondment she lived with her husband in their home in London. Her husband continues to live and work in the UK. When Elizabeth returns to the UK after her secondment she returns to live with her husband in their London home. The London house was Elizabeth's home throughout the period of her secondment.

A12   You should note that if you have a home (either in the UK or overseas) that your family do not visit as they live in another of your homes, this will not mean, when taken in isolation, that the home cannot be your home.

A13   If an individual moves out of their home temporarily it may still remain their home.

Example A5

Asif has lived and worked in the UK for many years, occupying the same apartment in Liverpool since the day he arrived here. Asif's father lives in Sweden and is seriously ill. Ten months ago Asif decided to take a career

---

> break to care for his father and moved to Sweden. He does not know how long he will be out of the UK.
>
> Since moving to Sweden Asif has not returned to Liverpool, but his apartment remains empty and available for him to return to whenever he wants. In this situation Asif will have a home in both Liverpool and Sweden even though he is spending all of his time in Sweden.

A14   A place that is used as a home will remain a home even if it is temporarily unavailable, for example, because of damage or renovation.

Example A6

Rachel and Tom's kitchen and dining room have suffered flood damage. The estimated clean-up and repair operation will take six weeks, so they stay with Rachel's parents while the work is being done. The property will remain their home even though Rachel and Tom are unable to stay there for the time being.

A15   Your home starts to be your home as soon as:

- it is capable of being used as your home, for example, you have taken ownership of it, even if it is temporarily unavailable because of renovation
- you actually use it as your home.

If the first point above is satisfied, but in fact you never actually use it as your home, then it will not be your home.

Example A7

Aneta moved from Poland to the UK and completed the purchase of her new house on 1 June. Whilst it was empty, she stayed with friends, until her belongings arrived. These were moved in by the removal firm on 15 June.

Aneta stayed in her new home overnight that night. However, as she had arranged to have some extensive refurbishment done to her bathrooms and kitchen, she stayed in a local hotel and with colleagues whilst the main works were carried out. She moved into her home on a permanent basis on 15 July.

For SRT purposes we would consider that the house became Aneta's home from 15 June.

A16   The key points are that:

- a place must be capable of being used as a home, even if it is temporarily unavailable, and
- an individual must actually use it as a home.

A17   What is not considered to be a home for the purpose of the statutory residence test?

If an individual moves out of their home completely and makes it available to let commercially on a permanent basis it will not be their home during the period it is let unless they or their family retain a right to live there. This can happen, for example, where the rental agreement permits the individual to use the property or part of the property as living accommodation.

Example A8

Ivan left the UK to work in Germany. He lets the flat he previously lived in to a tenant on a two-year lease. After 18 months he was made redundant and returned to the UK. The rental agreement on his flat gave exclusive use of the property to the tenant so Ivan arranged to stay with relatives and friends until the lease expired. For the period his property was let it is not his home.

However, if the rental agreement had allowed Ivan to use the flat and he had stayed there when he visited the UK it would have remained his home throughout.

A18   A place that has never been capable of functioning as a home cannot be a home. For example, a property purchased in such a state of disrepair that it is not capable of being lived in as a home, is not a home until such time as it becomes habitable.

A19   If an individual completely moves out of a property and makes no further use of it whatsoever it will no longer be their home.

Example A9

Harry's new job requires him to travel extensively around Europe. He spends some time working in the UK but most of his work is carried out in other countries. He decided to sell his UK property. On 3 June he put his furniture and belongings in storage and two weeks later he handed the keys to his estate agent. He did not return to his UK property after 3 June and stayed in hotels or with friends on the occasions when he came back to the UK. The property is not his home from 3 June, the date he put his furniture and belongings in storage.

A20   A property which is used as nothing more than a holiday home, temporary retreat or something similar is not a home. So a holiday home where an individual spends time for occasional short breaks, and which clearly provides a distinct respite from their ordinary day to day life will not be a home. However if there comes a time when an individual's use of a holiday home or temporary retreat changes so that it is used as a home it will become a home from the time of the change. It will then continue to be a home until such time as circumstances change again and it ceases to be used as a home.

Example A10

Jenny lives in Birmingham and works from home. She also owns an apartment in Spain which she rents out apart from two to three weeks a year when she takes her holiday there. The Spanish property is not her home.

However, Jenny then decides to live in the Spanish apartment throughout the British winter time, from October to March. Her use of the property has changed from being somewhere she used for an occasional short break to somewhere she uses as a home for part of the year. The property is her home from the point she commences using the property as her home.

A21   A property, vehicle or other 'home' that an individual never stays in will not be their home. For example a property purchased solely as an investment or a property bequeathed to an individual and which they never stay in will not be a home. This will not be the case if they start to use the property as a home.

Example A11

Jamal purchases a house in the UK as an investment. Although the property is furnished it is currently standing empty because he cannot find a suitable tenant. Jamal has never stayed in the property. The UK house is not his home.

A22   A building, vehicle, vessel or structure, or the like, can be an individual's home even if it is not owned by them. Ownership or a legal form of tenancy makes no difference. For example a property that an individual rents or in which an individual lives with their parents, another member of their family or others will be a home if they use it as their home.

A23   The statutory residence test accommodation tie

This section provides information about what HMRC considers to be an accommodation tie in the context of applying the SRT to an individual's circumstances. It should be read in conjunction with the SRT legislation in paragraph 34 of the Schedule to gain a comprehensive understanding.

A24   This guidance is intended to help individuals apply the sufficient UK ties test (paragraphs 31 to 38 of the Schedule) to establish their UK residence position.

A25   If an individual cannot determine their residence by reference to an automatic UK test or an automatic overseas test they will need to consider the sufficient ties test. The sufficient UK ties test sets out a number of defined connection ties that need to be considered when determining their UK residence position.

A26   One of the ties is the accommodation tie. Any accommodation that is available for an individual's use while they are in the UK:

- must be available to them for a continuous period of at least 91 days during the tax year and
- the individual must use it for at least one night during that tax year.

Example A12

Peter left the UK last year to travel the world. He let his UK property on a two year lease and has no rights to use the property. Peter has no home in the UK.

Before leaving the UK Peter agreed with his cousin that he could stay with her on any occasion he was in the UK. This is more than a casual offer; Peter's cousin is fully prepared to put Peter up for several months at a time should he need it. He made two visits to the UK this year, each for ten days, and stayed with her. Peter has an accommodation tie this year.

A27   The main difference between the term 'home' for SRT purposes and available accommodation is that accommodation can be transient and does not require the degree of stability or permanence that a home does.

A28   If an individual does not have a home in the UK they may still have an accommodation tie if they have a place to live in the UK.

A29   The principles and characteristics of accommodation as a UK tie

Although this guidance gives some general examples of what an accommodation tie may or may not be, whether somewhere is or is not an accommodation tie will always be dependent on the facts and circumstances of its use by the individual. HMRC may choose to enquire into those facts and circumstances.

A30   Accommodation can be a building, a vehicle, vessel or structure of any kind which is available to live in. It can also be a holiday home, temporary retreat or similar.

Example A13

Mary has lived and worked in the USA for many years. Her uncle has a holiday houseboat in the UK where he has agreed Mary can stay any time she wishes, for as long as she wishes, when she comes here. Mary's uncle does not allow other people to stay in the houseboat.

Last year Mary came to the UK twice. She made arrangements to stay for three weeks with a friend and for four weeks with her brother. Although the

---

houseboat was available for a continuous period of at least 91 days, Mary did not use it at all. Therefore, she had no accommodation tie in respect of the houseboat last year.

This year Mary again visited the UK twice, spending her five-week summer holiday on her uncle's houseboat. This year Mary has an accommodation tie as the houseboat is available for a continuous period of at least 91 days and she has stayed on it for at least one night.

A31   An individual does not have to own the accommodation. Ownership, form of tenancy, or legal right to occupy the accommodation makes no difference.

A32   Accommodation can be any type of accommodation. For example, accommodation provided by an employer, a holiday home, a temporary retreat or something similar.

Example A14

Simone has lived and worked in France all her life. She and her brother purchased a cottage in the UK several years ago as a holiday home. The cottage is let for most of the year but June, July and August are always kept free so that Simone or her brother can stay there. There is sufficient accommodation in the cottage to ensure that Simone is able to stay there, even when her brother and his family are also there.

Simone spent two weeks in the cottage last year and three weeks this year. Simone has an accommodation tie both last year and this year.

A33   Accommodation is regarded as available to you for a continuous period of 91 days if you are able to use it, or it is at your disposal, at all times throughout that period (subject to the 16 day gap rule covered below). If a relative were to make their home available to you casually, for a social visit, say, it will not mean that the accommodation would be regarded as being available to you. However, if it is available to you for a continuous period of 91 days and you use it casually, it will be a tie.

A 34   Similarly, a casual offer from a friend to 'stay in my spare room any time' will not constitute an accommodation tie unless your friend really is prepared to put you up for 91 days at a time (whether he actually does so or not).

Example A15

Sacha visits the UK on business and usually stays in different hotels. On one of these visits he takes an opportunity to attend the Wimbledon Tennis Championships. A business associate who lives in Wimbledon invites Sacha to stay at his flat for three nights rather than use a hotel. The arrangement is a one-off invitation and the accommodation is not available to Sacha for 91 days. It is not an accommodation tie.

A35 If there is a gap of fewer than 16 days between periods when accommodation is available the gap period is ignored and accommodation is regarded as being available throughout.

Example A16

Hyo lives and works in Poland. He is his company's European sales manager. This year he will be responsible for launching a new product in the UK and will need to spend time here. His sales force are on the road the last week of every month so he books a room in the same hotel for the first three weeks of June, July, August, and September.

Hyo has an accommodation tie this year.

A36 The rules change slightly if an individual stays at the home of a close relative. Close relative means parent, grandparent, brother, sister and child or grandchild aged 18 or over (whether or not they are blood relatives, half-blood relatives or related by marriage or civil partnership). Child includes any adopted children.

A37 If an individual stays with a close relative the accommodation will be an accommodation tie if they spend at least 16 nights there in any one tax year and it is available to them for a continuous period of at least 91 days.

Example A17

Ravi can stay with his grandparents whenever he is in the UK. They will put him up for more than 91 days if he wishes. He usually comes from India every year to visit them and stays with them for the whole summer.

Last year Ravi spent only the first two weeks with his grandparents then went on a one-off visit to his uncle (who would not be regarded as a close relative for the purposes of the SRT) for two months before returning home. So, although accommodation at his grandparents, who are regarded as close relatives, was available for more than 91 days, Ravi stayed with his grandparents for only 14 days, and therefore had no accommodation tie.

This year Ravi spent the whole summer with his grandparents.

This year Ravi has an accommodation tie.

A38 If an individual stays in UK accommodation held by a spouse, partner or minor children then they will be considered to have an accommodation tie if they spend at least one night there.

Example A18

Peter and his civil partner Andrew share an apartment in London. Last year Andrew moved to the USA to take up a university place to study marine biology.

This year Andrew came back to the UK for a three-week holiday which he and Peter spent in Scotland. Andrew spent the first night and last night of his holiday in their London apartment.

This year Andrew has an accommodation tie.

A39 It is possible to have more than one place in the UK that counts as available accommodation. However this would still represent only one accommodation tie no matter how many different places of accommodation are available.

Example A19

Julie has lived in Canada with her husband for many years.

Julie and her husband own a holiday home in the UK which they do not let out and in addition Julie can stay with her parents whenever she is in the UK, for as long as she wishes.

This year Julie visits the UK and stays with her parents for four weeks and then spends a further three weeks in her holiday home before returning to Canada.

This year although Julie has two places that count as available accommodation she has only one accommodation tie.

A40   When accommodation is not considered to be an accommodation tie

Accommodation owned by an individual but which they have wholly let out commercially would not be considered as available to live in unless they retained the right to use the property or part of the property.

A41 Accommodation that is available to an individual but in which they have not spent at least one night in the tax year will not be an accommodation tie.

A42 Short stays at hotels and guesthouses will not usually be considered to be an accommodation tie. However, if an individual books a room in the same hotel or guesthouse (and does not cancel those bookings) for at least 91 days continuously in a tax year it will be an accommodation tie. (See Example A14)

HMRC Guidance Note: Statutory Residence Test (SRT): Section 7

7. Record keeping

7.1 What records should I keep for SRT purposes?

You will need to keep records and documents to support the statements you make when you are:

- considering the statutory residence test, or
- giving specific responses to questions in the Tax Residence Indicator (TRI) tool.

In many cases your circumstances will be straightforward and you will not need to retain paperwork over and above any documentation you might normally be expected to keep for your own or your employer's purposes.

7.2 Home

When considering whether you had a home in the UK or abroad, HMRC would look for evidence to establish your presence at a particular home and whether or not a home existed. The following information would help establish the facts.

- General overheads – utility bills which may demonstrate that you have been present in that home, for example, telephone bills or energy bills, which demonstrate usage commensurate with living in the property.
- TV/satellite/cable subscriptions.
- Local parking permits.
- Membership of clubs, for example sports, health or social clubs.
- Mobile phone usage and bills pointing to your presence in a country.
- Lifestyle purchases pointing to you spending time in your home – for example, purchases of food, flowers and meals out.
- Presence of your spouse, partner or children.
- Engagement of domestic staff or an increase in their hours.
- Home security arrangements.

- Increases in maintenance costs or the frequency of maintenance, for example having your house cleaned more frequently.
- Insurance documents relating to that home.
- SORN notification that a vehicle in the UK is 'off road'.
- Re-directed mail requests.
- The address to which you have personal post sent.
- The address to which your driving licence is registered.
- Bank accounts and credit cards linked to your address and statements which show payments made to utility companies.
- Evidence of local municipal taxes being paid.
- Registration, at your address, with local medical practitioners.
- What private medical insurance cover you have, is it an international policy?
- Credit card and bank statements which indicate the pattern and place where your expenditure takes place.

7.3   The above list is not definitive; no one piece of evidence will demonstrate the existence of your UK or overseas home with the requisite time spent there. HMRC will consider the weight and quality of all the evidence as, taken together, a number of pieces of evidence may be sufficiently strong to demonstrate your presence in a particular home.

7.4   Where your home has changed from a holiday home to your home, for the purposes of the SRT, the change in occupation could be evidenced by, amongst other things, utility bills which may show an increase in usage, or changes you have notified to local municipal authorities, or to the company providing your buildings and contents insurance.

7.5   Working hours and location of work done

Where your residence status is determined by the automatic tests relating to working full-time in the UK or overseas, you should keep information and records relating to:

- the split in your working life between the UK and overseas, particularly noting days where you worked (including training, being on stand-by and travelling) for more or less than three hours
- the nature and duration of your work activities – a work diary/calendar or timesheet is likely to indicate this. You may find that it would be beneficial to ensure your diary is sufficiently detailed, maybe reflecting hours worked and the nature of your work, for example reviewing and responding to emails, meetings, or filing travel claims
- breaks you had from working, for example between jobs, and why
- your periods of annual, sick or parenting leave
- time you spend visiting dependent children (those under the age of 18) when they are in the UK
- time you had to spend in the UK owing to exceptional circumstances
  - what your circumstances were
  - what you did to mitigate them where that was possible, for example making alternative travel arrangements

- your contracts of employment, and documentation/communications which relate to these, particularly to curtailment or extension of these or other changes to them.

7.6   The sufficient ties test

Where you have connections to the UK, such as family, accommodation, work or time spent here, you should keep information and records that will allow you to work out:

- in which countries you have spent your days and midnights, for example
  - your travel details
  - booking information, or
- tickets, and boarding cards
- if you left the UK to live or work abroad,
- the date you left the UK
- visa or work permit applications, etc if you had to make them
- contracts of employment
- if you come to live or work in the UK
- the date you arrive here
- visa or work permit applications
- documentation relating to you taking up employment or ceasing your previous employment
- when you were present at your home or homes, or other available accommodation
- how long you owned or rented those homes, for example when you purchased, sold or leased those homes
- the time your home was unavailable for your use, for example because it was rented out.

HMRC Statement of Practice SP 1/90 Company Residence

[9 January 1990]

1. Residence has always been a material factor, for companies as well as individuals, in determining tax liability. But statute law has never laid down comprehensive rules for determining where a company is resident and until 1988 the question was left solely to the Courts to decide. Section 66 FA 1988 introduced the rule that a company incorporated in the UK is resident there for the purposes of the Taxes Acts. Case law still applies in determining the residence of companies excepted from the incorporation rule or which are not incorporated in the UK.

A. The incorporation rule

2. The incorporation rule applies to companies incorporated in the UK subject to the exceptions in Schedule 7 FA 1988 for some companies incorporated before 15 March 1988. (This legislation is reproduced for convenience as an Appendix to this Statement). Paragraphs 3 to 8 below explain how the Revenue interpret various terms used in the legislation.

Carrying on business

3. The exceptions from the incorporation test in Schedule 7 depend in part on the company carrying on business at a specified time or during a relevant period. The question whether a company carries on business is one of fact to be decided according to the particular circumstances of the company. Detailed guidance is not practicable but the Revenue take the view that 'business' has a wider meaning than 'trade'; it can include transactions, such as the purchase of stock, carried out for the purposes of a trade about to be commenced and the holding of investments including shares in a subsidiary company. Such a holding could consist of a single investment from which no income was derived.

4.   A company such as a shelf company whose transactions have been limited to those formalities necessary to keep the company on the register of companies will not be regarded as carrying on business.

5.   For the purpose of the case law test (see B below) the residence of a company is determined by the place where its real business is carried on. A company which can demonstrate that in these terms it is or was resident outside the UK will have carried on business for the purposes of Schedule 7.

'Taxable in a territory outside the UK'

6.   A further condition for some companies for exception from the incorporation test is provided by Schedule 7 Para 1(1)(c) and Para 5(1). The company has to be taxable in a territory outside the UK. 'Taxable' means that the company is liable to tax on income by reason of domicile, residence or place of management. This is similar to the approach adopted in the residence provisions of many double taxation agreements. Territories which impose tax on companies by reference to incorporation or registration or similar criteria are covered by the term 'domicile'. Territories which impose tax by reference to criteria such as 'effective management', 'central administration', 'head office' or 'principal place of business' are covered by the term 'place of management'.

7.   A company has to be liable to tax on income so that a company which is, for example, liable only to a flat rate fee or lump sum duty does not fulfil the test. On the other hand a company is regarded as liable to tax in a particular territory if it is within the charge there even though it may pay no tax because, for example, it makes losses or claims double taxation relief.

'Treasury consent'

8.   Before 15 March 1988 it was unlawful for a company to cease to be resident in the UK without the consent of the Treasury. Companies which have ceased to be resident in pursuance of a Treasury consent, as defined in Schedule 7 Paragraph 5(1), are excepted from the incorporation rule subject to certain conditions. A few companies ceased to be resident without Treasury Consent but were informed subsequently by letter that the Treasury would take no action against them under the relevant legislation. Such letter is not a retrospective grant of consent and the companies concerned cannot benefit from the exceptions which depend on Treasury consent.

B.   The case law test

9.   This test of company residence is that enunciated by Lord Loreburn in *De Beers Consolidated Mines v Howe* (5 TC 198) at the beginning of this century:

'A company resides, for the purposes of Income Tax, where its real business is carried on ... I regard that as the true rule; and the real business is carried on where the central management and control actually abides'.

10.   The 'central management and control' test, as set out in *De Beers*, has been endorsed by a series of subsequent decisions. In particular, it was described by Lord Radcliffe in the 1959 case of *Bullock v Unit Construction Company* (38 TC 712) at p. 738 as being:

'as precise and unequivocal as a positive statutory injunction ... I do not know of any other test which has either been substituted for that of central management and control, or has been defined with sufficient precision to be regarded as an acceptable alternative to it. To me ... it seems impossible to read Lord Loreburn's words without seeing that he regarded the formula he was propounding as constituting the test of residence'.

Nothing which has happened since has in any way altered this basic principle for a company the residence of which is not governed by the incorporation rule; under current UK case law such a company is regarded as resident for tax purposes where central management and control is to be found.

Place of 'central management and control'

11.   In determining whether or not an individual company outside the scope of the incorporation test is resident in the UK, it thus becomes necessary to locate its place of 'central management and control'. The case law concept of central management and control is, in broad terms, directed at the highest level of control of the business of a company. It is to be distinguished from the place where the main operations of a business are to be found, though those two places may often coincide. Moreover, the exercise of control does not necessarily demand any minimum standard of active involvement: it may, in appropriate circumstances, be exercised tacitly through passive oversight.

12.   Successive decided cases have emphasised that the place of central management and control is wholly a question of fact. For example, Lord Radcliffe in Unit Construction said that 'the question where control and management abide must be treated as one of fact or "actuality"' (p 741). It follows that factors which together are decisive in one instance may individually carry little weight in another. Nevertheless the decided cases do give some pointers. In particular a series of decisions has attached importance to the place where the company's board of directors meet. There are very many cases in which the board meets in the same country as that in which the business operations take place, and central management and control is clearly located in that one place. In other cases central management and control may be exercised by directors in one country though the actual business operations may, perhaps under the immediate management of local directors, take place elsewhere.

13.   But the location of board meetings, although important in the normal case, is not necessarily conclusive. Lord Radcliffe in Unit Construction pointed out (p 738) that the site of the meetings of the directors' board had not been chosen as 'the test' of company residence. In some cases, for example, central management and control is exercised by a single individual. This may happen when a chairman or managing director exercises powers formally conferred by the company's Articles and the other board members are little more than cyphers, or by reason of a dominant shareholding or for some other reason. In those cases the residence of the company is where the controlling individual exercises his powers.

14. In general the place of directors' meetings is significant only insofar as those meetings constitute the medium through which central management and control is exercised. If, for example, the directors of a company were engaged together actively in the UK in the complete running of a business which was wholly in the UK, the company would not be regarded as resident outside the UK merely because the directors held formal meetings outside the UK. While it is possible to identify extreme situations in which central management and control plainly is, or is not, exercised by directors in formal meetings, the conclusion in any case is wholly one of fact depending on the relative weight to be given to various factors. Any attempt to lay down rigid guidelines would only be misleading.

15. Generally, however, where doubts arise about a particular company's residence status, the Inland Revenue adopt the following approach:

(i) They first try to ascertain whether the directors of the company in fact exercise central management and control.

(ii) If so, they seek to determine where the directors exercise this central management and control (which is not necessarily where they meet).

(iii) In cases where the directors apparently do not exercise central management and control of the company, the Revenue then look to establish where and by whom it is exercised.

Parent/subsidiary relationship

16. It is particularly difficult to apply the 'central management and control' test in the situation where a subsidiary company and its parent operate in different territories. In this situation, the parent will normally influence, to a greater or lesser extent, the actions of the subsidiary. Where that influence is exerted by the parent exercising the powers which a sole or majority shareholder has in general meetings of the subsidiary, for example to appoint and dismiss members of board of the subsidiary and to initiate or approve alterations to its financial structure, the Revenue would not seek to argue that central management and control of the subsidiary is located where the parent company is resident. However, in cases where the parent usurps the functions of the board of the subsidiary (such as Unit Construction itself) or where that board merely rubber stamps the parent company's decisions without giving them any independent consideration of its own, the Revenue draw the conclusion that the subsidiary has the same residence for tax purposes as its parent.

17. The Revenue recognise that there may be many cases where a company is a member of a group having its ultimate holding company in another country which will not fall readily into either of the categories referred to above. In considering whether the board of such a subsidiary company exercises central management and control of the subsidiary's business, they have regard to the degree of autonomy which those directors have in conducting the company's business. Matters (among others) that may be taken into account are the extent to which the directors of the subsidiary take decisions on their own authority as to investment, production, marketing and procurement without reference to the parent.

Conclusion

18.   In outlining factors relevant to the application of the case law test, this statement assumes that they exist for genuine commercial reasons. Where, however, as may happen, it appears that a major objective underlying the existence of certain factors is the obtaining of tax benefits from residence or non-residence, the Revenue examine the facts particularly closely in order to see whether there has been an attempt to create the appearance of central management and control in a particular place without the reality.

19.   The case law test examined in this Statement is not always easy to apply. The Courts have recognised that there may be difficulties where it is not possible to identify any one country as the seat of central management and control. The principles to apply in those circumstances have not been fully developed in case law. In addition, the last relevant case was decided almost 30 years ago, and there have been many developments in communications since then, which in particular may enable a company to be controlled from a place far distant from where the day-to-day management is carried on. As the Statement makes clear, while the general principle has been laid down by the Courts, its application must depend on the precise facts.

C.   Double taxation agreements

20.   In general our double taxation agreements do not affect the UK residence of a company as established for UK tax purposes. But where the partner country adopts a different definition of residence, it may happen that a UK resident company is treated, under the partner country's domestic law, as also resident there. In these cases, the agreement normally specifies what the tax consequences of this 'double' residence shall be.

21.   Under the double taxation agreement with the United States, for example, the UK residence of a company for UK tax purposes is unaffected. But where that company is also a US corporation, it is excluded from some of the reliefs conferred by the agreement. On the other hand, under a double taxation agreement which follows the 1977 OECD Model Taxation Convention, a company classed as resident by both the UK and the partner country is, for the purposes of the agreement, treated as resident where its 'place of effective management' is situated.

22.   The Commentary in paragraph 3 of Article 4 of the OECD Model records the UK view that, in agreements (such as those with some Commonwealth countries) which treat a company as resident in a state in which 'its business is managed and controlled', this expression means 'the effective management of the enterprise'. More detailed consideration of the question in the light of the approach of Continental legal systems and of Community law to the question of company residence has led the Revenue to revise this view. It is now considered that effective management may, in some cases, be found at a place different from the place of central management and control. This could happen, for example, where a company is run by executives based abroad, but the final directing power rests with non-executive directors who meet in the UK. In such circumstances the company's place of effective management might well be abroad but, depending on the precise powers of the non-executive directors, it might be centrally managed and controlled (and therefore resident) in the UK.

23.   The incorporation rule in Section 66(1) FA 1988 determines a residence which supersedes a different place 'given by any rule of law'. This incorporation rule determines residence under UK domestic law and is subject to the provisions of any applicable double taxation agreement. It does not override the provisions of a double taxation agreement which may make a UK incorporated company a resident of an overseas territory for the purposes of the agreement (see 20 and 21 above).

Appendix to SP 1/90

[The Appendix contains the text of FA 1988, s 66 and Sch 7 and is not reproduced here.]

INDEX

[References are to paragraph number and appendices]